Rose Macaulay in 1958

LETTERS
TO A FRIEND

FROM
ROSE MACAULAY
1950–1952

EDITED BY
CONSTANCE BABINGTON SMITH

COLLINS
ST JAMES'S PLACE, LONDON
1961

209973/10/1

Contents

Preface

These letters were written by Dame Rose Macaulay to the Rev. John Hamilton Cowper Johnson, of the Society of St. John the Evangelist (commonly known as the Cowley Fathers), and they are essentially a record of her return to Christian faith and to the sacramental life of the Anglican Church after nearly thirty years' estrangement. But they are also a lively chronicle of Dame Rose's enormously varied interests and doings.

She had known Father Johnson for about two years at the beginning of the first world war when he was on the staff of St. Edward's House, Westminster, but they lost touch soon after 1916 when he was transferred to the Cowley Fathers' community at Boston, Massachusetts. He remained there and they never met again, but occasionally he read her books. In 1950, after reading the American edition of *They Were Defeated*, he wrote to her, and her reply is the first of the letters in this book.

After Dame Rose's death in 1958, Father Johnson was anxious that the letters he had received from her should be put into safe keeping. He believed that if these letters could be published (after careful editing) they would be of help to many. He had met me once, through the introduction of Dame Rose who was my third cousin, when I was in America in 1956, and it was this personal link which led him to arrange with Dame Rose's god-child Miss Emily Smith, whose home was near Boston, for the letters to be dispatched to England and entrusted to me.

Miss Jean Macaulay, Dame Rose's sister, and the only surviving member of this branch of the Macaulay family, was then consulted, as well as others concerned, and it was decided that the letters should be prepared for publication. The editing was to be my responsibility, and I thereupon entered into correspondence with Father Johnson, in order to discuss various matters of policy. I received much helpful advice from him until his health failed (during the year preceding his death in March 1961), and his enthusiasm for the publication of the letters was a constant encouragement to me. It should also be mentioned here that the Father Superior of the Cowley Fathers' American Congregation, the Rev. G. Mercer Williams, S.S.J.E., was kept informed of the planning as it progressed.

The correspondence falls naturally into two parts, the letters written in close sequence between 1950 and 1952 and the less frequent letters of the subsequent six years. The present book consists of the first of these two parts and the second part of the series will be published in a later volume. There is no question of publishing the "other half" of the correspondence, namely the replies from Father Johnson, as they were among the papers which, according to Dame Rose's instructions, were destroyed after her death.

The Introduction to this book is intended to give such biographical background as is needed for an understanding of the letters. While preparing it I have had many talks with Miss Jean Macaulay, who has given her whole-hearted approval to the entire project, and with Miss Dorothea Conybeare, Dame Rose's first cousin, to whom I have turned repeatedly in connection with family history. Both Miss Macaulay and Miss Conybeare have given me much valuable information from memory, and have made available various family diaries and other records; I am deeply grateful to both of them. I would like in addition to express my gratitude to Miss Emily Smith for organizing the dispatch of the letters on Father Johnson's behalf, and to those of Dame Rose's friends who have helped me in many ways, especially by lending letters in their possession. I am also very grateful to Miss Mary Barham Johnson for providing historical details about the Johnson family, and to Mrs. Frank C. Paine for advising on some of the references to Father Johnson's life in America.

In editing the letters I have omitted references which might cause embarrassment to living persons and in order to distinguish such omissions from ambiguous cases where ". . ." appears in the original I have added [*sic*] in these latter instances. The only other omissions are on pages 50, 51, 172, and 335 where Father Johnson had made deletions.

The letters were sometimes sent by surface mail and often by air mail. This is constantly referred to in the correspondence, so I have identified those which were airmailed by the symbol † placed alongside the date of the letter.

Some of the original letters are typed but many are handwritten and in the deciphering of these I was ably assisted by Miss M. F. McKnight. In the handwritten letters there are frequent contractions; I have extended most of these and have also corrected occasional typing errors, apparently unintentional mis-spellings, and punctuation which might be misleading. In general however I have not amended quotations, book titles, etc. where they are written incorrectly or in contracted form. Upon such problems of editing I have received invaluable advice from Mr. A. F. Scholfield who also assisted me in translating the Latin quotations and I am warmly grateful to him. I am also very grateful to Professor Bruce Dickins who has taken a most helpful interest in my work, to Dr. F. Brittain and Dr. F. J. E. Raby, whom I consulted when preparing some of the footnotes, and to Canon Charles Smyth and Professor Patrick Duff, who kindly advised on various other footnotes. I am furthermore indebted to the Father Superior of the Cowley Fathers' English Congregation, the Rev. F. B. Dalby, S.S.J.E., for allowing me to examine material belonging to the S.S.J.E. Library at Oxford, to the Rev. A. P. Hill, S.S.J.E., for facilitating this work, and to the Rev. E. A. Thomas, S.S.J.E., for his advice on some of the editing. I would also like to acknowledge the permission kindly given by Brother Paul, Oblate, S.S.J.E., to reproduce his photograph of Father Johnson, and by Mr. Cecil Beaton to reproduce his photograph of Dame Rose.

Constance Babington Smith

Cambridge, 1961

Introduction

" No wonder," Rose Macaulay herself once wrote, " that I feel
an interest in religion, considering how steadily and for how
many centuries ancestors versed in theology have converged on
me from all sides." On the Macaulay side—the side which
stemmed from a Scottish clan and whose motto was *Dulce
Periculum*—her grandfather and great-grandfather had both
been Anglican parsons and her great-great-uncle Zachary, father
of Lord Macaulay, had been a lay member of the Clapham Sect.
Before that there had been two generations of Presbyterian
ministers: John Macaulay (Rose's great-great-grandfather) was
a minister at Inveraray when Dr. Johnson visited the Hebrides
and their meetings are recorded by Boswell.

It was in the generation of Rose's father that the long line of
Macaulay clergy came to an end; neither he nor any of his
brothers took orders. George Macaulay chose an academic
career and in due course became recognised as a sound and
accomplished scholar in the field of English studies. After reading
Classics at Cambridge he had been briefly a Fellow of Trinity,
but in 1878 he relinquished his fellowship to marry his cousin
Grace Conybeare.

Rose's mother came of a family with roots in Devonshire
and some French Huguenot blood and with an even longer
tradition of scholarly divines than the Macaulays. Some of the
Conybeares were notably versatile. Rose's grandfather, William
John Conybeare, well known in his day as co-author of a life
of Saint Paul, also wrote a novel in three volumes; her great-
grandfather, William Daniel Conybeare, who became Dean of
Llandaff, was a distinguished geologist and a Fellow of the Royal

Society; while his brother, John Josias Conybeare, also a clergyman, was Professor of Anglo-Saxon and of Poetry at Oxford. Rose's great-great-great-grandfather, John Conybeare, a noted preacher in the first half of the eighteenth century, was Dean of Christ Church, Oxford, and later Bishop of Bristol. In the less distant past Rose's uncle Edward Conybeare was an Anglican parson who towards the end of his life joined the Roman Church, and her first cousin James Conybeare was for many years Provost of Southwell. Rose was also related, through her maternal grandmother, to another great family of ecclesiastics, the Roses (this is why she was given the name of Rose, in addition to her first name Emilie).

After George Macaulay's marriage he worked for nine years as an assistant master at Rugby during which time six children were born: Margaret, Rose, Jean, Aulay, William, and Eleanor. Emilie Rose was born on 1st August, 1881, and her mother, who had been passionately hoping for a boy, was much disappointed at the arrival of a second girl. On 18th September Emilie Rose was baptized: her godparents were Mrs. Archibald Moncrieff, Miss Ada Currey, and her uncle Reginald Macaulay. Of these three her godfather was to play much the most important part in Rose's life.

Uncle Regi like her father had been a classical scholar. His fine intellect, applied to business matters, contributed largely to the expansion of Wallace & Co. and of the Bombay Burmah Trading Corporation, which brought him considerable wealth. He was a very kind and generous man with a jocund manner and a lively sense of the ridiculous; religion was a target for his gay mockery like everything else. Another of Rose's uncles, W. H. Macaulay—'Uncle Willie,' of whom she also became very fond—was a Fellow and Vice-Provost of King's College, Cambridge, where he was renowned for the astringent precision of his remarks.

Some of the Macaulay attitudes appeared early in Rose and according to family legend when she was three years old and her mother first told her about God, her comment was "I don't know that!" But as she grew older her mother's religious teaching made a profound mark. Grace Macaulay, who had been brought up in a High Church atmosphere at Weybridge, under the influence of her much loved uncle Edward Rose, had all the imagination and originality of the Conybeares and was also a brilliant teacher. Her Sunday-school classes were notable for her vivid rendering of Bible stories and for her clear and simple interpretations of Christian theology. Church-going was of course taken for granted in the Macaulay household and also the tradition of family prayers; parents, children, servants, and any visitors joined in these prayers every morning. Psalms and prayers were said and a hymn was sung—often an ordeal for musical visitors, for the Macaulays were all tone-deaf, and Grace Macaulay at the piano played many wrong notes, though it is said she had a sense of time. At night, when the children went to bed, she used to visit each child alone for a talk and prayers, and she encouraged them to learn hymns by heart.

In 1887 the whole family went to live in Italy. The main reason was Grace Macaulay's health; tuberculosis was threatening and her doctors had advised her to live in a warm climate. They took a house at Varazze, a small fishing village near Genoa, and George Macaulay set to work on a translation of Herodotus. For the next seven years the children ran blissfully wild; sea and shore were their home as much as the unconventional " Villa Macolai," where life was simple partly because the Macaulays were not well off. The children's education consisted mostly of lessons with their parents, though for a short time Margaret, Rose, and Jean attended the local convent school.

The years in Italy, when "Rosy" grew from a child of six into a gauche tomboy of thirteen, set the course for much of her later development. The love of the sea-shore and of bathing, the attachment to "abroad," especially the Mediterranean countries, the happy-go-lucky untidy ways, the frugal standards of living, the boyish hobbies, the farouche demeanour—all these can be traced to Varazze. At Varazze too she gained lasting impressions of religious ceremonial, and in later life she often recalled the festivals, the processions, and the candles at the local church. But deepest perhaps of all the legacies of Varazze was the bond between the young Macaulays. Margaret, as the eldest sister, was rather more "grown-up" than the others, but Rose and Jean, Aulay and Will shared constantly in every game and adventure, and with Margaret they thought of themselves both then and later as "the five." Eleanor, several years younger and seldom included in the doings of "the five," was thus very much the odd one out. While the family was in Italy Grace Macaulay gave birth to another daughter, Gertrude, but to her great sorrow this lovely child died at Varazze at the age of three and a half.

The family returned to England in 1894, largely in the interests of the children's education, and they settled in Oxford where Margaret, Rose, and Jean were sent to the High School. Rose at this time was excessively shy. Although there had been visits to England during the time in Italy, Varazze had truly become home for her, and the contrast between the life there and the conventional Victorian ways of her contemporaries in England was sharp indeed. "Rosy," the family decided, was too childish a name and for some years she was known as Emily. She was also told sternly by her father that she must not talk about her longing to be a boy and join the Navy.

When Emily was fourteen she and Margaret were prepared for confirmation by the vicar of the Church of St. Philip and St. James in Oxford, where they used to attend the children's service. Emily felt many religious doubts (so she later disclosed), but was too tongue-tied to discuss them, and decided to submit to confirmation in silence.

In July 1899, according to a note by Grace Macaulay, "Emily left school and put up her hair." But she was loth to grow up. Never interested in clothes, she was a gawky, boyish figure, far happier on the hockey field than on the dance floor —by this time Aulay was at Woolwich, and he sometimes invited his sisters to dances there. Then in 1900 when Rose was nineteen came an important new development: Uncle Regi offered to send her to the university. During her three years at Somerville College, Oxford, when she read History and acquired a great love for the seventeenth century, a remarkable change came about in her. The painfully shy and awkward young girl became a vivacious talker and letter-writer, an adventurer in ideas and experiences, a popular companion who made friends wherever she went. When she came down, in the summer of 1903, she again lived at home. By now her father had an appointment at Aberystwyth so living at home meant rural Wales. Rose very much missed the stimulating company of Oxford and before long she was starting on her first novel. *Abbots Verney*, a sombre story in an Italian setting, was published in 1906. " If you want to be really interested and entertained," she wrote to a Somerville friend, " publish a novel; it's quite worth it! . . . It's a fearfully amusing occupation—so amusing that the financial side of it seems of very minor importance, except as a sort of justification, to turn it from play to earnest." She was also at this time " extracting an occasional guinea or two " from the *Westminster Gazette* for her poems; they were many of them in a wistful mood with religious undertones and nostalgic echoes of the Italian shore.

George Macaulay's next appointment was to Cambridge as Lecturer in English and in 1906 the family moved to Great Shelford, then a secluded village. By this time both the Macaulay boys had started careers; Aulay was with the Royal Engineers in India, and Will had just set off to farm in Canada. Jean, after a certain amount of protest from her mother (whose extreme possessiveness was becoming more and more of a trial to most of her children), had left home to become a nurse, so only Margaret, Rose, and Eleanor were at home.

Rose was writing more novels and being acclaimed as " a writer of no common ability," and life at Shelford was continuing as usual when in February 1909 came news of a shocking tragedy: Aulay had been murdered on the North-West Frontier. He had been journeying on duty through a lonely ravine when he was attacked and shot by thieves who wrongly believed he was carrying a large sum of money. The whole family was naturally devastated with grief, but to his nearest sisters the foundations of life seemed shaken. The inviolable unity of

" the five " had been violated. Rose for the first time turned spontaneously and with full seriousness to religion. Impulsively she offered herself as a missionary to the Universities' Mission to Central Africa, but her offer was declined, on grounds that she was unsuited for the work. Soon after this with Margaret and her mother she attended a retreat at St. Alban's, Holborn— a High Church stronghold—and it was at about this time that she first gave herself to the " Catholic " approach. In Cambridge at this same time Father Waggett, the Cowley Father, was at the peak of his brilliance as a preacher and was also a powerful social influence; Rose got to know him, and she and her mother often listened to his sermons. Meanwhile Margaret who since Aulay's death had often been doing mission work with the East London Deaconesses decided in mid-1911 to become a probationer with their community (she was ordained Deaconess two years later). Eleanor by 1912 was also away—in India, where she was teaching (later she became a missionary)—so Rose was now the only daughter at home. At this time she saw much of her father whom she greatly loved and also much respected for his scholarship of which a typical manifestation was a four-volume edition of the Latin, French, and English works of John Gower. Rose made several trips abroad with him; in the spring of 1912 they went together on a memorable Hellenic cruise. But during the years just before the war she was also coming to London more and more, joining with delight in quite a different circle.

Chiefly through Naomi Royde Smith, the literary editor of the *Westminster Gazette*, she met " a brilliant and vocal group of people "—Walter de la Mare, E. V. Knox, J. C. Squire, Middleton Murry, Hugh Walpole, and many others. " I liked them all," she later wrote. " They were all gay and intelligent and young or youngish, and haloed to me with the glamour and sophistication of London; they chattered of the literary and political world and its personalities as initiates—or so it seemed to me, who was a Cambridge provincial." By now Rose herself was beginning to make a mark as a novelist. Her book *The Lee Shore* was awarded a literary prize in 1912 and she had already established a reputation for " brilliant cleverness, yet with depths of thought" when her godfather, wishing to help her in her career as a writer, gave her a *pied-à-terre* in London, a tiny flat of her own off Chancery Lane. The year 1913 when Rose was dividing her time between the settled home at Cambridge and her exciting new life in London was a year of such happiness that she later called it her *Annus Mirabilis*.

Another tie in London was with St. Edward's House, Westminster, the Cowley Fathers' London headquarters, where Father Lucius Cary was her confessor, or in his absence Father Hamilton Johnson. In a letter to the writer of this Introduction dated 6th August 1959 Father Johnson has described his memories of his ministry to Rose as follows:

When I went, just before the first war, to St. Edward's House . . . Father Cary, who only occasionally came to London from Oxford, told me that he had told a few of his penitents to come to me when they could not easily get at him. Among these was Rose. She was living in Cambridge, and wrote notes to me from there at intervals to make appointments for her Confessions when she was coming to London from Cambridge; *nothing else at all in her letters*. This she did about half a dozen times, from the summer of 1914 until the autumn of 1916. Once (I think in Aug? 16) I found her (to my surprise) in a little *Retreat for Women* (or perhaps *Ladies*)—in some little Sisters' house, somewhere in the suburbs—I quite forget where—which I had been sent to conduct. I think she came to make her Confession at a time when others were doing so, and then asked me if she could come again to talk a little. This she did. We sat upright on chairs facing one another, both of us stiff and shy—much more stiff and shy than in the addresses in the little chapel, talking, I think, of nothing save only of how a young lady living with her family might most suitably conduct herself. That, I think, was my *one and only viva voce conversation* with Rose, (she sitting, and not kneeling) . . . Oh yes, and I remember looking out from the little parlour where I was put, into the little, dull, square garden, and seeing Miss Macaulay pacing up and down very gravely and slowly, I think *on the grass*, for a long while, in *steadily drizzling rain*, tall and grave and thoughtful, wearing some sort of dark tweed suit—no overcoat or rain-coat. This she did for a long time.

A few months after this, in November 1916, Father Johnson left for the United States, to join the Cowley Fathers' community at Boston, and his departure coincided with the beginning of a new stage in Rose's life. During the first years of the war she had tried various kinds of war work near Cambridge, first as a V.A.D. and then as a land-girl, but she was not well suited to either job. Meanwhile in 1915 George Macaulay had died and her mother afterwards moved to Beaconsfield. At this point Rose took a job at the War Office, and thenceforward London became her home and the literary set her natural milieu.

Before the war ended there came another important turning point for her. Until this time, though she already prized her independence in London, her family and the family home had been the axis of her life. Her affections, her writings, her travels, her hobbies, were all primarily related to home and family, though once, just before the war, she had almost become engaged. By 1917 she had written eight novels, all more or less auto-biographical and all—along with the " brilliant cleverness "—somewhat introspective and sad; there had also been a book of poems, *The Two Blind Countries*, which showed a searching thoughtfulness and melancholy. Underlying many of her writings was the theme of family relationships, especially of brother and sister, and there was a sexless quality about many of the leading characters in her novels which she underlined by giving them Christian names appropriate to either a man or a woman, a habit that later reasserted itself. But in wartime London Rose fell in love with a man who, she later learnt, was already married. For some years she struggled to combine their friendship with her now habitual religious practice. In the early twenties however their secret attachment deepened and eventually she broke away from the sacramental life of the Church. For nearly twenty years, until his death during the second world war, he was the dominant personal influence in her life. They met frequently in London and also abroad and her attachment became well known to her sisters and to her mother (who died in 1925) but was seldom discussed. Among her intimate friends in London the companionship was tacitly accepted, but outside Rose's immediate circle nothing was known of it.

The new pattern of Rose's life during the '20s when she took to living in a flat in Marylebone and also travelled much —sometimes with friends, sometimes with members of the family—was reflected in the change that came about in her writings. In 1919 her second book of poems, *Three Days*, was published, but subsequently there was no more poetry. Instead came a spate of witty, high-brow novels: *Potterism, Dangerous Ages, Mystery at Geneva, Told by an Idiot, Orphan Island, Crewe Train, Keeping up Appearances*, and *Staying with Relations*. There were also innumerable articles and reviews and she became famous for her flippant wit and sparkling satire as well as for her wide erudition. She often made mock of religion, especially of its incongruities and excesses, which won for her the reputation of an agnostic; nevertheless all through the time of her estrangement from the Church her instinctive leaning towards the religious continued to assert itself. Her ever widening circle of intellectual friends such as Gilbert Murray, E. M. Forster, and the Harold Nicolsons, for many of whom she had a warm admiration and affection, included few practising Christians, and to all appearances, during the inter-war years her life had hardly a point of contact with the Church. But Rose, with her talent for the paradoxical, had friends among the clergy even at this time. Occasionally too she attended church services, and much enjoyed listening to good preachers.

In 1931, Rose's fiftieth year, her book *Some Religious Elements in English Literature* was published. It is a brief work written in a vein of academic detachment, in which she set out to illustrate her theory that religious literature is usually the outcome of some kind of clash or conflict. *They Were Defeated*, her only historical novel, was published in the following year and together these two books marked the beginning of a new, more serious stage in her writing, with fewer novels and more essays and works on historical subjects and travel.

The second world war was a time of great personal stress for Rose. In 1941 her sister Margaret died which left Rose and Jean as the only surviving members of the family in England (Will had settled in Canada but never married; he died there in 1945). Jean's work as a District Nurse had recently brought her to Romford in Essex, so the two sisters were able to meet often and they became very intimate friends. Then soon after Margaret's death Rose's flat in Luxborough House, Marylebone, was bombed. Almost all her belongings were destroyed, including all her library and some unpublished manuscripts. Her many friends rallied round with gifts of books towards a new library but the shock of the loss had been desolating. At this time an additional distress for Rose was the fatal illness of the man she loved.

After his death she herself was seriously ill; in spite of the demands she always made on herself she was not at all physically strong. But before the end of the war she was hard at work again, busy with the research for her book *They Went to Portugal*. She did not write any fiction during the war but in 1950 came *The World my Wilderness* with its theme of loneliness and despair. In that same year Rose received the unexpected letter from Father Johnson which set off the correspondence that was to guide her gradually back into the Church and to lead to the inner transformation of her life.

When the correspondence began, and indeed for the first eighteen months of it, neither Rose nor Father Johnson had any idea they were related. But by chance Rose mentioned that her name had been chosen because her mother's mother had been one of the Rose family. It then came to light that through the Roses she and Father Johnson were fourth cousins—they had the same great-great-great-grandparents, Dorothy Vaughan and Joseph Foster Barham. This was a delight to Rose who was enormously interested in family relationships, but even more so to Father Johnson, to whom cousinship represented a very important family bond: in his own family a vast network of cousins was intricately complicated by intermarriage.

Father Johnson like Rose herself had innumerable clerical ancestors; he himself was the son, grandson, and great-grandson of Norfolk parsons. His great-grandfather, John Johnson (" Johnny of Norfolk "), was a cousin and close friend of William Cowper, the poet, for whom he cared devotedly throughout his last illness. In temperament the Johnsons tended to be sensitive and diffident, but possessed of unusual insight and understanding.

John Hamilton Cowper Johnson was born in 1877 and was the eldest of six brothers. His father found the expense of educating this family of sons a considerable burden and when Hamilton was seventeen a post was procured for him with the Eastern Telegraph Company. He worked for five years in Malta but then came to the conclusion that this was not his vocation and decided to take holy orders. After studying at home to qualify for entrance he went up to New College, Oxford, where he was a little older than the average undergraduate, and while at Oxford he came under the influence of the Cowley Fathers. He then trained at Cuddesdon and had two years in a curacy before joining the Cowley Fathers in 1906. Until 1914 he was at Cowley; he then spent just over two years at St. Edward's House, Westminster and in 1916 was transferred to the American branch of the Society. For the rest of his life (until his death in March 1961)—nearly forty-five years—he remained in America, beloved and respected by all who knew him. For many years he lived and worked at the S.S.J.E. Mission House in Bowdoin Street, Boston and later at the Monastery in Memorial Drive, Cambridge. During this time his outstanding gifts as spiritual director and confessor became well recognized and were given full scope.

His talent as a prolific letter-writer was very exceptional, and his letters, which were not confined to spiritual guidance, convey vividly his own vitality and sense of humour, also the joy he took in every detail connected with his correspondent. Until a few years before his death, when his health became increasingly precarious, he liked to keep in touch by letter with many of his numerous cousins, for example with John Cowper Powys (whose mother was his aunt). His relations with his Powys cousins were always warmly affectionate though there were sometimes "pitched dialectical battles" on the subject of Christianity. John Cowper Powys in his *Autobiography* has mentioned the intense pleasure it gave him to visit his cousin Hamilton in America, and also alluded to Hamilton's "astonishing knowledge of Latin."

Father Johnson's strong sense of family and his pleasure in reinforcing family bonds led him, when he discovered the cousinship with Rose, to introduce her by letter to one of his cousins in England, Mary Barham Johnson. The following extract is quoted from a letter he wrote to his cousin Mary on 24th February, 1952:

On Saturday I had a letter from our fourth cousin . . . I do so hope that you will meet her and make friends with her one day. I have not seen her for 36 years, and then only in a professional sort of way. In the summer of 1950, I wrote to her to tell her how much I had been interested by her historical novel *They Were Defeated*—now quite old. She welcomed my letter, and after a month, or 2 or 3 months, I was able to give her a little push back to where she belonged, *inside* the church door, instead of standing in the porch; and she has been grateful to me ever since, and has written me letters which have quickened and polished up my mind more than any school, college, or university ever did; besides making me laugh—for she is never *not* a humorist. She is also no small scholar; Cambridge made her a Doctor of Letters last June. *Moreover*, I feel sure that, *by nature*, Religion *is*, and always has been a bigger thing in her total make-up, than any of those other things, in which her pre-eminence is recognized.

After Rose's death in October 1958, for more than a year the present writer was in correspondence with Father Johnson, in connection with the plans for a book of Rose's letters. He had definite views on the subject and on 24th November, 1959, he wrote:

Throughout all this book-business, which you have so kindly undertaken, as nobody else *could*, I have felt that it is *most important* that it should be a book *about Rose—not* about Rose *and me*, which would be utterly misleading. Her letters to me began by her writing to me at a time when she was wanting a priest; just as if she had gone into a church in that state of mind, and had seen a priest whom she recognized go into a confessional-box, and then had suddenly thought that this might be the opportunity for which she was waiting, and had gone into the other part of the box, and had told him about her situation, without attempting to make her confession or asking for absolution—not until five months later, and *then not to him*. And so these letters began and continued, and gradually came to contain more secular matter, such as, in the case of Rose Macaulay, might well be of interest to people who have never seen the inside of such a box as that, or ever knelt at a prayer-desk with a crucifix above it. I am glad that my letters were not preserved.

It is much to be thankful for that Father Johnson should have given detailed guidance such as this on the question of how the letters should be presented, and should also have given his blessing to the publication of this book.

CONSTANCE BABINGTON SMITH

23

1950

August

20, *Hinde House, Hinde St., W.*1
30*th August,* 1950

Dear Father Johnson,

(I hope you don't dislike typed letters, because I type so much better than I write that I think it is only kind to my friends to do it.) I got back from a month in Italy last night, and, amid a pile of (mostly unwelcome) correspondence, found your letter, a very bright spot. It was indeed nice to hear from you again. And to know that you like that book of mine. Its real name (as published here) was *They were Defeated*, but the American publishers didn't like the word "defeated" (I think they were just emerging from a slump!) so called it *The Shadow Flies*, taking the words of course from the poem I quote. Rather foolish of them, I thought. *They were Defeated* is what it is about. Every one defeated—Julian Conybeare, Herrick, the Royalists, the Church, etc. I liked writing it, especially the part about Cambridge, which was very real to me, so were—and are —all the people in it. It was a lovely century in Cambridge; or anyhow those immediately pre-civil-war years were. So much poetry, so much flowering of Anglicanism in the middle of Puritanism, so much idealism on both sides. I'm glad you liked it.

I wonder if you would like my newest novel, to be published in America soon I believe. It is called *The World my Wilderness*, and is about the ruins of the City, and the general wreckage of the world that they seem to stand for. And about a rather lost and strayed and derelict girl who made them her spiritual home. Anyhow, on the chance that you may care to see it, I am getting my publishers to send you a copy. Perhaps you won't like it at all. Do not bother to write about it. Though anything you wrote to me about any subject would have interest and pleasure for me. If you were in England, I should probably ask if I might come and talk to you sometimes, and I wish you were. I remember that Retreat so well—though, like you, I don't remember its position in space or time; but I think the time must have been either just before or soon after the beginning of the first war; the place I feel, for some reason, may have been somewhere in Surrey? But I don't know. What I do remember is how much what you said helped and stimulated me. It is now very many years since I went to a Retreat or anything at all of that nature; I have sadly lost touch with that side of life, and regret it. We do need it so badly, in this queer world and life, all going to pieces and losing. Most of my younger friends have never had it, and haven't, therefore, that ultimate sanction for goodness, unselfishness, integrity, kindness, self-denial, which those brought up to believe in God accept at any rate as ideals, even if they have lost the belief. Like the generation of my father and uncles, parsonage-bred (like you), and, though agnostic, so *good*. I like to think of an uncle[1] who died a few years ago; he was Vice-Provost of King's, and the one I dedicated *They were Defeated* to; he had been an agnostic (very noble in character) from his undergraduate days on; but when he was dying he said to his sister, who had mentioned God and a future life, " Well, there's nothing so rum it might not be true," which pleased my aunt very much.

I rather wish the rising generation of clergy were more intellectual; so many seem rather chumps; or do I generalise from inadequate experience? I don't really know many. But I have a feeling that one's scholarly clerical ancestors might rather turn in their graves at the thought of them—or of many of them, for I know intelligent ones. I wonder how it is in America as to this. And, in Puritan New England, how much high Protestant Episcopalianism flourishes, and when you say mass in the garage-chapel, whether it is Anglican or P.E. (I know of course that they are affiliated). In any case, please go on occa-sionally remembering me when you think of it, for I value that extremely.

[1] W. H. Macaulay, Vice-Provost of King's College, Cambridge, 1918-24.

I have built up a library again, partly from family books, partly buying them; though some I can never replace. But one feels rather like a ghost, all papers and letters gone, and all belongings. I found this flat at once after being bombed out; it is small but pleasant, close to Manchester Square. I am now busy with a book on " The Pleasures of Ruins "—interesting to do, but a vast subject. I was looking at some in Italy. Do write again some time, when time has a gap. Thank you for telling me about Fr. Cary[1]; I hadn't heard.

Yours very sincerely,
Rose Macaulay

September

20, Hinde House, Hinde St., W.1
28th September, 1950

Dear Father Johnson,

It was good to get both your letters; thank you so much. I am glad my Anglican and R.C. " Church-going "[2] recalled to you those two lovely things—cathedral choirs and organ, and the primitive chanting drone. The setting of the first was actually King's College chapel—hence the Eton-and-Cambridge lector. It is so beautiful always; the candles, and the boys' voices, and the vaulted roof. I used to go a lot when we lived in Cambridge, and my darling uncle was Vice-Provost. I heard him read the First Lesson once; it was about Adam and Eve, and he sounded so surprised by it. The second kind of worship, the Latin chanting, goes further back in my memory, and, as you too feel, causes emotion when recalled. You can sing it; I can't, only in my mind. Perhaps religion should come to us in one of these frames—not too directly. I think the Quakers make a mistake, in having no frame, only direct communication,

---

[1] Rev. Henry Lucius Moultrie Cary, S.S.J.E. (d. 8th Jan., 1950).
[2] See R. M.'s *Personal Pleasures*.

which can be doubted. I like Latin for prayer; and I like the 16th and 17th century language (as in the collects); both have dignity, and one gets it, so to speak, at one remove.

You are right about everything being " rum "; that is a great thing to hold to. So one can select what one likes, out of the extraordinary possibilities. Thank you for reminding me of those Lucretius lines; I have been looking them up; they are beautiful, and apt to us; indeed, he so often is.

I liked the celluloid prayers[1]: he must have been (be) a nice candle merchant; because one can't see how celluloid prayers can be part of his business; or profitable. I shall keep them by me. I believe you would think my approaches to religion far too subjective. (But I should find it difficult to explain in a letter what I mean by this.) Here is a world perishing from lack of goodness, and we want a God who can help us to this. And we want to be sure that God wants us to be good. And that he is there at all.

I don't think I could go and talk to Fr. Wilkins[2]; I have no claim on him, and he would wonder what I was at. And he would rightly think, if this woman has lived so long without making up her mind about God, she isn't likely to do so now. He even might induce me to think I had, but it would be a delusion. But, if ever I should find myself in Memorial Drive, Cambridge, Mass., I should telephone to you, and would like to talk about all kinds of things (I don't mean over the telephone !). The changes in the collects, Latin and English, the Anglican Church, heaven and hell, books, God, the American liturgy, everything. By the way, I hope you will receive safely *The World my Wilderness* that I sent you. Tell me sometime anything that strikes you about it, if you have time to read it. And, if it *doesn't* reach you, say in the next month, do let me know, and I will look into it. I'm not sure how long books take; it was sent at the time I wrote before, or a few days after.

[1] Father Johnson had sent R. M. some of the celluloid " cards " printed with Latin prayers distributed by the Mack-Miller Candle Co. Inc. of Syracuse, N. Y.

[2] Rev. Bernard Dashwood Wilkins, S.S.J.E. (d. 7th June, 1960), one of the Cowley Fathers then at St. Edward's House, Westminster.

I am struggling with my book on " The Pleasure of Ruins." It is a vast subject, and difficult rather, but fun. I am now tackling the artificial ruins of the 18th century, an enchanting fashion, nonsensical, but charming. I would have liked to lay out my garden with ruined temples and grottos and fragments of an ancient abbey and a model of a Roman arch.

> " O how charming the walks to my fancy appear,
> " What a number of temples and grottos are here! "

as a contemporary of Pope's wrote. It was a lovely fad.

The people I love most have died. I wish they had not. But there is nothing to be done about it. Not only my parents —that was to be expected, of course—but my favourite sister, two brothers, and the man I loved. This seems one of the many reasons for wanting, so to speak, a link with another sphere of life. But I mustn't bother you with this. One should consume one's own smoke. But it was so nice to hear from you that I got led on. Thank you for writing so kindly.

Yours very sincerely,

Rose Macaulay

October

20, *Hinde House, Hinde St., W.*1
28*th October,* 1950

Dear Father Johnson,

I am writing in the train, on the way to the christening of an infant cousin at Eton, so please forgive my shocking handwriting: as you know, I usually spare my friends this by typing. (Train not moved yet: if it becomes too bad, I will stop writing.) *Your* handwriting is so clear—and with it so nice to look at— that it is better than type: mine, alas, *not*.

Thank you for your two letters—one at Michaelmas, the other 12th Oct. Both full of interest. I look up all your references that I can find. I looked up Mr. Dunstan[1] (who, I think, was quoting—or I was—Boehme) and that Roman missal collect (you say the 1st Xmas Mass—in my missal, the 3rd) and the Hebrews verse you wrote under poor Isie's O'Shaughnessy[2]; but I don't remember where is "*Cum de ruinis damnosisque*,"[3] etc., and would like to. I like to pick up and follow your trails, in hope. If (when) we meet "*coram*,"[4] I shall pick up some more. What, too sadly likely, I may *not* pick up, is the power to believe those things—I mean, the actual facts, (as you put it, what God has *done*). How I wish I could get there. Partly my difficulties are intellectual—I just can't make the grade—partly, I sometimes think, the blindness that comes from the selfish and deplorable life I've led. Who knows? It's all a kind of vicious circle—badness keeps one from the realisation of God; perhaps nothing but that could cure badness—well, so there one is. "*Quos sub peccati jugo vetusta servitus tenet.*"[5] And I expect one has to find a way through by some other road, that one can more easily accept. Who knows? Now this train is really *too* mobile; I must stop, and continue later.

Hinde House. Back on *terra firma* again. I like the Deposited Book baptism service,[6] which seems always used now. And I like Eton College chapel. And I like babies; this one is called Michael Conybeare, and is, so far, an agnostic, and doesn't much care for holy water or Holy Church (or so he seemed to indicate).[7] He makes a mistake: it is a glorious service—all those tremendous promises his godparents make for him (I was not one), and that are so seldom kept.

[1] Possibly this refers to Edgar Grieve Dunstan, editor of *The Wayfarer*, the Quaker monthly journal, 1929-45.

[2] The reference to "poor Isie's O'Shaughnessy" is nowhere elucidated in the letters, but it may relate to Father Johnson's habit of writing texts etc. in the margins of any book he was reading.

[3] "Since concerning ruins and destructive forces."   [4] "Face to face."

[5] "Whom their ancient slavery keeps beneath the yoke of sin."

[6] The Baptism service as revised in the 1928 Prayer Book.

[7] A slip by R. M. The Conybeare baby, a grandson of R. M.'s first cousin Bruce Conybeare, was named John Bruce not Michael.

*Father Johnson
at Foxborough,
Massachusetts,
in 1950*

Of course Fr. Palmer[1] is quite right. I think, when you are on the Gulf of Mexico, I shall voyage there—I have felt for some ? years (*how* many?) that I should like to talk to you again. Don't you preach missions too, as well as household chores, and services near home? If not, I don't know why not.

They have just re-published a novel I wrote in 1920— *Potterism*—and I am sending you a copy, as you seem to have a kindly toleration for my books. This one is very old, rather " dated," and I expect rather crude—I think it preaches, too! Still, I send it.

Thank you for " remembrancing " me sometimes, and please go on.

Yours very sincerely,
Rose Macaulay

November

20, *Hinde House, Hinde St., W.*1
27th *November*, 1950 [*probably by airmail*]

Dear Father Johnson,

Now I have *two* letters from you, which is lovely. Yes, I got that of 9th Nov. the other day; how sorry I should have been if it had failed to be collected, because it is so stuffed with good things of different kinds, all of which I want to talk about, sacred and profane. I see I was stupid about the Horace. I have now looked it up; I might well have included the 2nd stanza; I suppose I felt that the one about how each generation is worse than the one before was more precisely to my point in that section of my book. It is interesting how religious Horace and so many Romans were: polytheists like J. C. Powys (so they are your cousins) and with how stern a sense of the Gods' commands—like the Greeks. Yes, that letter from Rufus *would* do for my Ruin book—" *quum uno loco tot oppid*[*or*]*um cadavera*

---

[1] One of the American Cowley Fathers then at Cambridge, Mass.

projecta jacent . . ."[1] it is such an awful picture. Thank you for reminding me of it, for I shall certainly quote some of it, to illustrate one of the ruin-pleasures. But what a letter of condolence to get on the death of a beloved child! I have always thought how Cicero must have resented it. I think Rufus had never lost any one very dear. By the way, Cassell's Latin Dict. says *Hem!* is " an exclamation of surprise, wonder, joy, grief, etc. Ah! well! only see! just look!" (Latin words nearly always seem to have so many meanings, some of them of opposite sense; this makes one's Latin lessons at school so difficult). As you say " my hat!" would often do. We might well re-introduce it; also *ne* and *num* might be useful. The trouble with " *hem* " is, people might think you were just clearing your throat.

As to the child St. Augustine heard, I don't think, do you, that he was necessarily indoors. Doesn't *domus* mean, besides a house, a house and garden, as the vast palaces and courts and grounds of the Roman emperors were called " *domus Tiberiana,*" " *domus Augustana,*" " *domus aurea,*" etc. I expect the child was picking figs or grapes, saying " take, gather." This does seem more likely than " read."[2]

I am afraid you may be right about Fr. Jacinto.[3] I liked him myself, and put him in for a joke, never meaning to be offensive, but I do hope R.C.s didn't mind, or feel I was being offensive. I believe there are some pretty odd *ladino* priests in South and Central America; but also so many good ones, and, as you say, it may well be that the Jacintos would not be allowed long. In pursuing a joke, one should remember the point of view of those who may resent it. I should hate to offend R.C.s, very many of whom are my friends, or even relations. What do they feel about Graham Greene's drunken priest in *The Power and the Glory*? That was Mexico, of course, and a persecuted, hunted church, which makes it different.

[1] Sulpicius Rufus writing to Cicero says: "(What? Do we puny human beings feel indignant if some friend of us men, whose life ought to be shorter, dies or gets killed), while on a single site lie the relics of so many towns overthrown?" See Cicero, *Ad Fam.* 4.5,4.
[2] See St. Augustine, *Confessions*, Bk. 8, Chap. 12.
[3] See R. M.'s *Staying with Relations*.

I like looking up your collects. Would you say "whose mysteries of light," or "the mysteries of whose light"? Perhaps it doesn't matter. But surely not "of which light." I shall say your collect, "*Per hujus, Domine, operationem Mysterii, et vitia nostra purgentur . . .*"[1] I like it.

You ask about the Conybeares. I am half one; I mean, my mother was one. The Dr. Conybeare in *They were Defeated* was the son of an Elizabethan schoolmaster who was my ancestor; we have the line of descent, and a little Latin book he wrote; it was edited and reprinted by my mother's cousin F. C. Conybeare, an atheistical Oxford don, who wrote a book called *Myth, Magic, and Morals* (the Latin book[2] was by the schoolmaster, not by Dr. C.). I invented Dr. Conybeare in a sense, but I made him as like as I could to my cousin Fred of Oxford, atheism, appearance and all. But I have no reason for thinking that he ever existed in the 17th c., or Julian either. Possibly he may have! Did you ever chance to come across W. J. Conybeare, late Provost of Southwell, now retired? He is my cousin, and wrote two years ago a little book of his reminiscences, called *Here's a Church—Let's Go In.* Thinking that, as you are interested in family histories and the past, it might please you to see

[*The next page of this letter was missing when the correspondence was received from Father Johnson.*]

---

[1] " By the operation of this Mystery, O Lord, may even our sins be washed away."

[2] *Letters and Exercises of the Elizabethan Schoolmaster, John Conybeare, with Notes and a Fragment of Autobiography by William Daniel Conybeare, Edited by F. C. Conybeare* (1905).

35

December

20, *Hinde House, Hinde St., W.*1
9th December, 1950

Dear Father Johnson,

Thank you much for your letter posted on 22nd Nov. For a moment I thought, when I saw the envelope, that a miracle had been wrought for me, and that it might be answering one I wrote you on 28th Nov.,[1] and that I dare say you haven't even yet received, posts between Hinde Street and Memorial Drive being what they are. But of course it wasn't, and I am glad to have it as an interim letter, pending your possible reply to mine, in which I put up to you a problem for solution and asked your advice. Whatever it is, I shall take it. Meanwhile, thank you for many good things in two languages in this last letter.

Yes, I suppose I *am* grounded in religious knowledge more or less, having been brought up that way; and also, perhaps, inheriting an interest in theology and church literature from a thousand (or so) clerical ancestors, who, I presume, had it all at their fingertips. Of late years I'm afraid it has got rather rusty; but I still do know days and psalms and creeds and even most of the major heresies! I am much better instructed than Rome Garden,[2] who didn't know the connection between ceremonies and doctrine. But the way you put it is much more illuminating than anything I had really grasped about the history of the High Church connection with ritual, or anyhow you express it better. I think the excitement of the new spirit, the beginning of Anglo–Catholicism, in the 17th century, especially in the universities, must have been extraordinarily moving; the

[1] Presumably this refers to the letter which R. M. dated 27th November see above pp. 33-35), of which the latter part (and the envelope) is missing.
[2] See R. M.'s *Told by an Idiot.*

36

return (tentative) of ornament and crosses, etc., and decency of worship in the churches and college chapels (as in St. John's under Dr. Beale) and in Cosin's diocese—but I think I have said all this in that book I wrote[1]; it has always held my imagination. All my researches while I was writing that book failed to discover a clear instance of the *Crucifix* (as a separate object, not a picture) in churches. I think those Dr. Cosin was accused of having were all in paintings; though in one account it is not altogether clear. How far, I wonder, did William Law go in ritual? The times were against him; but such clergy as he and Dr. Cole (Horace Walpole's antiquarian friend) were very much inclined that way. I gather that the Tractarians were rather austere about ritual, weren't they? My father's father was a High Church rector; but there was no adornment in his church, and I think my father always said that he preached in a black gown. I suppose it was Fr. Stanton[2] and his contemporaries who really got all that going. I remember reading that Tyrrell didn't like it, when he worked in the East End under that ritualistic vicar, before his conversion[3]; too much "millinery," he thought. I have always liked it myself.

It is interesting, that ancient belief in blood as the sealer of covenants. Doesn't it go back beyond the Jews, to the Greek mysteries, and the Egyptian? It means something very profoundly deep in human religion, I suppose. I can't quite get at it ever; I mean, just why. But there must be something, and it has gone on and on, not only in Christianity, but in childish agreements, sealed with a drop of blood squeezed out by a prick of a needle, as I remember. It seems fundamental.

Later. In a train. As you were (unlike some of my correspondents) quite tolerant of my last train-letter, I am taking this one to go on with on a week-end journey. If it gets too shaky, I will

[1] *They Were Defeated.*

[2] Rev. Arthur Henry Stanton (1839-1913), Anglo-Catholic curate at St. Alban's, Holborn, famous for his preaching.

[3] Before he was received into the Roman Church in 1879, Rev. George Tyrrell, S. J. (1861-1909) lived for some months in an Anglo-Catholic mission house in South-East London organised by Fr. Dolling.

stop. I wish I wrote like you, who are legible even with a blue stilus.

That question about *knowing*, I have often asked it of believing friends and relations. They say it depends on what you mean by " know." They *feel* certain. Or, in some cases, are putting their shirts on a *hope*, because if it's not true, they feel they might as well lose the shirt along with everything else of value to them—they are quite right, of course. I wish I had as much guts.

I believe I like the English of that " chain of our sins " prayer even better than the Latin—the beautiful monosyllabic run of " though we be tied and bound by the chain of our sins "—and " loose us " at the end. It is one of the very best collects, I think, both for sound and sense. Is the other (" *absolve, quaesumus* "[1] . . .) perhaps better in Latin? I don't know. I like both—and the " *liberemur* "[2] at the end. They are prayers to use.

Thank you for writing, and for letting me write to you. I value it very much. It is a wonderful *revenance* from the far past, which I never supposed would cross my orbit again. It gives me a lot to consider—— But I wrote of all that in my last, which you will be getting sometime soon.

I am approaching my goal, so will stop.

R. M.

20, *Hinde House, Hinde St., W.*1
15*th December,* 1950

Dear Father Johnson,

Thank you so very much for your letter (air) of 9th and 10th, which came yesterday, by the same post as your letter of 27th and 28th, and the two numbers of *Cowley*, which interest me much. I find in them, inter alia, two pictures of you, which I like; one reading in the Refectory; I wonder what book.

Thank you for everything you say, and for being so immeasurably wise, good and understanding. I am relieved that

---

[1] " Absolve, we beseech thee."   [2] " May we be set free."

you can say "*nequaquam miror*."[1] I might have known that, of course. But when I wrote that rather difficult letter, I wasn't sure.

I suppose I too have lived " well in " a treacle well,[2] another kind of treacle, I mean, a climate of opinion and attitude in which the people one knows—and often likes or loves—do that kind of thing often, and don't think badly of it in themselves or others. So gradually, if one is doing it oneself, one sinks more and more well in, and can't even see clearly what it really is. One gets clogged about; treacle is so clinging. No doubt I am still partly in; though it is over, one can't struggle right out. To change the metaphor, long years of wrong-doing build a kind of blank—or nearly blank—wall between oneself and God, and the task is to break it down, or at least to make holes in it large enough to see through. It isn't, of course, God who puts up the wall; it is one's own actions and rejections. So blank is the wall—though less so than a few weeks ago, and this is your doing —that even communion might be barren and almost meaning- less—not seeing through a window, but from far off, through a telescope with a very murky glass. As to absolution, I suppose this would make holes in the wall. Absolution from Memorial Drive, which I feel I have (however undeservedly), has already made some.

If I go to confession, hadn't I better go to some chance priest, in some church where I could join an anonymous queue, not to someone I should have to make an appointment with and give my name, such as Fr. Wilkins? It would seem easier. Or is it better to go to someone whom one has reason to believe might be helpful? I don't know. And I shouldn't know what priest, being well out of that world. Meanwhile, as you say, I can go to church, and hope to get at something in that way.

Well, I think this is quite enough about me, anyhow for the moment. There are, as usual, a lot of interesting things in your letters. Dear Fr. Waggett :[3] he was a great friend of ours at

[1] " I am by no means surprised."
[2] See *Alice in Wonderland*; the Dormouse's story at the Mad Tea Party.
[3] Rev. Philip Napier Waggett, S.S.J.E. (1862-1939).

Cambridge, before 1914. Wasn't he sent there to counteract the influence of Hugh Benson at the R.C. cathedral, who was making converts? Every one loved him (Fr. Waggett, I mean). He was the most brilliant and enchanting person. We used sometimes to sit under him at St. Giles's; he could, by the turn of a phrase, set the whole congregation laughing (which he once said he deplored, but I think can't have). I remember his bicycling out in a snow-storm to stay the night with us, to take a Lent service at a church two or three miles outside Cambridge, and how we enjoyed having him. He used to call me " the hockey girl," because of sometimes meeting me coming in with my hockey stick after some match. We had that little book of Holy Week addresses[1]; I don't know where it is now. I recognise the passages you quote. How vivid they are, and how good. " Theft and envy "; that was so like him. He was, wasn't he, rather broken down by his war chaplain time, and later returned to Cambridge (we had left it then, after my father's death) in poor health and form. He was a unique person.

I must read that " English Reformation " book. Oh dear, if only the Ref. had happened differently, under the leadership of More, Colet, Erasmus, if only Somerset hadn't been as he was, if only they hadn't had that orgy of smashing and spoiling, if only the Marian persecutions hadn't sent Protestants fleeing to Amsterdam to be infected with Calvinism, or if only they hadn't come back. Then the Anglican Church might have developed differently from the first, been from the first more lovely, fine and learned, without puritanism, sabbatarianism or fundamentalism. Still, we could scarcely have had a better prayerbook and liturgy. I wonder if any R.C.s deplore the Counter-Reformation. In some ways, one could; and obviously (as we think of our own) it could have been much better done. I like those Tridentine sentences. I have never been enough into the Council of Trent to know how many of its declarations said something fresh (e.g. about the Mass) or how many were merely reaffirmations. And I wonder what ex-R.C.s, such as your

[1] P. N. Waggett, *The Heart of Jesus* (1902).

Canadian priest, feel about the differences between the two churches. . . .

I like *Blackfriars*[1] when I see it. And, usually, Dominicans when I see them. I sometimes do, as Archbishop Mathew, the R.C. arch. of East Africa, and his brother Gervase O.P. are friends of mine. Both very able. The arch. is good on history, particularly on R.C. life in England since the Reformation; he writes with learning and style, and has an affection for the C. of E. . . .

If I come on the Everyman More I will send it, but fear it may be out of print. I have read that Dialogue[2] in an Arber reprint, and liked it very much I remember. No, I could never write a novel about that period, because the language they talked was just too different from ours to make easy dialogue which wouldn't sound affected. By the 17th century this isn't so. And there is such a mass of letters, diaries, memoirs, plays, essays, of this period that one can soak oneself in the language and easily reproduce it. In the early 16th century there is much less available of colloquial talk, and one doesn't quite hear them talking. I should have to make them talk modern English, as I don't like the usual compromise, and I should hate to do that, it would be all wrong, and would modernise the idiom of their thought too.

Thank you for imprecating my reviewer! You are the friend whom every author wants. It is so comforting to have someone indignant with the reviews which one tries not to feel unfair and anyhow can't with dignity complain of oneself. I did see that review, I forget what paper, but someone sent it me. I suppose the reviewer didn't happen to like the book, probably didn't read it all, perhaps was in the wrong mood for it, or was the wrong reader. And no doubt much that he or she said was justified, tho' obviously he is weak on French geography. One mustn't be too hard on reviewers, who are generally in a hurry. But some of the American reviews have been very nice. I enclose one (don't want it back) I forget what paper it comes from.

[1] A Dominican monthly review.
[2] Probably *Dialogue of Comfort against Tribulation* by Thomas More.

I would like to know what you think of Victor Gollancz's anthology *A Year of Grace*, so am sending it you. It has a lot of interesting things in it—religion from all angles, from all ages, all races. V.G. is a brilliant and philosophic Jew, with Christian leanings. Not a *practising* Jew, but believes in God.

There is snow here. I am just in from tobogganing down Primrose Hill with two small girls and their parents. We only had a tea-tray.

Christmas posts are so dubious and slow that I think I will make this a 3d. letter.[1] It brings my Christmas greetings, and a good many things that I haven't said and can't say, but that I hope you will understand.

Yours very sincerely and gratefully,
Rose Macaulay

20, *Hinde House, Hinde St., W.*1
23rd December, 1950 † [2]

Dear Father Johnson,

Thank you so much for your letter of 13th. I hope that by now one of my two former letters has reached you—one air, the earlier ordinary mail. But I am writing again, because there seem so many things I want to say, and you make me feel that you put up with my badgering.

Thank you for copying "*pro vivis et defunctis.*"[3] I haven't got a full Roman missal. I suppose "*venia*"[4] is the pre-requisite for learning fresh things and making fresh advances. One likes to think that if the dead go on at all, in any mode, it must be progressive—perhaps more quickly and with fewer set-backs than in life. I think, if one felt that one had received *venia*, the next stages would show themselves, and one might be shewn what one had to do and be, to make up a little for the past. And I see that it should be officially notified, not a matter of private

[1] Marginal note here by R. M.: "No! I see I am mistaken about this rate."

[2] This symbol indicates that the letter was sent by airmail.

[3] "For the living and the dead."   [4] "Pardon."

enterprise; it is more satisfactory like that, and freer from danger of self-deception.

I am leaving a lot of things till I hear from you again, perhaps with further recommendations as to procedure.

I always use the P[rayer] B[ook] version of the psalms, when I read them. I like Coverdale's translation better than the A[uthorized] V[ersion] (Tyndale's?). I have been reading the 119th. Was it all by one author? There is a great difference of mood; between, e.g. "*Adhaesit pavimento* "[1] and "*Legem pone* "[2] on the one hand, and "*Principes persecuti sunt*,"[3] with its stress on "I have kept thy commandments." Yet in the very next section he says "I have gone astray . . ." Perhaps the expression of different moods. By the way, you mention the verse in Ps. 73, "Yea, and I had almost said even as they: but lo," etc. You will think me dense, but I have never quite known what it means. I wish you would tell me. Perhaps it is a muddled translation? Or perhaps I am merely stupid.

I liked your account of Fr. Humphreys's[4] Requiem and burial in the little woodland cemetery. Are the Fathers all British, or are there Americans among them? This is the kind of thing that Fr. Pedersen[5] will be able to tell me, if, as I hope, I see him when he is here. He will also give me news of you, and I should much like that. Do ask him to make himself known to me, either by letter or by *coup de téléphone*, when he is in London, and we will meet. My address is in the telephone directory, so he can look me up, if he would really like to be so kind as to spare the time.

In a train. I wonder if you agree with me that *Potterism* is rather jejune and too much of a tract. I feel I hammered away with a kind of angry fervour. I could probably rewrite it better now. I am glad you prefer the *Wilderness*. Thank you for that nice, kind review, which I hadn't seen, and am glad of. I haven't

[1] "(My soul) cleaveth to the dust." Ps. 119. 25-32.
[2] "Teach me (O Lord, the way of) thy statutes." Ps. 119.33-40.
[3] "Princes have persecuted me." Ps. 119.161-68.
[4] Rev. Robert Fletcher Humphreys, S.S.J.E. (1884-1950).
[5] Rev. A. L. Pedersen, S.S.J.E., of the American Congregation at Cambridge, Mass.

heard how the book is doing over there; probably not very well, it is so British! I am just now writing, (by fits and starts) poetry: a disease of which I have always had periodical attacks. I tried to make a complete poem of those 3 lines I used for the title-page of the *Wilderness*, but didn't do very much of it. Then I turned to Hadrian's Villa, Tiberius and Capri, Sybaris, etc. All rather time-wasting, but I like it. It is probably the " primitive droning," that meets so deep a need.

Christmas Eve. I am just off to the country, to spend Christmas with a charming and gifted family, great friends of mine, in what probably will be the deep snows of the Kentish weald. I am driving my car, and hope the roads won't be iced.

Oh dear, how I wish you were a little nearer at hand!

Yours,

R. M.

1951

January

Dear Father Johnson,

Your air letter posted 29th reached me to-day, which was quick; thank you so much for it. The letter before that (posted 15th) came about ten days ago; I answered it (air) on Christmas Eve. You *should* have got before you wrote on the 29th my sea letter of 12th or so, answering yours of 29th Nov., and talking about Fr. Waggett and how we knew him at Cambridge, and other things of not much importance; in yours you had most obligingly and consolingly cursed a reviewer for me. Posts are rather uneven; some letters seem to take longer than others sent by the same route. But, however and whenever they arrive, *all* your letters are better to get than I could easily tell you. They all seem to light some fresh candle.

The one that came to-day was, also, a great relief to my mind; before I got it, *timor mortis conturbaverat me*[1] a good deal, so thank you for reassuring me. Of course your phrase was more likely to be generally precautionary, but it might, on the other hand, have not been so. As to your semi-seriousness, in Latin or English, I find it very much to my taste; and certainly should in the confessional. Anyhow, please out-live anyone whom you can reasonably out-live. I like the people I am fond of and rely on to live well into the nineties; unfortunately they tend not to do this, and the more I want them to the more they don't. My oldest living relation now is an aunt[2] of 83; she may well live into the 90s, but then I don't really particularly want her to.

Thank you for producing a bishop[3] for me—and such a

---

[1] " The fear of death had confounded me."   [2] Mary Macaulay.
[3] Rt. Rev. K. E. Kirk (1886-1954), Bishop of Oxford 1937-54 and formerly Regius Professor of moral and pastoral theology in the University of Oxford.

47

bishop, for whom I have an immense respect. Too much respect, I suppose, because the difficulty is that I should never pluck up courage to write to him—or, anyhow, to post the letter if I did. I should feel too presumptuous. He must get thousands of letters from his own diocese, and wouldn't his secretary (if a good one) turn down out of hand any ultra-diocesan request of that kind? If he did answer, I am sure it would be kindly, because I should mention your name, but I should still feel I was encroaching on his time and attention. To ask a bishop (and him of Oxford, too) to turn from his weighty affairs and intellectual preoccupations to attend to a stray person from another diocese, and me not even a clergyman—wouldn't it seem to him rather cool? He would probably do it, and do it splendidly (because of you) but the feeling that I was presuming might make me too shy to utter. So I don't think I can. Don't think me ungrateful and choosey. But I now think (as you take a poor view of anonymous QUEUES) that I will adopt your earlier suggestion, and ask Fr. Wilkins if I may come and see him. So I telephoned to-day to St. Edward's House and enquired about him, and was told that he was at Oxford this week but would be back after that. So I might then write him the ominous letter; if I mention you, I should feel the assurance given by the introduction of a friend, and should be within the Society, which I should like. It will anyhow be difficult, making a confession covering about 30 years, years full of all the usual crimes of commission and omission (most of which I have of course forgotten), as well as the major business. How do people do it? Oh dear. Well, I suppose it will get done somehow. I wish you were here.

3rd January. Snow, frost and sleet; I expect Memorial Drive is deep in snow. I have been wandering about the Abbey, where one keeps on finding fresh pleasures. I believe the Dean and Chapter are in hiding, being liable to imprisonment in the Tower for not guarding the coronation stone better[1]; but there

[1] The Coronation Stone was removed from Westminster Abbey by Scottish nationalists on 24th December, 1950.

was evensong, sung very beautifully among the soaring vaults among the crowd of listening marbled ghosts and the fat little cherubs mourning them. As a point of theology, *ought* cherubs to weep for the decease and entry into heaven of these eminent beings? I am sorry such tombs are over. Are there any like them in our late colonies? No, I suppose baroque, in that exuberant form, never settled in New England among the Puritans. What beauties they missed! I like to hear that I have more letters coming to me. *Good.* Thank you all the time.

Yours affectionately,

R. M.

20, *Hinde House, Hinde St., W.*1
9th January, 1951†

Dear Father Johnson,

Thank you very much indeed for your air letter of 2nd Jan. How I miss your various sea-letters that have never come— I suppose mine haven't either—e.g. mine of 15th Dec., thanking you for yours that I valued so much. And if your letters posted *before Christmas Day* haven't yet reached me, it must surely mean that a ship has been sunk without trace, which probably happens oftener than we think? But I dare say Christmas is a bad season for posts, and that I shall get them one day—I do hope so, because I like them v. much.

Fr. Wilkins is hearing my confession on Friday 12th. In his reply he sounded very pleased that we both know you; so am I. Perhaps I may see him on some later and more auspicious occasion, and talk of you. He says he saw you in Boston in '48.

I have been very stupid always about that verse in Ps. 73, because I vaguely supposed it to mean that "even as they" was what he had almost said: and connected it with the verse before, about his having been punished every morning; so I couldn't make sense of it. I should like the psalms published with quotation marks for the speeches, and with names of the supposed speakers; they really *are* confusing sometimes. Till your explanation it hadn't, for some reason, occurred to me that it meant "I had almost said what *they* say", of course it is quite clear, and very logical and good. I have a Psalter interleaved with blank pages, that my father used at Eton, and that is inscribed in his round childish fourteen-year-old hand with the explanatory notes of his instructors—as Ps. 24, v. i—"idea then was that the earth was flat, surrounded by sea and round like a plate, with water underneath"—Ps. 8, 5—"Cicero says, *homo mortalis deus*"[1]—etc., etc. But nothing about Ps. 73. I like the sense of that verse now. Oh dear, I do hope it is true what you say, that I have never in my books "condemned the generation," etc. I have certainly never *meant* to—but one writes too carelessly, and gives impressions by mistake sometimes. I'm not proud of that book about the Buchmanites and the Basques,[2] I think now it is rather a *bad* joke, I mean about the Groupers; one shouldn't really make fun of people who, however aesthetically repellent to one's taste, are, after all, on the right side as between moral good and evil. To do this would be to condemn all the generations of revivalists, "enthusiasts," salvationists, excitable pietists—and look what practical good they have done in a wicked world. All very difficult. Moral; don't write about such people at all; I mean, *I* shouldn't. I hear that Monsignor Knox's book on "Enthusiasm" is v. good, and doesn't lack sympathy at all. But I'm very glad you feel I have avoided irreverent levity, if only narrowly. And I'm glad too that you saw the religious motif in the *Wilderness*. To me it was important. But of course most readers don't see such things, they are too busy with other aspects. Their heart is as FAT AS BRAWN. You are the most discerning of readers, and see all I mean.

10*th*. You will note with relief that I have rejoined my type-writer, from which I was temporarily severed. Wish I could hand-write better. Still no sea letters from you, is it not odd. I feel I am missing what I could have very well done with just now. All this digging into the past is painful ... with my many privileges, it is bad. I suppose the worst betrayal was when I

[1] "Man is a mortal god."   [2] R. M.'s *Going Abroad*.

... went to confession, and went away ... meaning to come back ... and I never after that returned to any sacraments ... I don't mean, can one be forgiven, but can one be good, honest, unselfish, scrupulous. Or is the whole basis and structure of character sapped by the long years of low life? I see horribly clearly how low it was, and how low I am.

I oughtn't to bother you with all this; I have got into the habit of uttering my thoughts to you, and just now I feel rather in a pit; *adhaesit pavimento*, etc. I suppose it will be better later. I like "he wanted to go home, where the food was better." I am reading Ps. 119 a good deal; very applicable to everything. "I will keep thy ceremonies"; but the way to them isn't easy.

Yes, I got home safely from my Christmas outing. Cars and lorries skidding all about the roads, but I conducted mine with admirable firmness and caution. Having manipulated all the wild and disconcerting roads of Spain lately, my faithful vehicle is not to be thrown out of step by a little ice in Kent.

If you were here, there are 1000 things I should say and ask you. As you aren't, I will now commit this letter to the air, putting no more trust in the ocean which swallows up all. You will observe from enclosed cutting that our Dean of Westminster is under suspicion of Stone-stealing. Would you think he did it? And what is the Hebrew for Tush? Is it *always* an interpolation in our psalm versions? I like the word; a pity it has gone out of use, like pish, twish, faugh and other terms of contempt. No derivation, says the O[xford] D[ictionary]—just "a natural utterance." What does one say to-day? "Nonsense," I suppose. And in Latin, according to my dictionary, "... "[1] but I don't remember this, do you. Now this must go. Forgive all this babble.

Yours affectionately,
R. M.

---

[1] In the original letter this three-letter word is undecipherable, but Cassell's Latin Dictionary which R. M. habitually used (see pp. 34 and 273) gives *phy* as the Latin word for 'tush.'

20, *Hinde House, Hinde St., W.*1
11*th January,* 1951†

Dear Fr. Johnson,

This is a P.S. to my letter posted yesterday by air, which contained lamentations that none of your sea letters had reached me; I should like it, if possible, to overtake that letter and arrive at the same time, because this morning the deep gave up your *three* sea letters (Dec. 22, 23, 25) and your air Epiphany letter too. I hope mine too have perhaps now arrived—(those that hadn't when you wrote on 6th Jan., I mean). I feel I should like you to get them all, even tho' of little importance; they said what was in my mind when I wrote them. Yours, I needn't say, are a great joy, all of them. I am writing at once, for the reason I said, and haven't even yet had time to read them with the care I shall give to them later, or look up the references, which I always do, and always rewardingly. They have come in the nick of time to strengthen my morale.

I know I was right (though it seems stupid and timorous) not to act on your suggestion of the Bp. of Oxon. If one could have met him with some good pretext—say on a retreat—it would have been very good; but my morale would have succumbed and disintegrated altogether if I had had to make an approach; and one needs to forget who one is seeing, and whether one may be thought presuming, etc., and concentrate on what one is doing. So it couldn't have done, tho' I should have liked to do it.

Now I will post this; I have a lunch date and must hurry to it.

Thank you *so* much for the letters. I shall write properly soon.

R. M.

Dear Fr. Johnson,

This is to be a nice leisurely sea letter, the treacherous deep having now, no doubt, recovered from its Christmas obstructionism that was so annoying. (Have you even now, I wonder, got all my ocean letters, as I have at last got all yours?) I told you, in a postscript air message that I sent you on the 11th, that there came that day 3 sea letters and your air one of Epiphany —just after I had posted you a letter written in some Dejection (like Coleridge). I feel much better now, thank you.

I was so glad of those letters, all of them. They were so full of a number of things—bits of autobiography that I liked very much and found very moving, in the same letter fragments from Coleridge and Donne and prayers from the Rom. Missal —" *remedium sempiternum*,"[1] " *O Sapientia* "[2] and the others. Do you remember that Candlemas sermon of Donne's about " those occasionall and transitory prayers " (some on celluloid; yes I have kept all those) being " payments of this debt, in such peeces, and in such summes, as God, no doubt, accepts at our hands." Remarkable Dean. I love the splendour of his phrasing. " Poore intricated soule! Riddling, perplexed, labyrinthicall soule! " " And therefore interrupt the prescription of sin; break off the correspondence of sin; unjoynt the dependency of sin upon sin . . . But thou shalt live in the light and serenity of a peaceable conscience here, and die in a faire possibility of a present melioration and improvement of that light. All thy life thou shalt be preserved in an Orientall light, an Easterne light, a rising and a growing light, the light of grace; and at thy death thou shalt be super-illustrated, with a Meridionall light, a South light, the light of glory." " Thus it is, when a soule is scattered upon the daily practise of any one predominant and habituall sin . . ." And then his poetry:

[1] " Everlasting cure."

[2] " O Wisdom," the first of the Greater Antiphons.

> " The Sun is lost, and the earth, and no man's wit
> Can well direct him where to looke for it . . ."

No wonder that those who sat under him in St. Paul's used to swoon with excitement and emotion. But what a bore he was about women—all that anger and hate and scorn; that eternal tendency to regard women as a peculiar section, instead of ordinary human beings. Language: how important it is. It's partly what I like so much in the psalms, that you have started me reading a good deal; also, as the Dean and you say, " to make an application"; but if one didn't like the language, one wouldn't so easily be able to. As it is, they seem to fit almost everywhere, in one way or another—(except the few smug bits).

Thank you so very much for your letter posted on Christmas Eve; about being in the Church, or coming back into it, and the acceptance of the " author of eternal salvation unto all them that obey him." You are so endlessly good to me; and your *absolutiones transmarinae*[1] *have* reached me, I know, and I can't see why they are *nothae*.[2] In fact, I know they aren't, whatever church law may say.

Speaking of church law, I am interested, and rather surprised, that Dr. Kirk says people mayn't be refused communion at the rails. I thought " notorious evil livers " had to be— though how evil, and how notorious, must be a delicate question to decide. My family was brought up on a story about a cousin of my mother's who was a vicar, and the local squire was a N.I.L. [*sic*][3], who kept concubines at the manor—perhaps I libel him and it was only one concubine (at a time, anyhow)—and he was also a regular communicant (as people often were, especially squires, for respectability's sake, in those days) and subscribed largely to church upkeep; and the concubines caused grave scandal among the villagers, so the vicar wrote to the squire and told him that unless he desisted from his notorious evil living he must warn him that he would be refused com-

---

[1] " Absolutions from across the ocean."   [2] " Illegitimate."
[3] A slip for N.E.L. (" notorious evil liver ").

munion, and begged him not to make a scandal by presenting himself. The squire was furious, and dared the vicar to refuse him, on pain of having an action brought against him for defamation. But the vicar did refuse him, and won the action, since he was acting by prayer book instruction; but of course he lost all future subscriptions. Would the Bishop of Oxford say he was wrong, I wonder? Possibly he was. But his point was that the Sacrament was being brought into disrepute in the eyes of the village. Didn't Conrad Noel[1] want to do this to employers who sweated their workers? Rather a dangerous path to start out on; it might lead to all sorts of difficulties and delicate decisions, and insults! If ever I do meet the Bishop, I might ask him about this point. I hope I shall, one day. I shall get some of his books out of the library; they sound what I should rather like to read. Having Scottish blood, I am interested in Moral Theology. He might one day have a Quiet Day perhaps; or don't Bishops do that? I do hope you don't think I made a mistake in not writing to him; I really was too shy, though of course I should have found him tremendously helpful if ever I had reached him. Actually, I should have found it easier, and more helpful still, to go to Memorial Drive, but that could not be.

I have been reading again your earlier letters. I have them all except the one you wrote me about 20 years ago, which I valued, and kept till the Luftwaffe got it. How many people do you " change " a year, I wonder? I expect, a lot. Beginning with talk about things in general, sacred and profane, and largely in a profane language; sacred things coming in more as time goes on; fresh lights on all kinds of topics, " a rising and a growing light " as Donne says, and a stirring of the conscience —till, before one knows where one is, one is surrendering to a new (or old) way of life and wanting to lead it. And all in about 4 months. I am prepared to believe that this happens to every one with whom you correspond; on the other hand, I was in part hitched on to old memories, which came back—that

[1] Rev. Conrad le Despenser Roden Noel (1869-1942), Vicar of Thaxted, Essex, well known for his Socialist views.

Retreat in 1915 (I think), which influenced me a great deal. In the light of subsequent developments in my career, you may not think much of this, but it is true. I even wonder sometimes whether, if you had been at hand later, the developments would have occurred; or anyhow, whether at the time I tried to make a fresh start and later broke all my resolves, I should have broken them. Who knows? Things are as they are, and have been as they have been, and will be as they will be. But I should like to say thank you for everything . . . [*sic*] I can't think why you bothered.

I'm glad '*Here's a Church*' arrived, though in duplicate. Dear old James Conybeare is a nice, simple person, very genial and kind. His father, my uncle, (about 14 years older than my mother, so we always looked on him, with his patriarchal beard, as an old man) went over to Rome about 1910 or so, which was rather trying for his family, as he was a Vicar and had to repudiate his Orders of course, and put a black handkerchief over his collar and stop being called " Rev.". James was grieved by it; he is a very loyal Anglican. Writing, of course, isn't really his strong suit.

I really shall be delighted to see Fr. Pedersen when he is here. Fr. Wilkins (with whom I had a moment or two of conversation, mainly about you) also said he was coming. I hope by then I shall have completed my Ruins book, at present I am living in a ruinous world of crumbling walls, broken arches, green jungle drowning temples and palaces in Mexico and Ceylon, friezes and broken columns sunk in blue seas, with crabs scuttering about among them. Such dreams of beauty are haunting, like poetry. If only I could *see* more of them, how lovely it would be! I am, by the way, grateful (perhaps I said so before) for your supplying of that letter to Cicero in B.C. 45, about the ruins the Romans had made in Greece. It is an earlyish indication of ruin-sentiment, which is just what I am looking for all the time. It is a fascinating book to work on, but a terrible lot of work. Next time I am in the Brit. Museum Reading Room I shall look at that Norfolk book you mentioned; it's not, it seems, in the London Library, my other source of literature.

I must remember John Bailey[1] too, who probably *is* in the L.L. I must say I do like to take books home to my flat and read them in comfort, not to have to sit always at the B.M. desks, among learned foreigners who lick their fingers to turn the pages and are no doubt engaged on writing some new epoch-shaking work (do I mean making?) like *Das Kapital* (composed entirely at those desks). I must now go and entertain a Spaniard at my club to tea, and try to induce him to join me in the swimming pool, which I like. I wonder how long this letter will take in transit, and what it depends on. Sailings, I suppose. I had other things to say, but space (and time) forbid, for which you will perhaps be grateful.

Yours affectionately,
R. M.

(I hope you don't feel this form of signature too familiar. I *feel* affection, and great pleasure that I know you, and a more formal adverb would seem inapt.)

20, Hinde House, Hinde St., W.1
18th January, 1951 †

Dear Father Johnson,

Thank you for your more than welcome air letter posted the 13th. How glad I was to have it, and am. I sent you a sea one on 14th, after all your barge, raft and trireme letters had arrived. Mine seem to have reached you almost at the same time. I'm so glad. I didn't like to think them sunk, either yours or mine. And yours, as I told you, came in the nick of time, just when my morale most needed them. Morale now greatly improved; food better, as the prodigal son decided.

Fr. Wilkins was very kind and nice. He didn't *say* anything; practically nothing but the absolution. Perhaps this is his way.

---

[1] John Bailey (1864-1931), the literary critic, was a friend of Father Johnson's father, Canon Cowper Johnson. R. M.'s reference is to his *Letters and Diaries* (1935).

I expect he thinks people should work out their own problems unaided, except for absolution when they work them out wrong. I'm not sure this isn't a mistake. Perhaps priests don't always realise the influence they could have at that receptive moment, and the good ideas they could put across if they chose; and one feels that Fr. Wilkins's ideas would be all good ones and would help. Of course he may have been pressed for time. However, I got the main thing. But those who can't see their way very clearly would be glad of a little expert aid. Thank God, you give this; if you didn't I should still be sticking in the wrong treacle well like a fly. Thank you for indicating those two psalms. Both very apt.

I have sometimes thought that there might well be consultant priests, like doctors, or like the hermits of past times, to whom one could take one's problems and get advice. If you were at hand, I suppose I should ask you a lot of things, now and later, as they turned up. Indeed, you may think that I do. Well, having such a non-resident chaplain, who allows me (as I hope) to do this, do I need a resident one? What I mean is, should one go regularly to confession, at stated intervals, or only when one feels in a jam? This enquiry for the favour of your best consideration, please. I just don't know. I do want to keep in touch, and not let that wall grow up again. But I want to ask things, not just tell them.

Am I "fundamentally religious," I wonder? I suppose in one way it would be difficult for any of my family to escape something of this, with our long lines of clerical ancestors on all sides. I think I naturally believe in some kind of mysterious world, interpenetrating this world, in and out of it and all round its margins. Writing this makes me think that perhaps I will send you *The two blind countries*, a book of verse that I wrote, together with a few other poems published separately. Many of them seem to be about just that. They were written at different times; many of them quite young. I wonder if you'll like them or not. I used to write a lot of poetry once; as a child it was my great outlet when things were almost too beautiful to bear; and I still write some. I like doing it; you can say things that way that don't go into prose. Am I to infer that you have been reading *Crewe Train*? It rather alarms me, all those old books coming your way. I don't remember them all very clearly myself, but suspect them of not being v.g. Have you come across *Orphan Island*, a novel of about 1924? A new edition is coming out this spring, and I might send it. It was the one of my novels I enjoyed writing most (except *They were Defeated*) because I indulged in it my morbid passion for coral islands, lagoons, bread-fruit and coconut trees, and island fauna and flora. You might get on with my Irish doctor, who, when inebriated, spouts Latin conversation. (I *don't*, of course, mean to imply that most Latin conversation is similarly inspired.)

You'll get soon after this, I hope, my sea letter of 14th, which answered your raft letters. I think the rafts must go quicker now; probably speeding along like the Kon-Tiki before the tides. I put in it some Donne that I like, complementing what you quoted. Dear non-resident chaplain, I would like to ask you, were it not so formidably vast a question, how people vitiated and weakened by a long course of knowingly wrong living, can become strong, intelligent, and moderately good. It really *is* a question. But I suppose I know the main answer, really.

Yours affectionately,

R. M.

20, *Hinde House, Hinde St., W.*1
22nd January [1951] †

Dear Fr. Johnson,

In one way, your letter of 18th, that came this morning, was the nicest to get of all your letters, because it reassured me that my letters aren't a nuisance to you. (This one, hand-written, may be; I am laid up with flue, bronchitis, and penicillin, with which I went down just after writing to you by air on 18th, and can't sit up in bed to type, tho' *writing* is o.k.) I wrote to you *by sea* after seeing Fr. Wilkins, because it was a longish, rambling letter, and because I didn't want to be a nuisance; you might well have said "what does she want *now*, after all is safely accomplished?" After your last letter, I see you wouldn't have said that at all, and wish I had made it air. But you see the immense difference between *my* getting *your* letters, which are sustenance and nourishment and *answers*, and you getting mine, which are questions and tiresome—or so I should suppose except for your apparently exhaustless patience. Anyhow, you will soon get both mine.

Thank you too for your letter of 15th, which is stuffed with good things, and seems to answer a question I put to you again, after you wrote but before I got it (" wells of salvation," and various psalms). I have looked at all your references except the Juvenal, which I am waiting for till I visit the London Library again.

Incidentally, you have the kindest impulses! To tell a person feeling *dejecta, abjecta, indigna, ignobilis*, that to some people (even to you) she may " seem to be somewhat " (tho' heaven knows why) seems the height of courteous good will. In consequence of my reference-hunting, my sick-bed is strewn with Psalters, Bibles, etc., calculated somewhat to surprise my doctor as they lie about among volumes on Syrian castles, 17th and 18th century travels in Greece and Asia (so exciting to trace the progress of the ruins we now see, century by century). " O! yes," I shall say to the physician, " I am reading about the Palaces of the Ptolemies in Alexandria, and about the wells of salvation in "—where? He mightn't quite understand, might even think my temperature too high. Ps. 119 I find more and more in. I care little about its acrostical aspects. What made the Jews like that, I wonder? An extraordinary gift of God consciousness. Could any other people *at that time* have so passed on their message? I think it was Belloc who wrote

> " How odd
> of God
> to choose
> the Jews "[1]—but of course it wasn't in the least odd

[1] W. N. Ewer, " How Odd."

Please go on bearing me in mind at the altar and offices; it helps me a great deal to think that you do, and all helps me to circumvent the imposing stumbling blocks in the road.

What I *don't* like to think of is your having hoped for a letter and not got one till so late—it seems so thankless. But you see my reasons. I am hoping that perhaps to-day (as I have yours posted 19th) you may have got my air letter posted same day. In it I didn't mean to imply that Fr. Wilkins in any way fell short and only that I suppose I should have found useful someone more loquacious. This probably never occurred to him, and was probably just a stupid idea of mine.

Time I did this up, for posting. Your to-day's letter *is* so cheering; I feel it might even improve the bronchitis. Now here arrives the Benger's Food—very good stuff. I do apologise for this illegible letter: don't try and grapple with it.

Yours affectionately,

R. M.

20, *Hinde House, Hinde St., W.*1
28th January [1951] †

Dear Father Johnson,

I am still not typewriter-fit, being still in bed, so forgive handwriting, which should, however, be better than last Monday's was. This is a sea letter (not so[1]) to thank you for yours posted 23rd, which came yesterday. I like it so much; particularly the bit about being inside the house, and the growth possible there—the gradual appreciation of one's inheritance. That comes home to me just now. I told you once that I couldn't really *regret* the past. But now I do regret it, very much. It's as if absolution and communion and prayer let us through into a place where we get a horribly clear view—a new view—so that we see all the waste, and the cost of it, and how its roots struck deep down into the earth, poisoning the springs of our own lives

[1] R. M. has interpolated " (not so)," because she later decided to send this letter by air.

and other people's. Such waste, such cost in human and spiritual values. The priest says "Go in peace, the Lord has put away thy sin." But of course one doesn't go in peace, and in one sense He can't put it away, it has done its work. You can't undo what's done. Not all the long years of happiness together, of love and friendship and almost perfect companionship (in spite of its background) was worth while, it cost too much, to us and to other people. I didn't know that before, but I do now. And he had no life after it to be different in, and I have lived the greater part of mine. If only I had refused, and gone on refusing. It's not a question of forgiveness, but of irrevocable damage done. Perhaps I shall mind more and more, all my life. Is this what absolution and communion do to one? I see now why belief in God fades away and has to go, while one is leading a life one knows to be wrong. The two can't live together. It doesn't give even intellectual acceptance its chance. Now it *has* its chance. I don't, you know, attach much importance to *details* of belief—I don't feel they really matter (or do they?). But I hold on to your remark—" we may be sure that at the bottom of the whole business there is a personal relationship," which is possibly all that matters. After what has occurred to me lately, I *know* there is. Why this, why that, why the other? Little is answerable, nothing is solved; one just has to leave it, and push ahead with what one has, hoping for more presently.

Did you mean, go to *confession* once a month? Isn't that too often? I shall find out, as time goes on, if Fr. Wilkins is willing to be talked to and to talk. I don't want to bother or embarrass him. He makes me feel rather shy, though I like him very much indeed; he gives such an impression of sincerity. But I think he would be a pocket-prophet not given to much prophesying. And I *like* prophecy. (*Later*: after your letter—I am convinced by all you say that he won't mind talking (and I seldom do!) so I shall take your advice).

How I bother you. I fear there is altogether a surfeit of R. M. in your life, what with letters, and what with all these books turning up. Don't let my poetry be a nuisance to you, or feel you must read it or comment on it. If I send it, let it be, unless ever you feel like glancing at it in an odd moment. But then you can't *have* any odd moments. I am remorseful to have taken so many of them, though with such infinite advantage to myself.

And No Man's Wit is much too full of Spanish politics. I wonder if you got to where Ellen turns out to be descended from a mermaid, but, only being partly mer, drowns in the sea. I think she was well out of this world, for which she was extremely unfitted. *Fabled Shore* (my Spanish travelogue) is being before long published in U.S.—but I could send you the English edition if you'd like to read it. I did love that trip. And (if I can lay hold of a copy—it's out of print) *Dangerous Ages*. And perhaps the little *Milton*. Oh dear, I seem to be adding to the surfeit. What insupportable egotism. Fr. Wilkins, in our moment of conversation, said he had found some of my books readable, which was nice of him.

The *Spectator* has just sent me for review a life of Thomas Fuller[1] (of the *Worthies*). I have always liked " the great Tom Fuller " (a very genial *collaborateur*); I did a BBC programme once into which he came, conversing with Milton and Roger Williams, the tolerant Independent who fled from Laud to Massachusetts (nearly the only real tolerationist of his age, I think). My theme was the contrast between the Milton of *Areopagitica*, that great libertarian, and the later Milton, who censored books and pamphlets for Cromwell, and suppressed those advocating " prelacy " whether Anglican or R.C. And even Fuller wouldn't have allowed R.C. or " heretical " writings (including Quakers). Only Roger Williams from Mass. was disgusted with them both. I have always loved the *Worthies* and *The Church History* [*of Britain*] and [*The*] *History of* [*The University of*] *Cambridge*, and *The Holy and Profane States*. This biography looks full, but it may lack style.

9th Jan. How splendid: your letter posted 26th has just come. Such a good letter. Thank you so much. I think, after all, having complained of illness, and in reply to your enquiries, that I will

[1] William Addison, *Worthy Dr. Fuller* (1951).

63

send this by air, and begin ocean-going after that. I'm much better, tho' the cough lingers about, so does that depressing remedy for lung-patches, M. and B., which is over, but still leaves a hang-over. I'm afraid the 1st page of this letter is rather dismal—perhaps M. and B. helped in that too. It is all accurate, but I try not to dwell on it, so don't mind it for me. I am now up, tho' inadequately dressed: declinicized, though not yet decubicalized—and well on the way to recovery.

I have been through all those prayers and am committing to memory " *et fac me tuis semper inhaerere mandatis*,"[1] etc. I shall like to think that you sometimes say it for me. In all these prayers, I can include my beloved companion.

I must get hold of *The Trumpet shall sound*,[2] which would interest me. I might get an American P[rayer] B[ook] too—I will ask Fr. W[ilkins] when I see him next. You have encouraged me very much about him.

Oh dear, why didn't you think to give me a *coup de télé-phone* in 1938? What a pity! I wish you were contemplating another English visit, like Fr. Pedersen. By the way—forgive my ignorance—is it done by those outside your Society to drop the surname in beginning letters, and simply say " Dear Father," or is this only practised within the Society? I like it, if it is usual: but feel quite at ease in either style and don't want to be forward! It really makes no difference to

Yours affectionately and gratefully,

R. M.

---

[1] " And make me always to abide in thy commandments."
[2] S.S.J.E. booklet (1950) by B. D. Wilkins, describing the work of the Society at home and abroad.

February

Dear Father Johnson,

Thank you much for your air letter posted Jan. 31st. I am sure you will be relieved to see once again these clear, typed characters. How I wish I could write a nice clear hand—but I can't. I am now sitting up at my typewriter, marvellously better, and surrounded by Bibles in various tongues and of various dates, in which I have been looking up your points. Certainly our English translations are rather loose sometimes. Why turn *pais* and *paidos* (my typewriter can't do Greek letters) into servant? Especially as the Vulgate had *puer*. I like *infans*; it suggests the Spanish royal *Infante*. But our earliest English translations had " servant," apparently—Coverdale (who has " He helpeth up " for *suscepit*, which I rather like), Tyndale, and of course ever since. I don't read the Greek Testament enough; it is worth while to, and I have been trying it with Hebrews, as well as the Latin. I am very unworthy of a great-grandmother of mine, who, from the time she was a girl reading with her father, till she died in her eighties, read the first lesson in Hebrew and the second in Greek, every day of her life. Of Hebrew I don't know a word. It must be a wonderful heritage to have, for a Jew; a cultivated Jew such as my friend Victor Gollancz, who, without being in the least orthodox, cares intensely for the past of his race. Knowing Jews like him makes one better understand that extraordinary faculty for God with which they were endowed. It had to be them, of course. The Egyptians, Chinese, Greeks, Romans, and the other ancient races never had that faculty to that extent, nor that concentration on ethical conduct as the meaning of life. And those few who had— Socrates, Plato, Marcus Aurelius, etc.—and who tried to obey the God within them, hadn't the Jewish aptitude for externalising God into a Spirit outside them who would help them. If it had been all entrusted to the Greeks, what would they have made of it, I wonder? Of course later on they did make a great deal of it; but it was the Jews who started it.

Certainly Juvenal's Jews must have been irritating, with their secret rites and scriptures and their contempt for all outsiders. They had indeed forgotten their vocation of " telling it out among the heathen." But how much had they done of this, during the 7 centuries between Isaiah and birth of Christ? I must read about this. As you will have gathered, I am shamefully ignorant of Jewish history. But what a people! And what a pity they stayed (in the main) outside Christianity. I was interested the other day to find that there were Christians living in Pompeii before its destruction in 79; in one of the houses an altar and cross were found. Would you think that family tried to spread the Gospel among the rather worldly and fleshly Pompeiians? And did St. Paul visit Pompeii? I don't remember that he did. I think that continuity, which you point out, of the missionary spirit (though interrupted) from Isaiah to the Apostle of the Gentiles is extremely exciting. And the similarities of phrase. It must feel extraordinary to have that heritage; and to be still waiting for its fulfilment.

Another book you set me looking at was Cowper's letters; the little Golden Treasury edition of 1884, that was my mother's. Quite full of your relations, of course; Heskeths, your double great-grandfather John Johnson (who must have been nice), Bodhams, etc. What a pity you can't establish the Donne relationship.[1] All those chests, all over the country, put away in country house attics, stuffed with old letters—how tantalising they are. There must be such a wealth of history stowed away; now and then some of it comes to light; but far more is neglected, and much destroyed, as it was during that silly paper salvage drive during the war. My father was once working on some papers in the Lytteltons' house, Hagley Hall; he said there were chests and chests of precious documents, which no one ever bothered

[1] The " supposed " relationship of the Johnsons to John Donne.

66

to go through. Sometimes of course some enterprising person really does rummage, and then appears an invaluable collection such as the *Verney Memoirs*. I was allowed to see, years ago, a lot of fascinating Macaulay papers in the house of an old cousin, the daughter of the historian's younger brother.

I don't think I should expect my *Wilderness* to make much of a hit in America; it is too English. Some of my early novels went well—*Potterism, Dangerous Ages, Told by an Idiot, Keeping up Appearances*—but *They Were Defeated* sank with scarcely a ripple, though it got across pretty well here; and every one says English books aren't having much of a time, on the whole, in the States at present. I don't much mind. I have had some quite kind and intelligent reviews, though probably not many. Reviews are chancey things at the best; just a question of luck into whose hands a book falls; and books are a matter of taste after all. It is one of the things about writing; one has to train oneself not to mind (much) what people say, or don't say, about one's books. Probably no writer ever succeeds in not minding at all! Some of them have *said* they don't; but . . . [*sic*] We have all a feeling for the children of our brain; even if we don't think them particularly good children, we don't like to see them slighted. But I find it matters less and less. What one does care about is that the people whose opinion one values should like them.

Now this must go down to the sea, tho' there is a lot more I could say.

Yours affectionately,
R. M.

You know, confession is a desperate business. You think in the middle that you can't go through with it, but somehow you do, and at the end you feel winded and dazed. I felt so much so, that, instead of going into the chapel after it I forgot all about this and just went home. I can only hope that Fr. Wilkins put this down to disturbance of mind and the highly unusual (for me) circumstances in which I found myself, not to mere distaste for prayer!

I told him, you know, that the whole thing was your doing; he seemed to think this quite natural.

20, *Hinde House, Hinde St., W.*1
9th February, 1951 †

Dear Father,

(Thank you: I rather like that. And I should be delighted when ever you chanced to feel like saying " Rose Macaulay "; lots of people do, among them many I have never met. I think one likes people to address one exactly as they feel like at the moment, don't you. Though, as to that, if one really followed that principle, it's not by any means every one to whom one would always begin " Dear . . ."; " Hated Sir " might sometimes meet the case better.)

I got your wonderful Candlemas letter yesterday; thank you very very much. I had posted you a sea letter the day before, answering yours of 31st. But this one is to be air, reporting how nearly recovered I now am. Still slightly bronchial, and not yet supposed to do anything energetic, like going out early or plunging into swimming pools. (Yes, I am vaguely ichthyous and mer; can't breathe under water, except through one of those lovely goggle masks with air-pipes, which I was using in the Mediterranean last summer, you get such a nice view of the fishes and sea-weed grottos; but I should notice it at once if a shark got into my pool, and should tell the Club secretary. I dare say some Conybeare rector in Devonshire once married a mermaid, tho' it doesn't seem to have got into the family records.)

All this nonsense. What I really want to say is, thank you for always saying the thing I need. And for *not* telling me to put the past behind me, now that it is absolved. And for understanding how one has to face there being no cheap and easy way back, and that Horace was right, and Omar and FitzGerald with their " The moving finger writes, and having writ, Moves on, nor all thy piety and wit Can lure it back to cancel half a line, Nor all thy tears wash out a word of it." And yet that they didn't know the last word, about the potter and his workmanship. I suppose all one can do is try to keep the eyes of one's understanding enlightened and try to have no more black-outs. I do see the point about monthly confessions; I wonder if Fr. Wilkins would see it too. I might tell him it was your idea, which would make him think well of it. And of course it *would* provide opportunities for asking advice. All you say of Fr. Wilkins sounds very reassuring and what one wants. If only I can make the mental effort to write to him and go there. I will try.

Thank you for what you say about my writing, all those years. You know, I have always felt " Anglican "; (heredity, no doubt, like Ellen's mermaidishness). I mean, I have been an *Anglo*-agnostic; and even were I an atheist should be an Anglo-atheist I suppose. For years I scarcely entered a church except to look at the architecture or to attend weddings, funerals or baptisms; but still I was an Anglo-non-church-goer. It was a matter of taste and affection, and perhaps a kind of loyalty, rather than of belief; and I suppose this attitude would emerge in what I wrote about it; it is in the blood and bones, at deeper levels than brain or will. Perhaps it is a good thing, now that brain and will begin functioning again, to have that heritage to draw on. A kind of spiritual capital, laid up for one by one's ancestors and upbringing, and by various influences since. Certainly no merit of mine. When people I know have said that if they turned from their present unbelief it would be to Roman Catholicism, I have often asked " Why not Anglicanism? " But they probably feel this insufficiently dramatic. And yet what a thing it is, that re-made pot! In reading that Fuller book (I'll send you the *Spectator*, with my review) I was taken again into that mid-17th century world. Fuller, of course, was something of a collaborator, which doesn't emerge much in this book. But he was able in that way to help outed clergy less fortunate or adaptable. (The *Spectator* has misspelt " Heylin," curse them.)

I am much looking forward to that packet, and particularly to the snapshots. (Which reminds me that, as a signature to those poems that you will get sometime, I appended a recent passport photograph.) I shall like too to have the American P[rayer] B[ook] pages, and the Juvenal. My classical library is not so well restored after its blitzing as it should be. The Greek is better off than the Latin, as Gilbert Murray (that very great and revered man is a most kind friend to me always) gave me a lot of Greek, with his own translations. I should love the Norfolk diary sometime, too. I told you in my sea letter how I had been meeting your relations in Cowper's letters.

I'm glad you like my Mrs. Arthur[1]; I grew fond of her myself. She was based, externally, on a nice woman who kept a small cigarette and sweet shop in Marylebone near me. She looked like that, and had that bonhomous air. The rest—character, career, conversation—I made up. Dear me, the liberties one takes with people scarcely known but just met; they provide a basis, on which one builds some fantastic structure, no doubt with no relation at all to the actual person. What would that nice, no doubt most respectable, lady think if she knew? But this habit of novelists only becomes dangerous when they use as a basis someone recognisable whom they know and who will certainly read the book; they invariably think it is *all* meant to be them, and will never believe they were only a starting-point and that the finished character is really something quite unconnected with them. A dangerous trade; one skates on such thin ice. *Keeping up Appearances* offended, I fear, a very nice young woman who worked in the . . . Library, and who thought I had drawn her in one of the Arthur girls, when actually she was definitely higher in the social scale than that. Of course some novelists . . . are completely ruthless; they put in not only real people but real situations, some of them supposedly unknown to the people's friends, such as secret love affairs, jiltings, etc., and leave a trail of misery behind them. Very cruel and unfair. Novelists should have a sense of responsibility towards those they might injure, like car drivers, and not run them down from behind.

Yes, thank you, I am well looked after when ill. A nice

[1] See R. M.'s *Keeping up Appearances*.

char, who will stay on if wanted, and a number of obliging friends, of all ages and sexes and avocations, who rally round with sick-room amenities, such as flowers and fruit, and offers to shop, post letters, get library books, come and get my meals, come and talk. This last I don't allow with flue; they would catch it, and their charming chatter would exhaust me. This is the result of living in London and being naturally gregarious (one need never lack for company). Actually, I rather like being alone when ill; it is more restful, and gives one a chance to read and to think.

Your letter set me thinking about the pursuing purposes of God, and I remembered Francis Thompson's " I fled him down the nights and down the days; I fled him down the arches of the years; I fled him down the labyrinthine ways Of my own mind; and in the midst of tears, I hid from him, and under running laughter. Adown Titanic glooms of chasmed fears, From those strong Feet that followed, followed after. But with unhurrying chase, And unperturbèd pace, Deliberate speed, majestic instancy, They beat, and a Voice beat, More instant than the Feet. . . ." And then, " I stand amid the dust of the mounded years—My mangled youth lies dead beneath the heap. . . . Yet ever and anon a trumpet sounds From the hid battlements of eternity; Those shaken mists unsettle, then Round the half glimpsèd turrets slowly wash again, But not ere him who summoneth, I have first seen. . . . Now of that long pursuit Comes on at hand the bruit; That Voice is round me like a bursting sea. . . . "[1]

Unhurrying pursuit; yes. It is we who refuse to be hurried. But it doesn't tire his kindness out, and he gives us these fresh chances, and lays these plans, in " the exceeding riches of his grace in his kindness towards us." All very odd. *Why*? That seems the enormous riddle of the human race and of God. Or, if not odd, very overwhelming.

Of course I am very sorry that I shall never see you in England; but I do understand how exhausting it would be, and it would be worse than anything to see you getting ill. I can

[1] *The Hound of Heaven.*

71

imagine feeling as you describe, though actually I am a fairly happy traveller. But what a fuss those set over us have agreed to make about our getting about. The young scarcely believe me when I say that before 1914 we had no passports, let alone visas or currency restrictions. Driving down Spain, I could never get off from anywhere before about 10.30, because the hotel didn't extract my passport from the police to whom they had sent it the night before, and who held on to it with the firmest Spanish apathy and tenaciousness. And the Americans putting half of us on Ellis Island for presumed un-American activities. . . [sic] All very irritating and wearing.

Fr. Wilkins said he knew a sister of mine in India.[1] She works in a mission (S.P.G.)[2] school at Ranchi. We are fond of each other, but quite unlike, and I suppose have less in common than I have with any of the rest of my family. She is devoted to her work and her untouchable pupils, and is very intelligent and good, and translates English books into a number of Indian dialects as easily as I could into French or Italian, which seems to me very admirable. No doubt Fr. Wilkins can do the same. When well enough, I want to attend Canon Raven's (C. E. Raven, Master of Christ's) Lent lectures on " Christianity in the world of modern science." Biology is his subject, and he is interesting. We used to know him at Cambridge in old days. He is a pacifist. I think I am too.

When I think of the time I must cost you, and the trouble, and the stamps. . . [sic] Well, you do know how grateful I am—— But I have been such a *job* to you, on the top of all your others —I am ashamed. But—well, anyhow, I am

Yours affectionately,

R. M.

---

[1] Eleanor Macaulay.   [2] Society for the Propagation of the Gospel.

Dear Father,

Thank you so much for your letter begun on Ash Wednesday, which came last night. I am so glad to have it. I wrote to you by air on the 10th, and by sea on the 7th. And on 30th Jan. I posted you poems, signed with a passport photograph. So we both sent packets; I much look forward to getting your two. I shall look closely in the pockets for the photographs, etc. I shall enjoy the *Norfolk Diary*[1], and hope this and the former packet won't tarry too long en route. Mine, I imagine, won't, as it was only a large envelope, not a parcel. Also, I told my publishers to send you *Fabled Shore*, but don't expect you to read it through; it's really a book for those who have travelled to the same places, or are about to. I am still hoping to send *Dangerous Ages*. I loved the trip. I too went to Granada, Ronda, and Seville—but Seville is too far inland to be described in my book. I shall get Mr. Cram's book from the London Library. By the way, *of course* don't bother to send the 2nd copy of *Here's a Church*—it was just a mistake of the despatchers obviously, and probably no one is the wiser.

I am sorry to say that poor Fr. Wilkins is ill; he wrote, in reply to mine, from St. Luke's Hostel, saying that he had been there 3 weeks with bronchitis, and wouldn't be allowed to work until some time after Easter. I am very sorry for this. I expect he, as I was, is being given M. and B., which is our name here for tablets which doctors prescribe for anything wrong with the lungs, and I suppose bronchitis too. It is a very effective remedy, but depressing to the heart, and lowering, and not to be continued too long. I hope he will be better presently. I expect he would love a word from you.

As to confession, I suppose I could go to someone else. If I did, should I explain a little about the past, or just leave it and

[1] *A Norfolk Diary: Passages from the diary of the Rev. Benjamin John Armstrong, M.A.* (*Cantab.*), *Vicar of East Dereham* 1850–88, *edited by his grandson, H. B. J. Armstrong* (1949).

start from now? I don't mean, of course, *confess* it again, but mention that there had been a long gap and that I was therefore rather at sea?

I read all your letter easily, though transparent. This doesn't matter if one puts it against a white background. Thank heaven, your writing has *not* become like my crabbed and indefensible script; it is always beautifully legible and clear. I am glad, because there is nothing you say that I want to miss. I didn't, you know, mean that some beliefs were "unimportant" objectively, or in themselves—of course they couldn't be, being all part of the whole business—but that they didn't happen yet to register with *me*, and so I didn't bother about them. I suppose I mean that (as you say) they haven't struck a match on my mind, or come to seem to matter. Life and one's point of view shift about, and one never knows what aspects of them will attract this or that aspect of belief (I think I am cribbing this from you, and that it is just what you said in this letter, which I have absorbed so well that I feel I am originating its observations). But, if my mind can't quite take certain things—such as the physical Resurrection—does it matter, so long as it doesn't get in the way of belief in Christ as master and saviour and helper, to be sought and served? I know it mattered to the early church, and was perhaps the only way in which they could be convinced—but should one try to force or persuade one's mind to it, if one feels one doesn't need it? You say "we cannot be expected to do more than yield to God the minds which we actually possess," so I suppose God takes them and does what he can with them. And of course in time they might develop new powers of faith; as you say, it depends on what happens to make connections. He keeps showing us new things, new light on the past, new roads for the future, and one hopes for new powers. But what moors, fens, crags and torrents lie all about.

You are so good to me, writing these splendid letters, which are like lanterns with many facets, shedding all kinds of light. And thank you for remembering my departed at requiem masses; I like to think of that. I suppose after this week I shall be able to go to communion myself again. What a magnificent

74

business all this must have seemed to the first Christian converts! And does to those who have lost it and begun to come back a little. I think I shall try and get hold of that little Lent addresses book of Fr. Waggett's[1]; it was so good.

I am feeling rather pleased and grateful because I have a letter to-day from the Cambridge Vice-Chancellor[2] saying that the Senate would like to give me an Honorary Doctorate of Letters, which I think is charming of them. So sometime in June I shall attend the Congregation in cap and gown and be en-doctored. I imagine it is actually more a tribute to my father and uncle, who were greatly esteemed in Cambridge, than to myself. But it is rather fun. After that, you could call me, if you so fancied, "my dear doctor"! Did I say, by the way, that I like anything you call me? (On the rare occasions of "my dearest R.M.," my soul has been greatly comforted.)

Later. I seem to have a slight return of cough and temperature, and shall go to bed; probably all right to-morrow. I hope no more M. and B!

I like my note-paper better than your new style one. But yours really is *quite* legible. I will send this by air again, to let you know about Fr. Wilkins.

Yours affectionately,

R. M.

20, *Hinde House, Hinde St., W.*1
16*th February,* 1951

Dear Father,

Being in bed again, with another spot of temperature, I will please myself by writing a *very beautifully written* sea letter, just to show you that I can, if I try hard. It is a bore, this relapse when I thought I was recovered, and very interrupting to my

---

[1] Probably his Holy Week addresses *The Hear tof Jesus*, but Lent addresses were included in his book *The Scientific Temper in Religion and Other Addresses* (1905).

[2] S. C. Roberts, Master of Pembroke College, later Sir Sydney Roberts.

life. However, I am not seriously ill, and have several nice books to read—one on Pompeii and Herculaneum, very detailed and exciting; one on the 1st Crusade (oh dear, what behaviour went on!); Wm. Law's *Liberal and Mystical Writings*; a rather good and ingenious thriller; and St. Augustine's *Confessions*. Do you think he really (as he says he did) liked sinning for sinning's sake, stole the pears not to eat them but because he liked stealing? That does seem to be what actuates some juvenile delinquents and young hooligans—all that wanton destruction they do—but it must, I think, be unusual, in a character like his. Most people do it because they want the pears, and let higher principles go by the board—but he "*non ob aliud, nisi quia non licebat*"[1]—or so he says. But then of course he kept bad company, ran about in a gang. What interesting reading he is. But what a labyrinthine, intricatory soul (as Donne would say). All that about ought he, as praise is unwholesome, to lead a low and degraded life that no one can praise? And all his involved enquiries into the nature of time. But when he writes of God and the soul, he is often magnificent. I imagine that Francis Thompson was affected by him when he wrote *The Hound of Heaven*. And he is soaked in the psalms, and quotes them so effectively—"*quoniam tu inluminabis lucernam meam, domine, deus meus, inluminabis tenebras meas*"[2] ... "*ut liberes nos omnino quoniam coepisti* . . ."[3] one couldn't want better "transitory prayers." (17th Feb.) Did Marcus Aurelius ever steal pears? I am reading him too; about all he learned from his good examples—"From my mother, the fear of God and generosity, and abstention not only from doing ill but from the very thought of doing it; and furthermore to live the simple life, far removed from the habits of the rich." From other examples, not to be taken up with trifles, not to believe wizards and miracle-mongers, not to keep quails, not to resent plain speaking, to be aware that he needed amendment and training for his character, not to commit breaches of good taste, to shew

[1] "For no other reason than that it was forbidden."
[2] "Thou also shalt light my candle: the Lord my God shall make my darkness to be light." Ps. 18.28.
[3] "But do thou set us wholly free, since thou hast begun."

himself ready to be reconciled to those who have trespassed against him, and meet them half-way when they seem to be willing to retrace their steps. Never to exhibit any symptom of anger or any other passion, but to be " at the same time utterly impervious to all passions and full of natural affection," to possess great learning and make no parade of it, and to look to nothing else, even for a moment, save Reason alone.

And so on. What counsels of perfection! He was surrounded by good examples of all kinds, best of all his father, who did not build for the love of building, gave no thought to his food, and did *not bathe at all hours.* " Thou hast but a short time left to live. Live as on a mountain." He would have been shocked by St. Augustine—except that Reason bade him be shocked by no one, seeing that men are as they are. They are an interesting contrast. Both commanding intellects, both full of good aspirations and self-awareness and God-awareness. I wish M.A. could have lived early enough to have met S. Paul; an interview between them would have been interesting. Both agreed on " Whatsoever things are, etc . . . think on these things."

The question of the developing sense of morality is fascinating. When do we get to the point of rejecting War? I have long felt that one great international gesture would be worth while; saying, just once, to potential aggressors, " Go ahead if you must and do your worst; *we* do not intend to behave like barbarians, whatever barbarians may do to us." This might mean occupation and domination by some barbarian power like Russia; very unpleasant, pernicious and horrible; but could not be more so than waging war ourselves, with all its cruel atrocities. And it just *might* help to start a new era. But I fear there is no hope of any such civility in a barbaric world, at present, and we shall go murdering each other by radio-active bombs, and destroying all that's left of beauty. We here rather dread the American state of mind; it might lead to some rash act.

I seem to be getting better to-day, and shall soon be fit to do a little typing. I fear this letter may have deteriorated in script as it proceeded. Oh I do get bored with being ill, it fogs the mind so—I should like to be intelligently systematic about prayer, e.g.

Don't you dislike all this eloquent bombast about defending " the British Way of Life "? After all, it's not so good, nothing to boast about. I prefer frank jingoism to sanctimonious patriotism, on the whole.

Well, I have enjoyed writing to you, and must now stop. " Not to write to Fr. Johnson at all hours," M. Aurelius's father might have resolved.

Yours affectionately,

R. M.

20, Hinde House, Hinde St., W.1
20th February, 1951 †

Dear Father,

Yesterday was a grand day—at breakfast-time your letter of St. Valentine's Day, at lunch-time the packet posted 31st Jan. with that dear little Juvenal, the American P[rayer] B[ook] and the photographs; at tea-time the *Norfolk Diary* with the reviews and photographs in the side-pockets, and the Penguin Norfolk, which had made very good speed indeed. So you see it was a good day, and very timely, as I was still half invalided and not yet out. This afternoon I have been out; I drove to the London Library and got the Hesketh-Johnson letters,[1] which I have been enjoying immensely. In fact, their elegant style is infectious. " Miss Macaulay's best compliments wait on Mr. Johnson, and takes the first opportunity to acquaint him that she received the Invaluable Items he was so obliging to send her, yesterday; they arriv'd very safe, and not even a little Damp, though they had crossed the Ocean. Miss Macaulay thinks herself particularly obliged to thank Mr. Johnson for the kind trouble he has taken. . . ." " Johnny of Norfolk " appears to great advantage in the correspondence, and must have been a

[1] *Letters of Lady Hesketh to the Rev. John Johnson, LL.D., concerning their kinsman William Cowper the Poet, edited by Catharine Bodham Johnson* (1901).

kind and charming person. I shall get pleasure out of this book. Also from the *Norfolk Diary*. Particularly with your annotations, and the photographs. I always feel there is something very nostalgic about those spacious old country rectories that one's ancestors inhabited. For you, familiar with all the ground, all the villages, it must be fascinating. But to me too, being familiar by hearsay with so much clerical life of that time. All those references to the E.P.,[1] Mr. Mackonochie,[2] the quarrels between the E.C.U.[3] and the Protestants, were frequent in my mother's reminiscences of her girlhood of the 70's and 80's (she was born in 1855) when she was a keen Anglo-Catholic and sat under Dean Liddon[4] and Fr. Stanton. Did you ever come across *Ecclesiastical and Social Essays* by my grandfather, W. J. Conybeare? He has an interesting essay (written, I think, for the *Edinburgh Review*, in 1851) about the three Church parties. He called them High, Low and Broad; or Tractarian, Evangelical, and—I forget what he called the Broad (which he himself rather inclined to). I see, by the way, that Mr. Armstrong[5] has a note on his grandfather's use of " Anglo-Catholic " in 1850 as remarkably early. But it was used before that. See the Oxford Dict., which mentions the " Library of Anglo-Catholic Theology," a series of reprints, 1841. Pusey speaks of " Anglo-Catholicism " in 1842; and Charlotte Brontë in *Shirley* of a dish " that an Anglo-Catholic might eat on Good Friday " (1849). But I think my mother and her friends used to call themselves simply " Catholics." Later, having married my father (an agnostic) she became " Broad-High." Mr. Armstrong would have called himself a Tractarian, I suppose. What a contrast to the clerical life of half a century before! I see he speaks (1851) of " more than 70 years ago, and in the midst of the church's dead-

[1] " The Eastward Position," the practice of the celebrant of the Eucharist standing on the west side of the altar facing east, then a very controversial matter.

[2] Rev. Alexander Heriot Mackonochie (1825-87), Curate-in-charge of St. Alban's, Holborn, 1862-82, and a leading Anglo-Catholic.

[3] The English Church Union, a society formed in 1859 to defend and further the spread of High Church principles in the Church of England.

[4] Rev. Henry Parry Liddon (1829-90) was Canon (not Dean) of St. Paul's.

[5] H. B. J. Armstrong, editor of *A Norfolk Diary*.

ness and imbecility." Which recalled to me the *Diary of a country parson*, also about a Norfolk rector, of the late 18th century, edited by J. B. Beresford, a most instructive and entertaining work in several vols. No, it was called *The Diary of Parson Woodforde*.[1] Notable points in it are the huge meals he ate, the few services he held, and the fewer people who attended them. Whereas Mr. A. had large congregations, very keen and attentive, regular services, and well-kept churches. While in Dublin both the "Romish" and "our own" were apparently filthy. This book is going to interest me a lot. He was a kind man, obviously. None of his comments are malicious. Whereas the diary kept by my Conybeare grandfather was full of such acid remarks about his acquaintances (most of whom he found stupid and ill-informed) that it couldn't possibly have been published; though I suppose it could now. Matthew Arnold was "a prig." his brother Thomas "a weak character," the Macaulays "given to talking for effect," most bishops and deans lamentable. He was a brilliant and charming person, but can't have been kindly. He was consumptive, which perhaps is bad for the temper.

I am so pleased to have those photographs. One I saw in *Cowley*, and like it. In fact, I like them all. I shall keep them in a pocket of the *Norfolk Diary*, so that the whole book is "abundantly delightful." I see that the gen. tree in the Hesketh book says your family *is* descended from the Dean,[2] by the way. I thought you said that Aunt Katie[3] said not. I think your family is the most wonderfully close-knit and involved of any I know of.

I like the P[rayer] B[ook] very much. Is it our 1928 Deposited Book? Or are there differences? (I haven't got that book.) The *order* of the H[oly] C[ommunion] prayers is certainly better; and all the additions are improvements. I'm glad they have that

[1] *The Diary of a Country Parson: The Reverend James Woodforde; edited by John Beresford* (5 vols, 1924-1931).

[2] The genealogical tree in the *Letters of Lady Hesketh* (see above p. 78n.) is misleading. In a later book, *William Bodham Donne and his Friends* (1905), Catharine B. Johnson pointed out that the "supposed" descent from John Donne had not been finally established.

[3] Mrs. Catharine B. Johnson.

sentence about " grant them continual growth. . . ." The Penitential Office too is good. I don't know if any churches here use the 1928 book; I suppose it is illegal, but perhaps they needn't take notice of that. I am sure Mr. Armstrong would have used it. Bishop Hensley Henson, whose letters I have been reading, would not, I imagine. It is probably on sale, and I might get one. I know too little of the history of the Anglican Church in America. Did it follow the developments of our Book of Common Prayer, and adopt the 1662 book finally? But I imagine its congregations were always small, compared with the Puritan sects.

On separate sheet (too transparent) I have illustrated my Church position. Plenty of churches, but the nearest seem the least suitable. I incline to Grosvenor Chapel, or All Saints, Margaret St. I think my landlords should have built a chapel in these flats. S. Paul's, Baker St., no doubt has midday communion, for those who can't go early. Is this all right? One probably couldn't do it at All Saints. I feel the important thing is to go *somehow*. But I am hoping to be fit for early going out soon. This second illness is tiresome. I see no reason for not going sometimes to Mass at St. James's; but I don't like it so well as ours, though it (I mean, the R.C. Mass) has many early associations for me, and I like much of the Missal, and use many of its prayers.

I wrote you a fair letter with mine own hand, very clear, when in bed the other day, and launched it on the sea. This one I shall launch on the air, to express my pleasure in the packets. I look forward to Johannes Monachus. All that Byzantine period of the church is fascinating.[1] I have been reading Procopius lately. He is hard on Justinian and Theodora —a thing I could not be, after seeing those glorious Ravenna mosaics.

Later. I passed Grosvenor Chapel to-day and looked into it,

[1] The *Liber de Miraculis* of Johannes Monachus, a 10th-century monk belonging to one of the monasteries near Amalfi, consisting of translations into Latin of various Byzantine legends, with which Johannes had become acquainted during a visit to Constantinople.

after many years, and liked it again. I see its early mass is 8.15, which is a better hour than 8, so I hope to get there. I was on my way back from having tea with Dr. Gilbert Murray at the Athenaeum; he had been at a United Nations meeting, where they had been deciding how firm U.N. ought to be. I am not for all this firmness myself. What with U.N., amending Aeschylus texts, and taking the chair at Hellenic Society meetings, he leads, for 84, a full life; but looks very frail now. How I hope he, and everyone else I am fond of, lives to be at least 90, like your Aunt Katie. Did you, by the way, ever come across Lord David Cecil's life of Cowper, *The Stricken Deer?* It is an admirable and sympathetic book. He must have been a trying friend, and Johnny and Lady Hesketh were very good to him. His life is a lesson (if one needed it) against adopting the unhappier forms of Calvinism.

My poems I suppose you may have got by now, or should have, as they were posted 30th Jan. But don't bore yourself with them, or feel you must try and like them. One has to write poetry (at least I always have) to express things that don't go into prose so easily; also, I like playing with metres and rhythms; it was, in childhood and youth, one of my forms of insobriety; and I still do it, though with less ease. I don't *read* nearly so much poetry as I did; I remember, as a child and girl, being poetry-drunk; it meant more than anything to me. It was so good for saying to oneself on walks alone. Alas, my memory is less good in these days; I suppose everyone finds that. *De senectute, eheu.*[1]

Goodnight, and thank you so much.

Yours affectionately,

R. M.

PS. I told you I could read both sides of the transparent paper quite well.

---

[1] " Of old age, alas! "

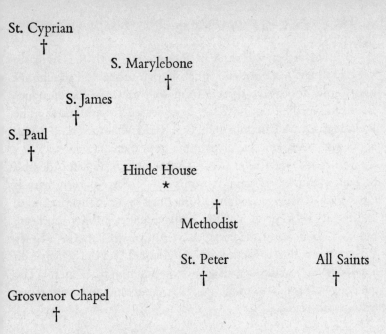

St. Cyprian
✝

S. Marylebone
✝

S. James
✝

S. Paul
✝

Hinde House
★

✝

Methodist

St. Peter   All Saints
✝   ✝

Grosvenor Chapel
✝

1. Hinde St. Methodist, 2 minutes.
2. S. James's, Spanish Place, (R.C.) 4 min.
3. S. Paul's, Baker St., 5 min.
4. S. Peter's, Vere St., 6 min.
5. S. Marylebone (parish church), 10 min.
6. All Saints, Margaret St., 15 or 20 min.
7. S. Cyprian's, Clarence Gate, 20 min.
8. Grosvenor Chapel.

Notes

In 1 and 2 I should feel something of an alien. 3 is, I believe, a little Low, but near. 4 is a charming little early 18th century building, built for a chapel of ease to S. Marylebone, but now attached to All Souls Langham Place, and probably doesn't have H.C. every Sunday.

5, my parish church, is 18th c. Palladian, and spacious, with pew rents. I don't know it at all, or what services it has. For 6 I should have to get my car out; it lives in a lock-up behind these flats.

The same applies to 7, which is, I believe, even more exalted than 6.

A little further still there is Regent St., with S. Thomas's, very small and extreme. So much so that probably I should not know how to behave there; I am told they try to reproduce Basilican worship, but how far they succeed I don't know. The Revs. Patrick McLaughlin and Hugh Ross Williamson. (I know about this because a friend of mine goes there sometimes.)

So I think when time allows, All Saints, and when it doesn't S. Paul's, and when there is a service, S. Peter's. Or there is Grosvenor Chapel, to which I sometimes went many years ago, and liked. I forgot to insert it, so have put it in now too near; but it is about the same distance as All Saints, I think. A pity the very near one is Methodist. Or I could bicycle, which I do a good deal in summer in London, but not in winter. The excitement of this is traffic-dodging, but on Sundays there is next to no traffic.

20 Hinde House, Hinde St., W. 1
23rd February, 1951†

Dear Father,

I think these air letters are an excellent idea; yours came in 3 days, which is certainly quicker than the normal, though this is chancey, and it might be 5 or 6 days next time. Your kind seems rather more spacious than ours. But one can get quite a lot on to them. By the same post came the stories (10 days). How nice they are. I enjoy them very much, particularly poor Eulogius, which reads very well, and I like the English.[1] One has much sympathy with the young disciple, who didn't like sitting in the village. And with the poor misguided, generous Abbot, and with Eulogius, who must have felt stone-cutting

[1] Father Johnson had translated into English some of the *Liber de Miraculis* of Johannes Monachus (see below p. 316). The story of Eulogius (a stone-mason) and Abbot Daniel occurs in chapter 27; that of the eunuch in chapter 28. The Latin text is accessible in an edition by Michael Huber (Heidelberg, 1913).

on one *keration*[1] a day a miserable downfall. The eunuch did better on his *paximatia*[2] and bean broth. Your arrival at toasted crusts was most ingenious; and how interesting to find the Greek mother had used it. I will try it (and *keration*) on a Greek restaurant I go to sometimes. But I must be careful not to *order* either, as I shouldn't want to eat them, not being a desert saint. I must get hold of the *Liber de Miraculis*. The desert ascetic life seems very like the same life in the 4th century; but there is more humanity in Abbot Daniel than in most of those Latin hermits. In fact, he must have been a charming person. So must poor Johannes, labouring over his translation. I suppose he lived in one of those beautiful monasteries round or in Amalfi. There was a close connection in his time between Amalfi and Constantinople, and the Emperor had a court there; that, no doubt, would be one way in which the Byzantine stories came west. If I find out more about J. I will let you know. These stories must be hard to put into such beautiful English, and it must be fun doing it. I shall like to see the third. *Margery Kempe*,[3] yes, indeed I know her, and have her. I think it was Logan Pearsall Smith, who loved the book, who gave it me years ago. It is fascinating. The religious side of the Norfolk life of which the Pastons represent the more secular side. What a lot comes out of Norfolk. Juliana, too. *How* good you are to suggest sending me some Latin. But no, don't. Such books are too precious to send away. I would love to come and see them, but, as you say, I shouldn't even be allowed to do that. I am building up my Latin books more now; and now I even have a pretty little Juvenal, for which I thanked you, and for the other delightful arrivals, in my air letter of 21st. What language do you generally read the psalms in? I think one wants both the Latin and English; both are so good. I *must* get a Greek testament, and read it properly ... [*sic*] Yes, Humbert Wolfe (now dead) was a very intelligent and understanding person; a poet himself; a brilliant and versatile Jew. I crossed out his commentary

[1] Locust fruit. [2] Literally "biscuits."
[3] English mystic (*c.* 1373—after 1433), author of the *Book of Margery Kempe*.

because it seemed to me a little foolish. But it is true that the inter-penetration of unknown worlds seems to have got a good deal into the poems, written at quite different periods.[1] Sometimes I meant the dead and the living, sometimes ordinary life and the kind of dream life beyond it, sometimes the Christian assault on the world (as in *Lady Day*)—the manifestation of the glory, as you say—sometimes the impact of some remote unbelievable past, sometimes of strangenesses one doesn't understand but feels. But many, of course, are quite matter of fact and earthly. *The Pond* records a summer afternoon in 1919, when we lay and discussed what on earth we should do about things.

The romance and adventure of that desert world is haunting. All that shifting-coloured waste of land, and a hermitage every few miles—" turn but a stone and start a hermit," and (by your Abbot's time) little round Byzantine domes. And beneath the desert, buried cities, silted over for centuries; some have been uncovered, others still wait. And, in the far distance, the glories of Byzantine cities. And lions roaming, making friends, it seems, with the hermits. Do you know Helen Waddell's *Beasts and Saints*, and her other Desert Fathers books?

I suppose the *Infans* was *only* a title, was it, and carries no implication of childhood—I mean, it wasn't the *Child* Jesus whom the abbot saw? It is rather a strange title; I remember no other use of it, except in the Spanish *Infante*, which doesn't imply infancy. Is it used anywhere in the New Testament (vulg[ate]), as an alternative to *puer* and *servus*? Perhaps one of its meanings is " son." I lack a medieval Latin dictionary. I like the immediate reaction of the abbot to the news of Eulogius's good fortune—" it is I that have done this murder." I expect he knew that E[ulogius] couldn't take riches well. It is a wonderful story. In my last air letter I sent you a drawing of my situation in re churches. I hope very soon to be able to go out early to Grosvenor Chapel. In the letter before that (I think) I told you about poor Fr. Wilkins being laid up with bronchitis; I hope he

---

[1] A collection of R. M.'s poetry, number six in the second series of the *Augustan Books of English Poetry* (Ernest Benn, *c.* 1925), included a prefatory note by the editor, Humbert Wolfe.

goes on pretty well. I have finished the *Norfolk Diary*, with great interest. One day I might make a Norfolk tour in my car, with that Penguin for a guide and instructor. Or I might go on pilgrimage to Walsingham. A Rom. Cath. I know once said he could not kneel and pray in the Anglican shrine there. I'm glad we have no such inhibitions about the R.C. one. Or, indeed, about the shrines and churches of any sect; it would be saddening. This letter draws to its close, and I have really got a lot on to it. And I would rather it reached you in 3 or 4 days than in 2 or 3 weeks, so it seems a good idea. Thank you again so much for Abbot Daniel.

Yours affectionately,
R. M.

March

[*Postmark: London, W.1*]
1st March, 1951†

Dear Father,

How lovely to get a nice long air letter from you yesterday. It came after I had visited Fr. Wilkins in St. Luke's Hostel, for he most kindly wrote to me at once on getting your letter (" a delightful long letter," he said) on Tuesday. He told me visitors came between 2 and 5, and that he would be glad to see me if I had time and felt well enough, before he went out on Thursday, when he was going down to nursing sisters at Hastings, till Easter or later, and after that hoped to be back at St. Edward's, I suppose allowed to do a little, but not to climb stairs, which doesn't sound v.g. Broncho-pneumonia acting on a rough heart-valve, as no doubt he will have told you. So I went there between 4 and 5 on Tuesday, and we chatted for half an hour, about India, the army, the old war, Cowley in America, you; nothing specifically professional, as I felt it scarcely the moment, and anyhow there didn't seem an opportunity; we talked about other things all the time, and I enjoyed seeing him. We didn't refer to church life, except that I think I mentioned that I had been on Sunday to Grosvenor Chapel and liked it. I suppose we are both rather shy; too shy to talk easily about anything not superficial and mundane. I know I am. People don't think I am shy, because I gabble away to anyone about anything or nothing; but that's different. I believe there is no one but you to whom I find it easy to talk (or write) on the subjects I have written to you about. To you it is entirely easy and natural. Partly it is that you have always met me half-way, or more than half-way, and one has the feeling that you really care. Then, you understand all I say or ask, with all its implications and overtones, and your answers always cover what I meant and add more to it; and I always understand what you mean. Incidentally, you have a knack, which pleases me, of making me laugh a little even on a serious subject; as, to take a small example, when in a recent letter you remarked that my communion would " *last* for a bit; but not for another 20 or 30 years." I doubt if Fr. Wilkins would have said just that. Still, I know it's no use letting my non-resident chaplain spoil me for a resident one, and I really will go to someone before Easter. You know, I rather liked . . . Grosvenor Chapel at High Mass last Sunday . . . And it would be easy to go there, as they seem to hear confessions regularly. And I like the atmosphere of the church; I used to like it long ago, tho' never a regular attendant. If I do go there, I could say what you suggest about the long gap, and get advice about how an earnest Catholic should comport herself. For I do feel a little vague about this; having been re-admitted into the freedom of this *Civitas Dei*, I should like to behave like a good *civis*, so far as I can, and get all I am able out of it. How much prayer, what church-going, at what hours—does a good *civis* communicate at noon, how often does she try to attend early mass—you know the sort of questions that arise in the unpractised mind. (I am talking, of course, of a *civis* in rude health; I shall soon be this, tho' this cough still hangs about.) Or again, I might seek one of the St. Ed[ward's] Fathers. Oh dear, I am indeed thankful you didn't

stay in this climate; if you had, and had died of it, I shouldn't
be in this *Civitas* now at all.

I answered your 10-cent letter,[1] which you despise unduly, by
a similar letter (6d.) on the 23rd; in it I thanked you for those
lovely Abbot Daniel stories; in an air letter on 21st I wrote of
the arrival of the *Norfolk Diary*, Juvenal, snapshots, U.S.
P[rayer] B[ook], etc., all good things. *Margery Kempe*, as I
said, I have had for some years, and find it extremely interesting.
(By the way, Fr. Wilkins says you can imitate Norfolk with the
nicest exactitude.) Thank you for being pleased about my quite
undeserved Cambridge Doctorate. Yes, it's true that I was
" educated at Oxford." When we were brought from Italy by
our fond parents who had decided it was time we had some
English schooling, we settled in Oxford because my father
wanted to search the Bodleian for a medieval MS. he thought
must be lost there, as indeed it was. So the girls attended the
Oxford High School and the boys Lynam's Prep. school, and
pretty dim it seemed after our libertine and bare-legged scram-
bling about our Italian shore and hills, complete with canoe
and pony. Having found his MS. and written his large book
about it, my father took a lectureship in English Literature at
Cambridge, his own University, and we all lived there, but I
was sent to Somerville, where I read history and enjoyed myself
hugely. So I always feel rather amphibious about the two
universities; tho' it is Cambridge that is in my blood, and
most of my ancestors were there, tho' the Conybeares seemed
to go to Oxford in the 18th cent. I am fond of both and on the
whole more of my present friends (male) were Oxonians.
I certainly meant no aspersions on Oxford by sending slightly
unamiable people there. But on the whole I am pleased that
my Hon. Doctorate will be Cambridge; filial piety perhaps.
I doted on my father. As children we endorsed what our Italian
servant said of him—" *proprio come il Signor' Iddio—sa tutto,
tutto!* "[2] And he told us the most entrancing stories from
Herodotus and Dante's Inferno. And grounded us in Latin and

[1] The " air-letter " forms used by Father Johnson carried ten-cent stamps.
[2] " Just like the Lord God—he knows absolutely everything."

cricket (a game however that I never liked much, it was too tame). I always feel like M. Aurelius about the example of my father; his integrity and unselfishness were so profound. One of those sons of the parsonage who read Darwin as they grew up and suffered Doubt, which remained with him thro' life. But the most magnificent principles. I am always glad he didn't live to think ill of me. It is odd; our generation, and perhaps the one after ours too, can reconcile God and Christianity with the revelations of science much more easily than the late Victorians could. I remember Dr. Raven writing that somewhere; he, of course, is a really good biologist and (modernist) Christian. Oh dear, this seems like the end; cut off in its prime, this letter is. My further valuable remarks must wait. Thank you much for all yours.

Yours affectionately,
R. M.

20, Hinde House, Hinde St., W.1
5th March, 1951 †

Dear Father,

Thank you so much for your 10-cent of 27th Feb. I always use these things for India (sister) and various Canadian acquaintances, but hadn't realised till lately that they went outside the Commonwealth, in fact to our late colonies such as Mass., Virginia, New York, etc., which was stupid of me. They are really very convenient, and seem about as quick as the others; yours, posted 28th, has taken 5 days only. Thank you a lot for having sent *Margery K[empe]*. When I came to look for my copy, I couldn't find it, and think I may have lent it to some reprobate friend who hasn't returned it, so I shall be really glad to have it again, and shall re-read it. *And* the two little podgy books, Horace and Ovid, how nice, and I do thank you. Of course, apart from their qualities, it pleases me to have these books from your shelves, *if you can really spare them*. I have now got from the Library John Bailey, which I have been reading (last night in bed) with much pleasure. I know some of his books, tho' never met him. But when he was dining out in London thro' the twenties, he kept meeting so many people I also have met that it makes one feel one was there too. What a number of sides he touched life on. And he had a good habit of putting in his diary the good things people had said to him, which is worth while, tho' I should never have the patience even to keep a diary. I like his references to your father, and one to you. I have been thinking about his constant idea that Christianity runs the danger of exclusion of many of the best interests. I don't see why this should be; surely it should contain everything good in itself. In fact, he does say this; but feels it often hasn't, and here of course he is right. One thinks of some of the early Fathers of the Church and their fierce concentration, which was I suppose a reaction against pagan licentiousness, but went stupidly far; as when Gregory scolded priests for reading the profane writers. He would perhaps have purged your shelves? J.B. wanted "a new interpretation of Christianity, with more of Plato and Origen in it and less Aristotle and Augustine." So did Milton; and perhaps that argument has raged always. Remembering Von Hügel, Acton, and so many great Christians of wide interests and range, J.B. needn't, surely, have been anxious. If our Lord had taught Greeks not Jews, would more of these general and artistic interests have got on the record? But it seems to me they have come in ever since, except among the fanatics, like Savonarola, puritans like S. Bernard who hated all decoration and beauty for its own sake as much as he hated Abelard and the reasoning philosophers; and the Protestant and R.C. puritans down the ages. Light, beauty, learning, and breadth of range—they are all there for those who want them. I don't remember that Margery K. did.

I am really getting nearly well now; coughing almost negligible, and putting on again a few lbs. of weight that I had lost. I do go to early church now, driving in my invaluable car. Grosvenor Chapel 8.15, Sundays and weekdays, so can go any day I like. (What about mid-day communion? Is it good?) Yes, I live very warm and cosy here; central heating, nice little flat, adequate plain cooking (tho' I am not nearly so gifted in this sphere as many of my friends, male and female) and of course pretty frequent lunching and dining with friends. As to milk, which I don't much like, there is any amount. I believe one should drink more of it.

I am interested just now in selecting short passages, fragments from psalms and Bible and collects and missal and general reading (in any language that I know) that seem to suit the occupations and emergencies and encounters likely to occur in the day ahead. If one collects a store of such, one can select at will. As Donne said, search in the wardrobe for suitable clothes.

Your rich and strange houses—no thank you, not often! I do sometimes frequent them for week-ends (summer, not winter, tho' I did at Xmas) and it is quite fun just for that time, because I like the people in them (or I wouldn't go there), and there is what J. Bailey calls " much good talk," but it wouldn't do for long, I like my freedom. Some of my friends spend most week-ends in one another's houses in the country; I couldn't do that. Tho' what an odd view it was of à Kempis's, that the more he had been among people, the less of a man he became. Perhaps the desert saints felt this too. Definitely un-Christian, it seems.

By the way, I was enchanted by a remark of yours in another letter about " some other reputable church ": it opened vistas of fascinating speculation as to what goes on in the less reputable and I thought of the temples of Daphne outside Antioch, and those of Sybaris, and indeed many more. I shall explore a little! Did I tell you, in my church list, of St. Thomas's, Regent Street, tiny and infinitely high, where I went with a friend some time ago and heard the Rev. Hugh Ross Williamson preach about " the terrible *narrowness* of Christ," into which we must enter? *Not*, I felt, my cup of tea. John Bailey would have been furious. Did you read the book he edited about Lady Frederick Cavendish (Lucy Lyttelton)? It was very good reading. We (my father, rather) knew lots of Lytteltons, and used to stay at Hagley Hall. He was at school with Edward Lyttelton, later headmaster of Eton, whom I greatly admired when young and when he was on the same Hellenic cruise as my father and I; I think 1913.

These 10-centers are intriguing; I look round corners and find a fresh bit; you have 4 little leaves in yours, unlike our kind. The Greek Test[ament] occurs on one of them. If you have a spare one lying about ever, I should love it. But I can and should buy one here, of course. I used to read in it long ago.

Bailey is crammed with interesting and suggestive remarks that set one thinking, wondering if one agrees with him, etc. I usually do, I find. Tho' some of his views on literature belong rather to his generation. But such a good and roving mind.

To-day there is actually some sunshine, tho' cold sunshine, I must now go out into it. It now looks as if spring might some-time come. Did I tell you I had sent you my Spanish travel, *Fabled Shore*? Rather tedious really.

Yours affectionately,
R. M.

20, Hinde House, Hinde St., W.1
12th March, 1951 †

Dear Father,

Your air letter of 6th and 7th came to-day; thank you so much. I am glad you like the idea of Grosvenor Chapel; I like it very much. The liturgy is varied on different days (I mean, the additions to the P.B. service are), and all good. It may, as you say, be Sarum.[1] I think the 1928 book is partly used. What I wish could be inserted into the prayer for the Church militant is the clause in the American version that you sent me, after " departed this life in thy faith and fear," about growth in love and service. They don't have that; in fact, they don't depart from the P.B. prayers, except for extras and a lot of v.g. semi-sotto-voce prayers, and responses; I must try and get hold of

---

[1] The Sarum Breviary contained the modification of the Roman rite which was used at Salisbury cathedral in the Middle Ages.

the missal used. . . . They do have a number of mid-day communicants on Sundays at the sung Eucharist, so I could do that if I felt unlike the 8.15 one. But I now am quite up to the 8.15; I get my car out, and it is only about 5 minutes' drive. It is every weekday as well as Sundays, so one can go any morning. It is really rather a beautiful service, I think, in that small 18th c. chapel, and very well taken. Should I make a confession before Easter? If I do, I might go there. I suppose I had better. I used to know (socially only) Christopher Cheshire, who was Warden of Liddon House[1] once, and have been to tea there. I remember (I think in the twenties) being embarrassed because he hadn't warned me who was coming, and there was an elderly lady whom he addressed as "Mam," and I thought she must be his mother, and greeted her in the ordinary way and sat down by her and chatted, and it turned out gradually that she was Princess Louise (I think) to whom I should have curtsied and waited to be spoken to first, etc. I apologised afterwards to my host, who said cheerfully, "That's the stuff to give 'em," but of course it wasn't at all! I think he is now a Prebendary. I never knew Fr. Underhill, though I met his sister Evelyn, who wasn't quite so good as her books. I don't know who is at Liddon House now. . . . The new All Saints vicar sounds very able; I might go and hear him preach some time. I have never known anyone there.

That Retreat that you have forgotten was very good. I kept notes of it for many years, till they got burnt in the '41 conflagration. I hadn't then looked at them for a long time, having been off the track of such things. But they had impressed me very much; they were about prayer, and goodness, and not getting separated from God. I remember I came away resolved to try to be good for ever; and I was rather in the middle of counter-pulls just then. Well, it didn't work out like that. But I seem to have met it all again now at last.

At Oxford I took the whole of English history (one has to)

[1] An Anglican centre for graduates and young professional men and women, founded in Kensington in 1907 and later moved to South Audley Street and attached to Grosvenor Chapel.

beginning with the Anglo-Saxon Charters, Villeinage, Sheriffs'
Courts, etc., etc. (these bored me rather) but my Special Period,
and my Foreign Period, was the 17th century. We had to do
Political Science and Polit. Economy, too. I was much interested
in most of it; unfortunately I fell ill at the wrong moment and
got an Aegrotat which was disappointing. I liked Oxford; the
river, work, people, Oxford itself, even hockey, at which I was
good. I wasn't much of a church goer in those days, so never
got to Cowley, which later I regretted. Yes, we went to all
kinds of lecturers and coaches; I remember particularly Dr.
Ernest Barker, who coached me in Aristotle and Political Science;
he is now at Cambridge. It was all fun. I never returned to
collect my B.A., as many people did; (women didn't get them
till 1921). I am reading some interesting books, among them
Dr. Kirk's *Vision of God*; what a stupendous learned work!
I like best the early part, about the pre-Christian pagan's thirst
for God; and then Philo and the Alexandrians. I read it in
bed, and its only fault is that it is rather heavy to hold. The whole
business of communion with God, so age-old, so irrepressible,
so partially achieved, so always sought after—it sheds such light
on the Gospels, and on the sacrament of Holy Communion.
I am glad you are sending me some notes on prayer; I rather
need them. I see what you mean about fasting communion.
Instinctively, I feel the early one is better, and seems to mean
more to me. I don't think, do you, that I ought to wrestle with
the Resurrection (as told in the Gospels) and the Virgin Birth,
both of which are rather outside what my brain can easily
take. So I just leave them in the neutral country beyond the pro-
cesses of thought, and don't find they matter to my personal
attempts at realisation of Christ and of God and the Incarnation. My brain being rather frail, had better not be strained. Or
should it?

All Saints has notices outside saying it is full of "thieves,
male and female," so I am loath to enter it, for fear of encounter-
ing these and being robbed, or of being taken for one and being
arrested. Perhaps the new Vicar will clean it up. I lunched at
a Cypriot restaurant the other day, and talked to a waiter about

paximatia; as you said, it is toasted bread, and has caraway seeds, and is popular at Easter. So the eunuch didn't eat badly. I look forward to the next Abbot Daniel story. Did you ever get a long MS. beautifully written sea letter that I wrote you from bed during my 2nd illness? Perhaps the sea letter you say you have sent was in answer to it. I read in some notice that Fr. Wilkins was to take a Quiet Day in Philbeach Gardens on 17th, and wrote to the church to ask if it was true, but of course it was a mistake, and he is still at Hastings recuperating. I thought I would go to it if he was taking it. Perhaps he will take one later on, after Easter.

Now I am off to a political meeting got up by Victor Gollancz, which may be interesting—he is a stimulating creature, of immense energy. I am recovering my usual bounding health, and the weather is, suddenly, less bitterly cold. I do hope you are well? *I* take iron, and codliver oil. Do you realise how your letters are to me the mental equivalent of these—only *much* nicer to take! A bad comparison really—I only meant that they stimulate and help me.

Yours affectionately,

R. M.

20, *Hinde House, Hinde St., W.*1
16*th March*, 1951 †

Dear Father,

Thank you for your very pleasing letter of 9th, posted 10th. I got out Darwell Stone[1] yesterday. Those spacious " Religion and Philosophy " shelves on the London Library's top floor, divided into so many sections, " Rationalism," " Judaism," " Metaphysics," " Biblical Criticism," etc., etc., etc., are nice to rummage about among, and I come on all kinds of things that I look into while there or take home if they seem worth it. Shall I like D.S.? He seems hugely learned; perhaps over legalistic and patristic for the layman; and, as you say, what

---

[1] Rev. Darwell Stone (1859-1941), Anglo-Catholic theologian.

undreamt of questions he answers! He distrusted *Lux Mundi*,[1] I see; thought it didn't square with Revelation. But all very interesting and instructive. Fr. Andrew[2] I didn't find, but think I may have looked for him stupidly under " Andrews," and shall try again. He must have been delightful. I love that answer to the worried Anglican. I was interested yesterday, in reading Dr. Inge's *Diary of a Dean* (full of amusing acidities, inter alia, such as that he felt when made Dean of St. Paul's " like a mouse watched by 4 cats," the cats being the 4 canons) to come on an entry by Mrs. Inge for 29th Oct., 1925: " One of our most successful little dinners. Lady Sandhurst, Mr. A. L. Mumm, Rose Macaulay, Sir Maurice de Bunsen, Sir Ernest Wild, Lady Burghclere, *John Bailey* [*sic*]." So I did meet J.B. I have quite forgotten doing so, and indeed that particular dinner; I obviously wasn't next him. I wish I had been— I should have enjoyed it. Yes, he was wrong, had got hold of the wrong end of the Christian life (as from the opposite angle T. à Kempis in some moods had). He should have read a v.g. book I am now reading, by the 18th c. Jesuit Père de Caussade, which is full of illumination and wisdom.[3] He speaks of " un Dieu toujours reçu dans *tout ce qu'il y a sur la terre* . . . Ce qui nous instruit, c'est ce qui nous arrive d'un moment à l'autre . . . Il faut donc écouter Dieu de moment en moment, pour être docte dans la théologie vertueuse, qui est tout pratique et expérimentale. . . . Le moment présent est toujours comme un ambassadeur qui déclare l'ordre de Dieu . . . *toutes les routes et toutes les manières l'avancent également vers le large et infini.* Tout lui est moyen; tout lui est instrument de sainteté, sans aucune différence." I like that idea, of each moment being an ambassador accosting us from God with a message how to deal with it. Of *course* it enlarges life; I don't need to tell you how much. It adds

[1] A series of essays on the Religion of the Incarnation edited by Charles Gore and published in 1889, which included new critical views of the Old Testament.

[2] *The Life and Letters of Father Andrew, S.D.C.; edited and compiled by K. E. Burne* (1948).

[3] *L'Abandon à la Providence Divine*, by J. P. de Caussade (1675-1751), first published in 1867. (English translation, *Self-Abandonment to Divine Providence, with Introduction by David Knowles,* 1933.)

another dimension to everything; or lights a candle behind things; both. I wonder if this will go on, in spite of the drag and suction of the hampering, corrupting past. One can't, of course, go on year after year, so many years, doing what one knows to be wrong, selfish, dishonourable, deceitful, unfair, against God's will; without being weakened and corrupted and partly blinded, and this must hamper and clog, perhaps prevent one ever becoming what one might have become. I really am trying; though of course not enough. But it will be a poor job at best. But never never shall I be tempted to think that religion doesn't cover and include everything, or could be narrowing. The *Imitatio*,[1] of course, is monastic in angle. I have only the English translation, which was given me by my godmother when I was 13. I was, I suppose, in some ways, an odd child; for I fell for this book; I remember sitting in the top branches of trees and reading about how I ought not to dispute about the Trinity, and how it was vanity to hunt after honours and climb to high degree (but I did aspire to being head of my form as a rule), and that I should withdraw my heart from the love of visible things (which was quite impossible, and he shouldn't have suggested it) must shun familiarity and company, and not be drawn by one's sensual desires to " rove abroad," for, " what carriest thou home but a burdened conscience and a distracted heart? " None of these precepts did I follow; indeed my mother threw cold water on them; but of course he is also full of excellent moral teaching for anyone. Yes, I agree about many de-Christianised novelists. I have just been asked to review Graham Greene's new book (not a novel, but a collection of essays, old and new, called *The Lost Childhood*) for *The Times Literary Supplement*. It may be interesting. He, of course, is *not* de-Christianised, but Romanised. . . . He has a great natural sense of guilt, I think. Did you read *The Heart of the Matter*, his last novel? . . . One sometimes wonders if Roman Catholicism is very good for the moral sense, with its almost mechanical view of the wiping out of sin by absolution. But of course this doesn't apply to the well instructed. All the

[1] The *Imitatio Christi* of Thomas à Kempis.

98

same, how much I prefer Anglicanism! (If you read it, tell me some time what you think of it.)

I think these sea letters are very dilatory, except sometimes. I sent you mine (from bed) on 18th Feb., and it hadn't reached you by 10th March. Not that it had anything of importance in it, I think it was just chat, about books I had been reading, etc. But it seems absurd to take all that time crossing the Atlantic; *we* don't.

Later. What extraordinary things clergymen sometimes want to know, and worry over! But it would have been worth while to write and put *any* question to Dr. Stone, to get such marvellous answers and learn so much about church law down the ages. The Resurrection bodies of the Patriarchs, should a baptized person marry a catechumen, did Dr. Pusey invoke the saints, are the Channel Islands in schism . . . [*sic*] all these queries evoking such a flow of profound knowledge. I am enjoying reading it, and, should anyone ever ask me any of these questions, shall be in a position to impress them greatly with my erudition. I fear I can't hope to impress *you*, as you have access to the book and would know where I got my information from. Goodbye.

Yours affectionately,

R. M.

20, *Hinde House, Hinde St., W.*1
21*st March,* 1951 †

Dear Father,

The most wonderful posts yesterday and the day before—first (early post on 19th) that delightful book parcel, viz. the charming little selections from Lucretius, Ovid, Propertius, etc., with just the bits from the *Tristia* that I chanced to be wanting to refer to just now, and so much else; then the dear little Catullus (what a handy book for bag or pocket on a journey); and the Greek Testament, also handy in size, which I am really delighted to have, and shall read it a lot. I hope you can really spare all these; they arrived so beautifully done up, packed with efficiency and skill well beyond my range, and must, I fear, have been troublesome and time-taking. You are endlessly good. By the same post came your letter of 12th. Then in the afternoon I came in to find *another* lovely packet—*Margery Kempe*, Horace, Ovid's *Metamorphoses*, and that very nice little book of psalms for offices and festivals. I am gradually committing passages from the psalms in Latin to memory. I expect you know most of them by heart already. Some, one prefers in English, some in Latin; *none* in metrical versions! Again, this is a very handy pocket book. Thank you immensely for *all* these books. My Latin volumes now make a much better showing in my shelves; I only hope they haven't left gaps in yours. Then yesterday afternoon came your air letter of 17th— a particularly good one—and the big envelope with the Abbot Daniel story and your notes and letter inside. The story is delightful; I like the Abbot's exquisite courtesy in thanking the Abbess for his unsatisfying meal—and how hungry he and his disciple must have been by that time! The inebriate *must* be related from life; indeed, the whole nunnery must. It *is* remarkable, the absence of specifically Christian devotion. Is it the effect of desert monastic life (or hermit life)? If so, it must have prepared the Thebaid desert monks and hermits to come under the Arabs with less difficulty; in fact, later they did, didn't they, become cut off from the rest of Christendom and form the Coptic Church. And many of them submitted to Islam. But one doesn't—I mean I don't—know nearly enough about it; I wish I did. The Byzantine period, in all its aspects, is so fascinating. I have read all your notes, with great attention and interest. They suggest all kinds of good ideas to me. One is that I shall get from Mowbrays *The Hours of Prayer*.[1] Another, to make an arrangement of Morning and Evening Prayer to say, bringing in the psalms for the day. The psalms are quick with meaning; more and more, I find. The 119th stupendous. (Would you think the Abbot Daniel said them?) That is interesting, about the neglect of the Eucharist leading to forget-

[1] The S.S.J.E Office Book.

fulness of Christ. To set against this, I suppose the Wesleyans, and later the Evangelicals, had a very fervent Jesus-worship, with very scarce sacramental life. But they, the best of them, had an intense personal faith in redemption that short-circuited sacraments. Odd, rather; I mean, to read those intimate appeals and prayers to Christ, in the most ardent language, from people —some of them clergy—who weren't moved to more frequent communion. Then, of course, the Quakers . . . [sic] Did you ever read the Life of George Eliot? She grew up in that fervent Evangelical piety, which completely captured her, before she became an agnostic, yet never losing that moral earnestness. But the Evangelicals thought that " This do . . ." meant only occasionally; it must have been impoverishing. One beauty of " This do " is that here is something that *can* be done, something definite and surrendering. And handing down a tradition: I tend to overlook that side of it, and to be too subjective, taking it as a means of learning what God wants me to do, rather than as a proclamation of faith. But I like to feel that we are helping to carry on the business too.

Thank you very much indeed for your letter of 17th. I turned to Catullus after reading it, and read that melancholy and moving lament of Attis, and a lot of 64. He *is* so lovely; so much the loveliest of the Latin poets. The mere sound transports one. He commands emotion more than any of the rest.

In one matter your letter came too late. Due to your having said to go fairly often to confession for the present, and to my firm persuasion that what you say must be right (it having worked out so), I thought I had better go before Easter, so did so on Monday, at Grosvenor Chapel. . . . I mentioned the long interregnum. I think perhaps it was a good thing to go. Thank you for your answer about the other thing I asked you, about not believing things. I am so glad you say that. It is what I think is best, too. To strain after conviction about things one doesn't easily believe worries and distracts, and tends to shift the emphasis from the things one does accept. As you say, it may all arrive later. Or never. I was interested in that " Christian Novelists " article. I think what one misses in most novels is a sense of right and wrong and the conflict between them. Compare the great 19th cent. novelists, such as George Eliot, whose chief characters are at perpetual war with themselves. The people in so much fiction now seldom appear to be this. Yet every one, almost, must be, I suppose, anyhow at intervals, however subconsciously and weakly. A good novel can be written without this, but the people in it seem to lack one dimension. One doesn't want preaching, but just a hint of that motive in life, to make it a true record of the "*condition humaine*." Those two Note Books[1] being written for me are a very pleasant thought; how much I shall like to have them! But I am very sorry about your cold; I hope it hasn't turned into anything very bad. You know, I sometimes feel remorse that I have pestered you with questions and remarks that may seem to want comment, when you have so little time. I do so hope you *won't* feel you must answer always; otherwise I should feel I was the last straw. Follow T. à Kempis's advice and commit me to God, as you anyhow do. I maunder on, making you the recipient of random speculations and problems, just because you have been so good to me, which is unfair. Unfair too is the abrupt close of this letter, when I have lots more to say. About Grosvenor Chapel, Mr. Wilkes, Lady Mary, etc.[2] I get there every morning now at 8.15. This won't last beyond this week! I know . . . and like her; tho' she has that confident, religious superiority so many R.C.'s have, as if they were in the best church, which they are not; *we are*. (How is *that* for religious superiority?)

Love and thanks,
R. M.

What a nice letter from Mr. Armstrong, enclosed with the Norfolk cuttings.

[1] Father Johnson was compiling for R. M. two "anthologies" of quotations, prayers, and his own compositions.
[2] Lady Mary Wortley Montagu (d. 1762) and also John Wilkes (d. 1797) were buried at Grosvenor Chapel.

Dear Father,

I have so many things I want to write about that I am making
the return of Fr. Wilkins's very kind letter an excuse for writing
a proper old-style air letter. I have had 3 delightful letters from
you lately—posted 20th, 22nd, 24th. These two last came this
morning; the other I was just about to answer, but left it a few
days so as to give you a little rest from my letters. *Of course*
you can't and mustn't go on writing often; I shan't expect it.
It has been so endlessly good of you, and good *for* me, all this
time, and I feel ashamed of taking so much of your time. I have
now made good resolutions about it. At intervals, when I want
your advice, or to tell or talk about something, or just to keep
in touch, I shall write a (sea) letter (air if in a great hurry!) which
don't bother to answer until you really have time. I feel we can
keep in touch without writing much—in fact, I see no way in
which I could get *out* of touch, exploring, as I am now, this
exciting country into which you have conducted me. When
things occur to you that you think I might like to hear, save
them up till you are at leisure. You are probably never this—
but more at leisure than sometimes. You see, my excuse has
been that it is a new country, and you have been, and are, my
guide in it. That is my *excuse*; my *reason*, I am afraid, largely
that I do like hearing from you, because your letters are (from
any standpoint) so good. They have every quality—range,
depth, breadth, humour, wisdom, interest, sympathy, even (I
like to think) affection. So much for letter-writing. Before I
embark on *Class*—to me always a most interesting historical
question, and one on which I have often speculated—I will proceed to a matter rising out of your letter to-day, and Fr. Wilkins's;
Confession; about which I feel in some danger of getting into
something of a muddle. You might gather from what Fr.
Wilkins says that it was in *conversation* that something passed
between us about confession; actually it wasn't mentioned when
I saw him. I had written to him, as you know, saying that you

thought monthly confession might be a good thing and when could I see him therefore. I added, as a kind of apology for bothering him again so soon, that I felt it seemed rather often, and was afraid he might too, but thought I had better take your advice, as I had been doing so. He replied to this telling me of his illness, and about how any of the S. Edward's House Fathers would be glad to see me, and gave me some times. I didn't answer that, except a line of sympathy for the illness, or do anything about it. Then after hearing from you, he wrote very kindly asking me to come and visit him before he left, which I did. But, as I said, we didn't speak of confession, except that he said, as we said goodbye, " I am so sorry to have failed you," and *I* said I was so sorry he was ill. I don't quite know where he got the impression that I had decided to come only before the Festivals, as these weren't mentioned; or that I was going to S. Edward's House; but I expect he thought that was what I wanted. And now, as I told you in my letter of 21st, I have been before Easter to Grosvenor Chapel, which seemed easier of access; and more given to regular times, than S. Edward's. . . . So now, how do I stand? What do I do before Whitsun? Does Fr. Wilkins expect me, and do I go to him? A professional opinion, please! Of course in a way it is rather nice to be all of a piece, and go to confession where one goes to church; then, it occurs *in* church, and at set times . . . Oh dear, I don't know. If Memorial Drive were round the corner, it would save me all this bother. . . . But, if I do decide to go on [making confessions at Grosvenor Chapel], should I write to Fr. Wilkins and explain? I like him so much, I should hate to seem off-hand or thankless. But I didn't actually quite know when he would be back.

I am so glad you took that cold (or flue?) to bed. I expect you should really have spent a week there, though. It is the best way of getting well, and of not having a relapse, or keeping a cough. And it is a rest. And a nice chance of reading and writing in peace, and thinking too; I did quite a bit of this last when I was ill in Jan. and Feb. I am so sorry your eyes are troublesome. I wonder if your glasses need changing? I wear them for reading and writing, and find I have to have them changed every few years, as the lenses get out of date. How nice you are to read and like *Fabled Shore*; I *am* glad you do. I think it is really rather dull for those who don't know the places, or aren't meaning to go there. It is so full of detail about the buildings, places, etc. I described it all because I loved it so much; it was like a lovely dream of beauty and interest, and I tried to put this across so far as I could. It was my first European travel since the war, and in a way lonely, because I used in old days to travel about Europe with a companion who liked all I liked and knew much more about it. He was very able. I think you would have liked him; certainly he you.

Now *Class*. Your remarks and speculations set me thinking about it again. I'm sure you are right that the marriage of the clergy helped to create a new kind of middle, clerkly class, to which lawyers, university Fellows, the more educated school-masters, and such, also belonged; what the French call " *les clercs*." It seems that the clergy social status went up gradually. Chaucer's " poor parson of the town " was brother to the ploughman; though at the same time there were the prelates from noble families. In 17th cent., there were the George Her-berts and others from the good families, and many from the poorer classes (like Laud) who went to the same grammar schools and universities as their social betters—I suppose this tended to narrow gulfs, this mixing up of classes at school and college, and now it is happening again. George Trevelyan points out, in his admirable *English Social History* (a book you perhaps know and would, I think, like), that the clergy rose very much in the 18th cent., when the close alliance with the squires began, and family livings, and this went on thro' 18th and 19th cents., when the Hall and the Rectory or Vicarage were the social centres of country and village life, and close friends often. I think the clergy are now getting rather more democratic, on the whole, aren't they? As to gulfs, social life in the Middle Ages seems to have been composed of land-owners and yokels and tradesmen and yeomen and farmers and " citizens." In the *Canterbury Tales* they all seem to have mixed up without embarrassment—the aristocratic prioress who ate so daintily that she let no morsel fall from her mouth, the rather coarse Wife of Bath, who however had a high opinion of her social position, and was offended if any other wife preceded her to the altar. I expect there were Scenes in church, embarrassing to the priests who executed Mass (I looked up "executed" in the Ox[ford] Dict[ionary]; in that particular sense it is obsolete but was once quite common, it seems). Somehow one gets no impression of class feeling from the prologue. Class must have developed more later, in the 16th and 17th cents. The propertied classes address the unpropertied very rudely, as "knave, churl, sirrah, fellow," etc., and regarded them as lewd fellows of the baser sort, no doubt; we have certainly improved in manners. All thro' C. 16 and 17 there was a sensible habit of the younger sons of the aristocracy and landed gentry often being apprenticed to merchants and tradesmen or to learn a craft, which mixed them up in a wholesome way; no horror of "trade" till C. 18 at least. And, with such bad transport, gentlemen and yokels talked their local dialect together, before accent was standardised by the public schools. I suppose that school class-segregation didn't really develop very much till late C. 18 and early 19th, when the poor boys were squeezed out of their ancient schools, such as Winchester and Eton, and these became class preserves. I think the extreme snobbism of the 18th cent. and of Jane Austen's Sir Walter Elliot would have become quite impossible by mid-Victorian days, wouldn't it? It gets less all the time, I fancy.[1]

(I am shocked by the look of the last page, so closely written, and feel it will be bad for you to decipher. I won't re-type it, but will this page use double-space instead of single, to make it easier.) G. Trevelyan says "The ideal arrangement, well established by the time of Jane Austen, was a good Rectory, with a bow window, built in a pleasant spot a mile from the manor house, and inhabited by a son or son-in-law of the squire. The religious needs of the village were served by a gentleman of education and refinement, though perhaps of no great zeal—

[1] Marginal note here by R. M.: "All quite unimportant and about nothing, and too closely spaced to read easily. Next page is better."

for it was only after the beginning of the 19th century that the gentleman-parson was likely to be 'serious,' that is, evangelical." How far back all that seems, recalling the water colours of the country rectories of one's ancestors, and of the rectors, with their nice faces, curled hair, and high cravats. What a coming home it must have seemed, New College after those years among rather different accents and backgrounds.[1] Mixing classes can be done, but it's not so easy and free, there's no doubt about it. Do you think the young man with great possessions felt snob about the fishermen and the other disciples? I think the Romans were dreadful snobs probably, don't you? All the same, some of the more educated freedmen seemed to be quite accepted socially, on the whole. I think snobbism must always have been a natural human addiction; the Romans were snobs about the British, the Normans about the Saxons, etc., etc. Extended egotism, I suppose. I shall read and think about the Christian beginnings. I *don't* want to be materialist about it, and I do see the cogency of the claims. I think my main point is that, to me, at present, it seems almost better and more congruous that God should have sent his Incarnation on earth in form fully human, with human birth and death. I would almost *rather* think He was born like us and died like us, and that it was His spirit only that lived after death, taking the form His friends would recognise. But of course this is no argument at all, and I don't try to make up my mind about it. I don't feel either way that it could make any difference to what I value more and more—the relationship that one tries to keep. But I will keep my mind open about it, and try and think it out. I felt, at the Easter mass, that here was Christ risen and with us, and I didn't care how. Is this very muzzy and illogical? I am trying out the arrangement of lesson and psalm-reading you suggest, and like it. I have an idiotic tendency to forget to say prayers at all— hang-over from past negligences, I suppose; I am capable of tumbling out of bed (after breakfast in it) and into my bath, dressing, reading letters and newspapers, and sitting down to

[1] This refers to Father Johnson's five years in Malta before going up to Oxford in 1899.

work on Ruins without a thought. Really shocking. I hope to get over this, however. Through Holy Week I went out early, but don't do this every morning now. (Should you say Sundays and Thursdays, perhaps? All experimental, so far.) I am interested in what you say of the Carthusian rite, and wish I remembered better what they did in that *Cartuja*.[1] I suppose the 2nd priest must have been serving. That is an interesting thought, the Elizabethan clergy inserting to themselves the bits of the Old Mass. I wish we had more light on what individual clergy felt about it all. There is a good novel there, if one knew enough. I am rather glad our Liturgy is now so flexible and susceptible to variety and additions. I myself add in pieces of your American P.B. pages that I like. The highbrows talking showily about the Trinity remind me of something I can't quite place—is it Langland?[2] Something about smart medieval table-talk—" They would tell of the Trinity a tale or twain . . ." So I suppose it was the fashion. No, it doesn't seem so now; unless in clerical circles? I believe you are right, and that Thomas [à Kempis] was beneficial to the little girl in the tree[3]; he set a standard to aim at. At the beginning of the book her god-mother had written," Remembering always that Baptism doth represent unto us our profession, which is to follow the example . . ." etc.—and that too set an impressive standard.

Yes, that was a bad lunar error, the Holy Week crescent. My uncle at King's said all novelists made moon howlers; he used to correct mine. But harmless howlers compared with some made by R.C. novelists about sin—" all right except for R.C.s," as you say. Such ungodly arrogance. At this point has arrived *Sheed and Ward's Own Trumpet*,[4] competing with the air raid sirens that are practising at full blast! Both they and S. & W. can be heard indeed. Thank you so much for the latter, which I shall harken to with interest.

Tho' I said, don't write, I *should* be glad of one letter about

---

[1] A Carthusian monastery described in R. M.'s *Fabled Shore*.

[2] William Langland (1330-1400), reputed author of *Piers Plowman*.

[3] R. M. aged 13.

[4] A quarterly " newspaper " devoted to the current publications of Sheed and Ward.

this confession business—as I see it, it is a (possible) obligation of courtesy, against what *I believe* to be greater benefit to myself. Which wins? However, Whitsun is not due yet. My sea letters will be better spaced and thicker paper. I am sorry about this one. It brings my love, and do let me know, when you write, *how you are*.

Yours affectionately,
R. M.

April

20, *Hinde House, Hinde St., W.*1
8th April, 1951

Dear Father,

Thank you so much for your air letters posted 28th March and 3rd April, both full of interest and what I wanted to hear. This, as you see, is to be a sea letter, in accordance with my new plan for writing, of which I told you in my last. I am glad that you think it all right to go to confession at Grosvenor (anonymous and appointmentless queues), and still to go and talk sometimes to Fr. Wilkins, if he will let me. I will write to him and explain. I should like to keep in touch with him, if he wouldn't feel I was wasting his time; I can tell him that I feel I belong to the S.S.J.E.[1], which is true. And I think he would be understanding and kind, as indeed he already has been. And there are all sorts of things I could ask him, if he didn't mind. As to " Staying with Sanctimonials,"[2] I feel you should send me this work, considering the number of mine that *I* send *you*. It sounds fascinating. . . . [About] the Resurrection, . . . [what] slightly puzzles me is that St. Paul, in 1 Cor. xv, does seem rather to equate it with *our* resurrection, as if the mode was the same

---

[1] Society of St. John the Evangelist (the Cowley Fathers).
[2] Father Johnson's translation of the Abbot Daniel story about the nunnery, which he had already sent to R. M.

(e.g. v. 15, " whom he raised not up, if so be that the dead rise not ") and yet he knew that *our* bodies stay in the earth (" thou sowest not that body that shall be . . . but God giveth it a body as it hath pleased him . . . flesh and blood cannot inherit the kingdom of God," etc., etc.) and, knowing this, and that for *us* there is no empty tomb, but that our bones are still there centuries later, he still does seem to analogize our rising again with Christ's, making the one depend on the other. Which made me think that he perhaps didn't himself believe in the empty tomb, but only in a purely spiritual presence of our Lord, clothed in the appearance which was familiar to the disciples, and which would convince them that it really was Him. Is this impossible—I mean, that S. Paul thought that—and does it impoverish the story? It doesn't to me. I mean, if His [resurrection] was bodily (however transformed and spiritualized, as of course it was in the story) it doesn't, to me, carry the same implication as to *our* immortality that it would if it was wholly spiritual, as ours, we know, must be. I wonder if this is nonsense. I never heard it or read it anywhere, so very likely it is. I expect Thomas à Kempis would condemn me for vain disputing! But you know I don't mean to be presumptuous, or set my understanding up against church tradition; though I suppose to say " it seems to me " has a terribly protestant ring. I dare say I shall come to see and accept it in time; you must forgive my rawness in these matters. I shall very likely grow into it, and into the understanding of the cosmic intervention in which everything was possible and everything part of the whole. Not that I feel, at present, that it could mean *more* to me than it does as I see it. Except that I like to believe what the Church believes, the Church being what it is.

What a heritage we have. I mean, we Anglicans. It is so incredibly beautiful. And such good fortune not to be an Anglican of a century or more ago, (or, indeed, a good deal less than that) or a Roman Catholic, or any kind of sectarian, or any Church without our liturgy, our particular ceremonial and dignity without fuss. I like it more and more.

Thank you for your advice about prayer. I am compiling

a kind of office (on the lines you suggested) that varies on different days; also, as I told you, a lot of scraps, all in one note book, so that all are at hand to select from as I want them. The ideas they give me expand indefinitely, one leading to more, and it is all rather exciting and enriching. I shall do all you suggest about prayer; I mean, I shall try to, and make it an aim. What is discouraging is the awful gulf between prayer and behaviour —not being able to " live more nearly as we pray."

I liked your account of your Harvard servers. How good for them it must be. I have a young cousin there—son of a first cousin who married an American wife and lives in N. York. A charming boy; they want him to come and have a year at Cambridge (King's), but don't know if they can manage this. He enjoys Harvard. I don't suppose his religious habits would lead him to the Cowley mission—indeed, I don't know if he has any; on the other hand, he may be religious and High Church, for all I know. How nice if you came across him ever. I'm sorry Harvard is irreligious. They are said to be *behind* Oxford and Cambridge in learning, and that the undergraduates of each age don't know so much, on the whole. I don't know if this is really so.

I am looking forward to my visit to Cambridge in June. I am staying at Trinity, with the Trevelyans; he is retiring from the Mastership at the end of the summer term. Yes, he is a cousin. And married to a daughter of that eminent Victorian novelist, Mrs. Humphrey Ward, who wrote so earnestly on Doubt. She knew all about that, as her father, Tom Arnold (from whom I drew, rather sketchily, the idea of my Mr. Garden in *Told by an Idiot*) spent his life migrating from one church or no-church to another and back again. My mother was brought up on my grandmother's stories of him; she (my grandmother) would come in saying, with sympathetic interest, " Poor Tom Arnold has lost his faith *again*," and so he had. Mrs. H. Ward was, according to my mother, a rather dull and ponderous woman.

Monday. This is Census Day, and soon the collector will come round for the forms, which ask all kinds of odd things, about bathroom taps, number of rooms, servants, occupation, etc., etc. They tell us it is all absolutely private, so that burglars can put " Occupation: burgling," without the least apprehension. I wonder if they do. It would be interesting if they enquired about religious beliefs and church attendance, but they don't do this.

Don't feel you must write in answer to this; not till you have a little time. But when you do next write, would you tell me how long this letter took, I should rather like to get a kind of average on this; of course they vary immensely, according to what boats go when.

I have finished *The Vision of God*, which is *enormous*, and full of interesting things. Now reading the 1948 Bampton Lectures, by Dr. Austin Farrer—*The Glass of Vision*. Interesting, but I don't quite always follow his thought. I shall try again for Fr. Andrew.

Did you mean by the S.S.J.E. Office Book, *Hours of Prayer*, which I bought? Yes, it *is* a little complicated to follow. But I use it.

I do hope you are well, and your eyes better.

Yours affectionately,
R. M.

20, Hinde House, Hinde St., W.1
16th April, 1951

Dear Father,

Such a lovely surprise to see your air paper on the mat this morning, all the nicer because I had with a noble gesture committed us both to the deep, and it felt some time since I had had a letter. And such a good letter, too. Further, by a coincidence arrived also on the mat at the same moment your large sea envelope posted 30th March; opening it was like unpacking a particularly nice hamper of assorted things. The Note Book: what a good idea! I have read it all, and shall give it more detailed attention later. I had already been compiling an office out of Matins and Evensong (P[rayer] B[ook]) on the scheme you suggested, and find it a good one. I don't usually read the 1st lesson, only the 2nd. Do you think that a pity? Perhaps I should *sometimes* read the 1st, when it is v.g. But one doesn't always want the O[ld] T[estament] stories as part of one's *prayers*, though some of the prophets and Wisdom and Ecclesiastes and Ecclesiasticus and Job and some other Books one does want. Do I miss things that shouldn't be missed, do you think? I am reading the morning psalms this month—sometimes in English, sometimes in Latin. Always the collects, of course. I must go further into this business of the Breviary; I haven't so far got one, though I have the Missal. I think I must get a Breviary. But I can get a good deal out of the *Hours of Prayer*; I think I shall take this to Fr. Wilkins when I go and see him, which I certainly mean to do. Having glanced at the *Ordo*[1] pages you enclose, I sympathise with those who were so much worried by the Pie.[2] It was complained of in the Preface to the 1549 P[rayer] B[ook] too, from which the 1662 preface [was] copied. Imagine the poor ploughman priests faced with such tangles. No wonder it was abolished under Edward VI. And the *Ordo* wears a rather Pie-ish look. How nice those P.B. prefaces are. I read them again. I like the piece about how the Liturgy stands "firm and unshaken, notwithstanding all the vain attempts and impetuous assaults made against it by such men as are given to change and have always discovered a greater regard to their own private fancies and interests than to that duty they owe to the publick." I don't know what altar book they use at Grosvenor; but . . . [the] extra prayers, prefaces and what-nots . . . all seem good, and to improve the occasion; would the P.B. preface-makers have classed them, I wonder, among the "impetuous assaults"? Also . . . [the service] always ends . . . with the Christmas Gospel from S. John, which sounds seemly at that point. I suppose it is a common practice. But I don't

[1] Abbreviation of *Ordinale*, a manual showing the Offices to be recited in accordance with variations in the ecclesiastical year.

[2] In the 15th century "Pie," or "*Pica*," was the name given to the *Ordinale* in England.

know much about altar books. . . . The last few pp. of the Note Book—Ronald Knox's fulminations against the doubting scholars, and your Galliambics against unintelligent reviewers— made me laugh a lot. I should think no one would have dared to mis-review Cybele when she drove out with her lions. Any more than they would dare attack the Sitwells, who also unleash ferocious beasts at their attackers. I must get some. R. A. K[nox] is very brilliant, and loveable when in that vein. I haven't read his last book, *Enthusiasm*, but am told that, though amusing and good, it is too prejudiced in favour of his One and Only Church. No, I don't think it does improve writers—converts, that is; the others are all right as a rule. Religious zeal doesn't always have the effect it hopes. I hear to-day from an elderly, moderate-Anglican, religious relation whose parish church (evangelical) has been having a "Mission." She writes, " I'm glad to say the Mission at the Good Shepherd ends to-morrow. I don't believe they do any good. They have an impertinent loud-speaker van, which, as I was passing, shouted out, ' Take care you're not blown off your bicycle, madam. We hope to see you at the Mission Service this evening.' I dislike those methods very much. They have a cinema show at the services, which of course draw crowds of children. I asked a neighbour if she was going to the mission; she said, ' No, I don't believe in going to church. I think my bed is the best place to ask for anything I want.' I felt I ought to have set the missioners on to her." Well, one can't say that such missions do *no* good; but it doesn't seem likely to be lasting in effect, and it does put off the more sensitive people. Like the Buchmanites. S. Paul had something better than that to hand people over to when he said " *obedistis autem ex corde* . . ."[1]

Thank you *very* much for those photographs. I particularly like to have the $\frac{3}{4}$ one, which I am putting in a little frame, to stand among a few others in my bedroom. It will make me feel still more in touch with the S.S.J.E., which, as you remark, has

[1] " . . . ye have obeyed from the heart (that form of doctrine which was delivered you. Being then made free from sin, ye became the servants of righteousness)." Rom. 6.17, 18.

so long dogged my steps. Do you believe that God has any hand in arranging these things? I mean, in putting it into my head to go to that retreat long ago, and into yours to write to me about a book? Or was it all just fortunate coincidence? And has God foreknowledge of what is to happen, and what one will need, and when? I suppose we can't know. But one would like to think so. He must spend a lot of time in retrieving situations and salvaging people, or what is left of them.

How nice to have more books arriving for me! How *could* I be anything but pleased and grateful for them, for the books themselves and for your thought in sending them? You know I love to have them. I like the account of your Day Out—old African lady, coffee, and small ice; it all sounds very fast and dissipated, and not what Oblates would be encouraged to have.[1] You should have had Mrs. Arthur with you; just what she would enjoy, and you would like each other; only she would have had, and wanted you to have, a *large* ice, and several cakes with it. She would have enjoyed Trimalchio's Supper[2]; as I do when I read about it. I'm delighted to think of that on its way; and the Munro.[3]

Now I have sent *you* a book. It was put into my mind by two things you say in your letter; you ask which book the young Portuguese at Silves had read, and it was (mainly) this one— *They went to Portugal*, published 1946. You also say that you came into existence because of the Great Quake of 1755. So, as a great-great-grandson of that Quake, you may like to read the chapter of the book about it, which includes a very charming account of it by a young English nun in Lisbon, whose convent was destroyed; she writes home about it most graphically, in the most shocking spelling. There is also an account of it by an English merchant in Lisbon. This MS. was lent me by his

[1] R. M. added a footnote: " Forgive this jest: *of course* I shan't show those typed rules. In fact, I should never show anything of yours to anyone, and never have."

[2] The description of a banquet given by a vulgar *nouveau riche* called Trimalchio is part of a romance by Petronius (contemporary of Nero in the mid-1st century A.D.).

[3] H. A. J. Munro, *Criticisms and Elucidations of Catullus* (1878).

descendant, an aged solicitor of slightly failing mind, who half thought the Quake had been 1855. My book is about English people who, for one reason or another, went to Portugal, from the time of the Crusades (when they behaved rather badly) down to recent times. Some of the chapters may amuse you. Our protestant missionaries there were pathetically eager and foolish. Borrow was unamiable; but there was (see end of book) a rather engagingly simple young officer of the Peninsular Wars who distributed Bibles to the Natives. There is a bit about J. M. Neale and his companion Dr. Oldknow, another about Whitefield, and there are Southey, Beckford, the Port Wine colony in Oporto, Queen Philippa of Lancaster who married King John of Portugal, Prince Rupert who took some ships to Lisbon bay to fight for Charles I, a Jesuit, a Scottish humanist poet and heretic, some diplomatists, etc., etc. I don't know if you'll find anything in it you care for, but have ordered its despatch. It entailed a good deal of hard work and research. I was very unhappy just then, and had to deaden it by work; I couldn't have done a novel possibly. I always talked over my novels with my companion, who stimulated my invention; when he died my mind seemed to go blank and dead. Oh why was there so much evil in what was in so many ways so good? Why did it have to be like that, all snarled up and tangled in wrong, when if we had been free it would have been the almost perfect thing. Idiotic question; I am sorry. Sometimes one is jerked back into the past by some thought or memory, and it all comes back, the happiness that isn't happiness any more to think of because of the wrong, and the whole awful mess it made of life, and yet it should have been so good. Forgive this maudlin whimpering. Remember to tell me sometime how the Great Quake affected your ancestors.

By the way, my aunt sent me the *Quarterly Review* for Oct. 1911, which has a rather interesting article by my father on English Bible translations. I already have a copy, so have cut out his article and am sending it to you, by this same post, in case you might be interested in it. It is about the influence the various versions, from Tyndale and Coverdale on, had on one another, and the relation of the A.V. to its predecessors. A fascinating subject.

17*th*. Next morning. Let me know sometime if you would have any use for a v.g. translation of Herodotus—much better and more accurate than Rawlinson's, who had the old-fashioned looseness and put things in on his own, and paraphrased. This one is by my father. Another copy was sent me, also by the aunt; of course I have one, and often read in it, it is such entertaining and good stuff. But I don't suppose you want any more books, or would have time for it. Books by the Macaulay family seem to bombard you. Now I have to go and broadcast on Travel. I rather like these sea letters, I can get such a lot into them!

Yours affectionately,
R. M.

20, Hinde House, Hinde St., W.1
24th April, 1951

Dear Father,

Returning from a week-end (fine, for a change) in Worcestershire, yesterday, I found on my mat exciting packages, which, being opened, produced the four little Latin books, Munro's *Catullus*, which looks very interesting, and (best) the Scraps, those from the walls, and those in the Scrap Book. A lovely rich collection; much of it supplements and adds to the book of R.M's Private Devotions (a book I will leave you in my will). Looking thro' your Scraps I am reminded of that passage from St. Augustine which you quote at the end of the *Liber de Miraculis* that came this morning—about memory and the *thesauri innumerabilium imaginum*[1] that it hoarded up for use. (By the way, in my St. A. it isn't *hujusmodi*, but *cuiuscemodi*, which of course does mean " of whatever sort ": I think yours must be

---

[1] " Treasures of innumerable images," see St. Augustine, *Confessions*, Bk. 10, Chap. 8.

a misprint.) Yes, it *is* just what one does when writing a novel. It is rather a lovely passage, all that chapter. I like the picture of reaching into the treasury for what one needs, and rejecting what one doesn't. And now your Scraps have much enriched my treasury of what is written down ready for use—more reliable than the *campos et lata praetoria memoriae*.[1] You will gather from this that I have received your Johannes Monachus—very nice stories, tho' I think I like Abbot Daniel even more. Unhappy Mary: but she was better drowned, she would have come to no good. What a long time it took Christians to grow up to the ideas of Christ, in some respects. How differently he would have treated the affair. And how differently Ananias and Sapphira would have been dealt with, I was thinking the other day when I read the story. Did S. Peter strike them dead, or did they fall dead of shock at being discovered, or were they really perhaps only in a faint, and buried prematurely? S. Peter had a lot to learn about Christian methods. All your pages at the end of Johannes are full of interesting things—S. Augustine, S. Monica, Carthusian rites, the pre-Tractarian clergy, about whom I fully agree with you and Fr. Palmer. There is a great deal of evidence of devotion and care; letters and memoirs (some in my family, as in yours)—and did you ever read the letters of Parson Cole?[2] But these are 18th cent. I am sure the neglect has been much exaggerated. It might be interesting to collect a good deal of evidence about this, and produce a book about it sometime. It is this tendency to see and present pictures in black or white that falsifies so much of history. I think I shall, when my present concern with Ruins is over, look round and collect pieces of evidence about this.

But the best thing I have had lately was your Air Letter of 18th and 19th, a delightful sight on my mat this morning, and better still when opened. How good of you. I'm glad my sea letter took so brief a time. I wonder what the next is doing, at present in transit on the seas, and what this one will do. How

[1] " The plains and wide palaces of memory."

[2] It seems probable that R. M. was referring to *The Blecheley Diary of the Rev. William Cole, edited by F. G. Stokes with an introduction by Helen Waddell* (1931).

stupid I was not to recognise at once your Staying with Sanctimonials; *of course* I remember the Female Inebriate at the convent
and the nuns' perplexity about her; my mind must have had a
black-out. Your comments on my use of "gotten" were made
to me years ago by an American friend—she said, as you do,
that it was only used in the perfect tense, and that you can't
say "I have gotten" meaning "I have got." I can't now think
how I dared attempt American speech at all; one can never
hope to get any speech right without long familiarity with it.
Does Fr. Pedersen talk American? But of course he does.
I shall like much to see him. The more he speaks of you the
better pleased I shall be. I think I should have guessed that you
were sensitive to apprehensions and anxieties and fears, especially
for other people. Not "*totus teres atque rotundus.*"[1] I feel this
is partly, perhaps, why you can do so much for people. There
are no miseries, apprehensions, anxieties, weaknesses, that you
couldn't understand and enter into and care about, not as a
professional job, but because you really do care. So perhaps it
is all worth while, though it would be *happier* of course to be
naturally phlegmatic and confident. I am not, at all; though
I fear my apprehensions are apt to be selfish ones mostly.
Fr. Waggett sometimes wrote (and talked, didn't he?) as if
he had been through, or was liable to go through, pretty
difficult patches. I suppose every sensitive and imaginative
person is.

Yes: the disciples did need the empty tomb to convince
them; I quite see that. So I won't let it worry me. They *had*
to be convinced, beyond all shadow of doubt. So I will think it
was probably so. I have lately come to think that anything may
be true; my universe has expanded so much. The Expanding
Universe, which is the name of a recent scientific book. Just as
they had to be convinced that he had left them and had "ascended
into heaven," which they believed to be somewhere above the
skies. Even as a child, the Ascension never bothered me, owing
to sensible teaching from my mother, who told us that it merely
meant that, when those 40 days were over, he stopped mani-

[1] "Whole, smooth, and rounded." From Horace, *Sat.* 2.7.86.

119

festing himself to them in that particular way. I believe it saves a good deal of painful disillusion and loss of faith to have been brought up in a liberal kind of theology—profoundly Christian, but liberal more or less. Not that one *didn't* suffer painful loss of faith in one's teens; I expect most adolescents do. I remember when I was being prepared for confirmation, the vicar of SS. Philip and James at Oxford[1] had us each for private interviews, so that we could ask what we liked; what I *wanted* to ask was, " as I really can't believe all this as I should, ought I to be confirmed? " but, being a shy child of 14, (nearly 15, I suppose) I could say nothing at all. I remember I had been reading John Stuart Mill, and rather absorbed his views. (The Thomas à Kempis period was then over.) I suppose most young creatures pass, each in his or her own way, through some such stages, *cuiuscemodi*.

That was a stupid review of Miss Goudge's book.[2] Not that it seems (I've not read it, nor shall) a good book, to judge from more intelligent and Christian reviews than that; it must, I think, be rather toshy and slushy and *fictional*; she speaks of " the tall Son of God "; as Wilson Harris points out in the *Spectator* (if I've still got that number I'll send it you), his height is nowhere mentioned. I wouldn't expect anything but a rather sentimental romance from this author of best-selling and rather sloppy fiction; but I may wrong her, as most certainly that Unitarian did. Imagine *sending* such a book to a Unitarian for review; his point of view disqualifies him at once. One *must* be open to belief in cosmic intervention.

Feast of St. Mark, in the evening
I have now acquired a very nicely bound little 4-volume 2nd hand Breviary, in which I shall root about among the days and seasons for treasures suitable for my collection and my needs. I am much pleased with it. I might take it to Fr. Wilkins for exposition, as I haven't yet sorted out quite how it goes. I really have a lot of varied topics to approach him about. I shall much

[1] Rev. Edward Conduitt Dermer.
[2] Elizabeth Goudge, *God So Loved the World: A Life of Christ* (1951).

like to have *Manuale Sacerdotale*,[1] which you have sent. I shall learn some of the prayers by heart; *narro memoriter*,[2] independent of having the book at hand. What good things you send me. I find your small Scrap Book immensely stimulating; *inventaque flumina monstrat*.[3] I like the way you correlate the Latin poets with the Christian and Hebrew devotions. You do enrich everything, and light things up, and integrate them.

"*Amor vincit omnia*"[4]—doesn't it here mean *conquers*? And in the Eclogues. I think it must. I expect the Prioress had read romances; but the motto has, surely, a religious meaning; would she have otherwise had it on her brooch? Or perhaps merely a moral meaning—love of one's neighbours. A very good motto, whichever way you take it. I always like the Prioress, with her pretty manners, good breeding and table manners, and tender heart. She must have been charming.

Poor Dr. Macaulay and her two colleagues in the business— a poet and a critic—are being exposed to a lot of attack just now on account of the selection they made for the National Book League Exhibition of 100 books representative of English literature for the last 30 years. We didn't really mean to say they were the *best* books, but of course a lot of people will have it that we did. I don't myself think it a v.g. list . . .. and it has obvious omissions and inclusions that are debateable, so we stand to be shot at, but on the whole people shoot with good humour. So you see Dr. M. has had enough of English literature just now, and, thanking Fr. J. for his kind offer, won't take his Manual of it. She scarcely even wants to receive an Hon. Doctorate of it. This should better go to Fr. J., whose letters are so admirable, whose Scraps so excellent, whose Latin so fluent. What a pity he can't hear the Public Orator of Cambridge describing my career—fortunately in the decent obscurity of a dead and

[1] A book containing the forms prescribed to parish priests for the administration of the Sacraments.

[2] "I recite from memory."

[3] "And (others) reveal streams that they have discovered." Virg. *Aen.* 6. 8.

[4] "Love conquers all things."

learned tongue. Good night. It is past one a.m. Thank you again so much for everything.

Yours affectionately,

R. M.

May

Dear Father,

How good it was to get your air letter of 28th April this morning! Of course selfishly I like to get air letters in answer to my sea ones, at least sometimes. A week or more ago (after I had posted a sea letter on 26th) there arrived a most delightful packet—the Vernal Breviary, which I love to have, the little Vulgate N[ew] T[estament], the Lucretius and the little Horace. And the 2 excellent little Latin books—Aulus Gellius and the stories from Phaed[rus]. Oh yes, and a lovely *blank* note book, beautifully made, which I am filling up. All are most valuable to me—and such a handy size—and my only doubt is if you could really spare them and still can, having yielded to a generous impulse and parted with them. Whether or not, to me they are delightful possessions, and I am most grateful for them. As, increasingly, for all the past books. I find more all the time in the little Scrap Book (accumulated for 3 or 4 years back). I continually read in it and pick out always something I want. It is an admirable collection, and I like that correlation of Christian and O[ld] T[estament] thoughts and prayers with the Roman poets. Yes: that American Lectionary calendar did reach me; didn't I mention it? It interested me.

What interesting things emerge in our correspondence! I am much intrigued by your story of Mr. Livius and the Earthquake. I wonder if his father *was* that Dutch minister whom Mr. Castres sheltered. I can discover this, I am sure, and will do so. I have never seen Q's book, and certainly shall get it from a library.[1] His "documents" are quite correct. I read those very letters in the Record Office (State Papers, Portugal, 89/50) when I was writing *They went to Portugal* and was working a lot in the R.O. You will find them summarised on p. 277 of my book. You will also find an amusing answer to Castres from his friend Sir Benjamin Keene, ambassador to Madrid, to whom he must have written with more freedom than in his Despatch to the Foreign Office. Keene answered, " I am enraged at your Dutch guests," and, " I assure you it never came into my imagination that the Dutch family should have the Dutch conscience to stay with you above a day or two till they could turn themselves elsewhere . . . I lose all patience with them . . . Indeed my friend, I would, after all this humanity on your part, send them and the horses of the Factory that are eating you up all together agrazing. . . ." The " horses of the Factory " were, of course, the British merchants and their families. Of these Castres writes, " the miserable objects among the lower sort of His Majesty's subjects,[2] who all fly to me for bread and lie scattered up and down in my garden with their wives and children. I have helped them all hitherto . . ." A complaint familiar to all ambassadors abroad at times of disaster. Castres emerges very well from his correspondence of which there is of course a great file in the Record Office. I liked him very much; he was humane, kindly, and humorous. I think you may find interest and entertainment in my chapter about him and Mr. Hay the Consul during the Quake, as also in the other two chapters in the Earthquake section, giving the accounts by a merchant and a young nun (this last I like particularly, if one can surmount the shocking spelling). I will let you know anything I discover about Mr. Livius. I hope he was the Minister; it would be amusing. I don't know when you'll get that book; I had it posted at the time I wrote to you (16th April). Sea letters seem to make v.g. time now; books much slower, naturally. But they get there in the end.

[1] " Q " (Sir Arthur Quiller-Couch), *Lady Good-for-Nothing* (1910).
[2] Footnote by R. M.: " those were not ' the better sort,' of whom he wrote."

Now it only remains to discover that some of your ancestors were also some of mine; I should like that. But I didn't have many in the eastern counties (except in Cambridge University); mine were mostly in Leicestershire, Cumberland, and Devonshire—my parsonic ancestors, I mean. Those were Macaulays, Herricks, Conybeares, Fergusons and Babingtons. And in the 18th century, before the first of the line (my great-great-grandfather) of Macaulays turned Anglican and became an English parson, the M's were of course Presbyterians in Scotland and " damned Whigs."

I am interested in the novels you are reading. I don't much care for Hugh Walpole really, tho' he wrote a capable story. I think *The Cathedral* is a better novel than *The Prelude to Adventure*; more mature. I wonder if you have read it, and what you thought of it as a picture of Life in a Cathedral Close. His father became a Bishop, of course. But I feel the picture is exaggerated. Graham Greene is somewhat different! I was dining with him last Friday. An amusing little company . . . It was in a restaurant, and . . . I was upholding the Anglican point of view against Graham's assertions that only R.C.s were capable of real sin because the rest of us were invincibly ignorant. . . . I never quite know what is his view of sin; I sometimes get the feeling that with him it is largely a matter of absolution or the reverse, and that he doesn't really think so much about the actual *sin*. But I may wrong him. So many questions that one would like to ask one's not-very-intimate friends, and of course can't. I told him what I felt about his position in my review in *The Times Lit. Supplement* (unsigned) of his last book. Someone had told him it was by me, and we discussed it.

You say you would like to understand what was in my mind in my poetry. Well, those poems were written at very different times, some when I was quite a young girl. I suppose I lived rather in a world of imagination and dreams; a good many of the poems deal with the feeling one has that another life, of shadows and spirits, presses about this one, breaking through now and then. Some, I think, are semi-religious—

"Lady Day," two missionary poems, and others. Others not that, but about foregrounds and backgrounds; see one called "Foregrounds," if you still have the book. It meant that one hides among colours and shapes and beauty from the assaults and intrusions of the spiritual world that might menace one's happy peace and enjoyment of this. Then one, (at least), called, I think, "Summons," is an appeal to a dead beloved (killed in the first war) to return and communicate with me. And so on, and so on. All rather fanciful, I suppose. But don't worry about them.

Of course I should, and do, write differently now. My outlook is different, as you can imagine. But also I don't write so much poetry as when younger; one doesn't, I think.

You must forgive my vain and profitless repinings for might-have-beens that I am afraid I gave way to for a moment in my letter. I have a bad habit of passing on to you my moods and thoughts, which isn't fair. But I suppose I have a feeling that you will somehow throw light on them, and of course you do, by reminding me of the *Remedium sempiternum* (see "Scraps"), and of the faith into which I have been traditioned (a good word, I think; valid, but obsolete now in that sense of handed into). Don't think too hardly of me. (An unnecessary request, to you of all people, who have always thought, said and done nothing that wasn't far too generous.) The thought that you will sometimes say "*in manus tuas illam, Domine, commendo*"[1] lights a candle in waste places of the spirit.

Talking of candles, I attended All Saints yesterday for High Mass; the first service, it seemed, at which the New Vicar preached. Such a forest of candles, such streams of incense, such beautiful choral and solo singing. A really magnificent service. Fr. Ross preached about why he had read the 39 Articles quietly to the churchwardens after the 8 o'clock Mass instead of to the full congregation now. He likes them very much, he said, but some of them need more explaining than he would have time for; such as the one about Christ not having ordained that the Sacrament should be reserved, lifted up, or carried about. That was because He was not going into details about it

---

[1] "Into thy hands, O Lord, I commend her."

at the Last Supper, but left all that to the Church. And so on. Personally, I *don't* like most of them very much. But I liked Fr. Ross—he seemed unaffected, able, sincere, and kind. What fine showy services they have there. But I really prefer the more quiet style of Grosvenor Chapel; no crowds, no choir (except a few singers up in the gallery), only one priest at a time (and sometimes a server); incense yes, and all very beautifully done. By the way, I wrote to Fr. Wilkins, and had *such* a nice, kind, understanding letter back. He says, come and see him any time, and talk about anything. I shall go soon after Whitsun, taking with me the Hour Book. I'm glad I belong to the S.S.J.E.

This evening I am going to see a performance of *Samson Agonistes* in S. Martin's church; or part of it anyhow, as I have to go on to dinner somewhere before the end. For the same reason I can't hear the Bp. of Oxford speaking at the Central Hall, which I should have liked. Always too many things to fit in, and I get little done. I am finding my way about the Breviary. And reading all sorts of things. And preparing a BBC talk about early bathing, sea and other. There is a nice letter from Cicero to his friend Trebatius, telling him that, enthusiastic swimmer tho' he is, he presumes that he won't bathe off the shores of Britain, where he is with Caesar. The Festival[1] seems a great success. Fr. Pedersen must go to it. I go to-morrow. But the weather is vile; cold and wet. This notepaper (off a block) is too small; I have to use too many pages of it! I must get a larger one. Yes, I must read the O.T. more, and shall. I am glad of Whitsun.

With love,
R. M.

[1] The Festival of Britain, trade fair held in London in 1951.

Dear Father,

An air letter (dated 7th) *and* that very interesting *Manuale*,
and the very nice little Epistles, done up in a brown paper cover
in your special manner, all have arrived in the last two days—
how nice! I have read a lot in the *Manuale*, and shall read more
in time. I copied a prayer or two from it last night into my
Scrap Book, to memorize. Dear Father, how good you are to
me. And your letters are the best of all. I am glad *They went to
Portugal* has already reached you—creditably quickly—and that
you like to have it. It *is* an odd coincidence that I had written
about Mr. Castres, and possibly Mr. Livius. I am now almost as
interested in Mr. Livius as you are. I wrote to the Dutch Embassy
to ask if they could tell me who was their Minister in Lisbon
in 1755; they reply that they have no such records in London,
but have kindly written to enquire of their Foreign Office in The
Hague, and will let me know. So then we shall know if your
Mr. Livius was the Dutch Minister who, with his family and
servants, encroached on the hospitality of our Envoy, or if he
was merely a merchant in Lisbon. I hope he was the Minister;
I naturally don't feel your slight vicarious embarrassment at his
having outstayed his welcome. But I don't understand why, if
he *was* the Minister, he was sent by Frederick the Great. Aunt
Katie suggests he might have been the *Prussian* ambassador; in
that case he isn't mentioned by Mr. Castres, though as time
went on a lot of people were sheltered by him whom he doesn't
refer to by name. A Moravian, I suppose, might be either a
Moravian by race (part of Bohemia, and under Austria at that
time), or more likely, by religion. A rather good religion, it
seems, and got about everywhere. If Mr. L. was simply a merchant, how did the legend start that he was the Dutch Minister?
I think he *must* have been this. But it is no use speculating, as I
hope we shall know before long. In any case, Mr. Castres was
Johnny's half-great-great-uncle, so I suppose some kind of great-

uncle also of yours. And a very nice, humane, able envoy he was.

That Quake produced some wonderful and tragic stories. I read a great many of these, by various people, when I was writing that book. Little Kitty Witham's letters, so ill spelt and ingenuous and vivid, have great charm; and Mr. Jacomb's too is an excellent account. Thirty years later foreign visitors complained that the Lisbon streets were still (in places) piled with rubble, in spite of Pombal's vigorous rebuilding. All the centre of the town is post-quake,[1] and very regular and straight and unlike the medieval jumbles of old houses and squares on the higher parts of the city on either side, which weren't destroyed. On one of these high parts, led up to by steep narrow streets of extraordinary picturesqueness, is the English College, the 17th century building where English seminarists have been trained for the priesthood since the days of James I, when they managed to escape out of England, and take up residence there. The *Inglesinhos*, as they call the college locally, has played a prominent part in Lisbon history. I wrote a history of them, but it was among the many sections which had to remain unpublished for lack of space. A chapter which interested me very much to write was the one about Floyd, the English Jesuit priest. Those English Jesuits were interesting studies; very conspiratorial and anti-English as a rule, and for ever busy with plots for invasion and conversion of their country, and with supreme courage, and spied cruelly on their countrymen abroad, ready to report them to the Inquisition authorities if they transgressed the Portuguese anti-heretic laws. They had a bad name among the English Factory in Lisbon—on the whole a very Protestant colony of merchants, though there were converts among them, often owing to the missionary activities of such as Floyd. One has to admire Floyd for his courage, but one can't like him. There is a great deal of dislike of him expressed in the letters of the English consul of that time, Hugh Lee. How lucky we are not to live any more in times of religious hatred; it would be odious, and especially if one was abroad. Some tiresome

[1] Footnote by R. M.: " The old print on my dust-jacket is *pre*-quake."

newspaper here has been getting up a campaign against Princess Elizabeth visiting the Pope; but it is very rare for any one to object to it. And when we were children in Italy the old *parroco* used to be most kind to us, and come round at Easter to bless our house and give us a great coloured candle of twisted wax; nothing could have been friendlier.

Thank you for calling my attention to I Peter. As a result I read it through, and then the first two chapters in Greek, in your little Testament. I like doing this. This enlargement of the tongues in which I read the Bible is worth while; and this, like so much else, I owe to you. What a good Epistle that is. That S. Peter could write in that way, from having been so *amathes*[1] a fisherman, so simple and rather crude—well, I suppose it was Pentecost that did it. (That is the day after to-morrow. I have already been shriven. I always find this a difficult business, but it seems to work.) Or did the Greek translators improve and complicate S. Peter's letters? How good Chap. 1 of the 2nd Epistle is . . . [*sic*] " and beside this, giving all diligence, add to your faith virtue; and to virtue knowledge,"[2] etc., etc.; what a fine progression to try for! Can Pentecost even do that for us? I suppose so—*en hagiasmo pneumatos*.[3] (My Greek characters aren't nearly as neat as yours; my typewriter ought to have them.)

The weather goes on coldly; but to-day at least there is sun. We are all agog with festival, Fun Fair, and Pleasure Gardens (this last not yet open). I took two small girls yesterday to the Fun Fair; it was much like others of its kind, but they hugely enjoyed themselves, and we came home laden with frightful prizes from coconut shies, dart shies, gambling games, and luckily none the worse (which I always used to be) after roundabouts and switchbacks, and sucking immense sticks of Festival Rock. I went another day to the South Bank; a very miscellaneous and experimental affair, some things worth seeing, others not. It might please more in warmer weather. It has had a very flattering press, I suppose to induce foreigners and ourselves all to visit it.

[1] " Unlearned."   [2] II Peter, 1.5.
[3] " Through sanctification of the Spirit " (I Peter 1.2).

Queer things one gets involved in. I now have an invitation to a wine-tasting party in the cellars of the London branch of a Port Wine shipping firm of Oporto. This, and my having been asked to write a foreword to their brochure, is what comes of writing so eruditely about port wine in that book: a fascinating subject of which actually I know less than nothing. But I did like those Oporto wine shippers; I stayed with one of them, and every hour [or] so when I was indoors port was brought in on a tray; it wouldn't do for long. Their Factory House (18th century) is a magnificent affair. (See my picture of the English wine shippers chatting in the street in 1834.) It seems to me the most romantic of the English colonies abroad.

I am going to ring up Fr. Wilkins after Whitsunday and go and call, as he said I could. How much difference is there between communicating and not communicating, when one goes to the service? Of course I know one sometimes does and sometimes not: but how nearly is it the same thing? This seems an ignorant and confused question; but then I *am* ignorant and confused still. I *feel* a difference between them; but could one communicate mystically? Then I suppose it wouldn't be a sacrament. I am probably talking nonsense. Anyhow I must stop. Did I tell you I copy out some of those short Latin prayers and put them in my prayer book and say them in church, which I like to do. It seems to link one with tradition and the whole Catholic church. Tho' for sheer *beauty*, I think our own liturgy and prayers beat any, owing to the fortunate language-period of our P[rayer] B[ook].

Goodbye, dear Father,

R. M.

(Sorry about my writing—
don't try and read it!)

Dear Father,

I took away with me for the week-end your letter of 11th
May, but not my typewriter, so will write to you in my very
best hand instead. I am sitting in a beautiful library, looking out
on a beautiful garden, and beyond it to a beautiful buttercup
field, and beyond that to a small grey perpendicular church, to
which no one in this beautiful old house ever goes, and which
I gather is almost pre-Tractarian in the rarity of its services. One
of my 3 hosts is R.C., the other two are nothing—they are 3
friends (male) living together, very delightful people, their
interests literature, architecture, art, and music. I am here to
help them to entertain the editor of the *Sunday Times* and his
wife, whom none of us know very well. We talk and read and
write and play a little croquet, at which I am becoming rather
a dab. But mainly we talk, and talk, and talk. Last night we
talked about how nearly all specifically *religious* writers to-day
(novelists, poets, etc.) were R.C. (" Catholic," they all call it
but me) and how few were definitely Anglican in tone and view-
point. Why is this, I wonder? I think because people 'vert to
the R.C. Church—the Anglican is what we were (mostly)
brought up in, and many take no notice of it, or just lapse from
it and don't come back. So it doesn't seep into their writing.
If they begin to believe Christianity again, then they do something dramatic, like going R.C. I can't help feeling that going
Anglican is better; anyhow I could never have done the other
myself.

Your phrase " nowhere to come back to ": it called up a
vision of desolation, of perpetual wandering homeless o'er moor
and fen and crag, with no kindly light to lead: a kind of waste
land. Yes: I am glad I didn't reject confirmation. I was " a
child that was an intemperate sucker " (a 17th century quotation)

of all that came my way, and not only honey from the rocks: but I'm glad I wasn't such a silly little sucker as to do that.

Your letter was a rather especially good one. I haven't yet heard again from the Dutch Embassy about the name of their Lisbon Minister in 1755, but hope to soon. If it wasn't Peter Livius, there might still be ways of finding out, from Lisbon records, who P.L. was. But I *hope* he was the Minister with " the Dutch conscience " who so enraged Sir Benjamin Keene.

I should be rather interested to read that history of the U.S. Episcopal Church, and shall get it from the Library. I know very little of it. I suppose Maryland and Virginia were the Church's main homes originally? New England was where the Puritans fled from Laud, and I suppose remained predominantly Puritan. I should like to improve my knowledge of it; when and why they altered the English P[rayer] B[ook] a little, etc. Another thing to discuss with Fr. Wilkins when I go and see him, which I shall try and do, if he is available, later this week. I suppose such as Fr. Pedersen would be *born* into the Church. How many New Englanders are this? Do the same dissensions rend them as us? Just now there is one about a United Church's Rally in Hyde Park (yesterday afternoon), led by the Arches of Canterbury and York, Bp. of London and other bps., and a great many prominent clergy, and strongly objected to by the *Church Times* and many Anglo-Catholics, who held, I believe, a protest meeting yesterday in the vestry of the Church of the Annunciation, Bryanston Street. They wrote a letter about it, signed by many protesters, clerical and lay, and 65 unnamed London incumbents, among whom I dare say were the incumbents of All Saints and Grosvenor Chapel, though I don't know. I don't myself see anything compromising in " rallying " with the free churches—it doesn't imply any abandonment of church principles, only Christian fellowship. People wrangle too much. It seems a mistake. Walking in bluebell woods, with cuckoos and wood-pigeons uttering their May songs, makes me feel very peaceful.

Yes, I shall write more novels. I want to begin one directly my present book is done. I like writing them, and one is independent of books and libraries, which is convenient. And one can say one's own things, and isn't tied to history, or geography, or anything else. One can let the fancy roam. How lucky I am, to have work I *like*, instead of having to drudge away at some job that bores me! It is unfair, really.

Later. A discussion occurred at supper to-night about whether Corpus Christi was (a) a feast in the P[rayer] B[ook] calendar (b) a feast commonly observed in the Anglican Church. I thought it *was* in the P.B., and *knew* it was kept in the Church. One of my hosts swore it was neither.[1] So we rang up the Dean of Winchester, E. G. Selwyn (a cousin of mine)[2] and asked him, and he said it was not in the 1662 book, but was (of course) in the 1928 Revised one, which is always used in many churches, and in his Cathedral. And he said it had been celebrated at Corpus (his college) for innumerable years. So I think *I* won the bet, and Raymond Mortimer thought *he* had. The argument began because I went to evensong in the little church and heard the Feast of C.C. announced—quite an ordinary, moderate village church, with a congregation of about 10 people.

I am driving back to London in the morning, and must now go to bed.

21st. Just home, and find a note from the Dutch Embassy, which says their Minister in Lisbon from 1753-8 was called Calmette. So Mr. Livius wasn't that, tho' no doubt was sheltered by Mr. Castres in his garden. I am rather sorry. Perhaps he was *not* Dutch, but really was a German sent on some mission by the emperor Frederick.[3]

I think I may have read that Oxford Movement book at some time. The Rev. T. Mozley, and Newman too, were great uncles of a cousin of mine, Canon J. K. Mozley of St. Paul's (now dead), and he always talked of them. But I think I will read it again. An interesting thing about them is how little

[1] The only point at issue, Raymond Mortimer recalls, was whether the feast was included in the 1662 Prayer Book.

[2] A cousin by "adoption."

[3] Frederick the Great, King of Prussia, was never emperor.

they were *ritualistic*, in the modern Anglo-Catholic sense. Did they ever use incense, e.g.? High doctrine, but what I suppose we should think rather austere ceremonial.

It is a lovely day, with that incredible bright green of May everywhere, and the gorse and chestnut tree candles all flaring —so beautiful, as I drove up from Dorset.

With my love,
Yours *R. M.*

20, *Hinde House, Hinde St., W.*1
25th May, 1951

Dear Father,

It *was* nice to get your air paper of 18th; and with it that extremely pleasing postcard photograph, which I can't say how much I like to have. I wrote to you last Sunday from Dorset, an MS letter I regret to say, but I hope it was legible without strain, or, if not, that you didn't struggle with it. Now I am home with my typewriter again, and, having just finished, with immense labour, a review of a book, turn with so much relief (at 10 p.m.) to writing to you; with the reflection that I so often have, how enormously fortunate I am to be able to, and to get your letters—I can't think what I have done to earn such good fortune as I have had during the last year. Nothing, is the answer. And now this splendour coming down every morning (every morning that I don't oversleep, that is). I do go to church most mornings now, actually; it is such a very good place to say one's prayers in after the service; I can there, when I can't at home. Thank you for pointing out "*Suscipe, Domine*"[1]; I have copied it out on a paper I keep in my prayer book, with some other Latin prayers from the Missal and Breviary. It is a very good one; and good, I think, especially for me. After church I now go and bathe in the Serpentine often, the weather now being less frigid. It is lovely there in the mornings at nine; very empty, and smooth and green—and rather cool, of course. The

[1] "Receive, O Lord, (the whole of my freedom,)" see below p. 135.

134

shadows of the may-green trees shine in the water, and the cuckoos cry, and the smaller birds warble, and all is peace and joy. Occasionally I meet some friends there who like bathing too; they haven't been to church, though, the heathen creatures. Grosvenor Chapel is just about half-way between Hinde Street and the Serpentine, so it is very convenient. A kind of shining peace prevails in both places. I felt this particularly yesterday morning, which was Corpus Christi; it seemed possible the *sacra mysteria venerari*[1] in the Serpentine as well as in church. How wretched it would be to have to pray and worship in an ugly church, or in one of those green painted chapels. One would need to be very spiritual and to have a very vivid sense of God's presence, and then, I suppose, one could forget the surroundings. Many people have to. St. Paul and his colleagues must have had a very wonderful time voyaging about those islands and places. I have a large edition of my grandfather's book about it, with lovely engravings. Imagine landing on Cyprus—perhaps Famagusta or Vounous—and preaching the Gospel there. And Antioch. And then Rome. And all about Greece. It must have looked so lovely that they must have sometimes forgotten their job of making Christians and just wandered about and gazed. Then they would have to pray " *suscipe, Domine, universam meam libertatem.*"[2]

I wonder if you have yet finished *Brighton Rock*.[3] The end is horrifying; the suicide pact, the horrible death, and then poor little Rose left alone with that awful gramophone record. In the film of it, which I once saw, the horror of that record is softened; the needle sticks, and goes on repeating " I love you, I love you, I love you," and never gets further. Film goers, it seems, demand a happy ending, or anyhow an ending not too unhappy and dreadful. But Pinkie is allowed to die in mortal sin, without time to save himself by absolution as he had counted on. This is certainly poetic justice.

I am sending you the *Spectator*, with a review by someone

[1] " Sacred mysteries to reverence."
[2] " Receive, O Lord, the whole of my freedom."
[3] Novel by Graham Greene (1938).

135

of a rather interesting new book about Cowper.[1] In the same number is a very kind note by the editor (see "A Spectator's Notebook") about my Cambridge Litt.D. It is nice of him to be pleased, though I don't deserve the kind things he says. As the Cowper book perhaps won't be published in America (I don't know if it will or not) I thought I would send it to you, because I think you might like to have it. I rather like it when a book comes my way that I feel you might like, and that I can send you; a very small return for all you have sent me.

On Monday I am going to see Fr. Wilkins which I shall enjoy. I think he will be very easy to talk to about anything I like. It is good to have such good prophets at hand. . . .

Thank you so much for offering me an Apocrypha. I have one, actually; my mother had a nice large-print one (she was very fond of it) and I have it now. It is a most valuable collection of books, and there are so many beautiful things in it. For sheer beauty of language and imagery, there are few writings to touch parts of Wisdom and Ecclesiasticus. I was discussing Bible translations the other day with a R.C. friend. He prefers the A[uthorized] V[ersion] to the Douai; I should think any one would. He also supposed the A.V. to have been translated all new in 1611, which seems an oddly implausible idea, considering the very Tudor—and earlyish Tudor at that—language of most of it. They wrote quite differently in 1611. By the way, you allude to Kitty Witham's spelling. I think girls and women, even of the upper classes, often did spell atrociously, even so late as that. Of course in the 17th century it was worse. I think the letter I composed for my young Meg Yarde to write to her brother at Cambridge, in *They Were Defeated*, is fairly typical of the ordinary upper class young female. Of course there were better educated girls and women, who didn't spell much worse than men; Lucy Hutchinson in C. 17, and many others; and more still in C. 18. Lady Mary Wortley Montagu spelt as well as her husband; I dare say better than her co-interee in Grosvenor Chapel, Mr. Wilkes. I remember some phrase of Steele's in the *Tatler*, early in the century, about a poem by a woman—" By

[1] Norman Nicholson, *William Cowper* (1951).

some negligence in the spelling, I perceived it to be a *female sonnet.*" And young Kitty Witham, obviously coming of an old Recusant family, probably hadn't even had a very adequate governess, and no [doubt] read little. But she wrote with great spirit and spontaneity. The more I muse on Mr. Livius, the more I think he was a German, sent to Lisbon in some official capacity.

I went to an Oporto wine-shippers' wine-tasting party the other day. Such nice people. They were most kind to me, and are sending me 6 bottles of port as a reward for the short foreword I wrote for their brochure. What does one do with port? In old days I think people took it to the Poor, along with soup, jelly, and flannel. I doubt if the Poor get any of these luxuries now, being so well cared for by the State. Perhaps I'll ask Fr. Wilkins if he would like a bottle.

I am going to an Oxford lunch next week to talk about Liberalism. I have no notion what to say about it. One can praise it as an ideal, elegize it as a deceased political party, tell stories about Liberals and Whigs of the past, talk about what it means in different countries (often so different from what we mean here), or just say how nice to be a Liberal because one can then be in opposition to any government that gets in, a healthy and profitable attitude, both for the government and oneself. One should never feel *submissive* to any government; bad for them and bad for us. They go blundering along, and it is our part to deride and criticize. That will in future, I fear, be the solitary function of our once-great party. That, and to try and spread a little light in darkness among Tories and Socialists. Well, they all have something, of course.

Now Fr. Gervase Mathew, a Dominican priest, is coming to call on me, with messages from his brother David, the R.C. Archbp. at Mombasa, who used to be a friend of mine. A very broad-minded R.C.; they both are, I think—unless they modify themselves for my benefit, which perhaps they do. But I think the Archbp. really *likes* the Anglican Church; he is certainly much interested in its history, and writes of it with great impartiality and respect. He (in fact both) likes *They were Defeated.*

I always feel moved now to say to R.C.s " I have something as good as you have, now. In fact, in my view a long sight better." Time was when I only had Anglo-agnosticism to put up against their great Church. But I don't really ever talk theology or churches to the brothers Mathew. They have a wide range of interests.

I must go to the library before it shuts (for it has now become Sat. morning). I must put my potatoes on before I go, so goodbye for now. You might be pleased if you could see me making frequent use of *all* your books, and of that nice note book. Nothing you have sent me is wasted, and all are loved and used.

Your affectionate

R. M.

June

20, *Hinde House, Hinde St., W.*1
1st June, 1951

Dear Father,

Thank you so much for your letter of 27th May, which came yesterday, just as I was going off to Oxford for the day. So I took it with me, and read it in the train when I ought to have been stringing together some remarks on the Function of Liberalism To-day for a lunch address to the University Liberal Society; I found your letter much pleasanter and more interesting than any such nonsense. However, I had a nice time at Oxford, first at this lunch, then going up to Boar's Hill with Gilbert Murray and strolling about his lovely garden, then being taken from one college to another by Gervase Mathew (a R.C. Dominican, an admirable Byzantine art scholar, and an archaeologist, who has just been digging up a ruined town in N. Africa). He took me to tea with a Balliol don, then to sherry with the Oriel chaplain, Austin Farrer,[1] whose Bampton Lectures,

[1] Dr. Farrer was then Chaplain of Trinity College, Oxford, not Oriel College.

The Glass of Vision, are interesting. So it was a full and entertaining and profitable day, and in the train home I talked with a nice American woman over here on a visit, who likes everything she has yet seen, even the weather; she had just been shown round Oxford by her son there. On the whole, I find Americans attractive.

But your letter. As always, it rejoiced me. And I shall love to have the Vincent Bourne[1]; I haven't got him, and never had. My father enjoyed him; he was a Trinity (Cambridge) man; my father's college. A most ingenious Latinist. That kind of Latin skill has sadly languished. I am pleased to be reading so much church Latin as I am just now, and learning some by heart. I know easily now several of those prayers. I say every day " *Domine Jesu Christe . . . et a te nunquam separari permittas.*"[2] Thank you for saying it for me sometimes. It is the perfect prayer for Mass, whether one communicates or not. So is " *Deus, qui nobis sub sacramento mirabili passionis tuae memoriam reliquisti,*"[3] which we often have in English at Grosvenor. I did look up Darwell Stone in the Library this afternoon, on non-communicating attendance; I see he says we can't " sharply distinguish " between the power to join in the offering when we communicate, and the power to do so on later occasions when only present, as the eucharistic life goes on from one occasion to the next, without break. Which is really what you too say. Actually I rather like only being there; it is so undistracted and uninterrupted. And after it is over is a wonderful time for thinking about something one has selected to read (prayer, psalm, a bit of the Gospels or epistles). It is so much easier in church. There is such [a] tremendous field of things to pray about, and it grows all the time. I rather want to get hold of a good Bible commentary, with the best scholars' views on meanings and authorship, etc. I am much too ignorant. Karl Adam doesn't seem to be in the L[ondon] L[ibrary] catalogue. Nor does that

[1] Vincent Bourne (1695-1747), Latin poet, was a master at Westminster School, where William Cowper was one of his pupils.

[2] " Lord Jesus Christ . . . and suffer me never to be separated from thee."

[3] " O God, who under a wonderful sacrament hast left unto us a memorial of thy Passion "; from the collect for the Feast of Corpus Christi.

American Church history, which I think I will suggest that the library gets. They are quite good about acting on suggestions. You see how I rush off at once to look for any book you mention. Another one is T. Mozley's reminiscences,[1] which you started me looking at again; I got that out of the Library to-day. I read it once before, or part of it, but it is full of interesting things and people and repays looking through.

I agree with you about *Brighton Rock*. It is damaged by the extreme lowness of its characters. Not the girl, of course; she is a different type. But he is obsessed by evil, as he says himself in his last book of collected articles. He has a new novel coming out soon; he told me something about it. Have you read *The Power and the Glory*, about a drunken priest in Mexico and the persecution of the church there? It is interesting. But works too far his theory about *goodness* having little or nothing to do with the grace of God and of the church, which redeem the wicked not by making them better but by saving their souls in spite of their badness. This does seem unsound. Somehow it premises, or seems to premise, an almost mechanical view of salvation, as if the operations of redemption worked not *on* evil but almost ignoring it, provided the faith is there. Rather Calvinistic, surely. All faith and no works—that is, no human works. A most dangerous view. . . .

I went to see Fr. Wilkins last Monday; he was very kind and nice. He cleared up some of the puzzles of the Office Book, and is going to send me the new *Ordo* he is working on. He also gave me *The Trumpet shall Sound*, which I like very much. They are expecting Fr. Pedersen very soon now, and he will let me know when he arrives and will be in London. He says he thinks the Scotch P[rayer] B[ook] contains that clause " that they may grow in thy love and service " too; I must get hold of one. Fr. Wilkins didn't mind a bit about my defaulting to Grosvenor Chapel, as you said he wouldn't. He thinks it good to go to confession at one's own church. Did I tell you the Grosvenor exterior and tower is in a very dangerous state, and is

[1] T. Mozley, *Reminiscences; chiefly of Oriel College and the Oxford Movement* (1882).

having to be repaired. I should hate it to fall down! Apparently much of the work in it was very shoddy, especially what they added at the end of the 18th century.

I like to hear about your book-binding and mending. I think your craftsmanship is rather like that of the Balliol don I visited yesterday; he spends some of his time making wonderful little models of period buildings of slabs of wood joined by putty, wonderfully neat; he shows you a Georgian house, then lifts from it one layer of exterior, and underneath there is a Stuart house, and below that an Elizabethan one, and then a medieval one. All very beautiful and clever and delightful; if I could do that I should do nothing else. I expect your book-binding is the same kind of pleasure; the covers you have sent me are very good. I wish I had some kind of handicraft; but if I had I should have no time for it, I can't as it is get much done of the work I am supposed to be doing, so perhaps it is as well that I am stupid with my hands. What I have always been good at is anything with my legs and arms, and I don't get enough time for that really; though naturally most of the active pastimes are a thing of the past. But I still like walking and bicycling and swimming—and even, in lonely and unobserved country, climbing up trees and sitting there. And rowing, gently and in moderation. I was teaching a little girl of nine to scull the other day, on the Fun Fair lake. But how one used to think one would miss running and active games—and one doesn't a bit when the time comes.

2nd June. A fine but coolish morning. I am just off to the Serpentine, to bathe with other *studiosissimi natandi*. After mass this morning I read those chapters 11 and 12 Hebrews about faith; how magnificent they are. You know, when I think of all my wasted years of turning my back on all that, I feel that kind of unhappiness that must be a shadow of what one will feel after death—the misuse of life, the missing of its meaning, and now too late, life never turns back. All those years all this was there, and I refused it in selfish blindness. Well, I shouldn't be bothering you with my unavailing regrets. Better go and drown them in those chilly waters of Lethe in Hyde Park. Next week I go to Cambridge, and shall return a Doctor; very oddly, it seems to me. General Omar Bradley will be also getting a doctorate—not lit: but something nobler, that generals get. No doubt I shall see him at the various festal meals and garden parties that are laid on for us. I dare say it will be quite fun.

I wonder why we (Cranmer? Was it one of his translations?) altered the sense of that Trinity collect. I never noticed it before. Of course *firmitate* must mean the firmness of the faith itself, and couldn't anyhow be a verb. I see that in the Latin trans. of our P[rayer] B[ook] (Bright and Medd, 1865)[1] they put "*nos in eadem fide confirmes,*"[2] following the English. The original Latin is better—more reassuring and assured. I have learnt it. It pays to compare with the Latin all our collects. This seems to be the end of this letter. *Fac me in memoriam tuam manere.*[3]

Your affectionate

R. M.

20, Hinde House, Hinde St., W.1

12th June, 1951

Dear Father,

Thank you so much for the delightful packet of books the other day, and for your letter yesterday (posted 5th June). I was so pleased to get it; it seemed too long since the last letter. But I shan't expect to hear again for some time, because of the Retreat and Chapter. The books are all charming to have. I have always wanted a Pliny's Letters, they are such good reading; I like so much all the descriptions of his various villas. And the sad death of his uncle from the eruption. In their way, the letters are as good as Cicero's, and not so stuffed with politics, which I always find excessive in Cicero's. Vincent Bourne is really a

[1] *Liber Precum Publicarum*, Bright and Medd's edition of the Latin Book of Common Prayer (1865).

[2] "(We beseech thee, that thou wouldest) keep us stedfast in this faith"; from the Collect for Trinity Sunday.

[3] "Make me to remain in thy memory."

treasure. How well he did it, and how pleasant the verses are to read! Being 18th century (and Westminster at that) of course he pronounced them in the most Anglican of pronunciations. Unlike the Public Orator at Cambridge last week, who rolled out his pieces of flattery to us in the most impeccable modern-style Latin. . . . In case it would amuse you, I am posting you the addresses. He had mugged up a lot of information about me, even about my partiality for swimming, and my upbringing in Italy, and not only my father but my grandfather (W. J. Conybeare) having been Fellows of Trinity, and Herrick and Bishop Heber and every one![1] The addresses must have been a great deal of work preparing; but he is a practised Latinist, of course. I do like the Latin exercise book of 1827. Much more interesting than most modern ones. The fables and the Bible stories and the excellent moral reflections are all just what one would be interested to learn. I shall read them all, as I go about in trains, buses, etc. Moral aphorisms sound good in Latin, don't they; better than in English, I think. And I particularly like the Bible stories. When my godchild gets on with her Latin, I shall read her some. By the way, I have an idea that I oughtn't to have stood godmother at all, while alienated from the Church. How is this, I wonder? Or doesn't it matter? Thank you too for the dear little St. John's Gospel, a *very* portable size. I could carry that and the little Greek Testament together without making a perceptible bulge in a bag or pocket.

I did enjoy your letter. We are gradually recreating Mr. Livius; you remember his portrait; all we aren't certain of is his nationality, and in my view he was a German citizen, sent to Lisbon by the emperor, as your aunt Katie said. But you think he was of Bedfordshire. In that case, isn't Livius an oddish name? However, if he served with Warren Hastings . . . [sic] Perhaps we shall discover more about him as time goes on. You might write to Aunt Katie about him? All you say about your family interests me.

[1] R. M.'s great-grandmother, the wife of Rev. Aulay Macaulay, was Anne Herrick, of the same family as the poet, and her step-grandmother (the first wife of Rev. S. H. Macaulay) was Bishop Heber's daughter.

I am glad my Dorset letter arrived as a birthday one. And the book about Cowper that I sent you can count as a birthday present. As for those two novels you mention, I will certainly look about for copies of them. They are out of print, and I seem to have only one copy of each myself, which I probably ought to keep for reference. But if another turns up, as it well may, I shall send it at once. *Dangerous Ages* is, I think, rather poor, on the whole, but it might amuse you just to see it. I will also send you *The Listener*, which contains a . . . . talk by Evelyn Waugh about our choice of 100 books, and a letter from me in reply to it. He said we were actuated by political (Left) motives. I answered him in a letter to *The Listener*.

Cambridge was fun. I met all kinds of people. At the Luncheon (in Pembroke, because that is the Vice Chancellor's College) I sat between Omar Bradley and Sir William Haley, the BBC Director. Omar B. was rather sweet. Edith Evans was there, and returned thanks at lunch for the new Chancellor's toast of us (11 of us) in a very charming and witty speech. Purely non-academic in background, she had never seen Cambridge before, and was delighted with what she called " the old grey walls and scarlet gowns." At the garden party I was glad of the scarlet gown, as it was rather a cool day. I liked staying at Trinity, and in the evening we went to the A.D.C. revue, which was very funny. The Master retires at the end of June. So now I am a Doctor, and can tell policemen so when they criticise me for leaving my car too long in a street; they will think I have been busy with an operation or a confinement.

Last night I went to see a poetical play in a church—little S. Thomas's, Regent Street. Rather interesting, I thought; by a young poetical dramatist Christopher Fry; I wonder if his plays reach America. After it, I was taken to a pub for drinks and sandwiches by a rather charming, entertaining . . . young assistant priest there. He told me that Anglo-Catholicism is now " much smarter " than Roman, so I feel much reassured. He is rather a new type to me; very social . . . and very extreme, which he finds rather amusing obviously. So extreme is St.

Thomas's that it has, it seems, come full circle, and they *sit* at Mass, or so he says. It must be very comfortable. However, it won't tempt me away from Grosvenor Chapel, which hasn't got so far as that, and is much less self conscious; in fact it isn't self conscious at all. I love it more and more. Even when I go on to church almost, as it seems, straight from some late night party, and feel half asleep, at first; as the service proceeds I wake up. Yes, I am very lucky in the lot which has fallen to me, and find the dwellings very amiable. All one wants is to be had for the asking, and it is very beautiful and satisfying, and I like its quiet anonymity. Yes, I should indeed find it difficult —in fact, impossible—to profess Roman Catholicism. It wouldn't suit me at all. I couldn't do it without being mentally dishonest. Besides, I don't like quite a lot in it. I am sure you are right that most R.C. converts are very ignorant of our church, and would probably find it satisfying if they really learnt what it can be at its best. If, for example, they had the privilege of corresponding with you, and having you point out to them the things you have pointed out and sent to me for the enriching of my knowledge and the suggestion of lines of reading and thought. I don't see any one who has had that *not* valuing and appreciating and beginning to understand the church, or wanting to leave it for any other, however plausible and showy and magnificent and *rotundum*. The very idea makes me homesick at once. You have rooted me deep in C. of E.

I haven't heard yet from Fr. Pedersen, but I expect he may materialize any time now, from what you told me.

13*th*. Now I have found a copy of *Dangerous Ages* in a cupboard. I have been looking at it, and don't think much of it on the whole. I am rather amused to see what a different view I took then (30 years ago) of the various ages people are, from my present view; naturally, of course. I wonder what you'll think of it. It won't make you laugh much, I suppose; I think it's more or less solemn throughout, and hasn't many jokes; I don't know why. I think *And no man's wit* is probably lying about somewhere too; if I find one (apart, I mean, from my own, that

I must keep) I will send it in the same packet. It is nice for me that you like to see my books; I am glad you do.

Will there ever be another Revised P[rayer] B[ook] instead of that 1928 reject? I hadn't realised it was so bad as that; but I scarcely know it. The Dean of Winchester (E. G. Selwyn) says they use it in the Cathedral. I will look up what Darwell Stone says about it.

I hope you enjoyed your marriage outing. Rather nice, marrying a girl you have known since a child. Naturally she wanted you to.

14*th*. I have been away all day, and must now end and post this, and also the large envelope with the Degree addresses and the *Listener* cutting. Thank you again, and my love always.

R. M.

20, *Hinde House, Hinde St., W.*1
22nd June, 1951

Dear Father,

Thank you so much for two air *papers* (12th June and 19th) and the air *letter* posted in the litter-bin on 18th, which was sorted out from the worthless mass of litter and safely posted. (You see how clearly I perceive the difference between papers and letters; careless talk on such a matter would be most reprehensible.) I'm glad they all arrived. And I'm so pleased that you like to have Cowper. I didn't know about that picture being the one in your dining-room; how nice that is! I shall now go and look at it—and at the Romney—in the National Portrait Gallery, and fancy it hanging in that recess over the chimney piece while you talked and were read aloud to. What a good idea it was to send it to you; I'm so glad I did. I didn't read a great deal of the book itself; I hope it is interesting and well done. I like your account of the picture, with the yellow breeches and the pen. The pictures one grew up with are for ever *perceived* in ourselves, I think. I use that word because I

146

wanted to say something about its earlier meaning, with reference to that collect. I like your rearrangement of the words, and your emphasis; it is *very* much better, and I shall adopt it. But as to the word " perceive," it seems one of those very many words in our P[rayer] B[ook] and Bible translations which have rather damaged their meaning to us to-day by their gradual slight changes in meaning during the last 4 centuries. It had in the 16th century in one of its senses a much *stronger* implication of possession, holding on to, taking root, than it has now, I suppose. Like the Latin *percipere* (*per* for through or thoroughly, *capere*, seize, lay hold of). I mean, this was *one* of the meanings of perceive, and probably the one intended in the collect, do you think? Obviously it often carried the sense of " take into possession "—as in a will of 1512, " I will that my daughters have and perceive all the revenues." I think the translator of *sentiamus* must have meant this; something much stronger and more firmly possessed than merely " notice," or even " feel " (in " perceive and know what things we ought to do," it is used in the modern sense, of course; they seem to have used both). Perhaps a re-translation of our prayers and collects —or anyhow a revision—would help to elucidate them; though I think one would miss the accustomed words on which one grew up—" prevent us," etc. To use the Latin versions avoids misunderstandings, of course; but simple people can't usually do this. I must look up some book on the translation of the collects, and find out which were Cranmer and which other people. I like your " continually " for *jugiter*. It is a prayer I very often say, in Latin, and now I shall use your English version, with its improved intonation. Did I tell you I bought an American P[rayer] B[ook] at Mowbrays? I am interested to note the differences. And I have found Karl Adam's *Son of God* in the London Lib[rary], and got it out to-day. It looks what I want. As to Dr. Addison's book on the American Church,[1] the Library has accepted my suggestion that it should get it, and are sending to New York for it; it's not published here. My only blank

[1] Daniel Dulany Addison, *The Episcopalians* (New York, 1904).

draw now is Fr. Benson's Cowley book,[1] and that will no doubt turn up presently; I would like to read it, and of course I ought to, being S.S.J.E. myself. Though when I imagine taking on such a career, taking such unearthly, stupendous vows, committing myself to such a life, I feel breathlessly out of step and unutterably tiny and puny. . . . [sic]

Oh yes, I am safe from the Order of Preachers—who, to do them justice, have evinced no desire for my conversion. It would be no good if a thousand preachers, or a thousand angels, or His Holiness the Pope himself, evinced such a desire, and spoke as golden as Chrysostom, offering me a Red Hat (in addition to the black velvet one I got at Cambridge); I should remain an unregretting and unenvious C. of E. member, S.S.J.E. disciple. Besides, didn't I tell you that I was informed lately by a young priest that to be an Anglo-Catholic is now " much smarter," which quite settles the matter for me. But no one has tried to pervert or convert me; as to the brothers Mathew, I really believe they almost prefer Anglicans.

No: I don't mean to use my " Dr." either on envelopes or elsewhere, so am still Miss. I might try the doctor on a policeman or two, when they contemplate summoning me for parking too long in the street; they would suppose I had been conducting an operation or a confinement in a near house, and would let me off. But otherwise I shall bury it, except I suppose on official occasions, when one has to produce titles, decorations, etc. Nevertheless, I rather like to have it, as a warming little greeting from Cambridge. Edith Sitwell has a D.Litt. (not Cambridge; I think Nottingham[2]) and likes to be called " Dr." When someone wrote of her in the *Spectator* some time ago as " Miss Sitwell," Osbert wrote severely " I suppose your correspondent means *Dr.* Sitwell "; but most people don't use it unless they are academically engaged, when it looks better to have it. I feel sure General Omar Bradley won't use his!

[1] R. M. Benson, *The Religious Vocation; edited by H. P. Bull with an introduction by L. Cary* (1939).

[2] Dame Edith Sitwell received an Hon. Litt.D. from Leeds University and also an Hon. D.Litt. from Durham University in 1948. In 1951 she received an Hon. D.Litt. from Oxford University.

I hope Fr. Manson[1] gave a good retreat. I know the kind of voice you describe. I think it's true that English speech has changed a good deal. It has become more *mincing*. Fr. Wilkins told me (in a letter) that Bishop *Viall* has arrived here; I think he got confused between him and Fr. Pedersen, and thought I wanted to see him. I hope he didn't puzzle the poor man by telling him so. No Fr. Pedersen yet. Instead, I have in London a dear little half-American first cousin of 15,[2] over on a visit to Europe; one of her aunts[3] and I share taking her about; she is delighted with London and all she sees. "Is that a *tea cosy*? Gosh! I've heard of those!" And, "Who'd have thought I'd ever be driving in a car with Rose Macaulay to the Tower of London? Gosh!" She is my godchild, and very attractive, intelligent, and gay. Her aunt, my cousin, is R.C., and very properly asked my leave before taking her to Westminster Cathedral to hear Gregorian chants. She seems less precocious in some ways than one hears that American schoolgirls often are; doesn't use lipstick, etc.; but she observed demurely, having met girls of her own age here, "when in Rome, I do as the Romans do"; so I don't know what she does when at home.

Here we are all agog about the two Missing Diplomats, Guy Burgess and Donald Maclean, who have vanished into space in very odd circumstances. As we most of us knew them, or one or other of them, we are intrigued. Are they also in the American press? They are commonly supposed to have fled beyond the Iron Curtain; but we doubt the trans-curtain authorities having much use for them; they are . . . not scientists, and know nothing useful like atomic secrets. Some of their friends say they have probably . . . been murdered in a Paris brawl. The police are interviewing and questioning all their close friends, so are the papers, and highly coloured interviews appear in the vulgar press. If they ever return, they will be able to collect a

[1] One of the English Cowley Fathers visiting Cambridge, Mass. at that time.

[2] Emily Smith (see Preface), grand-daughter of R. M.'s aunt, Mrs. C. S. Smith.

[3] Jean Smith, daughter of Mrs. C. S. Smith.

handsome sum in libel damages. It is really pretty sad, because they are clever, and have many attractive qualities. . . . How odd it is, this disease that seizes on so many able people. Both these F.O. men were secret communists.

I am, at intervals, trying to persuade an acquaintance not to turn R.C. She had seen me in Grosvenor Chapel, which surprised her; so she tackled me on the matter of Rome, which is beckoning her through some priest she knows. I told her I didn't see that Rome had anything good that we haven't got. Then I found myself confronting such a miasma of sheer ignorance and misconception about both churches that I scarcely felt able to say anything. Isn't it odd. Here is a woman of mature age and genteel bringing up and position . . . who really seems not to know the simplest theological or ecclesiastical facts. . . . But what goes on in such minds, and why should they consider such a change, having no knowledge of its implications? It is what you said the other day—misconception based on ignorance and lack of interest. . . . But they might give *Ecclesia Anglicana* a chance, these impulsive and unreasoning people. She wants me to go to lunch and talk it over. I am amused at being consulted as an ecclesiastical guide! And am rather glad of a chance to testify for my own Church.

23rd. Vigil of St. John Baptist, and so cool and dull a morning that I didn't bathe after Mass. I read an article in *The Times* about S. John, which I enclose. Is it correct in its view, about *his* views? I also enclose a photograph of us, all dressed up, processing along King's Parade. I and Edith Evans are somewhere in it, but I can't distinguish us. But it may amuse you to see it.

My love always,

R. M.

I sent you last week the Public Orator's Latin addresses to us all.[1]

---

[1] R. M. has added a note on back of envelope: " *No*. The *Punch* ' R. M.' [Richard Mallet] is not me, but some man. We are often confused."

July

20, *Hinde House, Hinde St., W.*1
12th July, 1951 †

Dear Father,

I was beginning to think it was some time since I had had
a letter, when your air paper of 8th July came this morning.
But I've not had the one you posted on 2nd July—if it has mis-
carried, it will be the first to have done that; but I suppose there
is still time, if it caught a slow plane. Anyhow, I now have this
one, which I love to have. I'm glad those two novels, bass-
sustained,[1] arrived safely. I do up packets very badly, lacking
your gift for it; but I think they get there all right, as a rule.
As I think I mentioned before, I don't believe *Dangerous Ages* is
much good; but I shall like to hear your views on it some time.
You know, I always do like to hear what you think of books,
mine or others. I'm very glad the Cowper is good; I shall get
it from the Library and read it carefully. I know N. Nicholson
is interesting; I like his poems rather, too. I should like to meet
him some time. How I wish you were here, so that I could meet
some of these people with you! But probably there would be
no time for that kind of thing; S.S.J.E. Fathers (to judge by Fr.
Pedersen) seem always occupied on their businesses. I hope Fr. P.
will turn up in London at a time when I am there too. I have
given up going abroad this summer, as I have to finish this book,
and, though I shall be away for short times (Isle of Wight and
elsewhere) I mean to be mostly in London, basing myself on
libraries and this studious and book-littered flat. It is the first
London August I shall have spent since the war, and may be
rather nice—quiet and uninterrupted and sunny (one hopes) and
a little shabby and derelict—old clothes and the Serpentine and
driving outside London to near country, and above all WORKING.

[1] Tied up with bast.

Last August I spent in Italy—and returned to find a letter from you, that started the train that led to this new country in which I now inhabit, and am fixed, I hope for good. Odd and grateful thought.

What you say about *Mary Lavelle* makes me want to read it, which I haven't ever done, though Kate O'Brien's novels always interest me. I fancy she takes what I call (unjustly, probably) the R.C. view of sin. Which is, no doubt, more to the purpose than the irreligious view, but still rather off the mark, perhaps. Not that I don't know many R.C.s who take the most sensitive and austere view of sin possible; agnostics too, for that matter; so perhaps it is, after all, partly a question of character. All the same, I believe there *is* something in the R.C. slant on conduct that is sometimes disconcerting. But when I read *Mary Lavelle*, I will see how it strikes me. Last night I saw that little play by Charles Williams, *The House of the Octopus*, acted in St. Thomas's Church, Regent Street. It was really rather moving and impressive; he takes the right line about Sin. Psychologically it is interestingly worked out; dramatically, full of tension and horror. They have the idea at that church (which isn't a parish church) of preaching the Gospel partly by drama; it is a very ancient idea, of course, and a good one. The vicar, Fr. McLaughlin, produces and directs the plays. The priest I know there is my bright young friend Fr. Gerard Irvine.

I go on brooding over the translations of P[rayer] B[ook] and N[ew] T[estament] words. Isn't there a case for altering " comprehended," in S. John 1. 5, to overcame or overpowered? That is, isn't it, what *katelaben* (can't type Greek letters) *means*. The Vulgate has *comprehenderunt*, which means the same. And we (starting with the early translations I suppose, tho' I haven't Tyndale's 1525 translation at hand, the earliest I have is the Genevan, 1560) rendered it " comprehended," which was used then often in the sense of captured, overcame, took hold of. The Genevan Bible uses it too in Philippians III. 12, " that I may comprehend that for which also I am comprehended of Christ Jesus." *App*rehend still has that sense; one can be apprehended by the police, taken possession of. But " comprehend " hasn't been used in that sense since the 17th century, and very seldom after the quite early part of the century, and still we have it in the passage that is read aloud daily after Mass, and it does seem rather unnecessarily misleading. I don't know what the R.V. has, but I believe some newer versions have substituted " overcame," which seems to be more sensible. I don't mind myself, as I can use the word in its obsolete sense easily; but what about . . . the simple uninstructed? Why be misleading, just for nothing? I wonder what Douai has for it, and Ronald Knox. I must look them up. Then, the Lord's Prayer. What made the Vulgate take *epiousion* (in S. Matthew's version of the Lord's Prayer) as meaning supersubstantial (*supersubstantialem*), and in S. Luke as *quotidianum*? Rather odd, with the same word. I rather wish it did mean supersubstantial; it is perhaps a better meaning than " daily "; but apparently it doesn't. Still, in saying it one can think of spiritual food if one likes, of course. But what I can't understand is the two different words in the Vulgate. For that too one might look up the Knox version. I do like your little Latin and Greek Testaments so much. What with them and all the English versions to compare, reading the Bible is an exciting job. Not only the meaning and the moral, but the forms of expression.

I'm sure Kitty Witham never looked much at any dictionary. But there *were* English dictionaries; the first, I think, Elizabethan, and various others through the 17th and 18th centuries, though of course none on Johnson's scale. There were spelling dictionaries and rhyming dictionaries; the rhyming ones I always find interesting as throwing light on period pronunciation; e.g. *barn* rhymes with *fern* and all the other *ern* words; in fact, all the *er* spellings were pronounced *ar*; and so on. Very illuminating as a guide to contemporary speech, and I don't think those people who sometimes do " Shakespeare as the Elizabethans pronounced him " on the radio make enough use of these dictionaries. In fact, no dictionaries, old or new, are used enough; I should like to force pronouncing dictionaries on the BBC, and on those dreadful voices who call out through megaphones at the London stations lists of places, pronouncing

them as they have seen them spelt (which Kitty at least escaped)
—" Ox-ford " (like the ford of a river), " Birming-ham," all the
oms to rhyme with *bomb* instead of with *come* and *rum*. Very
jarring. I should think Norman Nicholson would be interested
if you, as a Cowper Johnson, wrote to him about his book,
wouldn't he?

I think I shall send this by air, as you might be wondering
why I hadn't answered the non-arrived letter of 2nd July—and
anyhow it's a long time since I last wrote, and this may as well
speed through the air. It brings my love.

Yours affectionately,

R. M.

20, *Hinde House, Hinde St.,* W.1
17th *July,* 1951 †

Dear Father,

This is a p.s. to my air letter (yes, letter: *this,* I know is a
paper) posted the other day, in which I said that yours of 2nd
July hadn't arrived. But lo, it came this morning. Why it
should have taken 15 days (longer than most ocean mail) I can't
think, nor can the P.O., where I am writing this on my way to
a garden party (hence the pen). Some delay must have held it
up. But I'm *so* glad it wasn't lost, because it is so especially nice
a one. I thought I would let you know at once, in case you
thought it had got lost.

Did I tell you the London Library got that U.S. Episcopal
Church book for me, and I am reading it with great interest.
Interesting to learn how the Church developed, and how the
English religious movements were reflected in it. Another book
I am reading is *From Puritanism to the Age of Reason* (Cragg),
tracing the English move away from Puritanism from the 17th
century to the 18th, through the Cambridge Platonists (delightful
people, one and all, I have always thought) to the Latitudinarians
and the 18th century theologians.

I shall get the *Mary Lavelle* Penguin. I've never read it,

though I do read, and like, K. O'B.'s books. She knows her world—that world of Irish R.C. governesses in Spain, having been one herself once.

When I've read it I shall write and tell you what I think about it; probably what you do. Do read, if you come on it, Simone Weil's books—or rather her correspondence, collected and published (in French, but translated) by a French Jesuit priest. I find her extremely interesting and moving, in her integrity, able brain, firm and concentrated thinking. She had objections to the Church, and refused to be baptised; but was a magnificent Christian. You should see the *film* of *The Third Man*; it is really very exciting. I've not read it in book form. Of course in the film the views of Christianity don't come in much. I doubt if he is interested in Christianity *in itself*—only in its interactions in the lives and souls of R. Catholics (them alone). (After all, I can't finish this now.)

18th July. In a fortnight my Chapel closes for August. Where shall I go to weekday Mass when in London? I expect All Saints. I met the other day Canon Hood (head of Pusey House) who lives in London, not far from me, during vacations. He helps at various churches, including the Annunciation, Bryanston Street, which is about my nearest (daily-Mass) church. I asked him what it was like: " very Roman," said he—tho', he added, it does throw in bits and pieces of the P[rayer] B[ook] into its mass, such as the Church Militant. To me (with my S.S.J.E. training) there is something rather silly about these near-Roman churches, so I think I shan't attend it. . . .

The most extreme church in London, about, is S. Magnus the Martyr's. The Vicar, Fr. Fynes-Clinton, has relics, and can liquefy blood![1] I'm glad my Chapel attempts no such nonsense.

My love always,

R. M.

[1] There is a collection of relics at the Church of St. Magnus the Martyr, amongst which is one alleged to be of the Precious Blood. The late Rev. H. J. Fynes-Clinton, rector of this church, did not, however, claim to be able to liquefy blood.

20, Hinde House, Hinde St., W.1
23rd July, 1951

Dear Father,

Though I wrote to you (air paper) on the 18th, and an air letter a few days earlier (before yours of 2nd had reached me), I feel inclined to write a sea letter this evening, partly because I got your air paper posted 16th the other day (on 20th, I think), in which you promise me an Ovid vol., and the one I should most like to have—*Tristia*, *Fasti*, and *Ex Ponto*. His laments from the Pontine exile always move me; how he hated it! It is good of you, and I much look forward to its arrival, also to the packet of newspaper cuttings. By the way, in case it might interest you, I enclose a review by someone in the *Listener* of that Cowper book, which the reviewer thinks well of.

Since I last wrote, I have read *Mary Lavelle*, and see what you mean about the end. I think the explanation is that the girl, though a Catholic, wasn't meant to be *religious*; I think no reference to religion crosses her mind throughout the book (or does it?). I imagine she took her religion, in which she had grown up, without much thought or understanding or deep caring; neither had she firm moral principles. One may perhaps think this odd in a well brought up Irish Catholic girl, for as a rule they are rather modest and puritan in feeling and conduct; and I think this is an artistic defect in the book. But the point is that I don't suppose the author herself, though a Catholic, is particularly religious; I don't even know if she is *pratiquante*, for I know her very little. So the religious aspect wouldn't naturally be prominent in her view. She does certainly seem to sympathise and approve, and (one gathers) plans a happy solution to the love affair; and it is a real flaw that the moral and religious aspect of it are so absent. To me a more unpleasant flaw is the extreme unreticence of the description of the affair; such details *should* be "*tacenda*," but seem increasingly less so. I don't like it; I agree with you and Cicero; I suppose we are all three old-fashioned, and brought up in a more reticent and fastidious tradition. I certainly was, and such things always jar on me. At the best, they cheapen and sully what should be a very private experience; at the worst, they are rather disgusting. What is good in the book is the lively picture of the Irish "misses" in Spain, and the odd little society they form together; obviously a study from life. The Spanish family too is well drawn. But if she hadn't fallen in love with Juanito, or if they had done so and given way to it and then been sorry and parted for good, it would have been a much better and more interesting book. The conflicts of human beings with evil, the evil in themselves, are an intensely interesting and important theme, and modern fiction ignores it too much. Love seems to carry all before it, and the author usually backs it heavily as a winner and it romps triumphantly home. But, to give R. Catholicism its due, this isn't a characteristic, usually, of R.C. novels; they do, as a rule, consider the moral and religious aspect, though not always to much purpose. It's odd about R.C.ism. It has somehow got a reputation for being more in earnest about morality than other churches; is it deserved? For instance, a cousin of mine the other day, talking about . . . a convert, . . . who often speaks irritably and unkindly to her old mother, said "I wonder how much she tries not to. I suppose she does, because she is a Roman Catholic." I said, why should R.C.s be supposed to try harder to be good than others, and she said, well they go regularly to confession, so must think what they are doing. This, of course, would apply to many Anglicans too; but one doesn't hear often "I suppose so-and-so tries to behave well, because he or she is an Anglican." . . .

No sign yet from Fr. Pedersen. I do hope he will turn up one day, while I am in London (I shall be mainly here, but partly in the Isle of Wight). I regard him as your angel, or messenger, and want to hear news of you. But no doubt he will turn up; I expect he has been mainly out of London so far.

I have been reading lately Ronald Knox's New Testament. It reads well, doesn't it; but some of his translations seem to me a little disingenuous and wrong, also his notes on them. E.g. S. Matt. I, 25, which he renders "and he had not known her when she bore a son," explaining in a note that a more

literal translation would be " *till* she bore a son," but this might
" impugn the perpetual virginity of our Lady." He shouldn't
be thinking about that, surely, in translating. The Vulgate has
donec, the Greek *heos*; both, of course, mean " till," not
" when." I wonder what the Douai has; I must look it up.
He refers to some Hebrew word " represented by till " which
he thinks was used, but how do we know what Hebrew words
were used? The whole note strikes me as propagandist rather
than scholarly. Still, I suppose his translation wouldn't have
passed the church authorities unless he had been very careful to
smooth over awkward points. For " the darkness comprehended it not " he has " was not able to master it," which is
quite good, but has a note that " master " may be taken as *over-
coming* or *understanding*. But can the Greek *katelaben* mean understand? I suppose he must be right, as he is such a good Greek
scholar; but no such meaning is in my Lexicon.

That prayer you mention, " *et fac me . . .*" is a wonderful
statement as well as prayer. Since you first told me of it, I have
used it continually, and always after Mass. I wonder sometimes
how often it is a good thing to make one's communion. At
present I go every morning, and am by way of communicating
twice in the week; I mean once as well as Sunday; either on
some saint's day or special day, or in the middle of the week.
But I have no thought-out rule about it. . . . I haven't thought
yet where I shall go when I am here in August and my Chapel
is closed. I don't much care for the idea of the Annunciation,
Bryanston Square [*sic*], but it has the advantage of being near
and in the right direction—i.e. towards, not away from, my
bathe. All Saints is in the wrong direction for this. When too
chilly for the Serpentine, I go to the Lansdowne Club swimming
bath, which is lovely, clear and green, with high diving boards
and a water shoot [*sic*]. I often go there on Sundays with friends,
and we improve at long-distance swimming under water, which
is very important, or might be in some emergencies. I can't
think how people who can't swim dare to go about at all, they
are in constant peril. And particularly of course when at sea.
I saw to-day the picture of a little jeep that swims; its owners

drive in it down to the Channel or the Solent, and then drive it over the water to France or the Isle of Wight, it must be lovely. But how dreadful if it sank, and left one swimming. I think I will bring that situation into a novel. But I must try and get a trip in one first. My plans are at present to be here till mid-August, then, when my sister goes to the Isle of Wight, to join her there for a few days (perhaps about the 20th) then back here, with occasional week-ends away. In a way it is rather peaceful not to be rushing abroad, with all the arrangements that this entails, and certainly I shall be able to do more work. My Ruin book presses on my mind, and I have been very slothful and neglectful about it lately. I really must go at it hard for the next two months. It is fun writing it, but hard work. Any letters that come for me will be quite safe, and forwarded by our good porter if I am away. It is rather remarkable that, I think, no letters of yours to me, or mine to you, have been lost finally, though some have been tardy. Touch wood here. I couldn't *bear* to lose even one! I wish I knew (complete change of subject) what this week's gospel about the steward, meant. Perhaps it is a muddled story, got down wrong by whoever wrote it.

I am using Bishop Andrewes's *Preces Privatae* a good deal just now. Some of the prayers are very good; and I like the way it is arranged. I am also interested in the Hellenistic environment of early Christianity—the Hermetic Books, etc.—and am reading what I can of it. Dr. Kirk is good on that, of course. The cultural background in which the early Church grew up; it is very illuminating. If you were here, I should be talking to you about this and so much else.

I have an invitation to go to Jugo-Slavia at the expense of the Jugo-Slav Peace Committee, to a conference in October. I am tempted, because of seeing Jugo-Slavia free; but then I reflect that the conference is in Zagreb, 150 miles from the Dalmatian coast which I want to see, that it is high up and will probably be cool by then, that Z. is a large town, not wildly interesting, and that I should have to attend the conference, which would bore me badly and be full of clichés and nonsensical platitudes about peace, and that I mightn't care for many of my colleagues there. So I have put the temptation behind me, much as my heart leaps up at the notion of seeing any part of Abroad (which, unlike you, I adore) for nothing. But the price would be this conference, and it is too high to pay. Had it been in Split or Dubrovnik, on the coast, with all those lovely islands off shore, then I must have fallen for it, conference and all. So perhaps it is as well that it isn't!

Do you take a holiday, and go away for a little? I hope so. Tell me sometime, and where you will be. It might be nice to visit your Florida mission house, and wander for a time among the Spanish moss and swampy lagoons and creeks, perhaps with a bark boat. I am ashamed of my own holidays, which are often so wonderful. Now I must stop this ramble.

With my love, yours affectionately,

R. M.

20, *Hinde House, Hinde St., W.*1
29th July, 1951

Dear Father,

I have had two very delightful letters from you lately (i.e. since I wrote to you on the 23rd); air letter written 18th, and air paper posted 23rd. So much I want to say; that is the worst of writing to you, there is always so much I want to say. I mean, your letters start so many trains of thought, besides the various happenings, and thoughts of my own, that I like to relate. I am interested in what you say about these new-style Anglican priests, and I am sure it is all true. They *are* zealous and keen, and go to endless trouble to have their services as they think right. For my part, I rather like the variety, but do avoid the *most* extreme kinds, such as St. Magnus the Martyr's and the Annunciation, Bryanston St.; that is, I so far have, but in August may go sometimes to week-day mass at the latter, as it is so near, and in the right direction for me. As you say, one explores in that way the rich variety of Anglican worship. I shall certainly prefer my chapel, and shall be glad when it re-opens on the 26th. What one admires in all these priests is the way they carry on daily with their early masses, however few come to them, and in the nature of things it can't be many. It seems that next Sunday's services at Grosvenor will be taken by the Rev. Cecil Wood, who functioned there during the war. I met a number of priests the other day at a St. Anne's Day gathering to which I was invited at St. Anne's House, Dean Street, a kind of centre of discussions, lectures, etc., connected with St. Thomas's church and run by the clergy there. Fr. Patrick McLaughlin, the vicar, is a many-sided kind of priest, whom I like. They get up lectures at St. Anne's (I was asked to give one, but refused, I was too busy). I see that during this past year they have had lectures from Dorothy Sayers, Norman Nicholson, Austin Farrer (a Balliol chaplain who produced some interesting Bamptons a few years ago)[1] and others. They produce these religious plays also; on the advisory committee are people like T. S. Eliot, Canon Demant, Fr. Groser, an archdeacon, and others.

At the buffet lunch they had after Mass . . . I met Fr. Ross of All Saints, a nice, gentle, kind, able priest whom I liked, and several more, lay and clerical, including Fr. . . . [sic] of St. Patrick's, Soho, the Unreformed Church across the street. So you see I move in these days in the best circles, and have to be careful what I say. I was interested in your memories of Canon Hood. I like him. . . . [It] is profitable and interesting . . . when and if . . . [all these various priests] talk on their own subjects, shedding fresh light on what they hold and what the church holds, and where they differ from some other church views, and discuss questions of Biblical criticism, etc. Fr. Gerard Irvine was talking the other evening to his brother (a young barrister) and me, at supper in his rooms after a religious play in the church to which he had invited a party. I said something about the confusion often made between Mary of Bethany, Mary Magdalene, and the "woman who was a sinner"; Fr. Irvine agreed that it was a pity and quite baseless,

[1] See above p. 138n.

upon which his brother charged him with having made the confusion (anyhow between the Magdalene and the woman of the town) in his sermon on the Feast of St. Mary Magdalene. He agreed that he had, because he thought it would be expected by his congregation, which seems, as his brother told him, rather immoral. His business certainly is to correct such confusions, not endorse them. The best Bible commentaries do correct this one. It seems especially hard on Mary of Bethany to be thus stigmatized, and I'm sure Martha and Lazarus would have been most annoyed. Perhaps the Magdalene story is too much now a matter of literary allusion down the ages (and Magdalene Homes, etc.) ever to be cleared up; but at least the other Mary should be immune. I remember my mother being very firm about this.

Your charming account of the young Wykeham-Fiennes[1] at Cuddesdon made me wonder what on earth his ancestor, the Lord Saye and Sele of the civil war, would have said to him— " Old Subtlety," who sat in the Westminster Assembly of 1643, and was a firm Puritan. He would no doubt have rebuked his descendant for " Popery," and have thought Cuddesdon a nest of this. But how Cuddesdon would have pleased Bp. Andrewes, Dr. Cosin, and Archbp. Laud. Not that, I suppose, it is extreme in any way—but then, nor were they. Fr. Fynes-Clinton of St. Magnus would probably have thought them regrettably protestant. Times change; what further phases will our Church go through, I wonder? I like it as it now has come to be; it has built a City of God round the Eucharist; one can enter into it each day and be a citizen of that glorious city for a time, and remember its language and its light through the day, if only at rare intervals in the racketty hustle and business of life as lived. Yes: I *must* keep that up through August so far as I can.

Those 6 collects: how good they are. I find I already have " *dirigere et sanctificare* "[2] in Latin copied into my scrap book, my *Preces Privatae*, as Bp. Andrewes named his. Mine is the Breviary version, not Bright and Medd's—but I can't remember now

[1] Rev. the Hon. William Cecil Twisleton-Wykeham-Fiennes.
[2] " Direct and sanctify."

where in the Breviary it comes. That is the worst of the Brev.: one loses prayers and can't always find them again when one wants to. Of the "Prevent us" one, I think I like the English best, on the whole. I like the Latin of "*Adesto*"; but prefer the changes and chances of this mortal life to "*omnes viae et vitae hujus varietates*"[1]—as you see, I am quoting from Medd and Bright [*sic*], not from the *Itinerarium*,[2] which I haven't yet looked up. I should like to come to your Masses; I wish it were possible. Do you say *any* prayers aloud in Latin? I suppose not. We don't at Grosvenor either. I expect it is better not; people wouldn't understand. But I like my Bright and Medd; I have one which my mother used as a girl, given her by her "*frater amantissimus*," a priest who nearly at the end of his life joined the R.C. church and was at last content. A strange man.[3] He made my mother learn Greek as a child (he was 14 years older) because he said she would have to talk it in heaven, it being the language of that country.

I like Karl Adam very much. He conveys a vivid impression of the faith those early Christians had been apprehended of. I have been reading lately part of that volume in which M. R. James collected the apocryphal N[ew] T[estament] writings; it makes one feel the wisdom of the selectors of the canonical writings. Nothing in the apocryphal ones can compare; nothing in them gives an account of Christianity which could have inspired the epistle-writers or the first missionaries with the faith they had. And much is silly. But I've not read all the book yet. I think *The Vision of God* (Dr. Kirk's book) has something on them; I must look it up. Another book I am reading is Evelyn Underhill's *Life of the Spirit*. One chapter in particular, "Psychology and the Spirit," is really excellent. At her best, she can be v.g. She is, of course, deeply soaked in Boehme, and in Law's *Liberal and Mystical Writings*, and has a very good intellect. She is never merely emotional. The emotional approach to religion can be so *vulgar*, if uncurbed by intelligence and

[1] "All the changes of this journey and this life."

[2] A brief office now included in the Breviary and prescribed for recitation by clerics about to set out on a journey.

[3] Rev. J. W. E. Conybeare.

education. I don't think the R.C. approach of simple people, through images, etc., that you refer to, is vulgar, it's only simple; but I turned on the wireless [recently] . . . and what should blare out of it but a Salvation Army service—really dreadful in its vulgar familiarity and sensationalism and irreverence (or so it sounded, but of course they never meant this). I don't think the BBC should put on such services; they must put off many listeners from Christianity, and it isn't fair. Shocking to relate, the *accent* of the conductor of this primitive orgy of sentiment wasn't much worse than that of the Vicar of . . . , the Rev. . . . , who broadcast a service . . . from his church, and preached on the Oxford Movement. I *don't* think . . . [he] should talk of Universitee, Pusee, trewth, naow. I am surprised that they don't learn to talk standard English at their theological colleges—but I don't know what Mr. . . .'s upbringing was. Well, perhaps the apostles talked uneducated Aramaic and were scorned by the Pharisees and scribes, and perhaps S. Paul regretted S. Peter's fisherman accent—no, he certainly didn't, he probably thought it just right for the people they had to convince. Anyhow, I am quite sure that uneducated Aramaic wasn't so ugly as uneducated English often is. Not always, of course; many country dialects are delightful; and probably it would sound good if Mr. . . . addressed us in West Country, or Norfolk, or Northumbrian; but his accent did sound particularly debased and wretched. Nor was there much good in what he said.

I'm sure you are wise not to begin corresponding with Norman Nicholson. Every fresh correspondence is a burden, and one simply hasn't the time. I feel rather glad that you too have many people you " very culpably don't write to "; I have so many myself. But how glad I am that you sometimes write to a doctor of letters; none among your Johnsons, Powyses, Upchers, or other of Johnny's descendants, or the nephews and nieces in Africa, or the people who can't pronounce Cowper, could value it more. I feel it is so endlessly good of you. Having pulled the doctor into the church, you might well have then left her to her own devices; but no. It must take far too much of your time; you won't ever feel, will you, that I am expecting to hear, because when I don't I shall always know you are too busy, and shan't be in the least surprised, still less hurt.

Now I await *two* parcels; the Ovid, posted on the 16th, and the other, containing 3 tiny books, and chapel photographs in a showy and pretentious case, which I shall love to have, and be very proud of. I'm glad it is more showy than yours. The first parcel might, I suppose, arrive any time now. As I shall be here—or at furthest in the Isle of Wight for a few days in mid-August—I shall get it directly it comes. I am beginning to despair of Fr. Pedersen, who has perhaps been too impossibly occupied all the time, and too much all about the place, to approach me. Fr. Wilkins (kind man) said he would be sure to remind him of me when he was in London, so no doubt he will, or has. I shan't bother him unless he writes or telephones, as I know he will if he has time.

It is time I went to bed.

30*th*. This done, I got up in due course and repaired to the last Mass for the present at my Chapel. Rather sad; I shall miss it. Then I went on to my swimming bath, and slid down the shoot —lovely. And now I must settle down to my Ruins, at which I am resolved to be extremely industrious this next month. But to-morrow evening I am seeing *The Gondoliers* at the Savoy; nearly the nicest of the G. and S., I think, don't you? Though I always think *Pinafore* the best of all. So goodbye for now, with my love and thanks.

Yours affectionately,

R. M.

August

20, *Hinde House, Hinde St., W.*1
3*rd August,* 1951 †

Dear Father,

Your air paper posted 30th July came this morning; thank you *so* much for it. I had been wanting to write again anyhow, (I wrote last on 30th, and before that on 23rd; both sea), to tell you that Fr. Pedersen has materialised! He rang up the other day from St. Edward's House, and I asked him to come to lunch at my club, as he had to leave London again next day. He was so nice, really delightful, and we had a most pleasant talk, largely, I needn't say, about you. I did enjoy hearing about you and your doings. He said, inter alia, that you were the most popular confessor there, which didn't surprise me at all. He also said that you were so much better in health than a few years ago; I hope this is true. He admired your Latinity, as he should, and is obviously devoted to you. He himself has been having very much of a busman's holiday in England, sent about everywhere on missions, retreats, etc. He said he actually rang me some time back when he was in London, but I was out. He is now (I think) gone to Norfolk, your family country, and will see your brother[1] at Norwich. Then he goes to Ireland, I think he said. (Or perhaps that is later.) Anyhow he will be in London again soon, and we made a date for 28th August (when I shall be back from my week in the Isle of Wight). He asked me to dine with him and go to a play, if I can find one worth while—if I can't, a cinema, but he wants a play. He has left it to me to choose one and get the seats. That will be very nice. I conducted him (drove him in my car) to St. Thomas's, Regent St., where he wanted to get a ticket for Christopher Fry's play that they are doing there just now, *A Sleep of Prisoners.* I think he

[1] Rev. Wilfred Cowper Johnson.

thought of getting the people who are responsible for it, and who are taking it to America soon, to give some performances of it at S. John's, Boston. He is such a nice *zestful* person. I like his expression " Good enough! "

Your letter is full of *salus* and *veritas*. What a lot of good those thoughts, and those verses and texts, might have done to the *Dangerous Ages* people in their various needs. I think none of them had religion, except Grandmama, who was an old-fashioned Broad Church Evangelical. Neville could have had, if she had been turned to it; perhaps her mother too, who would have found in it the help that the psycho-analyst didn't permanently give. Had I been writing the book now, not then, I think I should have brought in something of this—or anyhow, if not, implied the lack they had.

I am reading just now what I think a very good book indeed, Evelyn Underhill's *The Life of the Spirit and the Life of To-day*. If you can come by it, I wish you would read it and tell me what you think of it. Excellent sections on " History and the Life of the Spirit," " Psychology and . . ." " Education," " Life of the Spirit in the individual," etc. Her point of view is particularly sympathetic to me, and I would like to know what you thought of it. If I can find another copy somewhere, in the bookshops new or 2nd hand, I would send it you. I *think* you would like it, and be interested in it.

Oh I forgot to say, the Teubner Ovid has come; thank you *so* much, I am delighted with it. I am looking forward much to the other " odds and ends "; the newspaper cuttings have come, and I read with interest Cecil Day Lewis on *A Year of Grace*, Alan Pryce-Jones on the future of fiction (I'm glad he doesn't think it over and like to die, as some people do), and other articles. Did you say " *tiresome* "? Goodness! You know how I love to get *all* you send me. For their own sakes, because I always like them, and because you have sent them, which, you know, adds so much to their value; I mean, the fact that you thought I might like them, and took the trouble to do them up and send them, and have used and liked them yourself (particularly this is so with the Greek Testament and the Latin, and all the religious books—but also with the classics). It makes a red letter day for me when I see anything in your handwriting on the mat, whether parcel or letter.

I miss Grosvenor Chapel sadly. I have been to two Masses since it closed, and didn't benefit by either really. They seemed unreal, and kind of *tatty*. At the Annunciation (Bryanston St.) . . . the celebrant . . . didn't say most of the prayers aloud, usually only " World without end " at the end of each, so I didn't know what they had been. He was a bearded monk. Another Mass I went to somewhere else was most peculiar, I thought. I find I grow more Prayer-book minded, C. of E., every day, under these influences. So now I say my prayers by myself in my Chapel, which is fortunately kept open, either on my way to or from my early bathe, and feel much more at home. The altar book used at Grosvenor is compiled by a member of the S.S.J.E., some years ago. It is very good, and I wish I had a small copy of it, but they don't exist. It has a beautiful variety of what I believe are called " propers " for each day, which I like much, so you see [I] am not wholly P.B. minded. I'm not sure it isn't really rather a good and profitable thing, for a change, to find silence in church and try to find God for oneself for a few minutes. In ordinary life, I don't usually get those minutes, everything is such a rush. Of course I say prayers, but not alone in church, and in the Reserved Sacrament chapel. I think it is a good training in attention, isn't it. My attention is apt to be very wandering and fitful. So I dare say being thrown on one's own resources is all for the best, though I shouldn't want it for too long. What a good word *fluctuationem* is for what God will deliver us from; much better than " fall." I need such deliverance badly. When you quote bits of psalms I look at them again, and they grow in meaning and vividness. I shall stop this letter and catch the post with it. Or, as I do want you to know about Fr. Pedersen *soon*, shall I air mail it? Yes, I think I will, for once.

With my love,

R. M.

Dear Father,

Thank you immensely for all kinds of things—your air letter posted 6th Aug., which came 3 days ago, and the lovely packet of books (so beautifully done up, as usual—your packages always fill me with shame and inferiority!). The very interesting and charming little Horace calendar and anthology pleases me much; it is interesting to see which things of his appealed to various writers of various periods and nations; and the calendar opens a fresh set of associations for each day—I like to be reminded of the anniversaries of the Roman conquest of Britain, the death of Augustus, the eruption of Vesuvius in 79, the death of Mark Antony, etc. (all this month), as well as of the Transfiguration, the Assumption, and St. Radegunde; it enlarges one's view. I would much rather commemorate at Mass the Roman conquest and the births of Cicero and Erasmus and the Feast of Lupercalia (15th Feb.) than some of these rather obscure, not to say potty, minor saints who are well thought of at St. Thomas's and the Annunciation and keep intruding themselves into the services there. Then, the Latin hymns—what a *very* nice book to have. I know few of them, and here are riches to study. Some, of course, are in English in our hymn-books; some I think of making, at my leisure (if any ever) translations of. Many are very fine and beautiful. Thank you too for the little Catullus; the translations are quite racy, and do catch the humour of the Latin very well. And the little wallet, so neat, so useful, containing the photographs of the Monastery chapel, very attractive, and the Holbein Erasmus. I'm glad you are an Erasmus devotee. I am too. If only he and Colet and More had had their way with the church in England, and it had developed in freedom and scholarly breadth and light, without the rude intrusion of the Reformation! Where would it be to-day? If no Reformation, then, I suppose no Counter-Ref., and none of those exaggerated excesses of fanatical piety; just a development into greater sanity, reason and light and spirituality and learning.

Would the Vatican have supported such a rational development, which would certainly have included and accepted all the new learning as it came along—Copernicus and all—or would it still have stuck its head in the sand and hunted down heretics and burnt them as it had through the Middle Ages? And would it be as reactionary and bigoted as it is to-day? We can't know. But whether or not, the Anglican branch of it would have developed more mellowly than it did, and with less conflict. Though I suppose there must always have been the Puritan element fighting against the Catholic. These questions of " If . . ." are intensely interesting, aren't they?

No thank you, my char isn't going to get any of those books; however much they might enlarge her mind. I want them all myself.

Your letter is full of interesting things. I'm glad Fr. Pedersen liked our lunch together; I did too, immensely. We are to meet again on 28th, for which night I have, at his request, got seats for a play, which I was to select. I chose *Waters of the Moon*, said to be v.g. and with a brilliant cast, including Edith Evans and Sybil Thorndike, so I hope we shall enjoy it. I wanted to find something Fr. P. would like; though, as to that, I fancy he would be prepared to enjoy anything, he seems full of zest. I wonder how he enjoyed *A Sleep of Prisoners*, the Christopher Fry play at St. Thomas's that he was going to. I must ask him. He is now at Oxford. . . .

By the way, the kind man has sent me such a very good book—the *Oxford American P[rayer] B[ook] Commentary*; most interesting. I haven't read much of it yet, but it is packed with information about the sources of prayers, dates of their adoption into the various P.B.s, etc.—just what I always like to know (as you know). It is good of him. We got talking about the American P.B., and this arose out of it.

I expect you are right about the swimming jeep as transport; anyhow, I see no chance of getting such a trip at present. Though, as to my occupation as *auctor historiarum commenticiarum*,[1] such an experience would help me in that, and might produce a good

[1] " Author of fictitious histories."

story about it, without those false touches that betray the romancer, and in which they said that Pythias indulged in his travel tales of the Outer Ocean and Ultima Thule, such as jelly in the sea, ice, slush, etc. (All quite true, in his case.) Still, I shall visit the I. of Wight in a steam packet this week, my car (strictly monobious) in the hold. I go on Friday 17th till 24th, with my sister,[1] who is spending a fortnight of her holiday there. If the weather is tolerable, it will be nice. I like the Island, with its air of Victorian gentility, its conservatory houses at Ryde (where I shall be), its beaches and bays on the north side, its lovely interior, full of history. I must take my book with me and my typewriter and do a little work in the evenings.

I am interested in your quotation from Erasmus about Colet and his possible reasons for infrequent Masses. I suppose it is true that different practices about it suit different people; and also the same person at different times. At present I am not doing very well with it. I went this morning (Sunday) to St. Thomas's, for the rather ignoble reason that it was at 9, but wished I hadn't, and shan't go again I think. I don't follow the service really, and missed the moment to go up to the altar; there was only one other person, and I wasn't noticing him, and I am used to the priest turning round and saying clearly " Behold the Lamb of God," then one knows, but at St. T. they do nothing of the sort, and perhaps don't really mean people to communicate. And they have too many Hail Marys and other prayers to the B.V.M., and I'm not really very Mariolatrous. The church I like best, after Grosvenor, is All Saints, where the service is very beautiful and dignified, and much more P.B., tho' the chairs are not adequately anchored, and slide about. But I shall go to it in future till my chapel re-opens.

About *Mary Lavelle* again—I suppose it is difficult for a novelist not to be, so to speak, overset by love, the strongest emotion that most people ever feel in their lives. So they are apt to lose sight of the other considerations that war against it; as in actual life we lose sight of these. To them it seems that everything must take a back place beside it, when it bursts on them in its

[1] Jean Macaulay.

171

full strength; and they visualise a future in which it will always be the strongest thing. For, of course, it does last a long time sometimes, even a wrong love; and its very strength blinds those who feel it to its wrongness, often, and might do so for many years. Everything else pales in its light, and it seems its own justification. Of course novelists should get outside this and look at it with detachment, in its right perspective against the standards of right and wrong that are really the ultimate thing and the eternal thing. But the Marys and the Juanitos don't do this in the first rapture of their love, and the creator of them and their situation throws him or herself into their feelings and writes of them as from the inside, instead of as the philosopher assessing from other standards their predicament. If she followed them down the years, she would presumably follow their changing feelings (so far as they did change)—only they don't always. And, as someone says somewhere, each wrong act brings with it its own anaesthetic, dulling the conscience and blinding it against further light, and sometimes for years. I am not defending Kate O'Brien . . . I am only trying to explain the sort of way such situations may work on the minds of those who imagine and describe them in novels. It is, I think, partly a lack of objectiveness. I never myself, I think, represented such things in a triumphantly favourable light in a novel . . . and this, I suppose, was how Mary Lavelle, and Juanito, and perhaps Kate O'Brien, saw it. Human passions against eternal laws—that is the everlasting conflict. And human passions use every device to get the best of it, and set themselves above the laws. All very tragic and pitiful; but writers about it should be on the right side—if they can. You know, I sometimes wonder why, knowing what you do about me, you care to know me at all. But I have long since accepted that, with gratitude. I suppose 45 years of going about in long clothing teaches tolerance and understanding, as well as the other things, such as handing on the word of God.

I have been looking again at the *American P.B. Commentary*, which is full of interesting information. I read that the collect for 11th Sunday after Trin[ity] was a Gelasian collect that ran " that we, running to thy promises, may be made partakers of thy heavenly treasure," and was altered by the 1662 revisers to " that we, running the way of thy commandments, may obtain thy [gracious] promises." I like " running to thy promises." I wonder how it goes in the original Latin. There is a similar change in Trin. 13. I hadn't realised how extensively the 1662 revisers revised the words of the 1549 P.B. Often, I think, improving them; sometimes the opposite. I see it says " the popular English name for Epiphany is Twelfth Day "; but actually of course it is never this, always Twelfth Night, surely.[1] In Trin. 4 " *finally* " was added to the Latin " that we lose not the things eternal." That seems a pity, as this commentary says; the eternal things are *now*. You see how interesting this book is.

I think I shall airmail this, and write by sea later from the Island. I wanted to tell you that your books arrived safely and give satisfaction, without delay. But I really will seamail the next. (Where are my good epistolary resolutions going to? I keep getting seduced by this so expeditious air.) With love.

Yours affectionately,

R. M.

20, *Hinde House, Hinde St., W.*1
15th August [1951]

Dear Father,

I want to write soon after posting my last air letter, as this will be sea, and I don't want it to lag *too* far behind. That is the worst of mixing the two. Also I want to answer your air paper posted 11th, which arrived yesterday. I am glad you put the case for these A[nglo-]C[atholic] Irregulars; I do see their point of view, tho' I think they make a mistake. They should, I think, be *glad* to differ from R.C. usage, which is UNREFORMED, backward, less enlightened, less civilised, more primitive. But

---

[1] Footnote by R. M.: " No, I am wrong. I see the O[xford] D[ictionary] does give 'Twelfth Day.' But it seems less common."

of course they are afraid of the C. of E. being despised and thought of as of no account, so abandon what should be its very strength. And how interesting if they were ever cured by a R.C. liturgical movement towards P[rayer] Bookery! I am interested in your interpolation with regard to this movement towards greater intelligibility (surely this word looks all wrong —what have I done with it?)—"very unwise, I think!" Do you mean it might set the congregation thinking and therefore criticizing? By the way, looking through Fr. Andrew's letters at Mowbrays—what excellent letters they are—I saw that he told someone (I think a priest) that he was glad All Saints used the P.B. mass, and wished all Catholic priests would do the same. So he agreed with us. But of course it is as you say—the treasure is the same (only slightly more difficult of access) and we must try and be lively stones, entering into what we can of it and tolerating what seems irrelevant, and helping to build up the spirit of the whole. And what seems affected and unnatural to old P[rayer] B[ook] fogies like me isn't really, of course, to those who use it: but I *should* like it if they said more of the prayers aloud. Never mind: I like my solitary praying in my Chapel. What a number of prayers I owe to your suggestions; some in your Scrap Book, others that you have pointed out, or copied out, for me. I like All Saints very much, and can go there with satisfaction (tho' in the wrong direction). I went there this morning at 9. I can't really take the Assumption; but it doesn't matter to the service. (*Do* we accept it in our church? I can't remember.) It seems to me entirely unnecessary.

Such a good sermon on the radio the other Sunday from George MacLeod, the minister (Presbyterian, but rather a lone hand) of the community of Iona. He called it "The Moving God," and it was about the gradual enlightenment down the ages of the spirit of man, from our animal days up—fresh convictions about right and wrong all the time; he referred to Drake setting out in his ship the *Jesus* to seize black slaves off the coasts of New Guinea, applauded by the whole Christian world; to the massacre of Huguenots approved by all R. Catholics, headed by the Pope, to the persecutions and tortures of heretics, to the ghastly public executions to which every one flocked with joy, to the savage treatment of lunatics and beggars and prisoners, to slavery, condoned by all until so late, and the gradual convictions dawning that these things were wrong. The thesis being that the spirit of God never lets man alone, but is for ever trying to pull him upward and on and out of his primitive nature. I found it inspiring: so much more hopeful than the theory that we were better once than we are now. Who first intruded the Fall into Christianity? Certainly not our Lord. And I can't find it in St. Paul. I must look this up in some theological encyclopaedia; it is ignorant of me not to know.

My ruins lie heavy on me. I have just done Babylon, and now have got to Mycenae. I love the fantastic ruin-pictures painted by the Jewish prophets—Babylon a desolation, full of owls, dancing satyrs in the pleasant palaces, bitterns crying in the lintels, a hissing of serpents, dragons all about. A gross overstatement, of course, like Tyre; but they liked to see it so, and piled it on. As to Mycenae, what a family life was led there, by Agamemnon, Atreus, and all the princes in succession! No wonder it inspired D'Annunzio with an idea for a novel about murder and incest. I must get on with my writing in the I. of Wight; but can't take many of the requisite books. However, I shan't have time there for much work. When I come back my Chapel will very soon be functioning again. I feel better with a daily Mass; it sees one through the day, ties things together, gives a meaning and horizons.

16th. No time to finish this letter, I have to go and get the car ready for to-morrow, and a hundred other jobs attendant on even a week of being away, and should like to post this before I go.

My love always. I shall write from the Island.

R. M.

Dear Father,

Being on this charming island, I take pen in hand (not having the typewriter out with me in this woody creek where we have just devoured a picnic lunch and I have bathed), to write to you a holiday line, in continuation of my short sea letter of the 15th. It is very nice here, and the weather good, though I could do with more hot sun, also with a sea that is more often *at hand*, instead of ½ the time being ½ mile away across wet and shingly and shelly and seaweedy sands, and when you reach it is so shallow that you may wade for miles and not get more than waist-deep in it. But of course normally I bathe only when it is high, and that is very nice: our hotel has steps that go straight down to it beyond a garden gate. My sister (who is a nurse, did I tell you?) and I have endless discussions on this and on that—politics, church, books, the future of the human race. She is a voracious reader, but gets little time for it. She is a *district* nurse, and how they do work them! She does much too much, of course, but never gives up. We (and a friend of hers[1]) drive round the island in my car, and see good places. Yesterday we went to Quarr Abbey (the monks were having Vespers, and we looked into the church for it)—a great red-brick building, built late 19th century, occupied by French monks in flight from France in 1901, but now has other nationalities.[2] But the interesting thing there, of course, is the ruins of the ancient, demolished Cistercian Abbey, which stand in fragments about the fields, some built into a farm-house, most separate; fragments of the choir, broken arches with trees growing through the stones, the refectory turned into a barn, here and there a window (blocked or open), in a wall, and the great wall running fitfully round the whole enclosure, which must have been enormous.

[1] Nancy Willetts.

[2] The monks of St. Mary's Abbey, Quarr, are an offshoot of the Benedictine community of Solesmes (Sarthe), founded in 1827. Owing to the persecution of the religious orders in France, the monks were forced to seek refuge abroad.

And woods all round it, and, from the end of the field, a wedge of the blue bay. Really a haunting and haunted place, and quite, of course, up my present street.

25th Aug. I never finished this, but put it away to finish when I had a moment of leisure, and now (last night) have come home (lovely voyage across the Solent) and what should I find but a letter from you, posted 19th, and the most *exciting* packets. It takes me back to *last* August, when I also came home (from Italy) at the end of the month, and found a letter from you, and how pleased I was, and how right I was to be pleased! And now I am still pleased, and even more than then. I have just looked up that letter. I see it refers (which I had forgotten) to the changes the 1662 revisers made in the collects—I suppose they are in *most* cases a pity—and anyhow should not get away from the Latin. Yes: " *dirigere et sanctificare* " is in the *Manuale*; I have just found it. What a good set of prayers that book has, for so many occasions. I often use them. And now I have looked up " *Homiliae et Orationes* "[1] in the Breviary—and read the " *ad tua promissa currentes* "[2] collect—and put a marker in that section, so that I shan't lose it again. I must say the Breviary *is* a little like a jungle, till one is really used to tracking one's path about it. So I blaze the trails to what I want.

All these lovely books! Unpacking your parcels is like opening those Chinese toys, one thing inside another—paper, stout envelope, soft packing, more paper (green, with elastic bands round it) and finally the book, always a lovely surprise. This time I have (1) a fine *green* wallet (the first was *red*), and in it a very choice blank note book, and 2 dear little American Bible Society paper booklets, the Appian Way decorating the Epistles, the River Jordan Proverbs—how very nice and compendious and pretty! (2) Statius (the *Achilleis*) (3) Rutilius Namatianus, with bits of Hadrian, Florus, and others—what a very attractive selection. I took *Desert Fathers* out of the shelf (H[elen] W[addell]

---

[1] " Homilies and Prayers."
[2] " Running the way of thy commandments "; from the Collect for 11th Sunday after Trinity.

gave me all her books in '41, after I had been bombed) and read that introduction again with interest, and her account of Rutilius N. How good she is (H.W., I mean). One does sympathise with Rutilius's view (and Lecky's) about the Desert Fathers; it is too easy to lose sight of the other side of the case (the Fathers' side, I mean). I don't know Statius's *Achilleis*, only the *Sylvae*, which has lovely things in it; probably actually more what he could do well than a long heroic poem. I like to have Florus's skit on Hadrian—" *ego nolo Caesar esse,*

ambulare per Britannos,"[1] etc., and

Hadrian's repartee—" *ego nolo Florus esse,*

ambulare per tabernas "[2] . . .

(4) the Martial (what an excellent collection of Roman poets I am building up, from your library) and (5) that extremely nice 2-vol. Tacitus, v. good to have. Thank you immensely for *all* these; it is good of you indeed, and I hope you can really spare them.

Your letter, as usual, v. interesting to me (and forgive my continuing mine as I began it, with a pen; it seemed easier). An interesting point about *have*. I see in Poole's *Parnassus*,[3] which includes lists of rhyming words (1657 is the date) that he puts *have* in a list of rhymes with *brave, cave, grave,* etc., so obviously it did rhyme then. I think the explanation of its having developed the short a (but *when?* I don't know) is that it was a quickly-uttered, often auxiliary, verb, apt to be lightly slurred over, and would easily become " *hev* " (as it is in much dialect speech), and then *have*. None of the other *ave* words are of this kind; and the tendency is always to shorten the sound of those light words. As " master " (maister) became " mister " when a *title*, but remained maister or master when not. This seems to me a likely development of have, don't you agree? What I would like to know is when it happened; unfortunately Johnson's Dict[ionary] doesn't give pronunciations (I think). (Or does it? I will look it up: mine, a 1st edition, was burnt.) One would like to know

---

[1] " I have no wish to be Cæsar and to roam through Britain."

[2] " I have no wish to be Florus and to be a pub-crawler."

[3] Joshua Poole, *The English Parnassus, or a Helpe to English Poesie* (1657).

what is the latest example in poetry of the have-grave rhyme; I must look out for it. I will look out too for Priscilla Sellon.[1]

Yes, that is the right Irvine: he was in the Potteries before S. Thomas's. A clever young prophet; Canon Hood knew him at Oxford and said he was so, and one can see he is. Very good company, too. . . . He introduced me to his mother when she was up here; "like you, she doesn't care much for Mariology," he said. A nice, cheerful lady: she comes up to see her son, "just to see how far he has now got," she told me. *Too* far, if you ask me. But I like him v. much. Fr. Ross too (tho' I've only once talked to him) . . . There is no company that interests me more (just now) than that of the intelligent clergy; and I like to discuss things with them when we meet, and they are interested, I think, to do this, both with one another and with the laity such as me.

Do you know *The Broadcast Psalter*, the revised versions of many of the Psalms that they use in broadcast services? I think many of the revisions are good. "O how *lovely* are thy dwellings," e.g.; and they make sense of what Coverdale rather left sometimes in a mess. They broadcast a morning service (10.15-10.30) daily, and I often make a pause in my work and hear it. The BBC does a good job for religion, on the whole; with scrupulous impartiality they try to allot equal time to all the Christian sects—but not (to the disappointment of Unitarians) to the non-Xian ones. For my part, I would very much rather have a Unitarian service than a Salvation Army one; it is a civilised kind of service, and I don't see why not.

On Tuesday evening Fr. Pedersen and I have our jamboree. I am interested in what you tell me of him; I must draw him out about his English experiences. He struck me as enjoying it all immensely. I shall be amused to note his reactions to the play; I expect he will be enthusiastic, as about most things.

I don't know if G[raham] G[reene's] *The End of the Affair* is a new novel, now just out in America and soon to appear here,

---

[1] Presumably the biography *Priscilla Lydia Sellon* by T. J. Williams (1950).

or if it is one we know here, under a new name. But I expect the former, and I shall like to read it when it is published here. He and Evelyn Waugh always praise each other of course. I enclose a column of an article on "The Temper of Modern Fiction" (in all countries) in this week's *Times Lit. Sup.*, that refers to those R.C. novelists.

On Sunday my Chapel functions again: I shall be very glad. I am wondering how much of the daily mass habit I shall be able to keep up through the winter, or how far coughs and colds and flue and weather will interfere. I don't want to be stupid and rash about it. On the other hand, I do miss it when I don't go. I must see. But anyhow there is a long time before the winter. Our ancestors were wise to have private chapels and chaplains, tho' the chaplain was often a nuisance. This [is] a shockingly long and ill-writ letter; forgive it. My love always, and my most grateful thanks.

R. M.

PS. Just found the little map diary, which had slipped down among the wrappers![1]

20, Hinde House, Hinde St., W.1
29th August, 1951

Dear Father,

I must write at once to thank you for sending me, by Fr. Pedersen, those two delightful books—Fr. Benson's and Fr. Andrew. It *was* good of you. I feel I should have got them for myself, and it is a shame, but I love to have them from you. I have dipped into Fr. Andrew in Mowbrays, and can now read him at leisure. A wonderful person he must have been. I haven't yet begun Fr. Benson, but shall to-night in bed. If I went to retreats, it would be a good book to take there; but I haven't this in mind at present. What a pity I lost those notes I took long ago of good retreat addresses!

[1] Note by R. M. on back of envelope.

Fr. Pedersen was so nice. We went to *Waters of the Moon*—Edith Evans, Sybil Thorndike, etc.—very amusing, and we both enjoyed it. Afterwards I took him back-stage for a word with Edith Evans, her face covered in grease. She really is a superb actress, and this was just the part for her. Then Fr. P. and I went to Soho and had a bite of supper and conversation. He does seem to have a good time here—rather a busman's holiday so far, full of retreats, missions and what not; but is now off to Italy for a few weeks' real holiday, which is very spirited of him, all alone; he seems to have planned to see every place—Rome, Florence, Venice, Milan, Siena, and bathe at Viareggio. He is great fun, isn't he. Just going to have his 40th birthday, he told me. He seems (I suppose all the Society is) quite in agreement with us about Anglicanism, the P[rayer] B[ook], etc., and doesn't care for excesses. I liked very much to talk with him, and hear about Boston, the Monastery, and you. He says you have been pretty well lately; I hope he is right. He also brought me a kind note from Fr. Wilkins, thanking me for some service I had done to a writing friend of his, and saying what an excellent retreat Fr. Pedersen had given them at Oxford.

Now I am busy writing on the ruins of Corinth and what they all said about them in the next century. They must have been the show ruins of the time, until J. Caesar built them up. Cicero deplored them; and his friend Servius Sulpicius Rufus, about whom you once wrote to me, used them (and others) as a text for preaching patience to Cicero about the death of his daughter. And Antipater of Sidon wrote a lovely lament, soon after the destruction of B.C. 146, of which F. L. Lucas, of King's, has lately published a good verse translation, beginning,

" Where are the towers that crowned thee,
    the wealth that filled thy portals,
  Thy beauty, Dorian Corinth,
    whereon men stood to gaze? . . ."[1]

Polybius's eye-witness description of the Roman Soldiers playing dice among the ruins, using the fallen pictures as tables,

---

[1] From "The Sea-birds crying above the Ruins of Corinth" in *Greek Poetry for Everyman; selected and translated by F. L. Lucas* (1951).

is very vivid and dreadful; though less dreadful than his account of the destruction of Carthage.

At this point the gay and Rev. Gerard Irvine rang me up, informing me that to-morrow is the day of my name-saint, St. Rose of Lima,[1] and suggesting that, as my chapel is still shut (opens 1st. Sept.) I should come to Mass at St. Thomas's. I might go, I suppose, though it rather fidgets me, but it is a friendly invitation.

Fr. Irvine read me an account of the achievements of my patroness, a poor little self-torturing Peruvian product of the Counter-Reformation, who slept on potsherds, wore a crown of roses with the thorns turned inwards, a girdle with nails, a hair shirt, etc., etc.; all the accompaniments of decadent sanctity. She wouldn't approve of my habit of bathing after mass; a firm hydrophobe, this was a practice in which she would have hated to indulge. Why did the Church canonise these poor little neurotics? On the other hand to-morrow is also the day of St. Pammachius,[2] a much higher type, who translated Origen and was a friend of Jerome's, and renounced his wealth to the poor, so I can think of him at Mass instead.

This is the last week of no-Grosvenor (it functioned on Sunday, but not yet on weekdays). I shall be glad to have it back. Here is a cutting about the Anglican Society, which seems a good Society. If one talks to R.C.s (intellectual ones) about the vagaries of their Church (very politely, of course), they say " the Church can carry all these things; it's big enough." Well, but why should it have to carry so much nonsense? Answer, because past and more credulous ages believed a lot we don't, and the Church (the Roman Church) can't go back on its past, except in private. Surely a fatal flaw in a moving, driving, upward-growing religion such as Christianity should be. The enlarging work of the Holy Spirit—they don't seem really to believe in this, but only in looking back at tradition. How dispiriting it must be. More and more I rejoice to be an Anglican. Oh dear, am I becoming like the Pharisee, who

[1] St. Rose of Lima (1586-1617) was the first canonized saint of America.
[2] A Roman Christian (c. 340-410).

thanked God he was one? But then it's the *Church* I am glad of, heaven knows not myself, except for my good fortune and good guidance.

I want to get this off, so must stop. My love and *so* many thanks for those valuable books—also for sending me nice Fr. Pedersen. As you know, he is tremendously attached to you, and will consent with pleasure to these embassies you send him on (book-buying and carrying) for your sake.

Yours always affectionately,

R. M.

September

20, Hinde House, Hinde St., W.1
3rd September, 1951

Dear Father,

Your air paper posted 29th Aug. came to-day, just when I was going to write and thank you for the lovely book packet that came two days before—I am particularly pleased to have the Latin *Imitation*; it would have been good for my Latin to have it when I was 13. Then, the very nice little Bible booklets—Job, Ecclesiasticus, Acts, Romans, Revelation (pretty picture of Patmos) and Corinthians (I have just finished my section on the ruins of Corinth and the effect they have had on people). And the Latin Literature primer—really admirably useful and compendious, and well written too. Thank you very very much, *Pater large et liberalis*; how good you are! I really do love to have these little books. As for the two larger ones sent by Fr. Pedersen, I have read quite a lot of Fr. Benson, and am very much interested. I like too Fr. Cary's introduction. More and more I marvel that any one should be found to enter into such an exacting life, and carry it through to the end; it seems one of those impossible careers, that any one would shrink from in prospect and fail under in practice; and yet it isn't so. Perhaps (as Fr. Cary suggests) the rule has been a little modified since then; I wonder how the Father Founder would have looked on the freedom and enjoyment of Fr. Pedersen's time in Europe; and, indeed, Fr. Waggett's social life in London and Cambridge, which did such immense good to people he met. And dear Fr. Cary I remember, years ago, going off for a holiday in Italy at Christmas time with two cousins of mine who were devoted to him; and how much they all enjoyed it! . . . But, as I say, the Rule must have been enlarged a little since the first, and I suppose became much less strict about such things as talking to " externs," looking at Nature, etc. But what a standard it holds up to poor selfish human nature! It makes one feel very much of a *homunculus* (or *muliercula*, as the case may be). Fr. Andrew I am enjoying very much; much more within one's grasp, of course, spiritually; I don't mean one can grasp it, because it is much too Christian and fine for that; but one could *try* after it. I should like to have known him. I wonder if you did. He would take a v.g. retreat, wouldn't he. As to a retreat by Fr. Benson, one would be terrified by the demands one would feel he was (even if unspoken) making on one's life. Did I tell you how good a retreat Fr. Wilkins said Fr. Pedersen took at Oxford? But what a " chore," as he says, it must have been! All those days; and speaking not to the laity, or even to secular clergy, but to Religious, and his own colleagues; and of course many of them so much older than he is. I expect he was excellent. A most likeable person.

I was pleased by your account of the little English girl (why did she stay on after the war, by the way?) and her catechumen lover. I should like to have seen you getting him ready with the swiftness of St. Philip! Why hadn't he been baptized before, though? I shall think of the wedding on the 14th. I like the way they all come to you to marry them. You ought to baptize their children too. Do you suggest a pre-baptismal general confession, or would that be too startling for him?

My last letter to you (sea) was posted on 29th, I think. But you should perhaps have got, by the time you wrote your last air paper, my sea letter of 16th; I hope it came soon after that.

Then I wrote again from *Vectis*,[1] but didn't finish or post it till my return, when I had got your letter of 21st. I think in my last letter I mentioned that Fr. Gerard Irvine of S. Thomas's had just rung me up inviting me to attend his Mass there on the feast of St. Rose of Lima—he thought my patron saint, but I have discovered a much better St. Rose (of Viterbo) of the 13th century; this prodigy raised her maternal aunt to life at 3 years old, at 7 she was living like a recluse, devoting herself to penances, at 12 she preached to and converted Viterbo, including a sorceress, whom she impressed by standing unscathed in a fire for 3 hours. Much better than anything done by her namesake of the Counter-Reformation. Well, I attended the S. Thomas's Mass, and managed this time to catch the right moment to [go] up to the altar; in front of me was one of those helpful women who know all the answers to unspoken versicles by the priest, and she even rang a little bell at the right moments. When I came out, another woman who had been there accosted me, with some ferocity. The dialogue ran like this:

" Is this a *Roman* church? "
" No, it's Church of England."
" What about the 39 articles? "
" Well, how do you mean what about them? They never say them at early service anywhere, I think."
" And what about all those *images*? "
" Well, churches do have images, don't they."
" Not *Protestant* churches. This is more like a Catholic one."
" Well, the C. of E. is both, I suppose."
" I call it a SCANDAL. Something should be *done* about it."

She departed in dudgeon; but what can she or will she do about it? Inform the National Union of Protestants, perhaps. I'm sure Fr. Irvine and the others would be delighted if they sent a spy along and had a protest in church. . . . Poor old C. of E., with Romans to right of it, Protestants to left of it, volleying and thundering. It does indeed stand to be shot at.

To-morrow I call for and drive Canon Hood to take Mass at

[1] Latin name for the Isle of Wight.

Grosvenor. When he stays in London he has a house near me, so I have undertaken to do this on the occasions when he helps at Grosvenor. I might ask him about the Annunciation, where I believe he also helps sometimes, and discover how far he likes its ways. I don't think Pusey House is very extreme or " fancy," is it; though I am sure much more so than Dr. Pusey ever was or would have thought of. Or Fr. Benson either? My grandfather, W. J. Conybeare, wrote an interesting article in the *Edinburgh Review* (1853) about the " three great parties which divide the C. of E."—Low, High, and Broad. He finds good and bad in all three; but prefers the Broad. He did *not* like the extreme Low Church; he quotes with ridicule such verses for children as " Haste, put your playthings all away, To-morrow is the Sabbath day. . . . Because, you know, you must not play, But holy keep the Sabbath day"; and " We must not laugh on Sunday," etc. The High Church he likes much better, and thinks they have done excellent reforming work in church services and buildings and the lives of the clergy. But he has some acid words on the more advanced section, who " pressed recklessly to the front, and soon left the mass of their troops behind them, and abandoned one by one the traditions of the Anglican divinity from which they started. After they had advanced beyond the High Church camp, they continued for nearly 10 years members of the C. of E., and formed a new party, which took from their writings the name of Tractarian. . . . Presently their leader, renouncing for ever the Anglican allegiance, passed over the Rubicon, and rushed into the heart of the Italian territory. But not all who advanced to that fatal frontier had courage to cross with Caesar; the rabble of his army remained shivering on the brink. . . ." The customs of this extreme party are described; and they seem all customs that are now usual in moderate Anglican churches, and throw a light on what was usually done then in those churches. Bowing to the altar is mentioned, talking of " the holy altar," " the blessed Virgin," having the offertory after the sermon, with little bags on poles, blazing candles on the altar, wreaths of flowers changing their colour with feast or fast, medieval emblems on the altar-cloth, genuflexions without authority of Rubric, credence tables, a novel usage in the reception of the consecrated bread (would this be wafers?) which sometimes caused a disturbance in church. And yet, he says, these very clergy would often omit morning and evening prayer, which the P[rayer] B[ook] orders them to say in church daily. Their main energies they devote, he says, to fighting Puritanism. They attack Bishops. "Greenwood and Penry were hanged by Whitgift, Leighton was whipped and mutilated by Laud, for the use of language against bishops mild in comparison with that which every pamphleteering curate now uses with impunity." My grandfather's hopes for the Church were certainly most with the Broad party, which was the most intellectual then; though he disapproved of extremes there too, and quotes as a scandal a clergyman of 1780, who, at his induction, read the 39 articles, then " addressed his rustic congregation as follows— ' My brethren, I have obeyed the law by what I have just done; and I now beg God's pardon and yours for reading to you so much nonsense.' " But the best Broads, such as Maurice and Arnold, and a number of bishops and writers, were the strongest force for enlightenment and progress in the Church, he thought. The whole essay is interesting, as showing one view held by an able clergyman of the C. of E. a century ago. Well, I am glad those Tractarians won so much of their cause, so that usages then extreme are now generally accepted. When did the *Church Times* begin, I wonder? Not so early as my grandfather's essay, as he enumerates some church papers, but not that. He wouldn't have cared for it! Do you mind these divisions in the Church? I don't think I do, so long as people are polite and tolerant and courteously anxious to make the best of other parties and not set themselves up. (It seems that some very High clergy—anyhow one—used, whenever they passed a dissenting chapel, to make the sign of the cross, as if they saw the evil one at hand. Not at all Christian.) But, apart from intolerance, people are so constituted, by nature and upbringing, that they must want to worship in different ways, as they want to read different books and hear different music; and heaven forbid that one should

187

disapprove seriously of any serious worship, either the Quakers at meeting, or St. Thomas's, Regent St. But one can greatly prefer one's own type, and be grateful to my grandfather's contemporaries who did so much to bring it about and make it accepted. When one thinks of the bad press they had then. . . . [sic]

4th Sept. (Feast of St. Rose of Viterbo). And I never reminded Canon Hood of her while I drove him to Mass! Nor, I fear, gave her a pious thought in church; how forgetful of me. It is a nice sunny warmish day; the Serpentine this morning was divine, with its smooth shimmer under the trees and soft sky, and its satiny ripples as I swam. How lovely September mornings can be! Can Father Benson really have meant that the Religious shouldn't look at nature and like it? I don't think he can.

I am looking at a Bampton Lectures [sic] about the Fall, trying to discover that doctrine's career in the Church, and pre-Church. I suppose it arose out of the theory that God must have created man perfect. But how illogical, surely. If one held that, why not hold that he must still be creating men perfect. It all seems so divorced from reality. Shouldn't there be more discarding and pruning of ancient beliefs, things believable by the Babylonians, Persians, Jews, and early and medieval Christians, but not really to-day? Our Lord doesn't ever imply that man's evil nature and deeds are due to a " fallen " state; man, he implies, must be redeemed from *himself*, not from the sins of Adam. Oh, if only He could come back to these spaces of the moon, just for a while, and clear things up!

On this wish I had better stop, and send my love.

Yours affectionately,

R. M.

Dear Father,

Thank you so much for your air paper posted 1st Sept.
—most interesting to me, with your views about the dubious
wisdom of the R.C. Liturgical Movement. I expect you must
be right, about the *majority* of simple worshippers, though it
might be very stimulating for educated young people; educated,
but not perhaps knowing enough Latin to follow the Mass
easily, and missing a good deal of it. Less and less, it seems,
people do know Latin. And this might be a revelation to them.
Of course a good deal of their missal is translated into English
already. As you say, the translations will lose something, like
so many of our collects. On the other hand, they will gain
comprehensibility. I would much like to go to some Mass
where they are trying it, if ever they do. Mightn't it lead to a
great revival of intelligent interest, and discount one of the
advantages our Church has over the other, for which I should
be sorry? I must try and talk to some R.C. about this. I don't
want us to forfeit any of our advantages!

I said to a young man the other day (a friend of mine, who
is on the National Gallery staff) did he like clergymen? . . . He
said promptly, " No, not much," and added, " except Roman
Catholic ones." I asked why he preferred these. " They're
mostly more intelligent," he replied. I said he didn't know
enough Anglican clergy, and probably had only met the average
country parson, whereas the R.C. priests he came across were
probably Jesuits, such as Fr. D'Arcy and Co., picked for their
clever conversation. He agreed that this might be so. But I find
this is a common view, and it's rather a pity. There seems to be
(I got this from Canon Hood) an Anglo-Catholic Progress
campaign this October, for a week, when priests will travel the
country brisking up the church and its members; I hope it will
have results. I think . . . Canon Hood . . . [is] taking part in it.
Another church event is, apparently, the jubilee of the Anglo-
Catholic Ordinand Fund, when the Bishop of Oxford is to

preach at 11.30 at Mass at All Saints. I might try and go and hear him; having read his *Vision of God*, I know I should be interested; having heard of him from you, too. Now there is the kind of highly intellectual bishop whom these young men ought to meet and talk with; it might change their views. I think I must try and be a go-between, in a slight way, between the clergy I know and the intelligent laity such as that. I was trying to explain last night, after dining with two young men friends (just back from Spain, where *Fabled Shore* had sent them), why I did believe in the Anglican church, and *not* only in the moral principles it embodies. Both are agnostics; but possibly the knowledge that a friend they quite like, and don't regard as half witted, has such views, may be a tiny influence, who knows. One of them shares a house with a R.C. convert friend, of whom he is fond, but he shuts off that side of his friend as one impossible to hold intercourse with. Perhaps he particularly feels like this about the Roman church because he is the son of an Irish squire, who was shot by the rebels in 1921. And he mainly knows the protestant Church of Ireland in which he was reared.

11*th Sept.* Here I went to bed, it having become past midnight, and now it is next day, and lo, on my mat this morning when I returned from Mass was your air paper of the 7th. How *nice*. I'm glad you could make out my written screed begun on the Island. Good to be reminded that we have been corresponding now for a year. How right I was when I said I should always like to hear anything you said! I always have, and still do. Heavens, what results have followed! Not that I don't feel just a little discouraged by your last letter for it makes me feel that you want me to behave as if I were very, very ancient. I am, of course; but I am really strong enough; I can walk for miles, go swimming every morning, even as late in the year as this (it was lovely this morning), and get up early for Mass. Of course if I didn't feel well enough, or had a cough or anything, I shouldn't go out; I am pretty well brought up about such things, and fairly sensible. I hope the time for retiring into Religion-in-the-flat is still far ahead, even in winter, though of course if I am ill I should. Last winter was a bad one; I had flue twice, and it went to the lungs, and I don't say I wasn't ill. But I hope this winter nothing of that kind will happen, and that on Christmas morning you can think of me first at Mass [and] then breaking the ice on the Serpentine! As to a drink of tea first, I solve that question simply by having it, practically always; I wonder if I am wrong. . . . I don't think I have ever thought it wrong, actually, though of course I know it is a church practice not to. And I can imagine how firm Dr. Darwell Stone would have been—no doubt *was*—about it. It makes a great difference to my powers of attention and alertness at the service, as well as physically. As to Religion-in-the-Flat, I know how important this is, whether one goes to church or not, and I am not good at it yet. Very bad at fencing off times; there always seems so much else to do. I see that Fr. Andrew says he values more than anything else his half hour of meditation after mass. I can't get as much as that, either in church before going on to bathe, or after getting home, as it would throw my morning's work too late. I suppose I spend about 10 minutes in church after the service, as a rule. Then the rest of the day is such a bustle; though I do try to get a little time in the evening, before going out to dinner if I am going; sometime between 7 and 9 if I'm not. I say prayers, and some psalms; and what riches to choose from! As I told you, I have a scrap book collected for use; a random collection of prayers in English and Latin, psalms or parts of psalms, and other things; and I try to read a bit of the N.T. appropriate to the general scheme. But it all gets crowded out too often; some days simply forgotten, other days put aside as too difficult, which is a mistake. When I have finished this very exacting book, I shall try and do better. And improve at mental prayer, I hope; I am very weak on this at present; scattered and shallow. I know I ought to practise it, both for its own sake, and in case I did have to stay at home through illness and join in Mass from a distance, though I should be very sorry for this. . . .

Oh yes, we *must* be able to recognise one another in the street. I should you, in a moment. You have my passport photograph, my only quite recent one; but in case this isn't enough for the purpose, I must look up some snap-shots, etc., and see if I have any (among my sister's photographs) to send you; I am afraid [they are] over 10 years old—no, 11 or 12 probably—but better than nothing. Too sad if you met me walking down Memorial Drive and didn't know me! Though, as I say, I should know you. And how lovely it would be to see you in the flesh again.

Yes, of course gender must come in to relationships; don't you think it does even between parents and children, and brothers and sisters? Certainly it does between friends, I don't think years make any difference to that; all they do is to get rid of *sex* in its strictly limited sense. I think it so happens that I have more men friends than women; and I am sure that their masculinity enhances the relationship. "Word after word has to conform"—yes, how right that is.

I have just remembered some photographs of myself taken about 1939, reading in my flat and gardening in my window-box outside it. I wonder if copies of these exist among my sister's bundles of papers; I will look them up, and send them if I come on them. I have some of you that I value much. So expect a little packet some day. Meanwhile, if I am in Memorial Drive, or you in Hinde St. or its environs, I am tall, and (as you say) rather thin, my hair is still brown, and I will be wearing a brown suit with carnation in buttonhole, so look out for me. What a lot there would be to say. Not that we don't get a good deal of it, on most subjects in heaven and earth, said in letters, at which I think we are both pretty good.

I shall think of you on Friday, tying up those children. I like these very young marriages; they can be boy and girl together for so long, which is fine. I do hope it will be very happy for always. As they are both Christians, it won't meet with one of those early and piteous ends that come now to so many marriages happily begun. Anyhow, I hope they'll never *want* this. "Two lovely children"—how nice that sounds. I was thinking when first you told me of them, that girls now have more difficulties to contend with than I and my friends did when young. We, of course, had love affairs, flirtations, even broken-off engagements and such; and difficult it often was; but young men and girls for the last 25 years or so seem, from what they say, to go much further than we did, on quite slight acquaintanceship. I mean, some of them seem to mean by an "affair" nothing short of sleeping together, and this is taken, often, so casually, as lightly as we took a kiss. Two great friends of mine, now aged 38 and 35, and married 11 years, told me that they had quite a long "affair" before deciding to marry; and both had had others before. This is, or was, extremely normal; though never, I assume, among religious young people ... Those I am talking about have no religious practice. It has been the great social change of the past 25 years or so. I suppose in America too. I wonder if you ever get girls who do that coming to confession; but I suppose if they did, it would mean they had turned over a new leaf, or wanted to. I mean, people wouldn't just go on doing it and confessing it as if it was losing their tempers or fibbing, I suppose.

I can't ever care a lot for Mary Webb myself, in spite of Mr. Baldwin. As you say, there is something unreal about her books. I like the descriptions of the country (Worcestershire), but the people are rather bogus.

Re *Fall*—I will soon know *all* about it, from that big book I have got from the Library. I will also read St. Augustine.

Now I must go out. I am reading Frs. Benson and Andrew with *immense* interest. It was good of you to give them me. Really, when I think of all you've done for me . . . [*sic*] Well, my love and thanks.

Always your affectionate
R. M.

Dear Father,

Your air paper of 16th [has] just come, greeting me when I came in from an afternoon grubbing in the B[ritish] M[useum]; thank you so much for it. I had, by the way, a nice picture p.c. from Father Pedersen from Rome, saying Italy was a glorious land, and Florence his favourite city. Mine is Venice—or I think so. I don't see how there could be another like it. Did you see the comment of the Russian ballerina (Stalin prize-winner) who was there the other day? There seemed, she said, to have been recent floods, and the houses still stood in water. Also, there were no vehicles to be seen in the streets, and all was very primitive. No doubt *Pravda* was delighted to print this account of a backward capitalist country. I am glad Fr. Pedersen is enjoying his travels; I expect he gets on very well with the people everywhere.

I am glad your wedding is safely accomplished; it must have been, as Fr. P. would put it, rather a chore, however delightful; all that journeying and bustle and strain.

I am glad you knew Fr. Andrew. He sounds the most delightful person; so ready to adapt himself to all kinds of correspondents, and give them advice of the most sensible kind. Real understanding and imaginative sympathy; and humour too. No wonder he was loved. It is interesting trying to construct, from his answers, the kind of situations his correspondents had written to him of. I don't think I could have sent all those letters from him for publication in a book; some of them seem too private, and, though veiled by anonymity, one would know that some of one's friends and relations would recognise things in them. But people feel differently about such things, of course. Fortunately; or we should have lost a great many valuable letters from spiritual writers in the past—St. Francis de Sales, Père de Caussade, Fénelon, and so many more.

So the election is now upon us, and will make a fuss and splutter for the next month. Rather a bore; but it's time they threw in their hands.[1] I think they'll get in again, and probably with a good-sized majority this time; their propaganda will be that the Tories will whittle away at the Health Service, lower wages, raise dividends, spare the rich at the expense of the poor. And there is some truth in it, of course. Not that the Tories will dare (or want) to touch the Health Service, except perhaps by making a few things payable-for, or partly. But they *will* want to reduce direct taxation, and won't be so indulgent to wage claims, and they'll run the country at less financial loss. I don't want them, or trust them. I want no one but the Liberals, and those I fear we shall never have again. I have a bet of 2/- with Mr. Jones, my dairy shop (of course an ardent Welsh liberal), that we shall send back fewer Liberals than last time; he thinks more. I think the great majority of working people will reject the Tories, and rightly, from their point of view. Except that I think Labour will drive on to the rocks our whole economy soon, and that will be bad for every one. I shan't take any part in Liberal campaigning this time; I am much too busy, and anyhow have come to see Liberal candidates as mere deposit-losers. Now I have just heard a Conservative party broadcast from Sir D. Maxwell Fyfe; he talked about nationalisation, housing, ending the class war; all quite sound. The class war, such as it is, is a particularly unpleasant Socialist stunt. I wish Archbp. Temple was still at Canterbury; he was politically and socially so good. . . . And surely the Church should take some part in *res publica*.

I have been reading an interesting book; a new translation, by Father Caraman, the editor of the *Month*, of the auto-biography of John Gerard the Jesuit,[2] who was sent here on the English Mission just after the Armada, and related his experiences in Latin (MS. at Stonyhurst and Rome) at the end of his life. I remember the former translation, published about 1880; this one reads more briskly. It is a thrilling tale of secret going about the country in lay dress, talking about falconry, etc., to unsuspect-

[1] The Labour Party had been in office since the General Election of 1945.
[2] John Gerard: *The Autobiography of an Elizabethan; translated from the Latin by Philip Caraman with an introduction by Graham Greene* (1951).

ing country gentlemen, living in Catholic houses, converting and saying Mass, hiding in secret chambers when the pursuivants called and searched, being captured, taken to prison, and tortured, and finally escaping from the Tower by a rope over the moat. He must have been a very persuasive missionary, for he made many conversions, and induced Catholic squires and their wives or widows to give him hospitality for months on end, at risk of their own freedom. What is lacking in the book is any hint of the political background, of the papal bull absolving Englishmen of their allegiance to the crown, and of the fact that the persecutions were really started by that. I have been reviewing this book for the *Spectator*. If it would interest you to read it (the book, I mean) I will send it to you.

I have also been reading Graham Greene's *The End of the Affair*, which you mentioned to me some time ago, and which has now been published here. It isn't good; much less so than *The Heart of the Matter*. The people are all rather low types, and not convincing. And the religion in it (such as it is) is brought down to a very trivial plane by two rather absurd miracles at the end, which are supposed to show the heroine's sanctity, though there are no other signs of this. As . . . remarked the other day when I met him in the Times bookshop, she did *not* seem a promising candidate for canonisation. He doesn't care for the book; I shouldn't, if I were R.C. It gives a trivial picture of the faith. What a mess his mind must be—nothing in it, scarcely, but religion and sex, and these all mixed up together. Religious adultery; as someone said about it, he didn't mind either in a book alone, but didn't like the mixture. It *could* be a good mixture, if properly done; but not as he does it. I think he needs a fresh outlook altogether. I don't think you'd like this book; I think you hadn't read it when you wrote to me of it.

I looked up some photographs for you (snaps and others) and found a few duplicates, which I will send along sometime, if you'd like to feel more sure to recognise me. In any case, they might amuse you—if, among your many scrap books, you keep a scrap book of such oddments. I feel pleased that you would like to see them; I like to have yours, as you know.

I read in some book lately that one shouldn't talk to people before Mass, but keep silence and think. And here have I, when I have driven Canon Hood (as I did 3 or 4 times last week . . .), been chattering brightly away to him all the way, about this and that. I hope he didn't mind! He chatted back, but perhaps from politeness. I must ask him next time if he likes talking—no, perhaps not, it would look awkward, since we have been talking all this time. I won't begin it next time, but will leave him to if he wants to. I feel I am such a raw recruit that I might easily blunder. Do you think people do mind? Well, at least he gets a lift. I like him very much. I wonder if that A[nglo-]C[atholic] Progress Campaign in October will be interfered with by the election.

I will get *The English Inheritance*[1] from the library. I am looking about for a book of daily prayers (different ones for each day of the week), which is dignified, restrained, a mixture of collects, readings, ancient and new prayers (to which I could add some Latin ones and others). Prayers not too devotionally sweet, gushing, counter-reformationish, abject, popish, mariolatrous, Faberish—you know what I mean, and what I don't like and find embarrassing. I wonder what the best book is. I remember of old one called *Sursum Corda*,[2] which I think was good. Then it might have a few sign-posts for meditation, which I should find useful. . . . I have the offices, of course, and the arrangement for an order which I put together on your suggestions; but this other book would provide more prayers for different days. To-morrow is St. Matthew's day. 21*st*. Or rather, to-day is. So lovely it was this morning early. The Serpentine very cool: but most beautiful; steel-colour blue, with great swans swimming about, sometimes raising their wings and half flying, half dashing, over the water; the trees tipped with gold; a

[1] G. S. R. Kitson Clark, *The English Inheritance: an Historical Essay* (1950).
[2] *Sursum Corda: a Handbook of Intercession and Thanksgiving arranged by* W. H. Frere *and* A. L. Illingworth, *with a Preface by the Bishop of Southwark* (1900).

cavalcade of black horses and soldier riders trotting in formation down the row; the sky pale grey-blue, the sun tipping the ripples with light; I can't tell you; it was poetry, swimming alone there among the swans. I shall be sorry when it gets really too cold for this. To-day the sun shines coolly, but shines. I suppose you have lovely Fall weather now.

Those books: Fr. Pedersen didn't say they were from him, but from you. I thanked him much for getting and bringing them, but not for *giving* them. Still, no matter; the behest was yours, if the cash his. He paid for that whole evening, theatre, supper and all, generous man. Has the S.S.J.E. ever produced a Father *not* generous, good and full of human kindness? Probably not; it probably can't. It must be either the system, or the kind of character that takes to such a life. Both, no doubt.

Don't mind about not commenting on all I say, ever. I just babble on, by way of talking, because I like to tell you things, and should never think that, because you didn't comment, you hadn't heard. It is the same the other way round.

Love. Yours affectionately,

R. M.

20, *Hinde House, Hinde St., W.*1
Michaelmas Day, 1951

(And St. Michael is the Patron of
the Clan Macaulay, by the way)

Dear Father,

Lovely to get this morning your letter of 23rd; and to be bidden to expect a sea letter written during the tray period. I am sorry you were laid up; but trays brought in by someone else are certainly a rest, after getting them oneself—and in your case, getting other people's meals too. My poor old aunt[1] (now 84) has got so that she loves her trays coming in so much that she asks for another directly she has finished with one. I suppose

[1] Mary Macaulay.

they must be nice events in the rather dull days of those who can't get about.

Not getting about: you know, that was all I meant when I said I had been a little "discouraged" by your remarks on Religion-in-the-Flat. *Not*, for a moment, by your references to age; I am indeed extremely ancient, and should never think of claiming to be anything else, nor, I am sure, would anyone take me for anything else. But what I meant was that one can be old and *vigorous*, getting about as well as one used to, and enjoying active pursuits, such as swimming, going to Mass, etc. If ever the time comes when I shall have (more than temporarily) to stay in and give up these things, I shall be much disconcerted and frustrated; though I suppose one would have to adapt oneself and make the best of it. But I should hate it! And I see no reason why I shouldn't "die in my boots," or swimming, or travelling, or whatever. Even as I wrote these words, a negro voice broke out in my ear, from my radio, singing with great gusto,

"Let me run, run, run round this great and fertile land,
   For the world ain't big enough for me;
      No, no,
   The world ain't big enough for me!"

Them's my sentiments, exactly. I expect I shall feel the same when I am 90. *Indeed* you weren't "rude"; only solicitous for my well-being, and kind. Time's winged chariot hurries much too fast, that is the fact. But I hope it will not hurl me into my bed or arm-chair for a long long time. "While we have time": yes indeed. But how little, really, we have. And heavens, how I have wasted much of my brief hour. I hate to think of that, and of how little remains.

I have been thinking lately of all those great Victorians. I have to review, for *The Times Literary Supplement*, Noel Annan's book on Leslie Stephen and his life and times.[1] He was born in 1832—a generation before my parents, two generations before you and me. And took Orders for the sake of his Trinity Hall

[1] N. G. Annan, *Leslie Stephen, his Thought and Character in Relation to his Time* (1951).

Fellowship, and a very odd parson he must have been, and, indeed, was thought. I suppose he never actually believed very much. Later, of course, he formally renounced his Orders, and was for most of his life an agnostic rationalist. An austerely virtuous man, like so many of his generation. Unlike Edward VIII, whose autobiography is also just out, he never " lived for pleasure," as so many of us do. The book has interesting chapters on Victorian Evangelicalism and Rationalism. How seriously they took their Doubt! It seems to hinge often on such oddly unimportant and trivial things—beginning by loss of belief in the Flood, or some other Old Testament tale, tales that we were only told as Hebrew legends. And that led on to loss of belief in God, which seems so irrelevant and odd. Our generation was much more wisely brought up.

I have just come to a sentence in his book which is much the same as one in your letter—" He was clear that a writer cannot be expected to preach . . ." Not " oracular utterance, but a vision of life so deeply perceived that all the writer's faculties were co-ordinated to express it." That should be, as you suggest, the idea. How I hope it may one day animate a book of mine.

I shall certainly get some book about the Liturgical movement; it would greatly interest me. I might ask Maisie Sheed about it. I seldom meet her, but like her very much.

I enclose a cutting from to-day's *Sunday Times* (for it is now Sunday) . . . which I like. I have read that book [it] . . . mentions, in French, and it is excellent. I think I shall get it; hitherto I only had it from the Library, and copied some of it into my scrap book. It is very good on waiting on each moment and meeting God in it. I wonder if you know it.

It is very late at night; I have been out most of the day, and only sat down at my typewriter in the evening, first writing part of a review, then I thought I would finish this letter, but it is now 12.30 and I am falling asleep, so I will stop it and go to bed. Then I can post it early, on my way to church. I have read *all* Fr. Andrew's letters, and have found a lot of admirable things in them, very useful, and I shall go on reading them again. Thank you for pointing out those verses in Rom. v. Yes: they

are true, thank heaven. " Access by faith into this grace . . ."
It sometimes seems too good to be true.

Good-night, dear Father. I look forward to the sea letter.

Love,

R. M.

I hope that wedding *wasn't too* exhausting.

October

20, *Hinde House, Hinde St., W.*1
2nd October, 1951

My dear Father,

I posted a letter to you yesterday, but to-day have your sea letter of 20th Sept. (a *lovely* long letter—thank you so much for it), so will add a kind of postscript. I didn't gather from your air paper that I answered yesterday that you had been so really unwell—you made nothing of it. But now I see that you were much worse than I care to think—turning queer at Mass, and a temperature, and a murmur. I don't like all this at all, and think you should have rested much longer, had more trays, more Religion-in-the-cell, or even in-the-bed. Do, do, (is *this* comma correct?) take immense care.

An attack of flue is one thing, one must have that now and then; but your attack seems to have been apropos of nothing, except (no doubt) over-fatigue and strain. Don't forget that murmur—even if it is (like a bat's squeak) something that only doctors (and angels) can hear.

I like your account of Mrs. Paine.[1] How delightful, and how kind and good and charming, she sounds. I'm glad she liked *The World my Wilderness*. If she did "put me in her prayers," it seems to have worked. (Or perhaps you put me into yours,

---

[1] Virginia Paine and her family had known Father Johnson, as a priest and a friend, for over 25 years.

and *that* worked.) I like the thought of perhaps having got into hers too. I hope you told her that I am now Well In.

To-morrow I am going to hear the Bp. of Oxford at All Saints, and then on to a Buffet Lunch, to hear about Canon Hood's Anglo-Catholic Ordinations Fund. I should be interested to know how our clergy are at present divided—how many could be called A.C., how many middle, how many Broad, how many Low. I wonder if there are any figures about this. Perhaps Canon Hood knows. The Anglo-Catholic Progress Campaign (13th-21st Oct.) has rather collided with the election, and I am afraid will get small audiences. As to the election, I am prophesying an increased Labour majority, but may be entirely confounded.

Interesting about Fr. Benson. That extraordinary power of concentration on prayer—it must be very rare, surely. Do you think it's a natural gift, like music, or mathematics, or that it can be developed by practice in anyone, up to a point? Only up to a point, I'm sure. Fr. B. must have had it in a high degree. And I expect your Mrs. Paine has it, from what you say. I wish I had! But I know I never could have—I should have always to fill my hour of prayer largely with reading. "Meditation" could never come easily to me. Will you promise to let me know when you aren't well, or I shall be thinking you aren't when you are and worrying.

My love and concern.

Your affectionate

R. M.

PS. I am interested to learn, in a letter from the head of the Flood family (Scottish) that Fr. Henry Flood, S.J. (this, it seems, was the correct spelling) is a many-times-great-uncle of mine; he was a grandson of my ancestor Aulay Macaulay of Ardincaple. My informant also tells me that he was very busy in the 1590's (before his Lisbon days) in fomenting pro-Spanish plots in Scotland. In fact, as our Lisbon Consul found, a very busy priest all his life! Not a quiet or a dull moment. It must all have been very stimulating, and our modern Jesuits must miss it rather. One is reminded of this by such books as *John Gerard*, of which I wrote to you earlier.

20, *Hinde House, Hinde St., W.*1
9th October, 1951

Dear Father,

I was so glad to have your air letter posted 1st Oct., and to learn that you are " all right " again; I hope this is really so. But I'm glad you aren't (or weren't when you wrote) going to Craigie St.[1] early. And also that you are, as I trust, going to bed earlier. I know the temptation to sit up late and write things; it seems such a nice quiet time (uninterrupted) to finish things off, or anyhow to get on with them. But it *is* tiring, there is no doubt, and perhaps we ancients shouldn't do it much. Anyhow, I do hope you'll have no more of these attacks of faintness.

Your letter much interested me. When I read this enclosed article in *The Times Literary Supplement*[2], it occurred to me that it might possibly be from your cousin[3], who is writing the book about Johnny. The extracts from his journal are very interesting. You may have seen the *T.L.S.* already, but I send it in case it doesn't come your way. Your cousin's ought to be a most interesting book. And how fascinating to see all those old letters brought by your Powys cousin. Those old Evangelicals were such *nice* people—I mean the grandparents, who wrote about " walking with God ". " Oh for a closer walk with God "—is that an Evangelical hymn? I see Dean Inge has been criticizing " Rock of Ages," which has roused a lot of protest from elderly Evangelicals who say it expresses the faith in which they were

[1] The convent of the Sisters of St. Anne in Craigie Street, Cambridge, where Father Johnson often celebrated Holy Communion at 7.0 a.m.

[2] Two articles, entitled *Cowper's Last Years*, were published in *The Times Literary Supplement* of 5th and 12th October, 1951. They consisted of extracts from a manuscript of the diary or memoranda of the Rev. John Johnson (" Johnny of Norfolk ") giving details relating to his cousin William Cowper, during the period 1795-1800 when the poet was suffering from melancholia and madness.

[3] Mary Barham Johnson.

reared. Inge, of course, doesn't like that form of theology. I don't know that I do very much myself; but look what fruits it bore. It freed slaves, reclaimed heathen, preached the Gospel abroad and at home, reformed prison and factory conditions, invented District Visiting and Ragged Schools, abolished suttee, communed with God. Later it did fall into excesses, of course (the ones that so annoyed my Conybeare grandfather), but it was a fine godly affair on the whole. And all that coming and going between the families in the rectories—it must be fascinating reading for their descendants. I think my sister has somewhere a lot of my grandmother's[1] old letters which I should like to read if ever time allows. She touched a very wide circle; many of them come into this Leslie Stephen book; the Stephens themselves were family friends both of the Conybeares and Macaulays; and of course there was the usual wide spreading out of relations and friends, in London, Oxford, Cambridge, Westmorland, Leicestershire, all about. My grandmother wrote very racy, packed letters always, and seemed to be always on the move, visiting relations and friends. Then we have too a number of letters written by my *great*-grand-mother, the daughter of Thomas Babington of Rothley Temple (a great Evangelical himself, and a friend of Wilberforce). So much *high-mindedness* was about. Heavens, what would they have thought of George Orwell's book![2] I do agree with you about that; I hated it. It is fantastically horrible, and so *im-probable*. Poor Orwell was dying of consumption when he wrote it (he died, I think, before it was published). So he took a morbid and almost hysterical view of life. No, I don't think he was a believer in God at all. A high-minded man, in many ways, and with a horror (which obsessed and warped him) of cruelty and tyranny. His only gospel was freedom and kindness and the good of humanity. He saw a possible future hell on earth, and described it obscenely. " My hope is in Thy word " would have no meaning for him; and the darkness he saw as com-prehending (in the sense of mastering) the light. Poor man. Many of his friends (and his young wife) were devoted to him.

[1] Eliza Conybeare.   [2] G. Orwell, *1984* (1949).

But that book is really dreadful. The kind of nightmare that sick people dream. I think I disliked it so much that I didn't read it all; but I remember its horrible end.

I shall certainly get and read *The English Inheritance*, and shall tell you how it strikes me. It is the kind of book I should like, I know. I will try the London L[ibrary] for it; or the Times L[ibrary] might have it. I have just been reading an address by Professor Marcel Simon, of Strasbourg, delivered to the annual conference of Modern Churchmen, about the Church of England and its function, seen of course from the French point of view. He admires it greatly, and particularly the P[rayer] B[ook]. He is not now (he says) a practising Catholic, but is Christian, and intensely interested in the progress of the Churches towards unity; he was bitterly disappointed by the breakdown, 25 years ago, of the Malines talks.[1] The narrowness and bigotry of the R.C. church are obviously repellent to him; he seems to think the Anglican church has a great mission to the world. A puzzling church, he admits, " where broad and high and lowly

All meet to disagree."

He doesn't approve all this aping of Rome; he thinks it destroys the true Anglican quality. He quotes Duchesne[2] on this —" the attempt to introduce into the Church of England all that I wish to eliminate from the R.C. church." He also quotes Tyrrell, on the problem of combining freedom and authority, science and revelation, respect for tradition and respect for conscience (moral and intellectual). " The church which solves it first will sweep the world into its net. . . . It is perhaps the C. of E. which seems most likely to win the race." He ends by begging the church not to " exchange the precious values imparted to her for some illusory jewels borrowed from elsewhere." The whole address is interesting.

I wish I could remember where I was reading the other day something about that Trin. 19 collect, and Cranmer's reasons

[1] The Malines Conversations, between Anglican and Roman Catholic theologians, took place between 1921 and 1925 under the presidency of Cardinal Mercier.

[2] Louis Duchesne (1843-1922), French historian of the early Christian Church.

for altering the order of the words; the writer thought it an improvement and I think it is; it strengthens the sound of it. The alteration of the *miserationis operatio*[1] to "thy Holy Spirit" is odder. It comes back to me that the book I was looking at (probably in the library) was partly about ancient Greek and other prayers, and pointed out how Cranmer (and our other collect-makers) sometimes took them over, or mixed them with the Roman ones, in the same collect. Perhaps this was an example of that; I will see if I can trace this book; it was interesting and instructive. I like the meaning that God's pity may work *in* our hearts. I find I have lots of old photographs (duplicates) so send a few to amuse you and help you to know me when we meet. I have some later ones, I think, too, that I might send sometime. The nun with me is my eldest sister; she died in '41. She was an East End Deaconess (Community of All Saints). I loved her very dearly. I think the gardening ones and the reading one were taken by some newspaper. I don't know which of them will go in this letter—I will see. I must try and see Fr. Pedersen again before he leaves; but I expect he is very busy. My car is out of sorts for a few days, and I go to Mass on my bicycle, and then ride on to the Serpentine. Rather *cool*.

My love always, dear Father. Say how you are.

R. M.

20, *Hinde House, Hinde St., W.*1
15*th October,* 1951

Dear Father,

I am really shocked that my letter posted 22nd Sept. didn't reach you till 9th Oct. It is reminiscent of the bad old days of last December, when they took about a month. This is 17 days, which is much too long. Yours posted 9th (air) came on the 12th, to my great pleasure. I *am* sorry you were worried by fearing your letter about health precautions and increasing age

[1] "The exercise of (Thy) compassion."

might have vexed me. Indeed it didn't; by now you will have got the letter in which I explained what I meant by calling it "discouraging"—nothing to do with age, but only with my reluctance to lead an invalid life until I have to. You know that it would be impossible for me ever to think anything you wrote to me "inconsiderate." All I would think is that you probably under-rate my toughness and vigour, and this would be from affection, so I really value it. I am very well at present. The ending of summer has stopped my Serpentine bathing after Mass, which I miss, but it really was getting a little too chilly. I have just been writing a BBC talk about "Swimming for Pleasure"; I began with the Assyrians, Greeks and Romans, then ourselves from the 16th century on, in rivers and sea, and so to to-day. I give the talk next Monday, on the Third Programme. A rather incongruous topic in this foggy weather; but one on which I like to muse. Islands in a blue sea, smelling of thyme and myrtle in a hot sun. Green water swaying and murmuring in rocky creeks. Etc., etc. I like those pagan religions which included a bathe in sea or pool as part of their initiation. Baptism once did, I suppose, and it was more beautifully symbolic actually than the modern rite, though less convenient. I like symbolism. At Mass this morning there was a densish mist outside; it brooded beyond the clear window above the chapel altar, among the trees; and inside was the candle-lit altar and the lit chapel, and the darkness comprehended it not (in the old sense of mastered) and I prayed "*Lucem tuam, Domine, nobis concede: ut, depulsis cordium tenebris, pervenire possimus ad lumen, quod est Christus.*"[1] Thank you for telling me of that.

I am sorry *And no man's wit* is put under lock and key! I am pretty sure that would be owing to R.C. influence, as they always exercise a lot of censorship over books over there, and, if they suspect the faintest taint of anti-Romanism (as they might from my book, though wrongly, as I was merely being objective and speaking through my characters, giving various types and their views) they suggest that it shouldn't be freely

[1] "Grant us, O Lord, thy light, so that the darkness of our hearts having been driven away we may be able to attain to the light, which is Christ."

given out at libraries. I have heard of so many such cases. It is one of the many reasons why I couldn't possibly ever be R.C. They *are* so frightened of adverse opinions. Do you know Simone Weil's book, just translated from the French *L'Attente de Dieu*, that I think I have mentioned to you before?[1] Simone, in her letters to Père Perrin (a Dominican priest who befriended her) gives reasons why she won't, though really a Christian, be baptized into the Church; one reason is the intolerance of the Church, and her horror of the word "anathema," and of the Inquisition, etc. Father Perrin, in the French edition, published her letters after her early death with a long and interesting introduction by himself. In the translation this introduction is replaced by a short one by someone else, and it seems that the Vatican forbade Father Perrin to introduce so heretic a book. And it is such an interesting and truly religious book. That is the kind of thing that drives some R.C. converts out of the church; as it drove (I mean, intolerance and bigotry did) Kathleen Raine, a young poet, who joined it a few years ago, out of unhappiness and loneliness. She told me the other day that she came out after 6 months, because she couldn't bear the intolerant attitude.[2] I wish she would now become an Anglican and come to Grosvenor Chapel! I must lend her Marcel Simon's address to the Modern Churchmen, that I think I wrote to you about last time.

I'm so glad you are interested in that novel.[3] You ask about the people in it. Ernie I knew slightly; he worked in a garage; but he was a Durham man and I made him Worcestershire, so he probably talked wrong. Dr. Marlowe was based on a woman doctor I knew, but only externally really; internally she was like a number of ardent public-spirited liberal women I have met. Ellen I invented entirely; I never knew a mermaid, or even a part-mermaid. All her conversation, such as it was, is such as I supposed a part-mermaid might utter, in such circum-

[1] Simone Weil, *Waiting on God* (1951).

[2] Kathleen Raine has explained that her reason for withdrawing from Roman Catholicism at this time was not antipathy towards the Church, but doubt as to the usefulness for her of any formal religious tradition.

[3] R. M.'s *And No Man's Wit*.

stances. The Frenchman too I invented. Hugh is rather like a man I know. The others are out of my head. Except that Guy *looked* rather like Guy Burgess, one of our two vanished diplomats of whom you may have read (vanished for good, it now seems).

I'll see if I can find *Farewell to Spain*[1] in a Penguin. *Mary Lavelle* is Penguin'd, so I dare say the other is too. I am sure, by the way, that *Mary Lavelle* is under much stricter duress at the libraries than any of my books—and rightly, I think, don't you?

Very unfair of the American soldiers to chalk your name on the bombs they dropped on Berlin. Anything more unsuitable! To drag the S.S.J.E. into the dreadful affair was very wrong.

I looked up those articles[2] again, together with the comments on them in the *American P.B. Commentary* that Fr. Pedersen gave me. It says "It is in articles 9–18 that the influence of Lutheranism shows itself most clearly." I suppose they are translated literally from the Württemburg Confession of 1552 (or the Augsburg of 1530?) and embody the Lutheran Doctrines of original sin, original righteousness, etc., that I find so improbable and groundless and opposed to reason. The whole theory seems to have been taken from Adam's imaginary career; it does seem time that we dropped it? I think it must be an intellectual stumbling-block to a number of people, who can accept original sin, in fact they know it in themselves and everyone else, and it isn't involved at all with any theory that man was once better than he later became; it is just " the law of sin which is in my members," and has been so all through the history of the human race, warring against the laws of God. Well, I suppose it doesn't actually matter much, but I have a feeling that that kind of thing (like " predestination," and " election "—St. Paul's fault, I suppose) is so much dead wood, that should be cut out of the living tree. Do you think there is enough *revision* of our current religious formularies, in the P.B. and elsewhere? As to the merits of the saints (relying on them to help us, I mean), I suppose it is a purely Roman doctrine.

[1] Kate O'Brien, *Farewell Spain* (1937).   [2] The Thirty-Nine Articles.

I do agree with Fr. Palmer about that! St. Dunstan, I am sure, had many merits; when invoked by school boys about to be flogged, he would cause the flogging master to drop to sleep, so that the boys got away. And didn't he throw an inkpot at the devil? But what it means to " rely on his merits " I can't imagine. Oh dear; all this jargon; away with it. I can imagine relying a little on the merits of St. Luke (his day is to-morrow, for this letter has stretched over 2 days, owing to overcrowding of jobs) in the sense of trying to emulate his gifts of tending the sick, etc.—but is that what it means? No; I feel such notions belong to a different climate and age, and that it is useless trying to get back to them; perhaps worse than useless. I'm glad you feel rather the same.

I am sorry I didn't see Fr. Pedersen again before he went. I rang up St. Edward's House, but by then he had just sailed. I would like to have said goodbye to him, heard a little about his travels and Italy, and had another talk. But I think he was mostly away from London after his return from abroad. I hope by now he is safely back, and has related to you his saga.

Here is a second instalment of Johnny's Diary.[1] What a devoted friend he was. I don't quite understand about the " tin tube " and " comfortable sounds," but I hope they comforted poor Mr. C[owper]. A pity he hadn't a radio.

Now I must really stop this drawn-out letter, to which I sit down at intervals to refresh myself between less pleasing labours. We have just emerged from a dense fog; it came on again last night, when I was driving a friend from Hampstead to the Old Vic to see *Tamburlaine*, and got so thick that I left my car outside my flat on the way to Waterloo and we took a taxi, which also groped its way with some difficulty, but I felt rather he than I. The play (which no one living has seen before) is a fantastic performance of sound and fury, spectacle and blood, and fine mouthed speeches, which I expect the Elizabethans enjoyed more than we do. One never sees an Elizabethan play without marvelling at Shakespeare—*stupor mundi* indeed! A kind of splendid miracle. The others, such as Marlowe, had no such

[1] See above p. 203*n*.

210

thoughts, no such poetry, except here and there in snatches (I mean poetry: they *never* had the thoughts).

My love and thanks. I keep on giving thanks for you, in my prayers, you know. As well as praying for you. As I feel you do for me sometimes, and how much better.

Your always affectionate

R. M.

Let me know when those old photographs reach you.[1]

20, Hinde House, Hinde St., W.1
24th October [1951] (Feast of St. Raphael)

Dear Father,

Thank you very much indeed for your air letter posted 15th, saying that mine of 22nd Sept. had just come, taking 17 days—disgraceful! Since then you will have got other letters, and I hope with more expedition. Your air ones, of course, manage pretty well as a rule. I enjoyed the last one very much, with its account of the visit of your young relations, your stories of J. C. Powys, your reassurance about Canon Hood and talking . . . I went to the Rally of the Church Union Progress Week campaign last Sunday; a number of priests who had helped in it spoke—including the American Father de Bois, who spoke for the American Church Union. They seem to have had great meetings, and to be much encouraged; they said they drew more people than the party election meetings in the same places, which is perhaps not always saying much.

Since I last wrote I have read *The English Heritage*,[2] or most of it, and found it interesting, and some of J. C. Powys's new novel *Porius*, about the Britons after the Romans had withdrawn, and the Saxons invading. I found it rather confused and confusing, to say the truth—too many Britons, and not enough

[1] R. M. has added a further note on back of envelope: " I have been reading Kitson Clark, with interest."

[2] This probably refers to *The English Inheritance* (see above p. 197).

diversity of character or speech, and I didn't really feel he had caught the Ancient British mentality quite—but perhaps I haven't either! This business of writing about people of whom we know so little, owing to their unfortunate literary unproductivity, is rather tricky. It is very long. I wonder if any American publisher will risk it. If I can get hold of the paper jacket, which has an interesting picture of J.C.P. walking among Welsh mountains and looking like a prophet, I will send it you. I didn't like to steal it off the library copy when I had it, as I always regard this as dishonest but I may persuade one of the kind Times Library young ladies to give me one. I think you would like to see it. Yes, he is certainly a prophet, and I dare say sometimes a dangerous one. He shouldn't influence people to live on writing poetry alone; no one, scarcely, can. I am on the committee of the Royal Literary Fund, and we are always getting applications for money from poets who either can't or don't want to do another job while they write. When they are young or youngish, this seems quite wrong. Of course we are mostly concerned to help old and elderly writers, or their widows; they aren't usually very *good* writers, though sometimes they are; but they are pathetic, having outlived whatever market they once had, often in ill health, with children to bring up. It is a difficult business.

I didn't feel *anything* "cheap" in what you said about J.C.P.; it seemed to me interesting and sympathetic. You indicated that he was a great personality, intensely genuine and prophetic and real. Does *every one* (who self-analyses at all) see their own personality as a "collection of poses," I wonder? I certainly do. But how does one distinguish between pose and genuine character? "Literary, comic, theological, sacerdotal" (no, not senile!)—you *are* all these things, in different moods, surely, and it is absolutely genuine; one would feel the difference if it wasn't; I mean those who know you, or who write to you, would feel the difference. Perhaps one *couldn't* really assume personalities alien to one, it would be too difficult, though I suppose one can stress and exaggerate them. It reminds [me] of that novel of E. M. Delafield's, *Zella sees herself*—did you ever read it? Probably J.C.P. would say the same thing about himself, wouldn't he? I must read his autobiography.[1]

10 *p.m.* I was out to dinner, and came in to find your letter of 20th Oct. arrived. How nice to have it in time to answer it in this. You mention two letters of mine which took respectively 16 and 15 days, so about that seems now the norm. I am thankful to hear that you feel fairly well now again; but I am glad you have handed over the Teas for a time. I think you ought to hand them over for a long time. They sound much too hard work. Your job should be reading aloud to them while they eat and drink; I suppose you sometimes do this, but probably not often enough. Think of all the lovely things, Latin and English, that you could read—Ovid, Virgil, Horace, modern novels. . . . [*sic*] They would have a lovely time over their tea.

You should tell the Father who complains of the English misuse of "expect" that the Oxford Dict. says "The misuse of the word as a synonym of 'suppose,' without any notion of anticipating, is often cited as an Americanism, but is very common in dialectal, vulgar, or carelessly colloquial speech in England." Also, it might have added in ordinary educated speech. We all use it so, and know it is wrong, but don't care. So that really usage has made it right; after all, what makes a word right but ordinary use by educated people? But the Father might be interested to hear that it is "often cited as an Americanism"! One of the examples quoted is from Jefferson. I wonder why we dropped "I guess," and why the Americans didn't. English use of it is quoted from Locke and others; but by 1814 Byron wrote "I guess (as the Yankees say) . . ." We seem to have no precise alternative to "expect" in that sense. "Suppose" isn't the same; nor is "think," which is too definite. So we must go on using it, I expect.

The Bishop of Exeter at that Albert Hall Rally said he didn't care for, or use, the name "Anglo-Catholic," because *all* C. of E. members are necessarily this: they are Anglicans, and belong to the Catholic Church; so he prefers "High Church." I think

[1] John Cowper Powys, *Autobiography* (1934).

I do too. At that meeting I sat next to a woman who told me her husband went to Grosvenor Chapel, but that she didn't, it wasn't high enough for her, it allowed mid-day communicants (it has always had these) of which she obviously disapproved. *She* goes to St. Cuthbert's, Ennismore Gardens[1], which is on the highest peaks . . . She was rather a spiky . . . lady, I thought. I much prefer Mr. Sam Gurney, also on a high eminence, to whom I was introduced by John Betjeman in St. Augustine's, Kilburn, and with whom we lunched afterwards. We all three went to see a Catholic Apostolic church, which is slowly dying because all the Angels and Deacons are dead, and nothing can carry on the tradition, but the verger thought, indeed fully expected, that the Second Coming would occur in time to save it. It is a fine church, built by Pearson; when the Catholic Apostolic dies, it will pass into Anglican hands.

Yes, I think that would be a good plan, to divide my *Preces Privatae* into parts for each day of the week; I will do that; and, as it grows, can add things on to each day as they seem to fit in. A different group of thoughts and prayers for each day, linked by a common approach. No, I won't try to emulate Fr. Benson; I couldn't, anyhow. All I can do is to come as I am, and this I do, and it seems to get better all the time. I suppose—I expect—that God just takes what each of us can give, so long as we try to make it as good as we can, with our limitations, and doesn't demand what is too high for us. I like All Souls' and All Saints', which we shall so soon be entering into. In Italy they lit the graves in the cemetery with little lamps, to cheer " *nostri cari defunti* " on All Souls' night. I wish people still went souling, as they used to when my father was a boy, singing " Soul, soul, an apple or two; if you haven't any apples, a pear will do." But they no longer even go maying, I think.

Did I tell you about Noel Annan's interesting book on Leslie Stephen, which I was reviewing for *The Times Literary Supplement*? I think you would be interested in it. I won't suggest sending you my copy of it, as you say you don't like to get

[1] R. M. means St. Cuthbert's, Philbeach Gardens.

books; but I will send you sometime my review of it, so that you can see what kind of book it is.

To-morrow is polling day; and all to-morrow night the results will be coming in; I shall be out at an election party to hear them, and shall probably only just get home in time to change into day clothes and dash off to 8.15 Mass. So now I expect I had better go to bed, and sleep while I may. Goodnight, dear Father, and my love.

Your affectionate

R. M.

November

20, *Hinde House, Hinde St., W.*1
All Souls' Day, 1951

Dear Father,

Thank you so much for air paper of 28th Oct. The last I wrote to you was on 24th, which you won't get for ages. But you ought to have got (when you wrote) my letter of 9th; I am afraid they are settling into their Christmas form (did you get the photographs safely?). I look forward to your sea letter of 25th, which I may get in about 10 days, with luck. I wrote to you again on 15th (I think), and I think I said I would send you a paper jacket of *Porius*, with a coloured picture of J. C. P[owys] among the mountains. I succeeded in getting hold of one of these, and enclose it in this; it may interest you to see it. I think I told you I didn't get very far with *Porius*, for lack of time; it is a book to take away on a long holiday, and read slowly and with care; it is too crammed with ancient Britons, and rather confusing. But some people have enjoyed it hugely.

Yes, it is a shame about those Latin errors. Even the English printers made some, which I listed in my errata list at the end, but the book was never reprinted unfortunately, so they remain. And the Americans expanded the errors, of course. No, American publishers don't send proofs to England. I can only hope that most American readers don't know the difference. The Latin in the English edition used to annoy me a lot; I had forgotten about it.

What a lovely Mass for All Souls! We use that altar missal compiled by a Cowley Father some time ago; it is extremely good. . . . [The] whole is a wonderfully beautiful service. Of course our P[rayer] B[ook] ought to have it; so should the American. I went to the 7.30 Mass this morning, in darkness and rain, which, when the lit altar shone out, seemed right for All Souls, and for " *Lucem tuam, Domine*. . . ." All Saints yesterday, too, was good; " the solemnity of all the Hallows." Do they still keep All Hallows e'en in America? It always seems rather odd that Presbyterian Scotland should have been the great celebrator of this festival and its rites. I think it has almost died out in England (?) but the Scots keep it with vigour. When I was at Oxford, it was the Scotch girls who used to give Hallow e'en parties. I wish these festivals didn't tend to die out. It's many years since I saw, for instance, the Christmas actors going round doing St. George and the Dragon. Or perhaps they still do it in the country; London is the killer of such gambols; though Guy Fawkes is still celebrated with ardour and fire. How about New England, the home of Puritanism? Did they leave such vanities behind them in the popish old world when they fled from its wickedness? One good thing which has increased greatly is the Christmas crib, now I suppose to be found in nearly all English churches, in varying degrees of magnificence. Not, however, in the Church of Ireland; I was told of an Anglican family living there some years ago who went into the R.C. chapel to look at the crib and was told next day by their butcher that he couldn't serve them any more, as they had been seen entering the popish church. I suppose he was probably Presbyterian (it was Ulster) but the C. of I. don't like cribs either. What a lot they lose.

I am now for a few weeks on the BBC Critics, who meet every week to broadcast a discussion on contemporary arts— a book, play, film, radio programme, and picture exhibition. It takes more time than I can afford, actually. Last week we had to see *A priest in the family*, which is an Irish play, a kind of domestic tragedy, in which the wicked old mother comes between the young couple, determined that her son should enter the priesthood, so tells him slanders about the girl. Unconvincing, but interesting; the young man does become a priest, discovers too late that he was deceived, wants to resign his orders, but doesn't, and goes off to Africa with a mission. All rather unlikely; but the acting very good and amusing, with dear old Maire O'Neill as a tipsy gossip. The Irish do act so well. I liked the play better than most of my colleagues did; at least it was about something important, a psychological and moral and religious problem, not merely an emotional one. I saw it with a R.C. cousin, who thought it excellent. Had it been going on when Fr. Pedersen was here, I would have suggested going to it rather than the play we saw.

What you say about the 1549 and 1552 P[rayer] B[ook]s set me reading again in the *American P.B. Commentary*. Have you that book? It really is excellent—so full of information, and good in comment. I suppose they did want to get right away from the medieval abuses connected with the idea of the Sacrifice; but after all, they didn't get away from it except in name. " A repetition of Calvary "—that was what they took against. I don't feel it matters much what they called it, do you? The offering is the same. Perhaps in time I may grow to grasp and understand it a little better; I hope so. But not fully understanding it doesn't hinder its working. Being allowed to take part in it daily seems one of those incredibly good things: just to go to church, and get all that.

Now I must put this letter up, with J. C. Powys and perhaps my talk on Swimming for Pleasure from the *Listener*, and then I will weigh it all and put on the right stamps, and then, after long long weeks of travel, it will reach Memorial Drive. Rather remote contact, I always feel, when the time runs into weeks. What was the record last winter? About 2 months, I think, for one of my letters—and quite an important letter too. I hadn't then learnt that important letters which must arrive quickly should go by air. However, we managed somehow, didn't we. And how well!

My love always.

Yours affectionately,

R. M.

20, *Hinde House, Hinde St., W.*1
13*th November,* 1951 †

My dear Father,

Your air paper posted 6th Nov. came this morning, and convinced me that sea letters are, for the present, a very slow proposition indeed, (I think I said this in my last letter, written on All Souls' Day). Anyhow, I shall use the air for the present. Even the air is slow! Yours of 6th Nov. took a week which is poor. It grieves me that you hadn't then got my letters of 15th and 24th Oct.—anyhow the former should have reached you. And what of a sea letter you told me of, written after Father Pedersen's return? And did you ever get those photographs I sent? And *The Times Literary Supplement* cuttings (two) containing the extracts from the diary of Johnny of Norfolk? Well, I suppose all these things wend safely home at last. I do hope none, either yours or mine, have met with disaster. But never think (a) that I want to write less often or (b) that I am ill. I think I will perhaps ask my sister (a nurse, at Romford), if she will send you a line (air paper) and tell you if I am ill—too ill to write myself, I mean. I know she wouldn't mind doing that. So, unless you hear from either me or her, I am *well.*

I read and enjoyed *In search of London.*[1] And *Flame touches Flame.*[2] Margaret Cropper is a connection of mine—a 1st cousin, on their mother's side, of the Conybeares. All those Croppers are charming, able, and good. They have Quaker blood.

Yes, Graham Greene is *not* New Testament but R.C. The

[1] H. V. Morton, *In Search of London* (1951).
[2] M. B. Cropper, *Flame Touches Flame* (1949).

N.T. hasn't got those *magic* solutions—being saved (or damned) at the last simply by whether you repent at the moment of death, etc., etc., and everything depending on joining the right Church. G. G. wouldn't understand or approve of " not everyone that saith ' Lord, Lord,' shall be saved, but he that doeth the will . . ." Doing the will means less than nothing to him, compared with saying Lord, Lord, before the right altars. That gets you to heaven, doing the will doesn't. No, St. John VIII (I have just been reading it) wouldn't mean a lot to him. It is all about *our Lord* being all that matters, the light, the truth, the giver of freedom—personal commitment to Him, not to the formularies of any Church. The Church (one section of it) is all to G.G., one feels. He has been hypnotized by it. Indeed, where should we be without it, but it's not the infallible dispenser of salvation that he thinks (or writes). It's the essential channel that God uses —but the Church in a much larger sense than G.G. knows. I find it (the Church) enlarges one's comprehension of God all the time—comprehension, apprehension, in both their senses.

I see you say that sea letter was posted by you on 25th Oct. —but has now only been 19 days on the way, so I can't hope for it for another 10 days, I expect.

Do you have many religious plays in St. John's Church?[1] Fr. Pedersen was looking out for some, and thought of *A Sleep of Prisoners* (or was it *The Octopus*, by Chas. Williams?) that they were doing in St. Thomas's, Regent St., but I don't know if he decided on it. Now there is to be another, at St. Martin's; the Religious Drama Society is very active, but doesn't usually get hold of v.g. plays, I think. I suppose there aren't many. G.G. might turn his hand to that, and have it acted in Westminster Cathedral.

I am too busy to be comfortable, what with Ruins, and BBC Critics, etc., etc. I wish I could get more *method* into my life. However, I have cut out so many late nights as I was having. One can't go to bed in the small hours and get up in hours only

---

[1] The Church of St. John the Evangelist, Bowdoin Street, Boston, which belongs to the S.S.J.E.

slightly less small, *and* work—something must go. Please never think that what is cut out is my letters to you.

My love always.

R. M.

20, *Hinde House, Hinde St.,* W.I
16*th November,* 1951 †

Dear Father,

Your sea letter (posted 25th Oct.) sailed in yesterday, and was worth waiting for, it is a splendid letter indeed. I sent you an air paper 4 days ago, saying I hadn't yet got your sea letter, but now here it is, and how I like to have it!

I'm glad you have Fr. Pedersen safely back. And that he thought me well balanced! Really most gratifying and surprising: I must have put on a capital act when I saw him. For I am actually about the least well balanced person I know. No doubt I was composed and in excellent equilibrium when we spent the evening together, and lunched together; no reason for agitation or excesses of prejudice or other manifestations of poor balance; but, alas, it *is* poor, and I am very ill poised in reality. So it is particularly gratifying to have so imposed on Fr. P. I'm glad he liked England so much; I am sure it was mutual. . . .

I'm sorry you erased (and so impenetrably) your Latin Psalter quotations. Now I shall have to guess what it was, from the context, which was concerned with perfect equilibrium. Perhaps the psalmist has something on that; I must look. Don't you think that idea that it was irreverent to use Bible phrases in speech (and I suppose Fr. Benson would have included light writing—like mine) was very much of his period? What I suffer from now is that one's scriptural phrases, often apt, are as likely as not to go unrecognised, which deprives them of their point. I think I am always doing it, even without knowing; I must be very scripture-minded, because Biblical phrases, like Shakespeare's, swim into my mind on all occasions.

As to Fr. Benson's Rule, I suppose the Holy Spirit, always

on the move, expanded it continually, suiting it and making it possible to the times it had reached. Isn't that what the H.S. does? Just as He makes us believe in all kinds of new facets of truth, some of which our Christian ancestors of past centuries would have thought quite incompatible with their religion, which hadn't yet filled up to that level. Isn't that what the R.C. Church lacks, and what makes it rigid and brittle and so apt to repel and shock modern minds—I mean, it lacks real belief in the action of the Holy Spirit; it thinks things got stuck at a certain point and can't move on. Do you get the storm we have here about the Pope's pronouncement about saving the child at the expense of the mother's life? It has fluttered medical and nursing services badly; also prospective parents. As my sister says, no husband wants to be left with a baby instead of a wife. She says it is a rare predicament, in these days, but does arise; and then the doctor sometimes asks the father, but usually saves the mother. I am sorry the Pope said it, because it has stirred up religious quarrelling. It seems an utterly false and inhuman notion; because the mother will perhaps have other babies and bring them up to have souls to be saved. Anyhow, this *mechanical* belief in baptism as a soul-saver is so odd. Well, where was I? Saying, I think, that Fr. Benson to-day would perhaps like us to quote Holy Writ when apt, so that you should, dear Father, have left in that Latin Psalter bit for me.

Yes; the S.S.J.E. has developed, hasn't it. I expect Fr. Benson is watching it with approval and pleasure. He probably likes Fr. P. very much. How good that the influence of the Society has made the girl B—— to be a church girl and to stick to it. She must have a lot of strength of character to take up that rather hard, poor, austere life, for love, when, from your accounts, she could no doubt have married into comfort and money. I am glad you told Mrs. Paine that the prayers you asked her to say for me had worked. That puts one in a nice relation with people.

Thank you for telling about Fr. Baker's book[1]; I don't

[1] Augustine Baker, *Holy Wisdom or Directions for the Prayer of Contemplation* (1657).

know it, and will enquire after it of Burns Oates. It sounds what I should like to have. So Fr. Baker was converted by Uncle Richard Floyd. Good. There were several Floyd brothers, all R.C.; I only know of Henry, John and Edward, but will accept Uncle Richard too. Uncle John was, like Uncle Henry, a Jesuit. I must look into Uncle R. When I next have access to Challoner,[1] or another of those R.C. biographers, I will have a search for him. Or I might ask my clansman who told me about Uncle Henry—Captain Flood-Macaulay who has all the family annals at command. I have looked up Fr. Baker in my *Dictionary of National Biography Epitome*, which only gives brief facts, but there will be a longer life of course in the full *D.N.B.* I see he became head of the Benedictines at Padua, which was rather grand. I can probably find a 2nd hand copy of *Sancta Sophia* somewhere.

I like your suggestion about concentrating on a word. To take *salutare* would be good. There is so much of it. Then, one can take any prayer slowly, and its pauses fill with meaning and new thoughts. E.g. " *Quid retribuam Domino pro omnibus quae retribuit mihi?* "[2]—a question one should always be asking one-self; and there can be more answers than " *calicem salutaris accipiam, et nomen Domini invocabo.*"[3] It is a good exercise to think up other answers; then, in the day that follows, one can put some of them into practice. The same with " *et fac nos tuis semper inhaerere mandatis,*"[4] and " *Dirigere et sanctificare,*" etc. And " Grant that we may both perceive and know what things . . ." But *all* the good collects in either language can be spread over great spaces of prayer and thought, if we only will try, and make the time for it. You know, I am very bad at this. " *Quid retribuam?* " Well, at least one should answer this question by trying to offer up prayers. I was thinking the other day that, among the best things " *quae retribuit mihi* " are your friendship,

[1] Richard Challoner (1691-1781).
[2] " What reward shall I give unto the Lord: for all the benefits that he hath done unto me ? " Ps. 116. 11.
[3] " I will receive the cup of salvation : and call upon the Name of the Lord." Ps. 116. 12.
[4] " And make us ever to abide in thy commandments."

your help, and your letters over the last fifteen months. Where should I have been without them?

I'm glad you think that the line of prayer chosen should be congenial to one's particular capacities and leanings. I do, too. That's why I always shun those rather florid, sentimental prayers and meditations; they might sink one altogether. There is much in R.C. devotions that I can't stomach; *nothing* in what a contemptuous convert called "Cranmer's little work." I have been collecting good ancient collects from various sources, for my collection. The *words* of liturgies can carry us, even without very strong feeling, in a way extempore prayer can't. As, best of all, the act of the Eucharist can. I felt that so much the other morning, when, during Mass, a dear friend of mine was, I knew, having the cornea of her eye cut out and changed for another (incredible, but true) under a local anaesthetic, so that she was knowing all about it though not feeling pain—and of course I could think of nothing else, I felt I was there watching it, and I couldn't think of the service at all. But suddenly I felt that we were both being somehow carried, by the mere words and act, however little we attended to it. Nothing we can do deserves that—but there it is, and how thankful one is that it is so. When I think that this time last year I knew nothing of this. . . . [*sic*]

I didn't know you hadn't seen *The Stricken Deer*,[1] or would have sent it you long ago. It is very good, don't you think? Please remember me to Fr. Pedersen, and tell him I took it unkindly that he never communicated with me again after his return from his European Grand Tour, which I wanted to hear about. But I know how busy and how mobile he had to be. Tell him too that that *American P[rayer] B[ook] Commentary* is among my more treasured works—I find it useful and informing at every turn.

I feel we are arriving at the time when sea letters are going to take an unconscionable time crossing the ocean (though yours was only 3 weeks), so I think for once I shall commit this to the air, or it will get tangled up with the Christmas mails. It grows

[1] Lord David Cecil, *The Stricken Deer; or the Life of Cowper* (1929).

late in the night, and I must stop this and go to bed. I am trying now to get to bed a little earlier, as I found late nights and early mornings didn't go well together. I am reading in bed a lovely book of travel in the east—deserts and ruins and ancient cities, that send me to sleep in a drifting dream of strangeness and beauty. Good night, dear Father, and my love always.

R. M.

20, *Hinde House, Hinde St., W.*1
19th November, 1951†

Dear Father,

Thank you very much indeed for your letter (air) posted on 15th, which came to-day. I am so sorry you were worried by the long gap between letters. Of course the one posted 17th Oct. ought to have reached you ages before it did. And you are right in thinking there was another I wrote on 9th Oct., and I do hope you have got it by now, because in it I enclosed those old snapshots I spoke of, some of which I thought might amuse you. I also enclosed, as you surmise, the 1st bit of Johnny's Diary, from *The T[imes] L[iterary] S[upplement]*.

What else was in the letter I forget: but I must have talked about your letter of 1st Oct., and the visit from your Powys cousin, and Orwell's book, and other things in your letter of 1st Oct. I hope you'll get it, because of the photographs. As you say, no letter between us has yet been utterly lost, only delayed. Still, it might happen, of course. In a recent letter, which you may have got by now, I said that, in the event of my being too ill to write, I would ask my sister to send you a line. So, unless you ever get that line, I am *well*. If just laid up with some mild complaint, I should write myself, and get it posted. Don't be anxious about me. Though it is a nice, warming feeling that you can be. I wrote you an *air letter* on 16th Nov. (as the sea seems to have settled into its winter sloth) but write this line now because I have got yours.

I was much interested in what you say about *Tudor England*

(I haven't yet got the Pelican, but shall). Is Bindoff[1] a Roman? Or just (what we are bidden *not* to call) Anglo-Catholic? They mustn't run down " Cranmer's little work " or try and deprive us of our Mass. The ceremonial must have been most comfortless, both to old-fashioned worshippers then, and would be to us now, but I don't agree about " blocking the last loophole," and " the forbidden vision of sacrifice." It sounds like the attempts R.C.'s make to deny the validity of our Eucharist.

" They had no sacraments," says Evelyn Waugh, of the Protestant Elizabethans. I'm glad you say that about its sufficiency and validity under the P.B. formulas; after all, they preserved and kept it down so many centuries, and if people like Laud, Hooker, Cosin, George Herbert, and Jeremy Taylor were satisfied and nourished by it, we needn't run it down, though it is good that we have given it now a more fitting and glorifying dress. We can't whittle away the profound Eucharistic experiences of our devout ancestors before the High Church movement took over. I must send you the address of Marcel Simon to the Modern Churchmen, praising the Anglican Church. I think I told you about it in one of my letters lately.

I sent you the picture of J. C. Powys on the jacket of his book, I forget in which letter. The Prophet in the Mountains —I must read his autobiography. I am afraid his financial circumstances aren't v.g.

Yes, I suppose *And no man's wit* is, in a sense, an indictment of the Franco regime, which was then very shocking and barbarous and unjust. It still is Fascist, of course, but time has toned it down, and it has improved. The position of the poor is deplorable, everyone says. I think I *should* probably write the book rather differently now.

Let me know if you get my letter of 9th Oct., with the photographs. There is still hope. It all seems very capricious. I think I shall use the air now, mostly, till Christmas is past or you won't get anything I write till 1952, which won't do at all.

My love always,

R. M.

[1] Professor S. T. Bindoff, author of *Tudor England* (1950).

Dear Father,

Thank you so much for your so good letter of 17th Nov., which came a few days ago. I am relieved to know that my letters had all reached you at last, including the one with the photographs, and the 1st *T.L.S.* cutting. So it was a strike that held them up; really it is too bad. It might in some cases do a lot of harm; imagine the people waiting anxiously for news of a sick relation or friend, or a lover for a word from his lady— the failure to get it might ruin lives. Very bad.

In dating this letter, I remember that (I think) on this date last year I wrote you a letter that started quite a lot. No; it didn't start it; it was really the carrying to its logical outcome something started before; still, it was important. And now here I am, thank you! And learning something new all the time. Not that one never passes sometimes into " the parched places in the wilderness," where one doesn't " see when good cometh "; those are bad times; but more often one has access to the river, and the river may reach the roots even if one doesn't feel it much; and one may hope (if sometimes rather forlornly) for the " fruit in due season." Thank you for the last page of your letter. It confirms much that I have known in myself was right to do. " Solid ground ": yes. I'm glad you said that; for sometimes it does seem to be a bit quakey and bog-like under one's feet. Especially after a bad night. But I try and remember that it doesn't depend on my feeling about it, but on the whole church in action.

When I got your last letter I sent you *John Gerard*, which you refused before; I had it for review, and herewith I enclose the review, in case you'd like to see what I said of it. I don't quite see why Fr. Manson thinks it will do harm. I suppose he means it will give a heroic picture of the Jesuit mission in England —but then it *was* heroic, surely. As I say in my review, the picture doesn't include the political background of Jesuit pro-Spanish conspiracy against the queen and country, the plans for invasion, etc., and I think it should; but what can one expect from a Jesuit autobiography and a Jesuit editor? Of course they keep that side of it quiet. It is a pity, because it loses a chance of enlightening a very ignorant public on an interesting historical situation; but of course they are too propagandist and too little historical or scholarly (or honest) to want to do that. All the same, I don't see its doing much harm. Though one of its publishers, a rather innocent young man in Longmans, did say to me, " I'm not a Catholic, but . . ." (I distrust that beginning.) He went on to say what fine people those priests must have been. He sees something of Fr. Caraman, the translator and editor of the book (editor of *The Month*) and I dare say . . . [might] be a convert before long. I think it is for the most part those rather ignorant people who have never learnt much about theology or history or the church, who are seized by the R.C. idea and carried by admiration and emotion into it. I am interested that Fr. Manson should feel as he does about it, as of course he must have come across far more of that kind of thing than I have.

I'm sorry that silence and gap in letters made you anxious. Don't ever enquire about me, or worry, as I promise you will hear at once, by air, from my sister (who now has instructions and your address) should I be really ill. I, of course, can be sure of getting news, when I ask, from St. Edward's House about you.

You know, I remember you very well 36 years ago. I didn't remember that you hadn't laughed; but at least it was obvious that you had a sense of humour. And you had gentleness, and understanding, and sympathy, and were infinitely helpful and intelligent in advice. And said quite a lot; which I liked. And I loved your retreat addresses. I can say now that I was very sorry when you disappeared, and when dear Fr. Cary returned to take his own people over, good as he was. You had supplied something rather different. And 35 years later you still did, and more. And still do. If you had any photographs of yourself *then* . . . [*sic*] but I suppose you haven't. I don't know what photograph of me was in a book of 1928; was it a Penguin, I wonder?

I have one taken about then, which may have been reproduced; someday I will send you a copy of that, perhaps.

Later. I am just back from the London Lib[rary], where I found that J. C. P[owys]'s autobiog. hasn't yet been returned by whoever has it; they have sent for it again. I also ordered *Tudor England* from W. H. Smith some time ago, but that isn't in yet either. I look forward to reading the autobiog., especially the things about you. *Orate Fratres*[1] I can get, no doubt, from Duckett. I shall have more time after this week for going about looking up books, as I shall have done with the BBC " Critics " that I have been on for 6 weeks, which takes so much time seeing plays, films, books, art shows, listening to radio. I have been doing Radio, but we all have to *see* the other things one's colleagues will speak about. This week I am complaining of some of the music hall jokes the BBC puts over, they are so vulgar sometimes as to be nauseous, and of course are greatly applauded by the uneducated public who are their audiences. Jokes like (believe it or not) " I told my girl-friend to walk *against* the wind when she comes to see me at the farm, so as not to make the goats jealous." Meaning, of course, that she smelt. Shrieks of applause and laughter at this sally, from the " workers " who hear " Workers' Playtime." Really, besides its fatuity and unfunniness, a joke of that kind is rather nasty. Or so it seems to me; but it seems to please the listeners. I believe little prep-school boys think it funny to call one another smelly; girls, I think, not.

Did you ever read Milman's book about Horace,[2] his life and farm, etc., well illustrated, and with a good many of his odes and epistles in it? It is really rather attractive; I got it from the Library to-day. A book I was asked to review is Professor Allison Peers's edition of St. Teresa's letters, in 2 vols. I declined it, for lack of time; but it is a book I should like to have had. I've not yet seen Kate O'Brien's Life of her. I read

[1] Formerly the name of the American R.C. liturgical journal *Worship.*
[2] H. H. Milman prefaced his edition of Horace's works with a life of the poet (1849).

Vita Sackville-West's *The Eagle and the Dove*, about T. of Avila
and T. of Lisieux (a tiresome little creature, who shouldn't be
mentioned in the same breath as her of Avila) and found it
interesting. Indeed, she was a wonderful woman, with a great
sense of humour and of humanity. I must read this new edition
of her letters. Now I must stop and drive off to Moorfields Eye
Hospital to read to my friend there who has been having her
cornea changed. I am reading *Howards End*[1] to her, which we
both love. I would like to continue this letter, but should also
like to post it to-night, so will stop it, with my love and greetings,
and hoping no more strikes will come between our epistolary
intercourse. Anyhow, this goes by air.

Your affectionate

R. M.

I think I have got all your letters up to this one, now.

December

20, *Hinde House, Hinde St., W.*1
6th December, 1951 (*Feast of St. Nicholas*)

Dear Father,

Thank you so very much for two air letters—such good ones
—posted 26th Nov. and 1st Dec. (?) (postmark a little smudgy).
I am delighted with your suggestion about Cynthia[2] trying to
swim; why *not tentantis*? Teuthras isn't known much about
by anyone, it seems; of course " the waves of Teuthras " *may*
then have had some local meaning, and refer to some pool or
bit of quiet sea near Cumae—but if so why has it been forgotten?
We know all about the Lucrine Lake, and Avernus close to it,
and the causeway of Hercules, and the shores round Baiae, but
Teuthras no. I think your suggestion is brilliant; he was probably

---

[1] E. M. Forster, *Howards End* (1910).
[2] She figures in many of the poems of Propertius (b. *c.* 50 B.C.).

still referring to the Lucrine Lake and its little quiet waves, where she might either row (more likely be rowed by that annoying *alterius*) or practise her swimming in safety; for none of them would seem to have gone in very much for the open sea. But I think *alterius* would still have companioned her, so she wouldn't have been so much safer from his *blandos susurros*.[1] She was undoubtedly something of a minx; the way she summoned poor P[ropertius] at midnight to make the dangerous (in the dark) journey across the Campagna from Rome to Tibur, was unpardonable. However, she seems to have been the life and soul of the villadom round Tibur, and they all liked her company, so she must have had wits as well as beauty.

I have now got hold of *J. C. Powys, his autobiography*, and am reading it with great interest. What an extraordinary character he has—or is it only an extraordinary view of himself? I read the part about you (p. 599) with much appreciation and pleasure. I note that he says you think better of him than he does of himself—or than your God does. I expect you are more nearly right. He must be a very loveable person, and with a tremendous sense of Right and Wrong, Good and Evil—perhaps that inherited sense of it that clergy families are apt to have, indeed, can scarcely avoid, whatever their personal beliefs. He has a very busy conscience, obviously. And beautifully keen sensuous perceptions. I like the feelings he had about the type of picture he loves, and that I love too—the 18th century Italian landscape with trees, ruins, distant water, light in the sky, a bridge; he describes it so well, and I too feel like that—a kind of sensuous joy in such pictures. On the high level, of course, Claude, Poussin, Rosa, and other 17th c. artists painted in this sort, and how lovely and romantic and breathtaking they are! And even on the more ordinary level, all those Italian landscapes that our 18th cent. ancestors brought home from their Grand Tours and hung about their houses, and that one sees now in the old picture and junk shops—there are lots about here—how they tug at the emotions, for some reason which has little to do with art, I fancy, and is perhaps ancestral pleasure in Abroad.

[1] *Soft whispers.*

Your cousin has many good observations such as those about this. I don't quite know what he means about the Christian doctrines (see p. 599) if " relaxed a little on the erotic side," may hold deep cosmic secrets. Does he mean they are too severe about chastity and such things? I suppose so. You told me he wasn't really sadistic and that that is all his fancy: still, why did he throw you into a bed of nettles? I think he is older than you, isn't he. I like his remark that the grand struggle of his life has been between Conscience and sensual desires. He has the face of an ascetic at war with the world, the flesh and the devil. As you said once, he might well have been a priest, had his beliefs been different. I like his perfect frankness, and his refusal to present a romantic picture of himself. And how beautiful his love for Llewelyn[1] was! I am still reading the book, and expect to find a lot of interest in it. Anyhow, his feeling for you endears him to me. I like his word " Cowperist."

I'm glad you like those photographs. Actually, I look older now than when they were taken. Though I hadn't realised that my hair now looks gray, though of course it has a lot of gray in it. How conservative one is; I suppose one gets used to one's hair being mid-brown, and it still seems to one to be so. But I am sure Fr. Pedersen is right. (Don't tell him I questioned it— it would seem like vanity, and I'm sure he must be right.) Perhaps I will chop off a tiny piece and send it to you to judge for yourself—*not*, I needn't say, to keep in an album in the old-fashioned way of our ancestors, but to cast in an incinerator when inspected. If I remember, before posting this I will do that— but again, don't tell Fr. P. Yes, it has, as is only right at my advanced stage, a lot of gray in it. Also, it is falling out too fast! *Eheu fugaces*.[2] I should now like a photograph of Horace, being steeped in descriptions of his farm and his surroundings, so that I feel I could find my way about every inch of the ground, along the cold Digentia, up the hill behind, through the woods towards the Fons Bandusiae, among the oaks and vines.

I supposed that Peter Livius must have been a Hamburg man.

---

[1] His brother, Llewelyn Powys.
[2] " Alas, the fleeting (years glide by) "; Horace, *Odes* 2. 14.

It is obvious that he wasn't a British merchant, as nearly all of these would be members of the British Factory, and there is no mention of him in the various lists of Factory members given in the book I have about the Factory. I wonder what Livius did in Lisbon. If he was a merchant, he would no doubt be a member of the *German* Factory; and I have no lists of the members of that. Or he may have been something diplomatic of course. He went there in 1709, I note. And George became wholly English, obviously, in spite of being half German and half Irish. I will look out for further information about Peter's Lisbon life. What happened to his other children, I wonder? George's godparentage looks rather diplomatic—our friend Castres, and Mrs Compton (wife of the Hon. Charles Compton, who was, I think Envoy Extraordinary from 1742-45. I have read some of his despatches in old days in the Record Office). But yes, do send me a copy of that paper about Peter in Portugal sometime; I should be interested.

I sent you *John Gerard*—oh perhaps I told you this last time— and my review of it. Yesterday I met Fr. Caraman S.J. (editor of *The Month*, and translator and editor of Gerard) at a party, and conversed with him at some length about his book. He had been quite pleased with my review; *he* says the only Jesuit plotting against the throne and country was on the part of Fathers Parsons and Allen; but he understates; there were more Jesuits than these involved in it. And great distrust and dislike of the Jesuits by many of the R.C. gentry and seculars in England; a point that the former translator rather slurs over. I was interested in the passage where Gerard avows the Jesuit doctrine of lawful lying; it seems very—Jesuitical, and is what we have always accused them of, and what modern apologists such as Ronald Knox say is quite untrue. Here they are convicted out of the mouth of a Jesuit of repute, who would certainly state the case correctly. Fr. Caraman . . . is a friend of Graham Greene's and Evelyn Waugh's. He doesn't think E.W. likely to write any more comic novels, which is a sad pity, as he can be so brilliantly funny.

What do you think about C. S. Lewis, of whom I have read

very little having had always a slight prejudice against him? But I think I shall now so far overcome this as to read *The Problem of Pain*, and something called *Beyond Personality*, which sounds interesting.

Thank you for giving me your interpretation of that prayer "*ut ad sancta sanctorum . . . introire*."[1] I have now added it to my collection of Latin prayers in my *Preces Privatae*, the ones I pick about among to say to myself before, during and after Mass. I like the thought of bringing in all the oddments of luggage and holding them up. That friend of mine who had her cornea changed still can't see out of that eye or the other, and is still in bed at Moorfields, where I visit and talk and read to her. The surgeon says her state is all right, as it is a very gradual process. Poor dear, she gets very weary of lying there blind, but she listens in a good deal, when there is good music, or anything interesting in the way of talks, and her friends and relations divide up the days between them to go and sit with her. She is very gay and amusing with it all, and enormously courageous; a person in a thousand. Not religious; but will admit anything to be possible, and has a splendid gospel of courage and pluck. And beautiful to look at, even with bandaged eyes. Anyhow, I take *her* in with me to Mass.

I understand exactly, I think, what you feel about sticking to the P[rayer] B[ook] service instead of adding all those supplementary prayers, etc. I think I do feel they enrich the service; the interpolated sayings are often so good, and seem to light up the P.B. prayers as if sudden flashes of light were directed on them. But even without these, what a wholly beautiful service it is. I can imagine feeling that it shouldn't be touched or added to in any way. And I can imagine too that, if I were a priest saying it, I might feel as you do—that this was my Church, and these the prayers it ordained, and I its minister and priest. Not being a priest, I like anything that is put into it so long as it is *good*. It always is at the Chapel. Unlike some churches, which insert translations from the Roman Missal which I don't always like. As you say, they are better in Latin: sometimes because of the

[1] " So that [we may] enter into the holy of holies."

" decent obscurity of a learned tongue," sometimes (as in the case of *honore*) because they really are better put. And if rather too Counter-Reformationist for my rather austere taste, they are *much* better in Latin. I wish they would hurry up and produce that Pelican of Bindoff's which I have ordered. Or perhaps they have it to-day; I couldn't get there this afternoon. I know it will interest me. But I now have Powys to read, so, as my reading time is so scanty, it is perhaps as well that Bindoff tarries.

The Archbishop of Aelia, Dr. Mathew (Apostolic Delegate at Mombasa), whom I have probably mentioned to you before, though I see him seldom now he is in Africa, writes to me to-day that he is dedicating to me the book he is now writing, *The Genesis of the Civil War*.[1] This is because he liked *They were Defeated*. I am very proud and pleased at this, because he writes so well and is so able. He is coming to England in Feb. for 6 months. I expect he will be a Cardinal before long. I like both him and his brother Fr. Gervase Mathew v. much.

I feel you are right about the Elizabethans *on the whole* not wanting religious changes. Though surely there was the Puritan wing (from the Lollards on) who really did. I suppose church abuses had annoyed and galled very many people; one can see that even in Langland and (less) in Chaucer. And the vulgar outcry against the Pope was only partly anti-foreign-power. Many of the ignorant rabble must, it seems, have confused Guy Fawkes with the Pope! See enclosed (part of letter in *The Times Literary Supplement*). It is hard to say from what springs these surges of popular feeling well up. But I have an idea that the feeling has always, in one form or another, been there. And then national feeling came in to strengthen it and give it drive.

The season has moved on from the Feast of St. Nicholas (which my father always honoured when we were children, because St. N. was the patron Saint of his old school) to that of the Conception of the B.V.M. (Immaculate? Do we hold with that? No: according to *Hours of Prayer*, not. Indeed, I am sure

---

[1] This book was later published (in 1955) under the title *Scotland under Charles I*; it has the following dedication: " For Rose Macaulay in memory of a long friendship."

not. I wonder do the very extreme churches, such as St. Thomas's, Annunciation, or even All Saints, celebrate that. I dare say they do. I must ask Fr. Irvine!). Now I must go out; I hope to pick up Bindoff before the shops shut.

I wonder what the Christmas air-posts will be like, and on what date I should write to you for Christmas Day. In about 10 days, I fancy—my love till then. I look back on last Christmas, that strange, dark, *suspended* time. . . . [*sic*]

R. M.

20, *Hinde House, Hinde St., W.*1
15th December, 1951†

Dear Father,

I've just got your air paper posted on 10th—well, it came last night, actually—and think I will now write for Christmas, and enclose my Christmas card, *which I like very much*, whoever isn't going to. I got it out of an old early 19th century Spanish book. I think the flautist looks so happy, and is leaping in the water with such spirit. I expect, as it was Christmas Day (though that is only my addition, and I dare say actually it was summer), he is trying to keep warm by motion. Anyhow, he brings my love and Christmas greetings, though I fancy he will arrive a little before time.

Thank you so much for your letter, which I peruse every word of with pleasure. I'm glad you will like to have Gerard, and also like my review. To-day there is one, rather to the same effect, in *The Church Times*, which I send herewith, though I think you very likely see this journal. As you see, the reviewer agrees with us that the political background shouldn't have been omitted; but he puts it with more feeling than I did, and I think seems to share Fr. Manson's apprehension of the harm the book may do. In fact, he sounds a little cross. It takes R.C. propaganda to cause *Church Times* reviewers to speak with so much sympathy of our Protestant martyrs. I like Fr. Palmer's thanksgiving for Elizabeth and Archbp. Parker and Hooker.

I think I should like Fr. Palmer a good deal, from all you have said about him.

I heard yesterday from Fr. Wilkins, suggesting that I should compile a set of short " acts," or prayers, suitable for people to say in buses and trains on [the] way to work. Of course I can't. But, as I told him, I wish someone would; we would all find such a collection useful. He mentions those (8, I think) at the end of *Sancta Sophia*,[1] which he thinks not enough in touch with what young church people want or can easily use. Nor, I suspect, old church people either, to judge by the one most familiar to me. I am sure good new collections of prayers are badly needed. Fr. W[ilkins] kindly said that I would, he thought, be able to do the kind of thing he has in mind. My view is that people had better make their own, since they alone know what they can say and use without difficulty and embarrassment. I have by now made for myself (largely assisted by your pointings out, especially of Latin prayers) a collection that I like very much, and keep adding to. I get them from all kinds of sources. And among them are verses from psalms, from the Bible, and some poetry, and other oddments. I have them in one of your homebound scrap books, which seems their suitable frame, since so many of them are suggested by you, and since it is so much your doing that I am well in. Yes; that is a comforting thought, that one can go through a Mass with mind straying elsewhere, and still be inside, and nourished by the treacle well. I, of course, never take part in offices (in church; I say parts of them alone) but I think it might become a kind of submergence of which one would be glad. " The rock that is higher than I "—how good to remember that we are set up on it, whether we are thinking about it or not. Yes: what indelible impressions those childhood homes of ours made. The hymns one's mother sang to us in bed; those tunes are so deeply planted in one's soul that I resent all these new ones to which they are now set and sung. I'm sure the old were better; anyhow, it is the old I know and love. One was well inside that small, dear world, and can never get quite outside its influences. Christmas brings them back, of

[1] *Holy Wisdom* (see above p. 221*n*.).

course. Cribs and Christmas trees and candles and stockings, and singing " Wreathe the holly, twine the bay " (which we all thought meant our Varazze Bay, the sea lipping on its sands) " Christ was born on Christmas Day " . . . [*sic*] and the lovely plaster sheep and cows and angels in the Cribs in the dark little shops in the piazza arcades, and the harsh bells clanging out from the 14th century church among them, and the orange and lemon trees shining on the terraces of the hills above the town. Those were the Christmases. Now, and here, it has become too much a racket—crowded, noisy, commercial, expensive. But it is still Christmas; and the first that I shall be fully taking part in for so many years. I shall go to my sister at Romford, as I usually do, for Christmas Eve, Day and Boxing. I hope there won't be fog. I got caught in it last night, dining with friends in Westminster; when we started for our homes, about 11.30 p.m., it was so dense one couldn't see a foot. Luckily I wasn't driving; those who were abandoned their cars in despair. I groped a mile on foot to St. James's Park station, and thence home in the safety of a train. Last Christmas was snow and ice-bound, I think; I spent it with friends in Kent. And felt tossed about with many a conflict, many a doubt, fightings and fears within, without. What a lot has happened this last year!

I tried again this morning to get *Tudor England*, but they've not yet got it in. It will be here before Christmas, though. Meanwhile I am reading Ronald Knox's *Enthusiasm*. A good account of religious queer sects; written with sympathy and a lot of knowledge. But I can never be deeply interested in Shakers, Muggletonians, and their kind. He begins quite early, and includes the Catholic heretical sects of the Middle Ages. Not Margery,[1] though she was certainly an enthusiast in his sense; but not a heretic, of course. I don't feel attracted by any of these people, they all seem rather too hysterical.

I hope you are going to have a nice Christmas, like me. I suppose, unlike me, yours will be all snow, like a Christmas card (at least, we *hope* unlike me, but there are still 10 days to go). I hope this letter won't be over-weight; because, besides

---

[1] Margery Kempe.

the Xmas card, I am putting in yet another little photograph, as you collect them. This pudding-faced tot (of which there are several copies in my mother's old album) seems to be 14 months old; no help in recognising to-day (if she should walk by).

Your affectionate
R. M.

I am being given a pair of rubber swimming fins—they shoot you through the water at a great pace, fixed on the heels. *Won't that be nice!*

20, *Hinde House, Hinde St., W.*1
Christmas Eve [1951] † [*Postmark: London W.*1. 27 *Dec.*]

Dear Father,

I am writing this before the midnight Mass, having put off driving down to my sister's till to-morrow morning, owing to it being a very dark wet evening, not too good for driving out of London among Christmas Eve traffic, with the dim lighting the streets now have. So I am staying here to-night, going to Grosvenor Chapel for midnight Mass, and driving to Essex in the morning. It is a very cool, wet, gusty old English Christmas. Probably you have crisp snow and low temperatures, and a real *New* England Christmas.

Thank you so much for your air paper of 14th, which was your Christmas letter. Mine was posted to you about 15th Dec., I think; (air). Yours (posted 15th) arrived this morning, and interests me much. I read *all* J. C. P[owys]'s autobiography, with great interest. Yes, he certainly had, and felt he had, a mission to the world. (Why do I put it in the past? No doubt he still does.) Now I should like to see a Life of him by someone else, someone who knows him well, and get another view of him. It is interesting, that contrast between people's own view of themselves and the view of them held by other people. (See Oliver Wendell Holmes on *The Three Johns*—the real John known only to his Maker; John's John, never the real one; and

Thomas's John, never the real one either. All 3 are important.) loved to hear of the " little river " at Northwold[1], and the boat. There were both in the garden of my Conybeare uncle and cousins at Barrington, near Cambridge, and when we stayed here it was as romantic as you found it; I fell in, I remember. Nothing is more glamorous than a bit of river running through the garden. Horace had the Digentia. I expect he had a boat, too. I'm glad J.C.P. wasn't really unkind about the nettlebed.

I wonder so much how you are spending Christmas Eve and Day. I suppose you are 3 or 4 hours behind us, and are perhaps now having tea. Or perhaps hearing confessions. I got mine over last Friday. And for a week have been running round with cards, parcels, all the Christmas litter. The jam in the streets has been terrific. Why is humanity so *excessive* in the way it does things? The golden mean seems out of fashion. Hence the decease of the Liberal Party, and also of the *Guardian*,[2] which kept, I suppose, the *via media* between High and Low Church . . . The *Modern Churchman* was deploring its death; of course it prefers it to the *Church Times*, with its Anglo-Catholicism (" sometimes disloyal," the *M.C.* points out); still, I fancy the *Guardian* was a little *dull*, perhaps.

This letter is really to wish you a happy New Year, which I do, so much. And so many more of them. I do like to know and feel you there, across the dividing salty sea, taking me sometimes with you into the *sancta sanctorum*. So long as you do that, I don't feel very much harm can hold me for long together. I am reading *The Problem of Pain*, which interests me. C. S. L[ewis] is a little slapdash, perhaps, but vivid and impressive, and has good images. Now I must pack my bag for to-morrow, and get some supper. Good night. Thank you for a wonderful year, dear Father.

Yours with my love,

R. M.

[1] Northwold Rectory (near the River Wissey) was the Norfolk home of Father Johnson's paternal grandparents when he was a boy.
[2] A weekly Anglican newspaper, founded in 1846, which ceased publication in 1951.

1952

January

Dear Father,

Thank you so very much for your air letter posted 27th Dec. and begun on Christmas Eve, acknowledging mine that enclosed my Xmas card, infant photograph, and *Ch[urch] Times* Gerard review. I sent you an air paper from Romford, where I spent Xmas and Boxing Day. It is rather restful to have Xmas over, it is such a rush; but I was very happy. It was such a good midnight Mass. Why, by the way, don't churches that are at all high have New Year's Eve Mass—watch night, they call it at the churches that have it? Some ecclesiastical principle seems to be involved; but I can't think what. I think it is a pity. People *like* New Year's Day, and take it seriously, often, thinking things over and taking stock and making resolutions. We always did this in my family, and I certainly do now. It seems one of those natural, as distinguished from church, seasonal days, that have deep roots, and I think should be used. Of course a lot of people prefer to merry-make, and see the year in with babble and revel and wine; but many others like to pray. I suppose Anglo-Catholics don't have watch night services because R.C.s don't; but why don't both? . . . Did you have it as a boy in Norfolk? When we were children in Italy, we didn't, of course; anyhow we were sent to bed before midnight. But my father always read aloud the part of *In Memoriam* about " Ring out, wild bells." Then, after we lived in England, the waits came round and sang and rang handbells, and all the bells for miles round rang. It really is an occasion. . . . I see you say you don't really like even Xmas midnight Mass. I do; there is something beautiful and mysterious in its being at dead of night, and the new year stealing in. And now it's well in, and I wish you such a happy one, with all my heart. Health, and joy, and every good thing possible.

I am interested in what you say about Fr. Wilkins's suggestion that I should compile a collection of Brief Prayers. If ever I did, it would have to be anon. . . . I could only compile such a book freely if I was Anon. Perhaps, after some years of collecting and sifting, I could. I absolutely agree with all your views as to what such prayers should be. Dignified, finely worded, often Latin, often archaic; when modern and vernacular, very restrained and austere and elegantly put. How interesting it might be, choosing prayers for occasions—as you say, not specifically mentioning the occasions, but suited to them. Yes. Ps. 119 could alone almost meet most occasions; what a treasure-house it is. I shall now add to my Scraps " *Benedictus Dominus die quotidie . . . Domini, Domini, exitus mortis.*"[1] It is more interesting and beautiful than the English " escape death"; because it includes the exit of death in what is His, not merely the escape from it. Your rendering turns it a better way up altogether, and I shall say it like that; it has more religion and more poetry. You know, that verse is one people might say when in danger —one could have used it during the bombing; when driving one's car or ambulance along dark streets with those things thundering down and flames leaping to the skies. I *was* frightened once or twice; but not often or very much, not, I suppose, being constitutionally particularly nervous about such things. I know some people were far more frightened—and therefore, of course, braver in enduring it. But the *exitus mortis* would be good in any case.

Do you believe that it is any use praying that someone (such as my friend who had her cornea changed for another) may see again properly? (She is progressing quite well, I think.) I mean, can one pray for purely physical results like that? I know they did in the Gospels, but then physical cures were then part of the business of showing that He was Christ. I do pray about such things, illness, etc.; one can't help it; but I wonder how much

[1] " Praised be the Lord daily: . . . God is the Lord, by whom we escape death." Ps. 68. 19, 20.

use it is. Perhaps one can't know that. Anyhow, one has to do it, for one's own comfort. But there are, of course, all sorts of " emergency " prayers which one can use, which don't ask for specific results.

I often wonder what was the state of mind of those Catholic secular priests under Elizabeth, whom you speak of. I suppose some of them were left pretty much alone, in country districts, so long as they didn't obtrude themselves. Certainly some were kept as chaplains by the recusant gentry. But sometimes they would get into trouble. They were much put about, no doubt, by the Bull of Excommunication, which made their position so difficult. And I expect they looked rather doubtfully on the " Jesuited Papists," as the missioners from abroad were called, with their Roman rites and even new pronunciation of church Latin, and transmontane views on church government and pro-Spanish bias. I suppose the more prominent Catholics were imprisoned (if Bishops) and weeded out from the Universities, and those who were left unmolested would be laxer—often not even recusants, but conforming Church Papists, believing in the old religion but not bothering to sacrifice much for it. Perhaps, do you think, the zealous seminarists on their Mission woke the consciences of some of them, and exasperated others. What one would like to know is how long it took Catholics to be absorbed, as most were, in the new church, and what they really felt about it. Sometimes it took two generations, sometimes more. How exciting a flashback to Elizabethan life would be; and the religious aspect most exciting of all. Could one have joined the Elizabethan church, or wouldn't it have seemed too desolately impoverished ? Later, in the 17th century, it would have been possible. And of course there was always Cranmer's Prayer Book with its translated liturgy, which must have seemed beautiful, surely, except to those invincibly set against the vernacular. . . .

Yes; the Great O's[1] certainly should be among our Brief Prayers. Or some of them. *O Sapientia, O Clavis David, O*

[1] The O-Antiphons (or Greater Antiphons), often sung before and after the Magnificat in the seven days preceding Christmas Eve.

Oriens (the best, I think). I only know by heart *O Oriens*; that I often say.

I don't know where those words of S. Augustine are; they are in the best classical tradition—Cicero or Marcus Aurelius might have said them. I must read *De Civitate* again. The *Confessions* I read through early last year while in bed with flue. I think many Brief Prayers might be got from him. (You see I am becoming rather taken by this scheme.) But would Latin do for the majority of possible users of the compilation? It seems less and less known, unfortunately. I was shocked to hear even a young priest, who sometimes helps at the Chapel, say lately that he scarcely knew any. How did he get where he is, or through his examinations? On the other hand, I met last night a most cultivated young ordinand . . . who knows all he ought. Cuddesdon seems to produce the best types, don't you think? Before that, he was Trinity, Cambridge, before that, Eton. His parents live in a beautiful medieval house in Majorca.

Is Bright and Medd's Latin trans. of *Lighten our Darkness* the same as the original in the Sarum office? I haven't got the latter—and I don't know if this collect is in the Breviary. The Breviary Epiphany collect is better than the P.B. trans. Trouble with the B. is that it has no index and takes a lot of hunting to find a particular thing—unless I have one of your admirably accurate signposts (such as you gave me to find the O's). I think I shall *index* my 4 little vols., by degrees, entering things as I find them. I wish I had more time for things. I am pressed on by my Ruins book all the time. *Resolve for 1952 to finish it within 2 months!*

My love for 1952 again. Thank you for making it to be what it is to me—this beginning of another year.

Always yours,

R. M.

(Mathew has a short a.)

Dear Father,

Thank you for your delightful letter begun on New Year's
Eve and posted 3rd Jan. *And* for sending me that really lovely
photograph of you standing in the forest glade at Foxborough[1];
I like it better than any I have of you, and have stood it on my
bedroom bureau; later it shall have a little frame to keep it
clean.

I can't pretend to explain the date on the postmark of my
air paper written on Xmas Eve. I don't now remember when
(or where) I posted it; but I agree with you that a 2-days'
passage seems incredible. Yours, posted on 3rd, reached me, I
think, on the 8th. Life in the air is highly unreliable, it seems.

You drew my attention to a lot of interesting matters in
your letter. I sent for *Pax* from its publishers (at Prinknash—
now, it seems, called St. Michael's Abbey, Farnborough—no, I
see it can't be, since Prinknash is in Glos.; but anyhow *Pax* is
now published there.)[2] I found the Eirenicism article[3] v. interesting. Searching about for more about John Barnes,[4] I found an
acid comment by Dom Bennet Weldon,[5] saying that Barnes's
project was " to mince the Catholic truths that the Protestants
might digest them without choking; and so likewise to prepare
the Protestant errors that Catholic stomachs might not loathe
them. He was hard at work on this project 1625-6." It seems
that Barnes died a prisoner of the Inquisition, in Rome. Obadiah
Walker,[6] on the contrary, died a prisoner of the English

[1] Probably the photograph reproduced opposite p. 32, which was taken at
the S.S.J.E. cemetery near Foxborough, Mass.

[2] *Pax*, the Roman Catholic quarterly review of the Benedictines of Prinknash, is published at Prinknash Abbey, Gloucester. The editor of *Pax* resides
at St. Michael's Abbey, Farnborough, Hants (since 1947 a subsidiary house of
the same order).

[3] Dom Gregory Rees, O.S.B., " Eirenicism in the Seventeenth Century ";
an article published in *Pax* (Autumn-Winter, 1951).

[4] English Benedictine monk, d. 1661.

[5] Ralph Weldon (1674-1713) became a Benedictine monk in 1692, where-
after he was known as Dom Bennet Weldon.

[6] Obadiah Walker (1616-1699), Master of University College, Oxford.

gov[ernment], in the Tower. So both these mediators copped it, from opposite sides. Walker, over whose rooms in Univ. undergraduates wrote,

> " Oh old Obadiah
> Sing Ave Maria," etc.

maintained that " my principles are *not* wholly agreeable with the doctrine of the Romanish church "—but they were certainly much less so with the C. of E. It is interesting that people on both sides were at work even then to reconcile the two churches. Laud, of course, would have liked to; but he didn't get down to it, he was too busy reforming the C. of E. at home. I am glad Dom Gregory Rees thinks " Roman fever " abated; I don't notice it myself, anyhow among the laity; but I expect he means among clergy, and I think here he is probably right. My experience is very little use, as it is only lately that I have mixed much in clerical or church circles and heard talk about it; but it does seem to me that there is an increasing self-confidence and independence among High Church Anglicans, and an increased pleasure in their own way of worship. I wonder what you think, and what all these Fathers who visit you from Cowley think, about that. Novels are still largely full of the view that if its characters turn religious, it must be R.C. they turn. But novels are mostly written by very ignorant people. Oh dear, ignorance is so odd, I mean it is so gross. . . . And a R.C. friend of mine who lives in Madrid, and whom I have been seeing lately here, assured me that we didn't [have a form for private absolution], and [that] the C. of E. never had, since the Reformation, believed in valid sacraments, e.g. Communion. I quoted what our catechism says about it, " verily and indeed," etc., and indeed what is to be found even in the Articles, and showed him a passage I was reading in Law's " Spirit of Prayer ",[1] which asserts very uncompromisingly that we receive the Body and Blood of Christ; and he was convinced, but surprised. We know much more about their church than they about ours.

I too read that C[hurch] T[imes] article about C. S. Lewis,

[1] Included in *Selected Mystical Writings of William Law; edited by Stephen Hobhouse* (1938).

and was induced by it to get some of his books from the Library. I found them interesting—more so than I had thought. He is very much in earnest about goodness. *He* certainly has no " Roman nostalgia." My own is very superficial, and wholly connected with memories of the dear Italian churches of my childhood, processions, etc. I know that I couldn't be happy, or honest, or religious, in the Unreformed Church; there would always be too much of what it teaches that I simply don't can't and don't want to believe. I notice this when I follow Mass in *The English Missal*, which is really a translation from the Breviary, I think; it has so many prayers, secrets, propers, saints, expressions, which I don't really say, nor could; they seem—what shall I say—*overdone*; excessive, sometimes sentimental. What I like is the large altar Missal used for Mass at the Chapel (of which there are no small copies, I think) and of course the P[rayer] B[ook], on which I agree with Sir Leoline Jenkins,[1] who wrote in the reign of Charles II " How excellent the composition is . . . how excellent the matter, the method, and the decorum of the whole liturgy. So that neither Rome nor Muscovy, Osburgh nor Amsterdam, have anything in the public services that can enter into comparison with it."[2] Though when I am abroad and go into churches there I do feel a certain wistfulness. But nothing to what one would have felt a century ago, of course.

I don't want a celibate clergy. Not only for selfish reasons— the self-preservation you suggest, for, as you say, you and I wouldn't be here—but I don't think it would be so good. It would keep the clerical element too much segregated, not pervasive, as we have always had it here—and when one thinks what the clergy families have supplied to the national life. . . . [*sic*] I think the celibate English clergy are the salt of the earth—but there is also the earth, which needs leavening. As to gentility, I fear that minishes decade by decade; fewer and fewer of the genteel seem to take orders; and perhaps in 50 years (unless the wheel turns) they will be a democratic company like the

[1] Sir Leoline Jenkins (1623-1685), civil lawyer and diplomatist.
[2] Presumably Augsburg.

apostles, with never an "Oxford accent" between them. Who knows? No, I suppose there will always be some. But on the whole we should be like the Italian or Irish priesthood in class. And what about in morals? That would depend, of course, on how many became priests from real vocation, how many just for a job.

Surely we too should be cooking up a quadrocentenary for the 1552 P[rayer] B[ook]. As Fr. Palmer says, it is the one we use. I forget if we celebrated the '49 book three years ago? And in 10 years we shall have to do the '62 one. But surely the '49 was the most important; no doubt we did do it honour, but I didn't notice, or have forgotten.

I suppose *Pax* is the magazine I remember being started by Donald Attwater[1] a good many years ago. Does he still edit it, I wonder? I liked him. He was (is, no doubt) a liberal kind of R.C. No, I suppose it couldn't have been the kind of paper it is, fifty years ago. I think the Unreformed Ch[urch] is looking up a little, I must say. Let us both—both churches, I mean—look up a little more, and who knows but we may meet? I read that life of Von Hügel;[2] it is quite good; but some critics complained that the writer played down Von H's modernism too much, as I thought too. After all, he *was* a modernist, and might easily have been in trouble with the Vatican; like Acton, he just avoided this, and settled down.

There is no case for "persue." Dom Gregory Rees must have been reading it in Middle English; they *did* sometimes spell it that way. But not, I think, since about 1500.

Well, I did ring up your nieces,[3] encouraged by your message, and, after several failures to make contact, owing to their being out, got on to one of them, who proved to be Catharine, and we had a nice chat; I gave your love, and she said she had been thinking of writing to you, so perhaps she has now done this. She knew I knew you, as you had spoken of me in letters to her father, so I wasn't quite out of the blue. One day we must meet.

[1] Donald Attwater was editor of *Pax*, 1922-28. Publication began in 1904.

[2] Michael de la Bedoyère, *The Life of Baron von Hügel* (1951).

[3] Catharine and Anne Cowper Johnson, daughters of Rev. Wilfred Cowper Johnson.

I liked the sound of her. I expect she and her sister are both very busy. I gather their father is visiting S. Africa, is he? Anyhow, it pleased me to speak with anyone of your name and kin.

How good of you to send *Tudor England*. I shall read it with interest. I have little time off from this book which I am resolved to finish in 2 months from now, but have made a little to rummage about among old prayers and devotional readings, in case I ever do tackle that compilation. I have been reading Law—*Mystical Writings*, the selection is called;[1] it is not the same as one I remember [best] of all, called *Liberal and Mystical Writings*, selected by W. R. Lilley, and introduced by Wm. Scott Palmer, I think;[2] but it has a lot of the same things in it; both contain " The Spirit of Prayer." I do think he is so good, don't you. I wish I had more time just now for such reading.

I must stop this and go off to the Library to hunt up some travel books about Sicilian ruined temples.

This time last year comes back to me. I sometimes wonder if any one ever had a better friend, in every kind of way, than you have been, and are, to me. Epiphany again, and it goes on and on.

My love always,
R. M.

20, *Hinde House, Hinde St., W.*1
19th January, 1952†

Dear Father,

Miracles increase! Returning this afternoon from the library at 5, I found your letter posted 10 a.m. on 17*th* (which means 3 p.m. Greenwich time?). So I now believe the 27th–29th postmark. Our air service is speeding up. I like getting a letter written by you only the day before yesterday; it brings one closely into touch with your current doings and thoughts. The

---

[1] See above p. 248*n*.
[2] *Liberal and Mystical Writings of William Law, with an Introduction by W. S. Palmer and a Preface by W. P. du Bose* (1908).

letter before this last was written 7th Jan. (postmark vague); it didn't make quite such good pace as the last. As to my mysterious Xmas air paper " from Romford," I think it was the same one that I began before midnight Mass, and which I suppose I took down to Romford on Xmas Day and finished there, and posted it in London on 27th after I got back. I don't remember, but this does seem possible. Did I mention in it that I was finishing it at Romford, I wonder? If I had finished it *here* I should, I suppose, have posted it here, before going to Romford. Anyhow, this is what I seem to remember.

I am glad if I have brought you to look with more favour on watch night services. What I feel is that the beginning of the year (as we have for so long made it to be) is connected with something very fundamental in our spirits, thoughts, and even bodies; we must take notice of it, even if we didn't want to; people always have. So why not cause us to take the best *kind* of notice, and use it for good, and let us start our year in the right spirit? This doesn't in any way detract from the greater importance of the Christian feasts and events and dates; they link together, nature brought into alliance with Grace. By the way, I was reading something the other day about the French word " *alliance*," used in the French Bible for our " covenant " or " testament," being better; but it doesn't seem to mean quite the same, surely? (Yes, I have just looked it up in the French dict., and " covenant " *is* one of the meanings it gives.)

Your nice story about " swayvighter " and " fortighter "[1] does bring dear Fr. Cary back. He was so full of good stories, as I remember him. My cousin who is now a Roman . . . reminded me of one the other day—[about] some very extreme Cornish parson whose Bishop remonstrated with him for imposing so many out-of-the-way saints and feasts on his rural congregation, telling him that " all this nomenclature " was a mistake. The parson, who was rather vague as to the meaning of this word, preached next Sunday to his flock, telling them to " drop all this *nomēnclature*; just get up and come along to Mass." I went, with this R.C. cousin, a Portuguese friend (also of course R.C., and a most

[1] Mispronunciations of *suaviter* and *fortiter*.

252

delightful man) and Fr. Irvine, to the opening of Church Unity week on Thursday at the Central Hall. I was disappointed, because no speaker made any concrete proposals for greater unity; they all spoke of good will, tolerance, courtesy, friendliness, co-operation between the churches, but got no further than that. They all spoke well, however; the Bp. of Oxford was in the chair, and as usual v.g.; there followed a Presbyterian, Dr. Maxwell, who was really excellent, and spoke very well for his church, saying how they valued their Orders and their Sacraments, and how much they would like union if it could be had without sacrifice of principle, which, he supposed, was what the other churches felt too. The R.C., Fr. Dwyer (who said he spoke with the full approval of his hierarchy) was a cheerful, friendly priest, full of fraternal good will and good jokes, deprecating inter-denominational sniping and desiring mutual peace and friendship. But did he even hint that any concessions from the Roman side might ever be forthcoming? He did not. Well he knew that he mustn't suggest any such thing. So we got no further; the plate came round and we were exhorted to put into it money to pay for this Unity, but how much it would cost we weren't told. I thought perhaps 2/6, though it wouldn't buy unity, would be suitable; if I had been given reason to think that Unity was really round the corner, waiting for the price to be collected before it materialized, I would have given more. But I am not at all clear what we are bidden to pray for this week. Inter-communion, perhaps. . . . Inter-communion would be nice, of course. So would fair play. My sister, who has worked, as a mission nurse, in S. Africa, says the R.C.s *don't* play fair, either there or in India; they persuade the natives to come into their church and desert the Anglican mission, telling them it is the same thing but better. (Gallant but untruthful men, as you say of the Jesuit missionaries of past years. I like that description!) Well, so much for Unity week. I saw Canon Hood on the platform, and a lot of Anglican Fathers (Cowley and Mirfield) and an abbot or two. So I suppose they hope for some result, *not* merely increased good will.

Yes, how bad those translations of Latin hymns nearly always are. The *Cultor Dei* trans. is very prosy and poor, compared with the Latin, out of which it should never have been taken.[1] Then, look at the hymn for Saturday Vespers for the Epiphany octave—the one we are saying now—*Deus Creator omnium*;[2] I don't know the Latin, but the English is very cumbrous.

"Nor envious fiend with harmful snare
Our rest with sinful terrors scare "——

what language! Who makes these translations? The Latin is probably very dignified. As to *Cultor Dei*, I am glad you discovered Gaselee's *totum* version; it is *so* much better than *rorem* which sounds foolish and weak.[3] What a pity you can't get it altered in *Hours of Prayer*. You might make an English trans. with *totum* and get the S.S.J.E. to adopt it. "*Totum subisse sanctum*" is very good.

I don't know if I could be much use to these young ordinands and ecclesiastics, though I suppose discussing things may be of use to both discussers. The Cuddesdon young man has now gone to Majorca for a holiday, and then will I suppose return to Cuddesdon; but I may very likely meet him again with his friend Fr. Irvine, and should like to pursue the acquaintance; I liked him. As to young Fr. Irvine (who began to call me "Rose" quite early, in the modern manner, so I call him Gerard), I have plenty of chance to talk to *him*. I am driving him to Herts soon—to see an artificial ruin he knows of,[4] and then on to see Howards End, which is the house in that novel of E. M. Forster's which I read aloud lately to my friend at Moorfields. You ask about that book; if you haven't ever read it, you should. It is quite delightful. It was published in 1910. I *think* you'd like it; the characters are so real, the style so excellent, the humour so delightful, the problems so serious.

[1] See *The English Hymnal*, Hymn 104: "Servant of God, remember The stream thy soul bedewing," from *Cultor Dei memento* of Prudentius (348-*c.* 410); translated by T. A. Lacey (1853-1931).

[2] "God, creator of all things," hymn by St. Ambrose.

[3] In the *Oxford Book of Medieval Latin Verse* (ed. I, 1928) line 127 of *Cultor Dei* included the words "*totum subisse sanctum.*" Subsequently, in an Errata slip, the compiler, S. Gaselee, replaced the proper word "*rorem*" (dew).

[4] The Indian-Troad Folly at Benington, Herts.

Do you not know any of his novels? He is one of my best friends, and I see him often when he is in London; he lives now in Cambridge, at King's. Next week I have promised to drive him to Abinger, which he likes to visit, as it was his home when he lived there with his mother, on his mother's birthday. He is a person of very strong and continuing affections. If you'd like to read *Howards End*, I would love to send it you.

If a new novel, *My Fellow Devils*, by L. P. Hartley, comes out in America (I think it is sure to) I wish you would read it and tell me what you think about it. I found it interesting; a good situation. It is one of those novels I spoke of in which the central character goes R.C. because it seems to her the only religion, and she needs one. The author isn't himself one, but probably thinks it would be the only thing to be if he did turn religious. Talking to him at a party lately, I said, if I had known his heroine I would have advised her to try Grosvenor Chapel. He didn't know about that; but he had heard of Rome! He is . . . C. of E. but never, I imagine, particularly interested in it, or in religion in general.[1] But, as I say, he has *heard of Rome*. So when he needs religion in a novel, as a *deus ex machina*, in comes Rome. Pity we can't spread news of the C. of E. like that.

Sunday. I looked up " *Deus qui nos redemptionis*,"[2] and certainly think the Latin is better; though there is a case for identifying the occasion as Christmas Day, no doubt. *The English Missal*, which I sometimes use, has " the yearly expectation of our redemption." I miss a great many good prayers, I suppose, through never attending Mattins or Evensong in church. It struck me the other day how beautiful many of those prayers are, whether in English or in Latin. Of course I read them, or many of them, in the offices; but never now join in them in church, of the psalms either. Perhaps I will take to sometimes going to Sunday Evensong somewhere; there is none at my Chapel, but

[1] R. M. was apparently unaware that L. P. Hartley, a practising Anglican, has always been much concerned with religious problems.

[2] " O God, who dost [gladden] us [by the yearly expectation] of our redemption."

All Saints isn't far off, and it is very beautiful there. I like those prayers; going to no service but Mass rules out too much. Did you mean, when you spoke of " *Absolutiones et Benedictiones* " at the beginning of each Breviary vol., those headed " *Ante Divinum Officium* " (one beginning " *Aperi, Domine, os meum* ")? I can't find any others just there.

Yes indeed, *what* marathon religious arguments John Gerard did have with his long-suffering (and apparently delighted, or so he thought) Protestant acquaintances! I wonder they stood it. But I suppose they were ready for conversion, or they wouldn't have gone to see him, or consented to the conversation at all. And no doubt he was an eloquent talker. What do you suppose he told them about the Faith? He doesn't tell us of any Protestant who remained unconvinced; but perhaps he preferred to forget these, if any. You are right: our modern country gentry wouldn't stand any such thing!

I must certainly try and see those young women your nieces; I would like to very much, if they would. I shall wait till I am a little less pushed for time, and then try and arrange it. At present I am so badly overdone with work that I find I am being impolite, if not unkind, to all sorts of people; one friend rang up the other evening to ask if she had offended me, since I had left her last two letters unanswered, in which she proposed a meeting. The fact is I looked at the letters in despair and simply put them aside till a chance seemed to offer of meeting, and then they slipped from my mind. Of *course* she hadn't offended me; that never happens; but perhaps it is worse to crowd people out simply from lack of time and the trouble of making a plan. One gets very inconsiderate, I fear, when behindhand with work one has to get done. Perhaps one should work in the country, away from everyone, but then there would be no books at hand to consult, and that is vital for my present work. To-day I lunched with people, and had tea somewhere else, and now it is evening, and the day is almost wasted as far as work goes. I suppose my neglected friend would say, if you can meet those other people, you can meet me—and of course she would be right. How difficult it is to be considerate and nice and courteous and painstaking about every one, in this bustle of a life, and oh how badly I do it.

You ask about Macaulays, Babingtons and Conybeares—so here they all are, in a genealogical table. As you see, though my parents were cousins, we weren't so intermarrying as *your* family. How very odd of J. C. Powys not to mention his fraternal relationship with his sisters. I wonder why. But of course he *has* a most odd mind. An interesting case of self-dramatisation, it seems like? I wonder how you will get on with *Porius*. Slowly, I guess. It is very long, and doesn't grip the attention; perhaps too remote from us. If ever I meet the author over here, I shall be much interested to talk to him. He is a good deal respected as a writer, and deservedly.

I was talking this evening to Stephen Spender, the poet. He rather interested me by saying that, though he couldn't *believe* much of what Christianity taught and held, he was an Anglican, because he thought it such a good " framework for moral aspiration," so that the Church should be supported. I believe he is right here; it *is* a good framework. I think that if people who can't really believe much of it held to it on those grounds, it would be very profitable. A great many do, I think. And no doubt some of them grow to believe more as time goes on. Apart from its other aspects, to be a framework for good actions and aspiration is a fine thing. And we aren't so *cluttered up* with devotional deviations as one sometimes feels the Roman Church to be.

Now I must go to bed. Do send me those family papers sometime; I should be interested, and would send them back with care. I am, as you know, interested in all you send or tell me, always. Because (a) it is always interesting (b) because you send it. My love,

Your affectionate
R. M.

That 2nd snapshot you sent isn't so good as the other, which I like greatly.

*20, Hinde House, Hinde St., W.*1
30th January, 1952 *(feast of the lamentable King Charles I)*†

Dear Father,

Lovely to get your air letter of 22nd, posted 25th. I do enjoy your letters. No one else writes such good ones. And, talking of letters, before I forget, I didn't get a letter from Fr. Pedersen at Christmas, but a v. nice Christmas card. I expect that is what he meant when he told you he had written to me. I was delighted to get it, because I liked him so much, as you know. And he was so kind to me; that American P.B. he gave me, in particular, I find of value and interest almost every day. I don't think I sent him a Xmas card (do you object to that shortening? Some do) in return, because I was living in a rush and was practically *non compos* with work, cards, gifts and everything combined; we have inflated Xmas to a mistaken size, from the external and material angle; it gets us all down. What would He have thought of it? But I love hearing and getting greetings from the people I like, even if I don't always return them. Did I send you my private Xmas card, of the swimming flautist? I hope I did, because I liked it. I should have sent it to Fr. P. too, only ran out of them. But, dear Father, you are inverting the facts when you say *you* wear an aura for him because of me; on the other hand, the only aura *I* had for him was because of his great devotion to *you*, which induced his kindness to me.

I'm so glad you have such a companion in interests as Fr. Palmer. I always enjoy hearing his comments and information about things—and anything in my letters that you share with him pleases me that you should. (What a sentence! Forgive my illiteracy.) I wonder what he thinks on the interesting question of the development of English Latin pronunciation. I shouldn't myself have the bumptiousness to think anything, except that I have been reading a rather good little book called *Latin in Church*, by F. Brittain (1934), lecturer (then) at Jesus Coll., Cambridge, which discusses the subject of the development of Latin in the various countries, from the break up of the

Roman Empire on. According to him, Latin speech was never uniform, but developed *very* early along national lines in each country. Hadrian, in the 2nd century, spoke it with a Spanish accent. By the 3rd and 4th centuries there were great variations. St. Jerome, writing at time of fall of Rome, said " *Latinitas ipsa et regionibus quotidie variatur et tempore.*"[1] After that the Church, of course, got about greatly, and spoke Latin in its services in the vernacular of each country. Classically pronounced Latin soon disappeared, probably even in Rome itself, certainly elsewhere. The clergy wanted to be understood by their flocks, and adopted the local pronunciation to that end, and also because it came easier to themselves. The liturgy gradually took a fixed and general form (or more than one, I suppose, in east and west?) but its pronunciation never. Latin broke up more and more into regional dialects—the Romance languages in embryo; the liturgies, though keeping the 4th and 5th century Latin, didn't keep the old pronunciation, but developed as the vernacular did. Italians took to the *ch* sound of *c* (before *e* or *i*), the French pronounced it like *s*, the Germans and English in their respective ways. And so with the vowels. The French *u* developed (which they use in French churches to-day), though most vowel sounds on the Continent are, of course, rather similar. But whatever the vernacular sounds given to vowels or consonants were in national speech, church Latin used them. My authority quotes from a book (1528) by Erasmus, " *De recta Latini Graecique sermonis pronuntiatione,*"[2] which gives examples of the Latin speech of the various races, and relates a story of an audience given by the emperor Maximilian to the ambassadors of various countries, who all made speeches in turn. The French ambassador was thought by the Italians present to be speaking in French; the German and others caused laughter by their national pronunciation; no doubt the English did so. Of course educated Latin-speakers of different races did manage to understand one another somehow, but it must have been often difficult. The French seem to have been the worst, until the English change of vowels.

[1] " The Latin language itself varies daily with places and times."
[2] " Concerning the right pronunciation of Greek and Latin."

This change occurred gradually through the 15th and 16th centuries, and no one, so far as one can gather, knows exactly when or *why*. We know that by the end of the 16th century the English *i* had changed from *ee* to *ei* (long *i*, I mean) and this seems such a great change that it is odd. The same with long *a*, which used to be pronounced *ah* and changed to *ay*; while *e* became *ee*. Of course there are exceptions, and some oddities about it; did you ever notice that though *rathe* (early) became raythe, as now, its comparative, *rather* (sooner), kept its old sound? All very chaotic, and what happened to cause it? But anyhow, whatever it was, our Latin sounds followed the changes in English, so had nothing to do with (as is sometimes surmised) the Reformation. Erasmus, in 1528, noticed that Colet pronounced *e* in Latin as *ee*. There have been many attempts to discover exactly how Shakespeare's plays were pronounced; but I think no one exactly knows, about most of the words. As to Latin, the puns of the plays acted by the Westminster boys show that the pronunciation was always English (when did they begin? I forget, and am too lazy to look it up just now). Milton, of course, was very keen on the Italian Latin sounds; but, he wrote sadly in 1661, " few will be perswaded to pronounce Latin otherwise than their own English." A thing in this book that interested me was the comparison between the English way that the hereditary English Catholics probably pronounced Latin, in their determination to be rather specially English and patriotic, and the Italian pronunciation probably introduced by the seminary-taught missioners (such as Gerard, no doubt) from abroad. The hereditary Catholics here went on steadily with the *anglicé* church Latin, and in the 19th c. (says Brittain) rather resented and derided the Italianate " chees and chaws " as they called them, of the zealous converts of the Oxford movement, who went to Rome and returned ardently Roman, both in pronunciation and " gew-gaws." Brittain says the Jesuits in England *still* use the English sounds; or did till quite lately. So did the Benedictines till late in C.19. I suppose the Latin used in Anglican churches is given the Italian sound, isn't it? Which do you use, in saying Latin prayers alone?[1] I use the Latin I learnt at school—kylee for *caeli*, etc. All that about Latin sounds following the vernacular everywhere interests me, and I seem to have written a very long screed about it, but think you are interested too.

I think we do know a good deal about 17*th* c. English speech, from rhyming dictionaries of the time, and largely from the letters of the not very well educated ladies, etc., who spelt phonetically. I studied that a lot while I was writing that book about them.[2] C. 16 is far more difficult to pin down.

1st Feb. I was at Romford yesterday, and didn't proceed with this letter. Returned, I found your air paper posted 28th, full of interesting information about Latin hymns, which sent me to the good little collection you sent me. But first let me go on answering your earlier letter. *Howards End* I find is a Penguin, and I have ordered it, and directly it comes (it is at the moment reprinting) I shall send it you. Oh thank you so much for *Tudor England*, which came before your letter, and which I am reading with great interest; it is good, isn't it. Well, I drove E. M. Forster to Abinger; it was the birthday of his late mother, and we took flowers to her grave. He was rather nice; he distributed sprays of mimosa also to the graves of his aunt, close by, and other deceased acquaintances, according to their deserts, taking some away when he recalled tiresome things they had once done, and being very careful to raise no jealousies; it seems that, even in the grave, feuds rage in country villages. It was a chilly day and grey, but not raining or snowing. But the day after, frost and ice set in, and Saturday, when Gerard Irvine and I were going into Herts, was impossible, with ice-coated roads and snow, so we didn't go. We shall choose a better day, later on. Yes, I drive these valuable persons with immense care.

You know how I should like it if you called me Rose not only to God, even though we are not driving or exchanging

[1] Footnote by R. M.: "I see you have answered this—you say them *anglicé.*"

[2] *They Were Defeated.*

cigarettes. I feel you have known me long enough for that, don't you? I really *should* like it, very much indeed, though didn't like to suggest it. Of course you could never be anything but "Father" to me; it is what you are, and have been now for well over a year (and were, after all, for a time many years back). I think I like you to call me exactly, at any time, what comes natural to you. All these young men (and older ones of course) call me Rose, almost at once; it is the modern habit; the young ones aren't at all deterred by the fact that I could easily be the mother of some of them. I prefer it; it seems easy and sensible and friendly. . . .

2nd Feb. How interrupted this letter is! It has become Candlemas, a feast I have always loved. At Varazze we always had a picnic on it, and lovely little coloured candles; I think I described them in *Personal Pleasures*. No picnics in this weather in this country, and no coloured candles like that, and the priest doesn't come round to bless them. At Grosvenor Chapel we only have the early Mass (by the way, did I say—I seem to remember that I did—that we don't have Evensong? This is quite wrong . . . I don't go to it, as it is only said, and one could do that as well at home, if one had the time. I do agree with you in liking the psalms well sung; if I had time I would go to All Saints, or St. Paul's, or the Abbey, every day. But I don't). But this morning I *made* time, for old sake's sake, and drove to All Saints at 11 for the distribution and blessing of candles, which we always liked at Varazze. Then the priests and choir proceeded, incense-swinging, round the church, while we all stood with our lit tapers. Mass followed, but I didn't stay for that, as I had to meet Gilbert Murray at the Athenaeum for lunch. At Varazze the procession was through the streets and piazzas, the weather being more seemly. But what a nice feast it is. It seems it was kept before Xmas day was; till the 5th c. the three main Xian festivals were Easter, Epiphany and Candlemas. And it was then simply a festival in honour of Our Lord; the Purification of the B.V.M. came in later. That much travelled lady, Etheria,[1] saw it cele-

[1] The abbess or nun (probably Spanish) named Etheria or Silvia, whose

brated at Jerusalem, in the late 4th c. The *Candelaia*, we called it in Italy. I suppose one likes it for the beauty of the symbolism, the idea of the Light of the world, lighting the small candles of every man that cometh into it, the light that has always lit man, and is now focused in Christ. All Saints, with its forest of tall altar candles in the dimness, and the forest of little tapers held by the congregation, looked very beautiful. Not for a moment would I not prefer my Chapel, which does seem to me to have even more of the *essential*, but one likes these rites and trappings too; they seem to express the tastes of the whole world at worship—like plainsong chanted.

Yes, I think on the whole I prefer the E[nglish] H[ymnal] version of *Deus Creator*[1]—anyhow some stanzas. But neither is v.g., and both a long way from the Latin. Why aren't verse translations more exact? I suppose, as you say, it is difficult to keep the metre, and the meaning; and add rhymes in addition (though why add rhymes, after all?). These trans[lations] do lack force, nearly always. Whereas St. Ambrose's doesn't. I have found the hymn in the 100 Best;[2] and have been looking again at others. It is a really good collection, and one I like to have. Isn't it a pity that neither *A. & M.*[3] nor *E.H.* have the whole of *Adeste fideles*.[4] They leave out those lovely stanzas about the shepherds and the Magi, and the next two. " *Stella duce Magi, Christum adorantes,*" etc.[5]—how beautiful! As to Jerusalem the golden, Dr. Neale was certainly in a less happy moment when he made the *E.H.* translation than the *A. & M.* one; I wonder which he made first.[6] Social joys indeed! What a prospect!

---

travels are recorded in the *Pilgrimage of Etheria*. English translation by M. L. McClure and C. L. Feltoe (1919).

[1] Hymn 49 in *The English Hymnal:* " Creator of the Earth and Sky " (a translation of St. Ambrose's *Deus Creator omnium*).

[2] *The Hundred Best Latin Hymns; selected by J. S. Phillimore* (1926).

[3] *Hymns Ancient and Modern* (1861).

[4] *The English Hymnal* includes two versions of " O Come, all ye faithful." Hymn 28 is a shortened version; Hymn 614 gives it in full.

[5] " The Magi, led by the star, adoring Christ."

[6] John Mason Neale (1818-66) made only one translation of *Urbs Sion aurea*, which is Hymn 412 in *The English Hymnal*, " Jerusalem the Golden". Hymn 376 in *Hymns A. & M.* was based on Neale's translation, but amended by the editors.

Yet of course these might be very stimulating, in such company as the blessed are promised. Only one would feel a fish out of water, invited to the great party among martyrs, saints, even angels, like common people invited to a party at a Bishop's palace. *Nescio, nescio*, indeed. I don't think " *con*jubilant with song" so hot, either. I haven't the Latin; it's not in the 100 Best, I think. Rather nice, that Medieval Latin primer sounds. I hope it includes some drinking songs.

Tell me sometime what you think of *A Room with a View*.[1] It is an early one, of course; actually written before *The Longest Journey*,[1] though published two years later. It is very amusing, and sometimes moving, and the family life of the Honeychurches delightful. The clergyman, Mr. Beebe, who starts a nice man, turns out very oddly, and isn't adequately explained ever. And old Mr. Emerson is a bit of a bore. But the detail, the conversation, the witty touches, the charming *writing* of it all, never fail to delight me. It's not on the scale of *Howards End*, which I mean you to have shortly.

Thank you for further references to the Breviary Absolutions, etc. I have found them, and like them. What a treasury the Breviary vols. are; I keep finding new things in them.

3rd Feb. Well now this letter, so long in writing, really is ended, and I shall take it and post it en route for High Mass at the Chapel. It's *very cold* here still. I do wonder what J. C. Powys thought of your letter about him when he saw it! I expect he would be interested and pleased. I've just been reviewing a Life of Flaubert. What an extraordinary character he had! Not likeable—but colossal in a sense. That intense, undeviating devotion to his art. But his hatred for humanity was pathological.

My love always.

Your ever affectionate
R. M.

---

[1] Novel by E. M. Forster (1908).   [1] Novel by E. M. Forster (1907).

February

20, *Hinde House, Hinde St., W.*1
11th February, 1952†

Dear Father,

Thank you much for your letter posted 5th Feb. On getting it, I wrote to my Conybeare cousins at Cambridge (Dorothea Conybeare knows everything about our relations) to enquire about that Canon Rose of Harpenden, of whose home you gave such a charming account. I thought he might be a cousin, but I haven't heard back from her yet. The only Canon Rose I *know* of was my grandmother's brother,[1] who was rector of Weybridge all my mother's childhood and girlhood; she and her mother lived at Weybridge, to be near him, and he was a kind of adored father to her, who had lost her own before she could remember. She always said that she owed all that she knew of good and of religion to his teaching; not that her mother wasn't good and religious too, but he does seem to have been a kind of saint. He died sometime in the 1880s. The Harpenden Canon may or may not have been a relation. I hope he was, as this would make us some kind of relations too! I will let you know.

How refreshing was your letter, coming into this present desert of royal funerals, royal accession proclamations, lauding of the late monarch and the new one, mournful valedictory music and words on the radio, official assumption that all other interests are in abeyance.[2] Most people are by now very tired of it; out of no disrespect to the good king dead or the new queen enthroned, for there is great feeling for both, but the feeling

[1] Rev. Edward Joseph Rose, Rector of Weybridge, 1855-82, Hon. Canon of Winchester, 1878.
[2] King George VI died on 6th February, 1952.

is inflated and blown up out of all proportion by our publicists. On the day he died, the BBC shut down altogether, but for periodical repetition of the sad news. A friend of mine, dropping into a pub for a drink, heard a woman there saying bitterly, " It's bloody murder, that's what it is, having no wireless. That's what drives a woman into the pubs." The funniest thing announced by the BBC (I read it in the papers) was that, during the period of national mourning, variety comedians on the air were to abstain from making jokes in bad taste. The comedians must be waiting eagerly for this close time for vulgarity to end. I fancy some of them can make *no* jokes in good taste! No doubt their public are waiting impatiently too. This solemn announcement was somehow very funny. Well, into this unnatural atmosphere arrived your good letter, full of interesting things. I looked up those Medieval Latin German texts,[1] and find they are, or some of them, in the Library, but not shelved all together, one has to look them up separately. I found one—about Clerical Discipline, but didn't have time to look at it much. It is a mistake not to catalogue and shelf them together, I think. Tell me some of the names of the authors some time, and I will look them up at leisure. Oh I see you mention Jakob von Vitry; I'll look for him. I should enjoy those stories and sermons.[2] Now I've just noticed again one of your marginal notes, and see that *Disciplina Clericalis* is mentioned by you, so I shall get that one out and read it.[3] The L[ondon] L[ibrary] hasn't, it seems, got the Beeson Primer,[4] or any other. Or I think not; but it was near closing time, I will look again. I have sent you *Howards End* (Penguin). I shall be enormously interested to know what you think of it, and of the other Forsters. He is profoundly a moralist, and

[1] The Latin texts in the series *Sammlung mittellateinischer Texte* (Heidelberg) which include *Die Disciplina Clericalis des Petrus Alfonsi* (1911), *Die Exempla aus den Sermones feriales et communes des Jakob von Vitry* (1914), and also *Johannes Monachus; Liber de Miraculis* (1913).

[2] The sermons of James of Vitry, cardinal bishop of Tusculum (d. 1240), often contained stories " for the entertainment and edification of his hearers."

[3] The *Disciplina Clericalis* of Petrus Alfonsi, a Spanish Jew who had been converted to Christianity (1106), is a collection of Oriental tales, proverbs and fables.

[4] Charles H. Beeson, *A Primer of Medieval Latin* (Chicago, 1925).

believes in People and personal relationships, and affection, and goodness. Not in God.

What good news about the Teas! I am delighted by this. Now you will have more time for reading, and looking up things I should read. What I am reading just now (when any time) is the letters between André Gide and Claudel—fascinating interchange between two distinguished and so utterly different minds. Claudel, of course, wanted to turn Gide into a Catholic. Then, later, he discovered that Gide was a homosexual, and was horrified. If you like reading French, do get hold of this book[1]; it would interest you and amuse you. One day I shall send you Simone Weil (in English[2]) which I have. I have lent it to my convert cousin.

Oh dear, why do these converts have to be so sure they have the monopoly of truth? But my cousin (who is a dear) kindly says that, though Anglican sacraments of course aren't *valid*, in the full meaning of the word, God can work through them, and does, so she feels I have got something good . . . By now she must know my ignorance is invincible, so that I am all right as regards my final end, and shall get more light after death. But I have a feeling that my ignorance will still be invincible! She is intellectual, generous, and really spiritual, and lives on a high level, mentally and morally. All [that is needed] . . . (as Dr. Cockin, the Bp. of Bristol, said to-day on the air) is a grain of wholesome scepticism about having the whole truth; a thing, as he says, which is needed by both Christians and secularists. And certainly by R.C.s. Well, they will know one day.

Thank you for saying " *propitius respicere* "[3] for me, dear Father. Please sometimes say too " *O Sapientia*." And " *O Oriens*." Light and wisdom. With those one can't go far wrong. Either in the car or out of it. Actually, my car is a life-saver in this wintry weather. If I *walked* (or bicycled) out to Mass each

[1] *Paul Claudel et A. Gide; correspondance, 1899-1926. Préface et notes par R. Mallet* (Paris, 1949). An English translation by J. Russell (with preface) was published in 1952.
[2] *Waiting on God.*
[3] " Look upon [us] with favour."

morning, in this cold, wet, sleet, winter wind, and whatever, I should likely enough get bronchitis, or at least a bad cold and cough. Whereas I trundle along cosy in my darling green car, and am only cold when in that blessed chapel. Then, in summer it runs me to my morning swim; and in the afternoon to my researches in a library, or what not, and in the evening to such " social joys " as await me. Social joys are rather diminished now in our time of national woe; all kinds of things cancelled, which leaves one the more time for work. Yes, I found those brief prayers, and have memorised some. Oh did I tell you how much I am finding in Wm. Law? I think I did. He is so very good. Have you got those *Mystical Writings* of his? If so, I should so much like to know if you like them as much as I do. Oh dear, I see this is the end. That is the worst of these convenient air papers; they run out all of a sudden, before ever one has done. This day last year, I think I lay on a sick-bed. I have been lucky this winter. I do so hope you are too, and will be.

My love and thoughts,
R. M.

20, *Hinde House, Hinde St., W.*1
13*th February*, 1952 †

Dear Father,

Further to my air paper of 11th: I have now heard back from Dorothea Conybeare, and know all about that Harpenden family. But you are wrong about their name, which wasn't Rose but Vaughan. Rose was the maiden name of Mrs. Vaughan, and that is what you must have been told, and you must have been related to *her* family, the Roses. She was my great-aunt Mary, my grandmother's sister, and she married the Rev. Edward Vaughan, who was Rector of Harpenden 1859-96; he was also a Canon of St. Albans. I don't remember ever seeing either of them, but my mother used to stay there as a child. And I have met some of their daughters (who all married except one,

268

and before you went there, for their children are mostly older than I and my brothers and sisters). The unmarried daughter was called Ellen. Of course some of the married ones may have been staying there when you went there. But isn't that interesting, and rather nice, that you used to go to the rectory of my great-uncle and aunt, so long ago. And, since you are related to the Roses, *we* must be relations, which is nicer still. The father of my great-aunt and grandmother was the Rev. E. J. Rose,[1] vicar of Rothley after (or before?) my great-grandfather Aulay Macaulay. The father of E. J. [Joseph] Rose was the Rev. William Rose, vicar of Carshalton, who would be my great-great-grandfather. Does this help at all in the quest after your Rose ancestors? I have two nice pastel portraits, one of my great-grandfather Rose, the other of his mother, the wife of the vicar of Carshalton. I assume it was to the Roses you were related, not to the Vaughans. *His* father was, I believe, a Dean of Llandaff,[2] and Master of the Temple, and his disciples were known as Vaughan's doves. But I have made you a Rose relation not a Vaughan. I believe great-uncle Edward[3] was rather evangelical, and used to embarrass my mother as a little girl staying there by praying, at family prayers, for " this little lamb of Thy flock now with us," which she considered in poor taste.

Well, so much for family history. We are under snow here; not deep, but it covered the streets when I drove out at 8 this morning. But now the sun has appeared, and it should melt it. *You*, in your New England winter, wouldn't hardly call it snow at all. I lunched yesterday with T. S. Eliot, of whom I am very fond; he has a great sense of humour besides his other gifts, and I always like seeing him. He was saying that he feels affected when he visits his American relations and friends, because he says tomahto, and they, of course, tomayto. But he was taught

---

[1] R. M. here means to refer to the Rev. Joseph Rose (1783-1823), see below pp. 305 and 308.

[2] R. M. here means to refer to the father of Canon Edward Vaughan, Rector of Harpenden ; but Charles John Vaughan (1816-97), Headmaster of Harrow 1844-59, Dean of Llandaff 1879, was Canon Vaughan's *brother*, not his father or his uncle (as R. M. herself discovered, see below p. 286).

[3] Canon Edward Vaughan of Harpenden.

tomahto, he says, in his Philadelphian (or was it New England?) childhood, for some reason. Do many Americans, especially in New England, pronounce it in this English way, I wonder? *He* says, very few. His parents must have been aping the English. His family went to America in 1667, and perhaps never stopped " tomahto."

Later. By afternoon post has come your letter of 7th and 8th— good! So you remembered " Vaughan " for yourself. The only thing you didn't remember was how " Rose " came in, and now I have told you that. But were you also related to the Vaughans? It seems like it; how odd, if so. But I would rather you turned out a Rose, please. " 150 years ago " takes us back to the vicar of Carshalton, or perhaps only to him of Rothley; I don't know their dates. I *am* sorry about that letter from Fr. Pedersen that I never got. Do tell him so. As to kindness when he was here, that was entirely his, and most generous it was, and much I enjoyed it. I am glad you and he are interested in what I reported from that Brittain book. If I can get a copy I will send it you; but it seems out of print; I will try and pick it up 2nd hand; it is quite small. Yes, he mentions that order from Rome about pronunciation. I have never learnt the old English way myself. I like to think of you struggling at Mass not to be a *diabolo incarnato* ![1] I shall attend a service at St. James's, Spanish Place, round the corner, and listen to those *diaboli incarnati* there pronouncing their stuff. The last ditchers as to talking *anglicé* will be the lawyers and judges, who are very staunch about it.

What you say about our young Elizabeth shames my impatience with all this " inflation." Of course you are right, and we do feel with her and for her, and certainly pray for her. Everyone feels so much attached to her that she will feel supported and loved. King George's coffin now lies in state, and miles of queue trail along the neighbouring streets all day and night to see it. How *cold* they must be! No, I don't think my

[1] From the 16th century proverb " The Englishman Italianate is a devil incarnate."

sex is really as tough as yours (if one can generalize on so individual a point). I think the heavy, cold, exhausting work that many working men (including miners) do, and the life of soldiers in the field, would kill many women, and utterly exhaust most. Women *live* longer, for some reason, as a rule, but they are more often ill and absent from work, and get much more exhausted with standing, for instance. Schoolgirls can't usually play games so hard and so much as boys without ill effects, I believe. Also they are nervously less tough, surely. But of course one can't generalize. *You* were probably not tough at all; and lots of girls are. Girls are certainly on the whole much less brave about pain and danger; they seem to mind them more. But what a *shame* to give small boys such hardships at school. " Cold and starvation "—it makes me angry to hear of it. How *can* people be so cruel? Thank you for saying " Rose." I like it, and, if we are cousins, it is more than ever suitable. Yes, you are quite right about my chapel . . . God must have directed me there. With it . . . here, and you there, I am indeed fortunate, and if I fail to thrive and grow, it will be no one's fault but my own. However I pronounce Latin, I am Anglican profoundly —born and bred to it, the heir to it, and now well in it once more. Nothing else would do. And it must be of this particular type—no *more* " gew-gaws " and no *fewer*. All this dignity and beauty—plus the Latin prayers I owe to you—what riches!

My love always,

R. M.

20, *Hinde House, Hinde St., W.*1
19*th February*, 1952†

Dear Father,

Now we really *are* getting on. Before your letter (posted 15th) arrived this afternoon, to cheer my convalescence from slight and brief flue (I am up but not yet out) there came this morning a most interesting and gratifying missive from your cousin (and mine) Miss Barham Johnson of the Norwich Training

College, enclosing an admirable genealogy of your Rose and Vaughan and Livius ancestry. I have written back sending her a copy of the one I had from Dorothea Conybeare, which I here enclose for you.[1] It adds a little to the other; between the two, we now perceive and know that you and I are 4th cousins, which delights me. It doesn't seem absolutely established that Canon Vaughan was related to his wife, or to you, but this seems probable; as Dorothea C. observes, our family has extremely often married cousins (tho' not so excessively as yours). Anyhow, our relationship thro' the Roses is firm. With your admirable memory of 1889, you are probably right in thinking that the old Canon told you about your Vaughan, as well as Rose, connections. And to think that we had all that correspondence about the Livii without realising that George Livius was my great-great-great-uncle by marriage! Your kind cousin says she will, when next in London, show me some letters from my great-great-aunt Charlotte Rose to her cousin Maria Johnson. In return, I said I would look up some letters from my great-grandmother Lydia Babington, of which there is somewhere a packet, and very nice they are. Some of them might throw a light on other of our common relations; she is, it seems, often mentioned in her sister-in-law Charlotte's letters.

Well, so there we are, and very nice too. Now for your letter, written before you got my air paper of 13th. Your letters are good for me in every kind of way. For one thing, you set me looking into interesting matters some of which thus occur to me for the first time, others on which I have speculated myself. " Compunction " is in the former class. I think your meaning of piercing or pricking was probably in Bede's mind. After all, there wasn't necessarily much *contrition* in C[aedmon]'s story of Genesis, Exodus, the Creation, the Fall, all the drama of Redemp-

---

[1] This genealogy was removed from the letters by Father Johnson. He substituted a note as follows: " R. M.'s great-grandfather E. J. [Joseph] Rose was 1st cousin of my great-grandmother, Maria Livius. R. M.'s grandmother, Eliza Conybeare, was 2nd cousin of my two grandfathers at Yaxham and Welborne and they were probably aware of one another's existence as relations. 'Eliz' Rose of Carshalton (of whom R. M. has a portrait) was actually the sister of Mary (Barham) Livius, the wife of George, the son of Peter the German! "

tion, and all his other Biblical tales; tho' of course there was that too. But they pierced the hearts and souls and consciences of those who heard them. And " compunction " *had* that active, sometimes physical, meaning *in English*, tho' now no more. You mention a large nail puncturing my front tyre (not, I may say, an example I much relish), and I find in the O[xford] Dict., under " In physical sense," another nail, also ill employed. " A sharpe naile, with which they prick the horse . . . such compunctions will even cause the best horse to plunge " (1617). And in Blount's *Glossography* (1656) " A pricking, or stitch." And Sir Thomas Browne, in *Pseudodoxia*, has " smoke of sulphur, that acide and piercing spirit which with such activity and compunction invadeth the brains and nostrils of those that receive it." There was also the adjective " compungent "—as now we have " pungent." Did you refer to Cassell's ? I see it has, under *Compungo*, " to prick, pierce on all sides," and a quote from Cicero about " *ipsi se compungunt suis acuminibus*."[1] So perhaps Caedmon's " *carmina compunctiva* " were piercing as well as contrite and suave. I have never actually found them so very much myself, tho' they have charm. I prefer Cynewulf, who has more sense of a *scene*—green grass and birds and flowers. But it was a day when the great epic of Man's Redemption held the literary field. I must look up the use of " compunction " in the *Imitation*. I think it is a very fine metaphor, that of piercing the conscience, for indeed that is what most poignantly occurs. So I am glad you have suggested that sense of the word; it gives it a new intensity.

As to " Gentility ", the odd opposition of its meanings comes out well in Bishop Jewel's[2] remark that " The Heathens in their rude Gentility thought that Bacchus and Ceres had first found out the use of Bread and Wine." " The Vaine opinions of the Gentilitee," too. " Genteel " in English (not " Gentile ") has suffered some curious changes of meaning. It was, only a century ago, complimentary; " A very genteel young man," or woman,

[1] " They prick themselves with their own stings." Cicero, *De oratore* 2. 38. 158.

[2] John Jewel (1522-71), Bishop of Salisbury.

meant, as it did with Jane Austen, one with gentlemanly or gentlewomanly manners and breeding. But now (largely pulled down by H. W. Fowler) it is applied to the class between high and low; it is "genteel" to say "sufficient" instead of enough, "serviette," "preserve" for jam, "wealthy" for rich, "photo," a thousand more such genteelisms; Fowler is full of them. (No, not "photo"; that is merely low.) A rather snob campaign of ridicule goes on against these, which, tho' often amusing (I have often taken part in it, adding words and phrases to the taboo list —John Betjeman has lately composed a poem bringing in most of them), is really perhaps a pity, and only exacerbates class war. It isn't, in fact, very good manners or *gentle*. And just now, when class feeling is rather irritable, and both the Poor and the Genteel are up in arms when they hear an educated accent (they think it "affected," but never suggest what those brought up to use it should do about it—it really *would* sound affected to put on Cockney or Lancashire instead, even if we could), much better not make fun of one another's phrases or accents or habits. Well, we are all Gentiles (except when we are Jews), and some of us are Genteel, and some Gentle (not that we don't use "genteel" about the educated classes, in fun; you and I both do that at times).

Thank you for that 1935 photograph. I like it very much; tho' still not so much as that one (the good one) taken in the woods last year, which stands on my writing bureau. But I like to have this. The bad one in the woods I threw away, not thinking it like you. What I would like is a nice *drawing* of you. You would draw well.

Thank you too for "*Hora Novissima*," which is a wonderful hymn. Did Neale translate the whole 3000 lines? Bits of it, of course, are in *The English Hymnal*—and how oddly jumbled up! Bits thrown in from other parts of the hymn—the order all wrong—and so much pure Neale added. I suppose he wanted just to get the general sense, and use the actual words as jumping-off grounds. How much better "*Hora Novissima, tempora pessima sunt, vigilemus, Ecce minaciter imminet arbiter ille supremus, Imminet, imminet . . .*" is than "The world is very evil, the times are waxing late, be sober and keep vigil, the judge is at the gate." It means the same, but lacks the majesty and urgency. I am very glad to have this hymn, and shall keep it with the 100 Best.

I am glad to have that list of late Latin texts. Those I have already seen are *Disciplina Clericalis*, and the Travels of Silvia or Etheria,[1] which are very pleasing; she must have been a most vigorous and eager and attractive tourist, and how she did get about! Now that I have the names, I shall easily find them in the Library when I am able to get there, which should be almost at once now. I ascertained that *Latin in Church* (Brittain) *is* out of print,[2] but I asked Mowbrays to advertise for it, and if it should turn up I will have them send it you. There is, of course, a great deal in it that I didn't refer to, and it all interested me. Yes, language as spoken changes all the time, and don't you think specially English? . . . Now, not feeling too good yet, I shall retire to bed (it is evening). I miss my daily Mass, and have a superstitious feeling that anything may happen on the days I don't go. However, nothing in particular has. Actually very nice things, like the discovery of our cousinhood, and to-day's letter from you. Love from your affectionate 4th cousin

R. M.

I *do feel pleased* about that!

20, *Hinde House, Hinde St., W.*1
23rd February, 1952†

Dear Father,

To-day came your letter posted 18th; thank you so much for it. I wrote last Monday to tell you that I had heard from your cousin that we are 4th cousins, which seems to me delightful, and enclosed a little genealogy sent me by Dorothea Cony-

---

[1] See above p. 262*n*.
[2] A second edition, revised and enlarged, was published for the Alcuin Club by Mowbrays in 1955.

beare. Now I have looked at her letter again, and see she says
" Edward Vaughan's father was Vicar of St. Martin's Leicester,
and was a *brother* of C. J. Vaughan, Headmaster of Harrow,
etc." So this last was Canon Vaughan's *uncle*, not father.[1] I have
been remembering that I believe there was a photograph in my
mother's old family album of Uncle Edward Vaughan, as well
as of Aunt Mary—did he, when you met him, wear a beard
rather under his chin, not over his mouth, and a small skull-cap?
I *think* this old clergyman in the album was Uncle E.V. Under
him (whoever he was) my grandmother, who had an interesting
habit of captioning her photographs with lines of poetry, had
written two Tennysonian lines " Kind like a man was he, And
like a man too would have his way." Great-aunt Mary looked
rather a charming old lady—as my grandmother also did. Of
course you are related to all those Vaughans, or the old Canon
wouldn't have talked about them to you in the governess cart,
nor Aunt Cecie about the Doves. And I think I must be too, so
in that case we are doubly related (you and I, I mean).

I don't know why you call your 1st page garrulous and
irrelevant; it is, as a matter of fact, all to our point, which is the
investigation of these family matters, and which is developing
so promisingly. Thank you also for your other interesting
matters, about the S.M.T. books,[2] for instance, which I can
certainly now trace easily in the L[ondon] L[ibrary]. I haven't
been out yet since I got this flue, but am now up and busy, and
(as you see) tapping away, and shall I think go to mid-day, tho'
not early, Mass to-morrow, Sunday. Quite time too. After
that I shall start my early exits again. The weather has turned
(unlike that of Cambridge, Mass.) mild and agreeable, and I feel
really all right again, and can start Lent in a seemly manner.
But no, I must own to you that I am starting it in an *un*seemly
manner, by having inadvertently promised over the telephone a
few days ago to go out to dinner with the Stephen Spenders
on Ash Wednesday. I only remembered some time later that
this was the date, and of course it *is* unseemly. *They* don't know
it's Ash Wed[nesday] and wouldn't care if they did, but I ought

[1] See above p. 269n.   [2] *Sammlung mittellateinischer Texte.*

276

to have. No day for *socialia gaudia*. I must try and make amends and the *sanctum Evangelium digne intimare*.[1] Yes, that is a good prayer to say; I think I must keep a copy in my car. Oh dear; this living life in two such different climates is complicated, and I don't do it well. One is too much entangled in one's past, and bogged in its ways. The wrong well. Please, dear Father, go on saying that prayer for me (*in manus tuas illam commendo*, I mean) and I will say the other for myself. I need them all, so badly.

Do you feel that people, particularly in crowds, are getting rather frightening? Or perhaps they always were. Mob hysteria seems to attack them so often and so violently, and they crowd round film personalities they see getting married, climb on to the bonnets of their car, shriek like Maenads, and block the traffic completely, so that police have to clear a way for the wretched victims. And the other day, when during the two minutes' silence for the King's funeral, two absent-minded people went on walking in Fleet St., the mob chased them when the silence ended, shouting "Throw him under a bus!" "Put him in the Thames," etc., etc. I believe the two people were terrified, especially the woman, who finally called a policeman to protect her (we aren't so tough, you see). But wasn't such persecution shocking, and aren't crowds rather dreadful. "*Méfiez-vous de la foule!*" said André Gide, and he was right. Are they as hysterical in your Continent? I suppose this mass hysteria has always been with us; it crops up all through history, and has taken many forms. The French revolution mobs shouting for the guillotine; the Jews shouting "Crucify Him!"; the wild religious revivalists of the Middle Ages; the Jacquerie; the anti-Jewish pogrom crowds yelling against Jews; to-day football crowds trampling one another to death at the gates; and all these terrible film fans screaming. I suppose there is a deep potential excitement in human nature, like a wild animal, and being surrounded by a crowd unleashes it, and out it leaps, feeding on the excitement of its neighbours and growing madder and madder, till people are chased and lynched, or chased and

[1] "Holy Gospel worthily proclaim."

kissed, and there are yells for blood and war, and anything may happen. Yet individually the mob are probably ordinary quite decent and kindly people. How horrible a thing it would be to be at their mercy, when they turn into a pack of baying wolves. *O Sapientia!* What are we made of? How can God endure us? And now we are preparing to try our ghastly new weapons of death somewhere, so as to perfect them.

My thoughts seem to have foundered rather into uneasy and stormy seas. Perhaps it is flue, or rather post-flue. And now I had better go to bed.

Sunday (*Quinq[uagesima]*). Well, I have been out to church, and it is a nice bright mild day. I see that R. Knox translates *agape* (sorry my typewriter can't emit Greek letters) by *charity*, like the A[uthorized] V[ersion]. I think the R[evised] V[ersion] is more *accurate* with " love," according to modern usage; but the old sense of *caritas* and charity was, after all, just love; " God is all charity," etc., and it seems a pity to abandon so good and lovely a word and its ancient meaning, just because the meaning has changed a little. I have just been reading that Chap[ter] in Greek, in the little Testament that is one of your most cherished gifts to me. But how many these are! Of all kinds, on all levels. I send you in return *Caritas*, and this air patter contrived between less agreeable works on the same typewriter.

Always yours,

R. M.

20, *Hinde House, Hinde St., W.*1
29th February, 1952†

Dear Father,

An untyped MS., *not* because I am ill still, but just feel a little tired, and am lounging in an armchair. I am going out and about now, and to-day a very nice spring day. And yesterday came your nice air letter written on St. Matthias Deferred[1] and

[1] The feast day of St. Matthias, 24th February, is celebrated, in leap years, on 25th February.

enclosing your cousin's September letter, that I read with interest and return. What a life she leads! I do admire it. All that hard work during term, and in the holidays looking after a blind and deaf mother, and, in any intervals, doing research among old papers and writing books for children on music. Admirable. I see the name *Castres* got into the family—was that from the Lisbon Consul who was George's godfather?

I must see if any of our Lydia Rose/Babington letters have anything of family interest for her purpose, and will look at them before we meet (I think in April sometime, she said).

Thank you also for letter of 21st, which crossed mine of 19th—both of us congratulating ourselves on the 4th cousinship, which I do like to have. Yes, dear Cousin Hamilton; but, though I do feel consanguine, and am proud to, I could never (as I said before) call you anything but " Father." Should further research disclose that you are my *brother*, I should still call you this. I am glad you like it too. I must ask the Conybeares if they ever heard of the two Yaxham and Welborne cousins, through our grandmother; they might remember her mentioning them; she was great on relations and keeping in touch— *much* better than anyone in the family since her. But what fun all this is, don't you think?

Don't be concerned for my health. The Chapel isn't really so cold; and anyhow I am as well qualified to bear it as anyone else, and very warmly coated. I am already going to it again. While I couldn't go, I tried to follow it in imagination (which I very much prefer, and always should, to having it brought me, which always seems to me to make rather a fuss, besides infecting other people with one's germs). Of course if one was really laid up for a month or two, or more, it might be worth while— but still troublesome. . . . I should feel more peaceful just following the service in my mind. Yes: I like your widening of " this congregation here present " (which is often so extremely small!) to include others—and to include oneself when absent, " *et pro omnibus fidelibus Christianis, vivis atque defunctis.*"[1] That is a good sequence of prayers—and I should always add my favourite,

[1] " And for all faithful Christians, both the living and the departed."

" *Quid retribuam Domino* . . . ? "[1] The trouble is that, when ill, one often feels headachy and bemused in the morning early, and can't follow or read with much attention. Then one has, I suppose, to fall back on saying by heart the prayers one already knows. But it is happier when one can say " *in ecclesiis benedicam te* "[2]; happily I can now do that again. How incredibly good, to be borne up and sustained daily like that. And before so *very* long, I suppose, I can be like Charlemagne again—" *frequenti natatu corpus exercens* "[3] after Mass. But not quite yet! I was telling T. S. Eliot of this custom of mine; he said, " Well, I hope you go home after it to a really good tuck-in." So I do. I devour my bacon ration after bathing, which I never do at other times, but hand the coupons to my porter, who values them, and doesn't really approve my new ecclesiastical-aquatic beginnings to the day. You know, I add all your suggested prayers, etc., to my private collection.

I was much interested in Peter Livius's statement. (I am returning it, in case you have no copy.) *How* careless they were about their children, letting them die like that! Everyone says Lisbon was unwholesome then—hot, dirty, undrained; no place for children. The Great Quake really cleaned it up a bit, for they built Pombal's fine new town where the ancient slums had been. I wonder how long George stayed in Lisbon after 1758. And who first introduced *Moravianism* into the family? I see that Wesley introduced it into England, having met some Moravians in Georgia (German immigrants). I don't know how the Livii picked it up. I don't think any *Rose* had it?

I am drowning in a storming sea of books, papers, work, that I can't make headway against; and now this wretched disease has thrown me back by several days. Oh for more time! Sometimes I feel altogether crazed with the amount I have to do, and the little I am doing. However early I begin, however late I work, I can't keep my head above it. I expect this drowning feeling is partly the after effects of flue; I feel no strength to

[1] " What reward shall I give unto the Lord . . ."; see above p. 222*n*.
[2] " I will praise the Lord in the congregations." Ps. 26. 12.
[3] " Exercising my body with frequent swimming."

tackle anything—I mean, mental strength; physical is coming back. A greater calm should be arrived at. And, oddly, tho' church takes time, it does help a little towards calm. (Of course it doesn't actually take time, because I should only be in bed, not working, at that hour.) Peace and strength are what one wants, and a little less time-wastage. I think there are plenty of collects about this; I must look them up.

I am right, aren't I, to return you these letters?[1] I thought you would probably want to keep them: I have been looking up one of our family genealogies, in an old family Bible, but no fresh light is thrown; it only traces back our descent through many generations of Babingtons of Rothley (which they got in 1544) to, of all people, Alfred the Great! I fancy he is the ancestor of most English people, tho' they can't always trace it.

Much love, dear Coz. and Father.

R. M.

March

20, Hinde House, Hinde St., W.1
6th March, 1952

Dear Father,

This is to go by sea, in the old-fashioned manner, and will enclose various documents you have sent me; you say *don't* send them back, but you *may* want them later on. I perused all with interest. Though slightly bemused with the forest of relations of both mine and yours, I try to hold on to the main clues in the labyrinth, the ones which lead us out into our 4th Cousinship; but I am a less skilled genealogist than you Johnsons and Barhams and Cowpers, and am sometimes rather bushed. Never mind, it is all great fun. If I come on any Fludd ancestors

[1] R. M. means the letter from Mary Barham Johnson and the "Peter Livius statement". But on the back of the envelope she has written "The Sept. letter made it overweight, so I have abstracted it. Also Peter Livius!"

for you, I shall be delighted. But that, I fear, is on the Macaulay side. I am glad my description of the photograph reminded you of great-uncle Vaughan; I am almost sure it was him. I wish we still had that old book, but, after removing from it the photographs of the people we *knew* or knew about—uncles and aunts, grandparents, etc., etc.—we threw it out with much else, when my eldest sister's house in Hampshire broke up at her death. Really, it is more interesting to keep *all* photographs of relations; you never know when you may want them. If I had great-uncle Edward, I would send him to you. . . .

Now I shall write you an air paper, as you won't get this budget for so long. I think, after all, I will *keep* Peter Livius's notes with the family tree on the back, and only enclose the *letters*.

Much love,
R. M.

20, *Hinde House, Hinde St., W.*1
6th March, 1952†

Dear Father (Father Hamilton, if you like—or Cousin, or just Hamilton),

I have just been putting up some of your papers and letters (tho' you say don't return) in a sea letter, which won't be overweight, and which you'll get in the ocean's good time. In my letter I commented on . . . the genealogies. This air paper is to fill the gap. Thank you very much indeed for your two of 28th and 29th Feb. You enquire about my health. My doctor has just sent me to have a blood test taken, as he is puzzled by these intermittent (tho' slight) temperatures, persisting so long after flue is over. It isn't important, and I don't feel ill, only a little tired, and feverish by night. I fully expect that the quinine I am now taking will effect a cure shortly. I ought to chew fever bark, or the laurel leaves that so went to the heads of the Pythian priestesses at Delphi, inducing such frenzied utterances. I am really quite all right, so don't be concerned about me; it is only that you said you would like to know how I am, so (always strictly truthful) I am telling you. After all, I didn't dine with the Spenders on Ash Wednesday, as I didn't feel well enough. I am sure your advice is right, and that I might have gone with perfect seemliness; it was just for a time that the idea somehow seemed jarring. But one mustn't turn into a prig!

I think " charity," using it in its earlier English sense, is the word I like, and I think the A[uthorized] V[ersion] was right. You know, I don't *try* to feel " love " for God; only the desire of the spirit and will to do His commands; Wm. Law says that is " the spirit of prayer and love," and that if we really have that then we are in a state of salvation. Only of course one doesn't have it, only very seldom, and when one's will and desires are directed quite elsewhere, God can do nothing with us.

Did you see an article in the *Church Times* last week advocating that a parish priest should, entirely on his own, refuse people communion, if he thought they were not in charity with their neighbours (or, of course, grosser sins). He said scandal was caused in a congregation when two families known to be quarrelling turned up to communion on the same day. His idea seemed to be first to warn them not to come, then, if they did, to pass them over! Talk of scandal! That would be a much bigger and better one in the parish. What extraordinary ideas people do get. I know Dr. Kirk says, refuse no one, neither the divorced re-married, the livers-in-sin, or the quarrellers. My sister says people should be refused if they have infectious diseases; she (as a nurse) is all for the entinctured bread and no chalice, which certainly seems more rational, though one likes the symbolism of the chalice.

I am interested in your account of your mother and aunt, and their so different ways. My mother too was prejudiced, both about ideas and people; certain people she could not and would not like. This often made life difficult, as she couldn't hide it. She was so charming and friendly and expansive to those she did like, that the difference was painfully obvious. Temperamental she certainly was! She could never get on with my father's youngest sister (now 84 and hasn't much longer) —but then no one could, she was a termagant.

I can't say our home was ever "beautifully run"; both my parents and all of us were naturally untidy; and Italy was a bad training. But my mother did amuse every one, as did my grandmother before her, and that is a great gift.

I feel pleased that you like to read *Volup. Min., R.M.*[1] in bed. You must get down to *Howards End* sometime. If I can turn up a copy of my Forster book,[2] I shall send it you; it would show you, anyhow, how I view his aims and interpretations of life. At the moment (did I tell you) I am reviewing a life of Hugh Walpole, mostly from his journals and letters.[3] I find it a fascinating lifting of the lid from someone I knew, tho' never intimately. He knew himself very well, and criticizes himself. I must send you my review when it comes out.

Gerard Irvine has persuaded me to go and hear him preach on Sunday night. He is doing nursery rhymes as applied to the Christian scheme. On Sunday it is "Jack and Jill," and treats of the Fall, on which he knows I am not really sound. He thinks there came a moment in the upward climb of the anthropoid when he became responsible enough to sin, and that was the Fall. My view is that the anthropoid, and the ape, could always sin consciously, and did so from the first, tho' of course not with the full moral consciousness that developed later. But at what point are we to say "This was man; he can sin, though he couldn't before?" These problems are very difficult, and I don't bother my head with them much—nothing like as much [as] I did when you first knew me, and long before that. The affair has ceased to be an intellectual problem, I suppose; I approach it otherwise, and leave what I can't take. I think, in my advanced years, that is the wisest way, don't you. So long as one knows the truth of the vital things, and so long as they mean what they do.

No; E. M. F[orster] won't come to it, I am afraid. On the

[1] R. M.'s *Minor Pleasures of Life*.
[2] R. M.'s *The Writings of E. M. Forster*.
[3] Rupert Hart-Davis, *Hugh Walpole; a Biography* (1952).

other hand, Christopher Isherwood, who has been over here from California for the winter . . . made friends with Gerard Irvine . . . which sounds hopeful. He is nice, clever, unselfish, rather sweet and touching.

No: you will *never* be " a mere relation " to me, whatever the kinship. Now I must put this up, and the sea letter too. My love with both, dear Fr. Hamilton.

R. M.

20, Hinde House, Hinde St., W.1
12th March, 1952†

Dear Father,

How well you understand things! Which means, at the moment, your letter of 4th March, with its agreement with my feelings about having Holy Communion brought to one's home. You describe the situation exactly: the lack of energy to tidy up, the lack of place among the books, etc., the general mess, so unseemly! I suppose in a nursing home or hospital it might be different, one wouldn't feel responsible. But even so I think I would rather join mentally in the service going on *in ecclesiis*. Largely thanks to you, I have now a lot of admirable bits and pieces, *preces privatae*, to say, which do me great service, both in and out of church. Is there a moment when Mass is not being said somewhere? I dare say there is: I haven't thought it out; but it may be so that there isn't. In Latin, in Greek, in whatever vernacular is used. It's a sustaining thought.

Thank you for your wise advice, and for understanding that drowned feeling under waves of work. I can cope better now that I *feel* better; my temperature is now quite normal and I get about as usual, and feel more vigorous daily, both in body and mind. You see, I *have* to get this Ruins book done; it is a commitment, and my publishers have been very patient, but I can't keep them waiting for ever. I think I see the end in sight now, but there remains a lot to be done. I *must* finish it before May, for then I go for a few weeks to the south of Italy, about which I have some articles commissioned. It will be lovely and exciting there; the Campagna and Calabria (the Gulf of Taranto, round the instep, between toe and heel, full of ancient, mostly vanished, Greek settlements). I shall have a friend with me, to share the driving. I shall write to you from there, but don't know about the time letters take between so ancient and so new a world.

Thank you too for your letter of 2nd March, enclosing the two about your mother's funeral, which moved me very much. I think you may really like to have them back, so I will enclose them, as I did the others, in a sea letter. All your family matters interest me greatly. I am going, when I get a moment, to write to Dorothea Conybeare asking if any of the family remember our grandmother ever mentioning those Norfolk Johnsons. She wrote so many letters, full of family and relations; I dare say if I still had those drawers full of her letters to my mother, I should find some references. But some of her grandchildren may remember some names; perhaps old James,[1] who is much older than most of us. You mention "Eliza and Mary Rose"; but they had many brothers and sisters—Edward (Canon) who was rector of Weybridge for very many years; Lydia, who married an Oxford don, Bonamy Price; Henry, who was a general; and I think others too. What families people had in those days! And now your air paper of 9th March. I looked up Wm. Bodham Donne in the D[ictionary of] N[ational] B[iography]; he was the Librarian of the L[ondon] L[ibrary] 1852-7, besides all his other activities and works. I read that book about him and his friends last year.[2] The *DNB* says he *was* descended from the poet Donne; but I think you told me this is wrong. I also read about C. J. Vaughan of the Doves, my great-uncle's brother (not of course uncle, as I rather foolishly said, I think).[3] Don't you think all those old relations of ours were very nice people? I feel they were, and that we may be proud of them. The only one I knew personally was my grandmother,

[1] William James Conybeare.
[2] *William Bodham Donne and his Friends*, edited by Catharine B. Johnson (1905), see above p. 80*n*.
[3] See above p. 276.

unfortunately. And she was delightful; very racy and unconventional and loquacious. I love the picture of your grandfather psaltering and gesticulating on the terrace.

Thank you for the piece from Asser. What a king![1] One of the more foolish things said in eulogy of our late King George was that he resembled Alfred the Great! Our nice late monarch was no scholar. How very good it would be if we should ever have a monarch who was, and who set himself to raise the level of taste by going to the best things, *not* only to the musical comedies and racing and the low-brow books. I suppose Wm. III was our last highbrow sovereign; Albert, of course, was only a prince consort. Perhaps little Charles will be highbrow; but I fear little chance.

How nice to have (when it comes) that Primer; I have looked for one in vain here, and should particularly like to better my understanding of medieval Latin. Now I have to go to the National Gallery, to be shown some drawings of ruins not on view, and will take and post this, so as not to miss a post. It is so nice to feel well again. But I'm sorry about your tooth, and hope it won't cause a lot of bother and fatigue. Goodbye, my dear cousin and Father, and my love.

Your very affectionate cousin,

R. M.

20, *Hinde House, Hinde St., W.*1
17th *March,* 1952†

Dear Hamilton,

This is the outcome of your letter of 10th and 11th March, which came to-day, thank you so much. Yes, I certainly like to call you this, and I don't feel that it interferes with or takes away from our other relationship as it has been for so long. We are now relations in another sense *also*, that is all. Anyhow, I

---

[1] The earliest life of Alfred the Great was by Asser, Bp. of Sherborne (d. *c.* 909).

rather like your name! It has dignity and a certain stateliness. (What is that poem of A. A. Milne's about a boy called Hamilton?)

I was thinking, wouldn't it be interesting suppose there turned up an old letter from my great-aunt Mary to my grandmother, mentioning that Hamilton Johnson, a charming little boy, had been to lunch, as he was at school in Harpenden. Better still, suppose my grandmother had chanced to be paying a visit to her sister when little Hamilton came, and had mentioned it in one of her (daily) letters or cards to my mother. But I fear you have no memory of this old lady stopping at the rectory when you went there. Dear me, how surprised I should have been at that retreat nearly 40 years ago had I been told that in the year 1952 I should be writing to Fr. Johnson, then become my 4th cousin Hamilton, about these family matters!

Yes, haven't habits about the use of first names changed. My father and his lifelong men friends (school and Cambridge) retained surnames to each other all their lives. I think it is in one of Angela Thirkell's books that a small prep school boy is asked by his parents what is the surname of another boy whom he always calls Philip. "I don't know," the boy replies. "You see, I don't know him really very well." A remarkable change in social habits. Now people, men and women, but especially I think men, seem to use first names about the 2nd time of meeting, very often. I like it, it is friendly and matey. Those old Edwardian novels, in which men call women, even while courting, "Miss so and so" read oddly. (By the way, have you tackled *Howards End* yet? I am longing to know what you think of it.)

My health is really all right now. The work remains, of course, but now that I feel all right I am not letting it get me down. I want to finish it, if possible, next month, before I go to Italy in May; but I won't get worked up about it. If I have finished it, I shall start for Italy with a heavenly feeling of freedom from care, and the new novel can begin to take shape in my mind, which will be a nice change and release. And Italy itself will be the best kind of nerve-rest; so many beautiful and interesting things to see all the time. So you must wish me well on my travels. Indeed no; staying with friends in the country is *not* a rest; far too sociable and gregarious and having one's activities arranged for one by kind hosts.

What a good thing " Cowper and Emily "[1] went into partnership! It is an odd thought that, without the particular union of two people, one could not have existed just as one is, that peculiar amalgam of millions of ancestors and drops of blood. " If you and Father hadn't married," we used to ask my mother, " which of your children should we be? " " Neither of us, of course," my mother replied. " You would have been quite different people." One gets giddy, remembering all one's ancestors who have played their part in shaping one, even the cake-burner! And oh all those armies of clergymen for the past 400 years! And marauding Highland chieftains, and godly ministers of the Kirk, and Devonshire parsons, and university dons, and bishops and deans, and French Huguenots in flight, and Evangelicals, and a few squires, and kings down to Henry III, and Highlanders hanged for stealing sheep, and heaven knows who else. No wonder every one is so odd and mixed. When your cousin comes to see me, early next month, we shall, no doubt, have a great family gossip, and I must show her some Rose portraits and look up some of my great-grandmother Lydia Babington's letters.

Do you think much about *time*? I do. I mean, from the point of view of the Christian scheme of salvation. I read somewhere lately, " the only gate to God is through the death of Christ." Which means, I suppose, that His death is being taken as an eternal thing, which took place from the beginning of time, and that He lighteth every man who has come into the world. For example, the psalmists, who certainly achieved and groped after " the way to God," more than almost anyone. And Job and even non-Christian mystics. So I suppose one can't think of His earthly life and death as events at a precise time on this planet; at least, as *only* that; it must have been available to those who lived earlier. It is so obvious that they too had their " holy

[1] Father Johnson's parents.

communion" with God; the psalms are full of it. I went to the first part of Evensong on Sunday at All Saints, Margaret St., just to hear the psalm for the 16th (*Quam dilecta*)[1] which they sang very beautifully. I never know which I really like best, that, or 40 or 42 or 43, or, indeed countless others, including parts of 119. They had "the gate to God" all right, tho' they didn't *know* about Christ's life on earth. I think it isn't confusing if one tries to take the long, eternal view. But sometimes people are too concrete about it, and then I get puzzled and uncertain. . . .

I am told that *Von Hügel* is very interesting, and mean to read it. I have also been told that the author makes too little of Von H.'s modernism and disagreements with the Vatican. As a devout R.C., he is likely to minimise these.

Now I must get back to my Ruins. I do hope your dentist is being nice and gentle. My love; and isn't it nice being cousins!

R. M.

*20, Hinde House, Hinde St., W.*1
22nd March, 1952

Dear Hamilton,

This sea letter is to send you some papers—the two letters that I think you may be glad to have back to keep, and my review of Hugh Walpole. He was a complicated and fascinating character; not wholly admirable (who is, after all?) but loveable, for all his rather irritating petty faults. I hope I haven't been disagreeable about him!

I was interested to see in one of these letters a mention of Mr. Jacomb-Hood, a lawyer. It was a Mr. Jacomb-Hood, a lawyer, who had, and lent me in 1943 or 4, the MS. account of the Lisbon earthquake by a Lisbon merchant ancestor of his, which I included in *They went to Portugal*. He was extremely old, even doddering, so the lawyer of the letter is probably his son or nephew or something.

[1] "O how amiable (are thy dwellings)." Ps. 84.

I mean to send an air paper in answer to your letter of 15th, a particularly good one, but will divide my comments on it between that and this sea letter. Thank you for what you say about the development of man and his power to choose between right and wrong. No; of course we *can't* know the moment when this began; it is (to me) an eternally interesting speculation; so is the development of conscience in the infant mind. (And, come to that, the dog's. I suspect that animals have more of it than we think—even those animals that, unlike domestic ones, don't catch it from us.) Perhaps the strange creatures from whom we descend had it, in embryo, and really did know it was wrong to bash their wives on the head with clubs, or bite one another; perhaps they too, had they known the words, would have said " *video meliora proboque, deteriora sequor.*"[1] Perhaps even the very jelly fish who are, it is said, our very early ancestors, had some such vague jelly-fish feeling; indeed, perhaps they still have. I am reading a French book about the loves of animals for one another (their mates, I mean), and, since they feel love, why not conscience?

The response of the conscience to God—that they scarcely know, I suppose. After reading your letter, the very good part about God's gifts of grace to us, which we are merely to accept, I was reading Wm. Law, " The Spirit of Prayer ", and came on passages which seem to apply to our response. " Here thou standest in the earnest, perpetual strife of good and evil . . . and wilt thou be asleep? . . . Heaven and hell divide the whole of our thoughts, words and actions. Stir which way thou wilt, do or design what thou wilt, thou must be an agent with the one or with the other. Thou canst not stand still . . . if thou workest not with the good, the evil that is in nature carries thee along with it: thou hast the height and depth of eternity in thee, and therefore be doing what thou wilt, either in the closet, the field, the shop or the church " (and of course the flat) " thou art sowing that which grows and must be reaped in eternity . . . The bells are daily calling us to church, our closets abound with

[1] " I see the better course and I applaud it, but I follow the worse." Ovid, *Met.* 7. 20-21.

manuals of devotion, yet how little fruit! . . . Your business is to give way to the heavenly working of the Spirit of God in your soul and turn from everything either within you or without you that may hinder the further awakening of all that is heavenly and holy within you."

That premises the initiation by God of His work in us, " No man can come to me except," etc.; the breaking in is His, and our mode of acceptance to try and work with it. . . .

Yes: I think you are right about my Wilderness being largely an unconscious prayer. Well, it got answered all right—more than one could have dreamed. Looking back, I can't think—I really *can't* think—how on earth I managed to get on for so long, turned away from it all, and not even realising, except at moments, how much I needed it and wanted it. Blind and deaf and choked with the vanities of time, turning away from the " riches of eternity." Oh well. Of course I have missed a lot, from missing all those years; but I couldn't *value* it more than I do now I have come to it at last. I can't agree that the vessels it came to me in were earthen, though; I have come across plenty of earthen vessels in my time, but not at *that* time. In fact, such is my weak nature that I don't believe I could have got hold of it if it had come in earthen vessels. It was regarding them as far from earthen that first persuaded me, and, I suppose, still persuades me. Even my Chapel, though crumbling (better now, by the way) is lovely and of heaven. I am afraid it is a real weakness, being so easily put off by a method of presentation that isn't to my taste, that sounds to me trashy, stupid, or over lush, let alone ugly or common. So I have to be careful not to expose myself. . . . [sic] Yes, it is a weakness, but there it is. And now you have put me on to reading Isaiah again—how beautiful he is. " I will go before thee and make the crooked places straight "; " Drop down, ye heavens, from above, and let the skies pour down righteousness." . . . [sic] I think I shall read the prophets for the rest of Lent. I like them so much better than the O[ld] T[estament] *narratives*. I was listening to the manna in the wilderness the other day. I wonder how much of that light wafer stuff one would have to eat before feeling one had

had a satisfying meal. A great deal, I suppose. Even then, one couldn't do hard work, or walk very far, on it. I don't wonder they got sick of it and wanted quails, a much better idea. The stuff didn't even keep through the night, except on the Sabbath. I do think it's rather odd to read these ancient Jewish tales aloud in church, intriguing though they are. I would like to revise the lectionary, and add to it a lot that isn't Jewish at all—Philo, the Neo-Platonists, and a lot of wisdom from the east; and, I think, the *Imitation*. And Jakob Boehme and other mystics. Why should the Jews be our meat year by year? I believe variety would make people prick up their ears and listen much more eagerly. But I would have the whole of Wisdom, Isaiah, Job, Ecclesiastes, Ecclesiasticus, a great deal from the prophets. But who will listen to my suggestions? No one.

Since writing thus far, I have written you an air paper, and am now going out to post both. They bring my love, dear Father.

Your affectionate cousin,

R. M.

20, Hinde House, Hinde St., W.1

22nd March, 1952 †

Dear Hamilton,

Your letter of 15th has come; thank you so much for it; it is full of things I want, and that no one but you can supply. I have answered it in a sea letter (to be posted with this; let me know the difference in times of arrival). I wrote a sea letter really in order to enclose some letters you sent, and my review of Hugh Walpole, and possibly, if it won't make it too heavy, an article from the *Spectator* by Mervyn Stockwood that interested me, about the kind of services he thinks it right and seemly to have in his church, where the congregation are strongly fixed to Cranmer's liturgy, unadulterated. I was interested in his idea for an evening service. Is he right that no one can understand the baptism service? Why not?

Thank you for your comments on the awakening of man's conscience, and on the free gifts of God. I have talked about both those things in my sea letter. And about Isaiah, which you set me reading again.

That Primer isn't yet to hand, but no doubt will be soon. I shall read it with great interest.

I have been asked to contribute to a discussion in *The Author* on the present cult in literature of violence and cruelty and obscenity. I agree that it is a contemporary fashion, and I don't like it. I suppose it comes from backwardness; uncultivated minds, whose only romance is violence—no, violence and sex; very much sex. The mass mind, too uneducated to look for or find romance and excitement in beauty, landscape, architecture, art, poetry, music; it can only thrill to the obvious physical excitements of horror and sex love, and craves avidly for more and more detail in the description of these. It not only disgusts me but bores me; so perhaps really I shouldn't join in such a discussion, I am not objective enough. American novels are *much* worse in this way than ours. I don't read them, but I gather that huge novels pour out weekly, full of cruelty, obscenity, words not usually uttered, descriptions of what it isn't seemly to describe (like in *Mary Lavelle*, but *much* worse) and general nastiness. Is it the effect of the growing influence of a tough, half-literate class of reader, who demands to sup of horrors? I hope that as we all grow better educated, this fashion will pass. . . .

About Italy. I am hoping to start there in my car early in May. I shall write letters and cards to you, but don't know when you will get them. I shall send them by air, of course; but don't worry when there are longish gaps; it will be the fault of the posts, which aren't very good from Italy. You can be sure all will be well; it always is when I gad abroad in my car. I was doing the same thing in 1950, if you remember, when I returned to find a letter from my as yet unrecognised cousin. This time I shall be going a little further south—Calabria. A lovely holiday, in splendid country, and set about with magnificent buildings, most exciting. How unfair, when I can have this kind of romance, to complain of those who can't finding theirs in violence and sex. Don't write me much, as letters may easily stray about and be wasted. I shall have a few points of call, where I shall enquire for letters, but haven't thought them out yet, of course. I imagine that Rome will be one. I shall give you the same that I give to my sister and to the porter of these flats, who will forward a certain number of my letters. No, perhaps he had better not; there would be the difficulty of adding stamps to them, of course. My companion will be, if he can get leave of absence from the British Institute in Madrid, a friend of mine called David Ley, who is interested in the same kind of things I am, and is also v.g. at jobs needing strength, like changing wheels, etc. If he can't come, I hope to take two cousins, a brother and sister. Oddly, all three of my possible companions are R.C. converts; so they will enjoy Rome, where they can spend their time while I am examining the Campagna (Horace's farm, etc.).

[*Here follows a line which R.M. has deleted, explaining her action thus:*] (I began to tell you something that it suddenly struck me I had told you in my last air paper.) For the rest of my answer to your letter of 15th, see my ocean missive, I am now going out to post both that and this. I am glad you are getting to like the Schlegels. He [E. M. Forster] has such an attractive mind, hasn't he. My love always.

Your affectionate Cousin,
R. M.

20, Hinde House, Hinde St., W.1
29th March, 1952 †

Dear Hamilton,

This is splendid! Two days ago Co-op[1] produced Beeson— it looks fascinating. I've only glanced through it so far, being laid up with another tiresome attack of some noxious fever.

---

[1] Father Johnson had ordered Beeson's *Primer of Medieval Latin* from the books department of the Harvard Co-operative Society.

The doctor thinks it may be Undulant Fever, which cows have, and which seems lately to have broken through from the cattle kind to ours. Symptoms are fever, up and down, but mostly up and up, dizziness, faintness, etc., etc. At least those are what *I* had for a week—but am now (to-day) so marvellously recovered, as you see, that I can sit up and write a letter, and in a day or so shall *get* up. It is a bore, going on like this, but such is life in winter-time. My doctor says this disease is carried by milk. " Milk," says he, " is *lousy* stuff——" and how right he is! I can't think why we pour it down the throats of helpless children! Still, never mind. My temperature rushed down last night, and I woke this morning below normal. Also woke to a white, blizzarded world—much like New England I guess. I listened to the Boat Race snugly in bed—obviously a v. fine race, neck to neck all the way till the end.

Besides Beeson (I wonder what Milton, who so loathed the sight and sound of M[edieval] L[atin], would have thought of it? Of course he was v. stupid about it, as about much else. A humanist like him should have taken pleasure in the development of an ancient tongue. Only he hated monks and the middle ages too much for this)—what *was* I saying? Oh, yes; besides this attractive book, for which I am really extremely grateful, I have 2 letters from you—one a[ir] p[aper] of 21st, and an a[ir] l[etter] posted (I think) 24th—both full of interest. I will get *Worship*[1] at Duckett—it will interest me greatly; and will tell how the article struck me. I think I agree with you they had better let things be; I can't imagine Italian peasants following the service in the way they want.

I was *extremely* interested in your O[rthodox] C[hurch] priest. Of course I knew they were in communion with us, but didn't know they were as near as that. I wish I knew some, I suppose there *must* be an O.C. church in London somewhere, and should like to go to it sometime. They, I suppose, are Greek Orthodox!

I'm glad you think there is a religious revival: I don't know

[1] A periodical published by the Monks of St. John's Abbey, Liturgical Press, Collegeville, Minn.

about this country. There are enormous numbers of young rationalists; but my Harvard cousin now at King's tells me the religious drift, when coming, is towards Anglicanism, not the Pope. He puts this down largely to T. S. Eliot. But, when I was young wasn't the drift stronger still? I don't know, but *think* so. Of course when my father was young, the drift was the other way. *He* drifted right out of it, despite the restraining ancestral hands (more clergy than you knew of!). Should I try and influence my small god-daughter, I wonder? (whom I now see it was wrong and presumptuous to take on, in my then position). Coulton's[1] book sounds exciting, and I will get it. You will have primed me well in M[edieval] L[atin] before we have done.

My "travel-chum" will *probably* be one David Ley, a youngish man, long a friend, who works at the British Institute in Madrid. Very stalwart, intelligent, companionable: R.C. convert, but *nicely*. I mean, not the English self-conscious type, like G. Greene. . . .

Remember I've driven on the Right (U.S. and about Europe) for 25 years, and find it, on the whole, *more* natural. And I've never had an accident—so far! *Dominus custodiet me, super manum dexteram meam.*[2] Still—*hi in curribus, hi in equis*[3]— and *hi* in neither, put their trust. Dear Cousin—and how I *like* this Cousinship—you mustn't worry about me in my chariot. Murmur a brief prayer for me occasionally, and it will bring me safely home. I shall write a better letter soon, this is a wretched one, *and* illegible. But it brings you much love and gratitude. I shall soon be *quite* well now.

Your affectionate

R. M.

---

[1] Dr. G. G. Coulton (1858-1947), medieval historian.
[2] "The Lord himself is my keeper: the Lord is my defence upon my right hand." Adapted from Ps. 121.5.
[3] See Ps. 20.7: "Some put their trust in chariots, and some in horses . . ."

April

20, *Hinde House, Hinde St., W.*1
1st April, 1952†

Dear Hamilton,

I was about to write to you to report progress, when arrived
yours of 26th; thank you so much. You had got my sea letter
on 25th, so it took 17 days. I am *much* better than when I wrote
my last air paper, in fact now practically all right, but don't go
out yet, nor shall, this vile winter weather. My arrangement
with Mary B[arham] J[ohnson] was that I was to wait for her
to let me know when she was in London " early in April "—
she knows I want to see her, and I do hope we shall meet, and
that I shall be feeling well. I am much interested in all you tell
me of her. I too feel a great respect for her.

That is interesting, about the pictures on books. What a
disconcerting thought, that *They were Defeated* might have a
picture of Cleveland and Julian in some embrace, or of Cleveland
and Francis fighting while Julian was knocked out on the floor,
that might embark some youth on a life of crime! There is
material for such pictures in almost *any* novel—including E. M.
F[orster]'s. But can criminals *really* be moved by such slight
stimuli? I don't believe it, whatever they may say. It would
be interesting to know the results of the Jesuit's appeal, if any
publishers consented; but I fear they are hard men, and wouldn't;
violent illustrations may or may not induce crime; but they
very certainly sell books. I will send you my contribution to
the discussion, when I have made it. I think I know the answer
more or less. As to the other business [homosexuality], who
does know the answer? I suppose those resisters of yours do, in
the end, get out of it. What you say to them seems exactly
right. ... [these] people buffeted to and fro, failing and recovering,
and still clinging on, instead of taking the easy way of non-

298

resistance. Yes, I am sure it grows commoner all the time. I suppose there was a good deal of it in the M[iddle] A[ges] among the Religious Houses; all the contemporary social satirists spoke of it; and, of course, it was one of the counts against them at the Dissolution—not that that says much, when so much was pure fabrication for a purpose. But I suppose one can't reject *all* the Visitors' Reports. Of course the M[iddle] A[ges] laws against it were very severe—they could be burnt alive for it at one time.

I see what you mean about Transubstantiation—that our feelings about it make it what it is. I mean, the feelings and associations of the whole Church and our prayers and hallowing. I believe that myself. I suppose we are less *objective* about it than the R.C.s. It is a mystery, and one can't really define it —certainly ignoramuses like me can't. All the sacramental life I at present get is from following Mass from bed and in imagination . . . you understood so well about the bedside table, the bottles and the books! But if I can't get out early by Easter, I must, I think, surmount all that. However, I hope to be able to go quite soon now. Deprived of the chief means of grace, I feel graceless.

There were one or two questions in your last air letter that I hadn't space to answer. Conybeare rhymes with *on*. (At least *our* Conybeares do.) I feel that once it must have been *un*, because I think nearly all the *on* and *om* words used to have the *u* sound. But I never heard of any Conybeare with it—I don't know why it isn't Cōneybeare, since we think it comes from *coney burrow*, from the Devonshire moors whence the family derives and the coneys who make their homes there—but I daresay it is nothing of the sort. Then you ask how I think of a novel. That depends on the novel. *Keeping up Appearances* had its genesis in the reflection how manifold is human nature, and that it might be fun to present one person as two, as far thro' the book as was possible. After that, the characters create themselves. *They were Defeated* developed from brooding on Cambridge life as it was about 1640; I had always read a great deal of 17th c. letters and memoirs. I got a group of people, most of them real, some half real; I took Herrick and re-imagined him as a live person, how he would talk and feel; then I built up round him the Yarde family, and Dr. Conybeare and Julian (Dr. C. was rather like my mother's cousin, F. C. Conybeare of Oxford). Then I thought up the Cambridge milieu—and what fun it was! *The Wilderness* was a meditation on Ruin, physical and material, with a lost waif for its central character. Now I have one at the back of my mind—two distinct *characters*, but not, so far, much of a plot. This will arise when I give it my attention. So, you see, it's sometimes one thing first, sometimes another. I wish I was now on my next.

I now await my travel companion, to discuss plans; he is coming in this afternoon. Now I must poach my egg for lunch. " Demeanour "—yes—that reminds me of how, on the rare occasions when we 3 little sisters, attending the local convent school for 6 months at Varazze, joined in a school walk, led by a nun, and met fishermen. But no space for this, or for more than my love.

R. M.

20, *Hinde House, Hinde St., W.*1
7th April [1952] †

Dear Hamilton,

Thank you for your letter of 31st March, in which you hadn't yet got the earlier of my two letters (I think posted 29th?) in which I told you I was laid up. I wrote again on 2nd April, telling you I was getting on nicely. I still am; but am still in bed, as this Undulant Fever is a v. slow and tedious business—it goes away and comes back. So I am spending Holy Week and Easter in the flat, as well as I can. . . .

What you say about [the] Passion and Holy Week is very helpful to me just now, and just how I am trying to look at it (necessarily from a distance). I won't get to Duckett for that book, till I am about again; I shall then. It's not a book anyone can choose *for* me, even if I could ask anyone to get so far. But

I can use all kinds of prayers, and try to follow the week, and the great proclamation of the Church's faith. And I try to get more and more *into* it, and to understand. Thank you very much for what you say of it.

That story about Fr. Gibbs[1] is very impressive. Surely an admirable way to die. And what presence of mind on the part of Fr. Pedersen! What did the congregation do? Wouldn't they naturally go home, if the celebrant was taken ill like that? But I suppose Fr. P. carried on almost at once. They must have been very anxious. Can a deacon administer the Ciborium, or only the Chalice? I suppose only the Chalice. The whole thing must have been a great shock to everyone. But much better, really, than a long, painful illness. And such a splendid moment to be taken.

I shall be glad when I get a letter from you, saying you have got mine of 29th or so. I am not meaning to worry you about my health, only I like to keep you *au fait* with my doings. I am really *much* better, and am hoping to be up after this week. Meanwhile, I am reading and thinking (rather incompetently). You know, really no spiritual reading can better the *Imitation*. I am reading, too, a good French book about Holy Week. Do you see *Theology*?[2] The March number has some interesting articles; one about a French community in Paris; another (called " Difficult Cousins ") about our relations with the R.C.s. Do read it, if it is published in America. I haven't got it, or would send it you! I rather hope Mary B[arham] J[ohnson] won't turn up just yet, as it would be a bad moment. She didn't say just *when* she would be in London. Now I am expecting someone who is going to do my shopping. . . .

My love for Easter,

Your affectionate
R. M.

---

[1] Rev. George Crocker Gibbs, S.S.J.E. (1878-1952), was stricken while saying Mass at the Church of St. John the Evangelist, Boston, on 30th March, 1952. He died the following day.

[2] Anglican monthly journal published by the S.P.C.K.

Dear Hamilton,

Thank you for 2 splendid letters (posted 4th and 7th April?) which cheered my sick bed very much. I was up (though not out) for 3 days, but had a return of this cursed fever in the night of Good Friday and am in bed again. That is the way of Undulant (or Maltese) fever—it comes in cycles. But I take an excellent drug (Chloromycetin) that gets it under, and will, I hope, kill it very soon. Did you, I wonder, meet it in Malta much? It is a frightful nuisance, tho' in no sense dangerous. Meanwhile, everyone is wonderfully kind. . . .

I can't answer your good letters adequately, being reduced in wits just now. But how good and timely are your observations on watching the great Paschal rites of the Church (which I have been doing from the wings). It is all very supporting and reviving and glorious, even to one dulled by Maltese fever. I follow the 8.15 Mass as best I can. I wish it were possible to get small copies of that large Altar Book we use (I think a Cowley one?) but it isn't. And the P[rayer] B[ook] doesn't contain a lot of it, of course, and *The English Missal* is really just the R.C. missal translated, and contains too much, and not all of the kind I want (I am not much good at the B.V.M. and the Saints, nor at all that Roman " enthusiasm," too Tridentine and sentimental). The American P.B. contains more (a collect for each day of Holy Week, e.g.) and *Hours of Prayer* a lot, and you supply me (thank you) with continual additions to my Brief Prayers, so I am really well supplied.

Now for a few points in your letters—*Howards End.* I think his [E. M. Forster's] philosophy of life is one of affection in personal relationships and sympathy and comprehension—not a bad one (though not technically Christian, but with many Christian elements). I agree, I never believed Margaret would have married Mr. Wilcox. I suppose he supplied the complement to the Schlegel aesthetic and unbusinesslike attitude towards life. But I have seen enough odd marriages not to be surprised at any of them. As to Helen's affair with Leonard—no, I don't really believe in that. She didn't love him—and surely her emotional reaction and pity wouldn't have driven her into that, particularly reared as she was. I always agree with a dear old lady I knew who said, disapprovingly, "I don't think Helen would have forgotten herself like that with that young Mr. Bast."

Delafield[1]—I knew her, tho' not very well; I liked her much. I think her mother (Mrs. Henry De La Pasture, a novelist who became Lady Clifford) was R.C. and sent Elizabeth to a convent school. Elizabeth threw it off young, I think, and was never R.C. when I knew her; one gathers she didn't much admire or like the convent school.

Donne was *certainly* "Dun"; there is every evidence, and I grew up so calling him. I expect your Donnes, like my Conybeares, were once *un* too. A losing battle is being fought between the old and the new—as in Romford that nearly everyone now rhymes with Tom. The change can happen very quickly—the O'Donovan family comes over here from Ireland—or one of them does; always called "O'Dunovan" in Ireland, he soon found that he couldn't get it done here, so gave up the struggle, and his children now call themselves *on*, and scarcely know they were ever *un*. A change in one generation. Just as nearly everyone calls the Trevelyans "Trev*e*lyan" (they call themselves "Trev*i*llian") and the Cecils not "Cicil" but "Cecil". As to Cowley, he lost the battle long ago, so the Fathers aren't "Cooley"; it is surprising that Cowper has kept the *oo*. I suppose his fame preserved it; I dare say there are modern Cowpers so debased as to rhyme themselves with *how*. . . .

I was much interested in your further account of Fr. Gibbs' death, and Fr. Pedersen's prompt action, and the beautiful burial. And in your account of the delightful-sounding Mrs. Paine. . . .

I hope it has been a nice Easter with you. In an odd sense, it has with me, in spite of this tedious disease. I suppose Mary B.J. didn't after all get to London, which is probably, in the circumstances, best. I am hoping soon to get hold of the Coulton

[1] Elizabeth M. Delafield (1890-1943).

303

book you told me of. Meanwhile I am coping with 6 French books, which I have to judge of.

I'm sorry for these illegible letters, but they bring my love and thanks.

R. M.

20, Hinde House, Hinde St., W.1
18th April [1952]†

Dear Hamilton,

Your letters came in like tonics (10th and 14th April), and I want to send a word in reply, though don't write much just now, being still in bed and still undulant. This disease goes on far too long. But may end suddenly, killed by Chloromycetin, the new drug. My doctor says there are several cases in London, and all the milk farms should be investigated for sick cattle. I feel good-for-nothing, can't eat much without bad results, can't use my brain to speak of. But I like to write to you, stupidly and lazily and with no less affection than when in health. Before beginning to, I rang up Duckett for The Words of the Missal.[1] Out of print, and they had just sold their only 2nd hand copy before I rang. They may come by another to-morrow, next year, or never. Isn't that annoying? But I feel I can get it somewhere, even if the L[ondon] L[ibrary] hasn't got it, which it doubtless has. It sounds a book to keep. . . .

Do we have those Easter Eve ceremonies in our churches? I have never seen them—but probably All Saints does. It must be a lovely ceremony—the lighting of the candle, etc. The English version of that prayer is good, though, too—" let the temple resound with the triumphant voices of the people " . . . Next year I must go to that service somewhere. I haven't got the Missal in Latin (only partly) and ought to have it all really —the Missale Romanum.

There is a lot to think about in your 2 letters, which I like to meditate over, and have plenty of time for that. Oh yes, the

---

[1] C. C. Martindale, The Words of the Missal (1932).

304

coloured photograph is of Lydia Babington, my great-grand-mother, who married Joseph Rose; a very nice, benign-looking old lady; I thought I would shew it to Mary B.J. when I see her.

I am missing a lovely little summer—perhaps the only one we shall have this year. Well, it can't be helped, and I dare say I shall be about quite soon now. I wonder why we imbibe this most perilous liquid, only safe when boiled. Do be careful of it. I send much love for Easter, and every good wish you can want.

Your affectionate

R. M.

20, *Hinde House, Hinde St., W.*1
21st April, 1952†

Dear Hamilton,

I wrote to you on Friday, three days ago only, but am sending this line to-day because I thought I would like to tell you how much better I am than when I wrote last. I do really now feel as if this illness was nearing its end, and that the last go of it has perhaps been had. I forget what I wrote on Friday, but think I was feeling pretty low. I dare say now I may be up in a few days. *How* glad I shall be! One gets so sick of bed, and of feeling ill, and of not being able to go about doing what one wants, and of feeling so mentally *dull*. I am now just begin-ning to be able to use my mind a little. . . .

Meanwhile, it has been nice to have [the Reserved Sacrament] . . . here; I lie on the sofa in the sittingroom, and feel the room has acquired a kind of lustre it had not before. I admit that I was wrong in my distaste for the idea. But then I was envisaging my *bedroom* with its bedside table so littered with bottles and books, and having to be cleared! The sittingroom, not much lived in now, and lovely with the daffodils that kind people bring, is much easier as a church substitute. On Saturday came the news of the sudden death of my cousin Alfred Cony-beare, the Vice-Provost of Eton. A happy life: Eton, then

King's, then straight back to Eton as a master, and there for all these years. He loved his work, and the boys, and had a great number of close friends among them always, and wanted nothing more. His only real griefs were when they got killed in the two wars. He never married, nor wanted to. Certainly a happy life, and fortunate in ending so suddenly, while he was still vigorously engaged in it. But a sad break, of course, in the Conybeare family circle.

No news yet from M[ary] B[arham] J[ohnson], so perhaps she isn't coming to London this time, and will come later.

Our little summer has fled, leaving behind it the usual damp and chilly April weather. I am glad, as the more summer now the less later, and I do like to have some at the proper time.

My Italy plans are still in the air—I will let you know.

I am reading Père de Caussade (18th century French priest—so good). All this sitting back from life gives one, I find, a rather changed view of it—some things matter less, others more. I am not fussing so much as I was about finishing my book. I hope you are well, even better than this leaves me. My love always.

R. M.

By afternoon post, after I had stuck up this, comes yours of 17th—thanks so much for it. Yes, I shall get a *Missale Romanum*. I am attracted by your idea of a collection of prayers. *But you must help with it*: it shall be a joint effort. Permanent chaplain also a happy thought!

20, *Hinde House, Hinde St., W.*1
25th April, 1952†

Dear Hamilton,

I thought to-day I would write a letter, not a paper, for a change: one reason is that I have none of those air papers at hand, another that a letter is more comfortable and spacious to write on. Your good letter begun on 18th came yesterday. I think I last wrote on Monday, when I was feeling better.

Alas, that didn't last; I have now relapsed into temperatures and weakness. My Doctor is consulting experts in this disease, and may turn up with some fine new remedy. The capsules I have been taking seem to have lost their power to keep the fever down; perhaps I am getting immunized against them! It is all a great nuisance.

I am a poor hand at Latin at present, and not up even to finding my way about the Breviary (or the Missal if I had it) to look for prayers. But I did find that collect for Easter Friday. Better than Fr. Martindale's version I like the one in *The English Missal* — " Almighty and everlasting God, who hast bestowed the paschal sacrament for a pledge of man's reconciliation: grant unto our hearts that what we celebrate in outward profession we may effectually fulfil." The meaning is a little different, isn't it, from Fr. M.'s—he says " the *covenant* that reconciles the human race "—the other makes it the *sacrament* that does this—I think the *Missal* trans. *sounds* better, too. But I like best your interpretation—if you could work that into brief collect form. A thing that I, at present, am quite incapable of even attempting. This illness reduces one to a great stupidity. I can't even tackle Beeson and medieval Latin yet, let alone translate collects. I wish I had got *The Words of the Missal*— but I asked Duckett to advertise for it, and it may turn up any time. I haven't yet got hold of Coulton's book, either; no doubt it's in the L[ondon] L[ibrary], but I can't get there.

By the way, do you use the American or the English P[rayer] B[ook]? I notice you say the Queen was not mentioned, so I suppose it is the American one, as indeed would seem more natural.

I did once, when alone in the Chapel, have a look at that Altar Book. I wish I had it. It would take some practice, finding the appropriate " propers," etc., for each day, but I do think they are so good and beautiful. I certainly never heard a Mass I liked better. . . . Certainly from no other church could I have got such good. . . . (alas, when shall I get there again?) . . .

No, it wasn't Lydia Babington that I said I had a pastel

painting of, but her husband Joseph Rose (my great-grandfather) and his mother, Mrs. William Rose. I believe there *is* a painting of Lydia, that the Conybeares have. She was a handsome old lady. I must show all those portraits to M[ary] B[arham] J[ohnson] when we meet. *Milk.* I hasten to register a patriotic protest—we do sterilize and bottle all our milk in London. But I suppose now and then an infected drop slips through, and such a drop must have come my way. Do Americans really say C*ow*per? (You see the connection!) How atrocious! How I hate cows!

Now I can't post this till someone goes to the P.O. and gets me a shilling stamp.

Oh yes, Paul Revere—how romantic he was! "Hardly a man is now alive, who remembers that famous day and you."[1]

I often pause with gratitude to reflect how *very fond* I am of you.

My love for now.

R. M.

May

20, *Hinde House, Hinde St., W.*1
2nd May [1952]†

Dear Hamilton,

Thank you for your very nice air paper of 24th April. Thank you for calling my attention to the None hymn in Latin; of course it is *very* much better. Also I have been reading the " *Libera nos* " after the Pater Noster—I like this plan of intermixing the Latin and English prayers. One day, when I am well, I may write out a private Missal for myself, with the Latin and English together, so I can use which I like. Who first intro-

---

[1] H. W. Longfellow, "Paul Revere's Ride."

duced our version of *audemus dicere* — "we are bold to say"?
A curious wording, which I think I rather prefer to the rather
commonplace "we *dare* to say" (which I have never heard,
actually).

Well, I don't seem to get well yet, and feel pretty weak. It
is really a most tedious and exasperating disease. At any moment
its end may come and I may take up my bed and walk, but it
doesn't seem to happen. . . . My intellect is going steadily down-
hill; I don't read much, and the books I do read seem vulgar
and trite, except a large 2-volume account of Indian architecture,
which is heavy on the chest.

I think there is a lot in what you say about the Evangelical
distrust of public schools. Zachary Macaulay felt it so much
that he sent T.B.M.[1] to a small school near Cambridge, which
was probably not nearly so good for him, as he was so easily
cock of the walk there; but [he] no doubt found his level at
Cambridge, where he failed to the end to pass the Mathematical
Tripos then necessary for a degree—or did he at the end just
scrape through? Perhaps he did.[2] I forget when the absurd
anomaly was abolished—that men had to take both the
math[ematical] *and* classical tripos. So many brilliant classics can't
do Maths, and vice versa. One of my uncles (later Vice-Provost
of King's)[3] was regarded at Winchester as a kind of idiot because
he couldn't learn Latin and Greek—and he turned out the most
brilliant mathematician. But no doubt (returning to schools)
the Evangelical distrust had good basis; they were, and are,
full of vice and temptations. Much less so now than then—I
wonder if Lord Shaftesbury sent his sons to a public school? I
wouldn't be surprised if not.[4]

The newspapers are awful reading now—Russian brutality
in shooting at passenger planes, murderers escaping from Broad-
moor and murdering children, bloody doings everywhere.

[1] Thomas Babington Macaulay (Lord Macaulay).
[2] T. B. Macaulay failed in the Mathematical Tripos and had to take a Pass
Degree.
[3] W. H. Macaulay.
[4] The 7th Earl of Shaftesbury (1801-1885) sent his eldest son to Rugby in
1845.

Libera nos indeed—*ab omni perturbatione securi*[1]—what a hope! Thank you for your concluding prayer for me; it sustains and strengthens—*in fidei luce et in mentis pace*.[2]   My writing is so shocking that I fear it may strain your eyes, and hope you *won't try* and *decipher* it.   But I do send my love, dear Father.

R. M.

20, *Hinde House, Hinde St., W*.1
6th May, 1952†

My dear Hamilton,

Thank you for your two most welcome letters (letter and paper) posted 30th April and 2nd May. I hope this too will be welcome, as it is partly to say I am *much* better, have begun the new Aureomycin treatment . . . and really for the first time feel on the way to health. I am normal in temp., can sit up and take notice, and feel I am climbing up. Last week I felt slipping down, to an extent I never mentioned to you: my doctor was going to give me a blood transfusion to arrest the process; but I suddenly turned a corner, and he is only giving me liver injections. It is quite absurd, the way this disease has affected me, but I suppose my resistance is low, and things get me down where they wouldn't a stronger (or younger) person. Anyhow I now feel I am really getting the better of it. . . .

Don't be vexed with poor M[ary] B[arham] J[ohnson]. She did nothing amiss. The arrangement was quite vague—*if* she came to London (and had time) she was to let me know. I suppose she didn't come, or hadn't time—and perhaps she will sometime later. I do hope you won't tell her she should have let me know, because she really wasn't bound to at all, and it was such a very *conditional* engagement. I should have done just as she did. I am sorry about your cousin Gertrude.[3] Such deaths make deep gaps—and she does seem to have been a fine and

---

[1] " Deliver us indeed—secure from all disturbance."
[2] " In the light of faith and in peace of mind."
[3] Gertrude Powys, eldest sister of John Cowper Powys.

central person in her family. One likes "those 2 little girls lie side by side again." . . . [sic] Eliz. Myers, who married L. Powys, was a very clever, interesting writer: I liked her books. They were very much the books of a consumptive (if you know what I mean—K. Mansfield was another). It was very right of your Aunt Katie to be named after St. Catherine of Siena. She was *our* patron saint (of Varazze, my home town) and her procession was the noblest of the year, even better than Corpus Christi. How I remember it, winding all through the town and along that sea road, St. C. carried in front and all the bells clanging, and ending where it started, in her pink-washed patronal Church just outside our house, at the foot of the hillpath. *Why* don't we have religious processions? Weather, or just stupid Protestant prejudice and apathy? . . .

I sit very loose now to "intellectual difficulties," and don't feel they matter. As you say, it is a personal relationship. I like Tyrrell's *External Religion*,[1] pp. 31-35: about how the Incarnation and Passion and Resurrection present for us in concrete terms the eternal age-old struggle of God in our souls, because men are too gross to realise the God within them unless He was externalised thus, so that His Passion and our sin and the final victory are shewn before our eyes, an eternal thing and a moment-to-moment battle to which we are committed and to which *He* has committed Himself. And [He] has "assembled" the sacramental rites for our strengthening. Yes; I like "assemble" in that collect. As to "*Pro uno defuncto*"[2] (how good a prayer!) the woman would seem to be more in need of purging from sin than the man, which is, indeed, the ancient and time-honoured view, both ecclesiastical and secular. Based, do you think, on anything more than the masculine-made view of humanity? These papers are very small and come to an abrupt end. But my love is not, and does not.

R. M.

[1] George Tyrrell, *External Religion : Its Use and Abuse* (1899).
[2] "For a man departed."

20, Hinde House, Hinde St., W.1
12th May, 1952 †

My dear Hamilton,

Thank you so much for your air paper of 5th May. By now you will have got mine of 6th, saying I was much better, and also that M[ary] B[arham] J[ohnson]'s conduct was perfectly right and reasonable and I should have done the same myself, in the very *conditioned* engagement we made, so don't let it vex you. Since I wrote, I had a slight return of fever, but it is now subsided, and I really am (I hope) in the way of recovery. I am interested to hear of the prevalence of the disease on American farms. *Never* again shall I touch that unwholesome drink wherewith Nature, that malicious harridan, has seen fit to nourish the mammal creation. (Unless it is *boiled*, that is.) " With milk and honey blest," indeed! I hope they boil it all there; if not, I shall stick firmly to the honey when (or if) I arrive in the golden city. I am practising all the *sapientiam* available, and going very slow and *suaviter*, in order to get entirely well.

I felt well enough yesterday (Sunday) to write a review of a very malicious and inaccurate little book by Sir Henry Slesser (judge, P.C., etc.) called *The Anglican Dilemma*. He was, as you probably know, a prominent Anglo-Catholic for years, and went R.C. a year or two ago, since when he has been a violent Anglicanophobe, and has now produced this contemptuous and ignorant book, proving how " Calvinist," etc., the Church has always been—I gather the " dilemma " is that no A.C. should stay in it. The Church is also Erastian (too true), impotent, immoral, ignorant, and without any roots in Catholic Tradition. I will send you sometime a copy of my review—perhaps the book too if you would like to see it as a curiosity. . . .

Oh yes, indeed—*veritatis tuae lumen ostendis*[1]—I have been saying that (in English) all last week, with thankfulness that I can now be shown it (progressively, dimly, but really). By the way (and returning to Slesser's book), am I right in saying [that] the 28th Article, in saying what it does about " given, taken

[1] " Thou dost show forth the light of thy truth."

312

and eaten, only after an heavenly and spiritual manner " and by
[saying that] Faith [is the " mean whereby the body of Christ is
received "], accepts the Real Presence? And does the mention of
Faith imply a " receptionist " view, any more than the words of
the Missal " *ut* nobis *corpus et sanguis fiat dilectissimi Filii tui*."[1] Sir
H.S., who insists on judging the whole Church and P[rayer]
B[ook] *by the Articles* (cf. the admirable commentator of the
American P.B. who says we must interpret the Articles in the
light of the whole P.B.), declares that the Articles, and therefore
the Anglican Church, deny the Real Presence, which was never
accepted till the Oxford Movement. He seems to have read none
of the 17th and 18th century Anglican devotional writers.
Particularly he should study Wm. Law's mystical writings. But
of course he is a . . . propagandist, and they won't see straight . . . .

Did you finish *Where Angels*?[2] A queer, *young*, interesting
book. E. M. F[orster] is coming to see me to-morrow.

Much love,

R. M.

20, *Hinde House, Hinde St., W.*1
16*th May,* 1952 †

My dear Hamilton,

Thank you so much for (*a*) air paper posted 10th (*b*) air letter
posted 13th, which came to-day (brisk work!). Both full of
interest. I hope both left you as they find me, in the rudest (or
almost the rudest) of health. I stroll the streets, I shop, and this
morning I drove to 8.15 Mass! How is that for a person who a
week ago was prostrate and undulating? I am delighted with
myself. Now I am bidden to put on weight; I am now 7 stone,
which is too light for my height (5 ft. 8) and normally I am nearly
8 stone. So I try and stoke up, but don't feel any very hearty
appetite yet. I suspect that thinness and under-weight may be

---

[1] " That *unto us* it may become the Body and Blood of thy most dearly
beloved Son."

[2] E. M. Forster, *Where Angels Fear to Tread* (1905).

a physical quality that you and I share; but I fear it may be the only one; I should like to think there were more (as you suggest) but I believe I take entirely after my father's family, and look very like him, and still more (I was always told) like his mother, who was a Ferguson, and had no relationship to the Roses. More chance of a family likeness in one of my sisters; they both took after my mother rather, and my sister Jean is a little like our maternal grandmother, Eliza Rose, who (I can see from his portrait) was very like her father Joseph. But I fear no one is going to find that side of the family in *me*; though, of course, there *are* odd fleeting looks, that it usually takes people outside a family to observe. For instance I am very like one of my brothers[1] (as children we could deceive our parents for a moment by wearing one another's clothes) but *he* was a little like my mother, and her uncle Edward Rose. So you never know.

I admired the Latin story you wrote to me (I mean, its Latin!). I expect one ought to practise writing in Latin, as our forbears did; but time lacks. By the way, did I tell you I have now read a lot of the Beeson, with great interest and profit? How terribly moral—and limited—those Dark Age writers and monks were! All those *Physiologus* allegories[2]—every animal having to be a moral image, or to represent Christ, or something. I suppose it was a stage in the evolution of a more enlightened Christianity that had to be worked through: like the eremitical stage, and extremes of desert asceticism and mortification of the senses which meant a lop-sided spiritual life and culture.

I'm glad Christianity has emerged into a fuller and better thing—*lumen veritatis*. After struggling, too, through Puritanic Calvinism, that deadly miasma—though of course it only affected *part* of the Christian church. But our Low ancestors! Yes indeed. Though I suppose they did practise the action of Prayer, going to church, and were sometimes sacramental. Didn't they at all believe in sacramental action on the soul—

[1] " Will " (W. J. C. Macaulay).
[2] *Physiologus* was the title given to a collection of some fifty Christian allegories, also known as the *Bestiary*. It was a combination of Natural History with allegorical interpretations of animals real and imaginary.

314

I mean, that Christ is (as Article 28 and the Catechism have it) truly and indeed present in it, though only in a spiritual manner?

By the way, *Collect*. The O[xford] D[ictionary] (referring back to the Latin *collecta*) says " in late Latin (Jerome) an assembly or meeting. In Med[ieval] Latin in the Liturgical sense (which was the first in English)." The Gregorian Sacramentary (late 6th century: I suppose), it goes on, has " *oratio ad collectam*,"[1] and sometimes merely " *collecta*," as the title of any prayer said at a station where the people were *collected* in order to proceed together to church for Mass. It meant simply a prayer at the collection or gathering of people. *Earlier* than this, in the *Gallican* liturgies, "*collecta*" was used as the title of a prayer (after the Mass) [which was a] collecting or summing up of thoughts suggested by the *capitula*[2] for the day. Thence the word, as an equivalent for *oratio*, passed into medieval French and English missals and breviaries, and thence again into our P.B. The odd thing is that in Jerome's " late Latin " it seems only to have meant assembly, so what does one make of that passage from Jerome? Could it mean "no other words he was wont to give the assembled people but . . ." etc.? But then surely *proferre* would cause *collectas* to take the *dative* case? I suppose the Breviary couldn't have altered Jerome, using *collectas* where he hadn't? Or needn't *proferre* govern the dative? I see we need further information about this. One should consult some Late Latinist —or see some good translation of Jerome's Commentaries. . . .

Virginia Woolf—yes, I was devoted to her, and am a great admirer. *Orlando* is nonsense, of course, but rather lovely and fascinating nonsense, don't you think? Orlando him-her-self was taken from Vita Sackville-West, who is coming to see me in a day or two; I am v. fond of her, she is v. beautiful and nice (Mrs. Harold Nicolson). I shall read Littleton Powys's autobiography[3]. I was greatly interested in J[ohn] C[owper] Powys's.

I told you, I think, that I had been reviewing Sir Henry

[1] " Prayer at the gathering of people."
[2] A *capitulum* was a short lesson from the Bible suited to the Office of the day.
[3] Littleton C. Powys, *The Joy of It* (1937). His second book of autobiography, *Still the Joy of It*, was published in 1956.

Slesser's anglophobe polemic *The Anglican Dilemma*. I had to condense a draft of over 1000 words into 550, which is difficult. This morning the literary editor of the *Observer* (a *young* man) rang me up to suggest a few alterations, as he thought one or two things I had written might "provoke a correspondence." One was my calling the Articles about predestination, election, Pelagians vainly talking, etc., "tribal cries from some far Scholastic jungle" which he thought might annoy some people. Then he asked "What are Pelagians, and how do they vainly talk?"[1] It did demonstrate the gulf between our generations, that he had, I think, never even *read* the Articles. Also, I was not to talk of the 1928 P[rayer] B[ook] having been "howled down by Parsee and Presbyterian M.P.s." So I cut that out. Then I said "Of course you don't remember that"—and of course he didn't—he was probably under 10 at the time.

I like that American addition to the "Church Militant," and always add it to myself—I wish it was in our Cowley Altar Book. I *must* get hold sometime of those books of Fr. Martindale's—it was annoying that I only just missed *The Words of the Missal*. But I expect they'll turn up sometime. By the way, I was interested in 2 numbers of the *Cowley* magazine that came for me, one with your Abbot Daniel trans. in it.[2]

I hope you don't mind these written letters. I don't feel up to typing yet, except for short business communications—but can you read me? Anyhow, I must now go to bed: I am trying to retire early at present.

Much love from your most affectionate and obliged cousin.

R. M.

Just found *Mind of Missal* in a little bookshop, and received some lovely flowers from your 2 nieces! *Did you suggest this?* I fear you must have![3]

[1] R.M.'s reference is to two of the Thirty-Nine Articles: Article 17 "Of Predestination and Election" and Article 9 "Of Original or Birth-sin." The teaching of the Pelagians (followers of the 5th century heretic Pelagius) included the denial of the transmission of Adam's original sin.

[2] See *Cowley* (Winter 1951).

[3] Note by R.M. on back of envelope.

My dear Hamilton,

Is not this grand, that I am typing to you again? I am sure you must have got very tired of trying to decipher my handwriting. Since I last wrote (17th) I have had your air paper of 14th and a[ir] l[etter] posted 20th. I must ask for that Pittenger book[1] at the London Library. . . . [Those] American-Oxford books are sometimes hard to get here; but the L.L. ought to have it, or get it on request. That translation of his of the B[lessed] Sac[rament] collect is a familiar one, I suppose; but, as you say, not good. " Experience " would be better (for *sentiamus*; " perceive " of course is obsolete English) than "perceive"; and of course "fruition" rather than "fruit"; and "continually" rather than " evermore." But it does sound a book I should much like to read, and shall. What you say about *Res* [is] interesting. I suppose one would translate it " substance," wouldn't one? " Grant me not only to receive the Sacrament, but its substance and virtue." It seems rather interesting that St. Thom[as] Aq[uinas] prayed that; for surely it amounts to saying that it *does* depend, as Article 28 has it, on our faith? I mean, that we don't *necessarily* receive the substance with the species. I am interested too to see in one of St. Ambrose's prayers (*Feria Sexta*—the one beginning " *Rogamus etiam te* "[2]) that it asks the Holy Spirit to make our offering into the Body and Blood. Is this the Epiclesis,[3] that they tried to put into the 1928 P[rayer] B[ook]? More and more one sees that there isn't really so very much difference of view—only perhaps of emphasis; after all, they speak continually of *memorial* of His Passion—" *recolitur memoria passionis ejus*,"[4]—as in the collect you quote. Of course not the same as " reminder." I don't mean that the Roman view isn't rather more objective than ours—but not much, surely? So the Slessers

[1] William N. Pittenger, *The Christian Sacrifice; a Study of the Eucharist in the Life of the Christian Church* (New York, 1951).
[2] " We also pray thee."
[3] The invocation of the Holy Spirit upon the bread and wine.
[4] " The memory of His Passion is renewed."

have no call to dismiss Anglicans as " receptionists." But the whole business is so tangled up with metaphysical and theological changing hairbreadth shades of meaning that one can't (and doesn't really want to) fully understand what it may have meant to different sections and ages of churchmen. I find myself more and more occupied in finding out a little of what it may mean to me and to Christians now. I naturally haven't got hold of much of it yet; but one explores it. And such books as the one you mention are a help. Meanwhile, what a glorious territory to explore daily! I am now back in the Chapel again, though I don't go except I feel up to it. *Nor* am I yet exploring the Serpentine afterwards; this will come in time. The weather now is delightful, on the whole. I am very busy, trying to catch up on arrears, and to get on with my Ruins. When more free I do hope to see your nieces, if they will. They may spell my name just as they prefer: they have probably never seen it written, except in connection with the historian, to whom they have no reason to think me related. I find in shops people always write it down wrong, tho' to me " Macaulay " seems the most obvious way. But Macauley is more liked, and better still McColley, or other oddities. In Italy they called it Macolai; our house they called the Villa Macolai. So we are all quite used to being mis-spelt. Alas, my chariot won't make for Tarentum this year; the time for that excursion has gone by and my doctor says (*fortiter*) *no*. At least not in June; and July and August I can't well go. Anyhow, I must now get on with finishing that book, from which I have been held so long. I hope Mother Rose[1] got to, and liked, the Chapel. Is she one who would be shocked at seeing communicants at High Mass? There have always been those there, I gather; and " spikes " don't like it. I think it is Christian and right, tho' I don't do it myself, from no principle but simply that I like early much better. I hope Mrs. Paine enjoys her English visit. . . .

I think I will try Mowbrays for Pittenger's book. I've acquired

[1] Mother Rose Anne, then Superior of St. Anne's House in Boston, Mass.

2 oz. of weight since I took up my bed and walked, and so go on from day to day getting a little fatter. . . .

My love always,

R. M.

20, *Hinde House, Hinde St., W.*1
30th May, 1952†

My dear Hamilton,

I meant to write a *letter*, in answer to your two of 22nd and 27th—but, since you say that Whit Monday is your birthday, am anxious to dash off a greeting, which probably *won't*, however, reach you on the Day. But I have no air letter stamp without going to the P.O., which I've not time to do (I found your letter on coming in at 4.30 from the L[ondon] L[ibrary], and have to go out at 6.45 to dine at 7 with a man at the Reform Club) so have only time for this a[ir] p[aper]. I'll write more later, to answer your interesting letters more adequately. But now, I do wish you a happy birthday, a great cake, and a really good year ahead. I shall remember you at 8.15 [on] Monday . . .

I have now read, with great interest, your review of [Karl] Adam.[1] If he sees it, he will be moved. Of course he wouldn't be likely to have our church much in mind; but what you say may give him to think of it. I liked it v. much. Fr. A. must be a v. different kind of R.C. from Sir H. Slesser! He would probably deplore the latter's book. But they will never accept us, will they? I don't see that they can, being tied as they are to their past pronouncements. Have you ever read Salmon's *Infallibility of the Church* (1888, but just republished, and reviewed in *The Times Lit. Sup.*)? I've not. The Abbot of Downside wrote to protest against the review. R.C.s don't like the book, which is very learned obviously. It is about the rise of the doctrine. But I'd rather read *Ways of Worship*, published by the S.C.M. Press. It is really a report of the papers read at the World Conference of Faith and Order, 1937.

[1] Review by Father Johnson of Karl Adam's book *One and Holy* (New York, 1951), published in *Cowley* (Spring 1952).

That is an interesting notion of Fr. Martindale's about *communio sanctorum*.[1] But can he be right? And can *sanctus* ever be a noun; and if it is an adjective (qualifying *res*?) shouldn't it be *sanctarum*? But perhaps *res* would not be the appropriate word for the things in question. By the way, I am interested to notice that *The English Missal* (for Anglican use, but much of it translated from the Roman Missal) translates the prayer " *Perceptio Corporis tui* "[2] (just before the priest's communion) by " *partaking*," and later in the same prayer *percipiendam* by *receive*. (No " perceive " there.) A modern translation, of course. . . .

Yes, of course Anglican Catholicism has never died; not even in the high 18th century. Though I suppose its *ritual* did almost die, till revived by the Tractarians. What a revival indeed, since then. I like all you say about the *oneness* of sacramental practices (such as confession) and of ritual, with the whole meaning and body of the Church. What about Confession, by the way? I must look into that. I mean, how far did a trickle of it run through the later 18th century, after the last Non-Juror died? A *very* small trickle, if any, I fancy.

Thank you for Catharine C[owper] J[ohnson]'s nice letter. Yes, she gets " Macaulay " perfectly. We *must* meet sometime. Meanwhile, I improve daily. I shall get Eliz. Myers's letters.[3] Also I must read a new collection of L. Powys's stories and essays that someone has just made.[4] I think I am heavier *for my sex* than you for yours. Male bones weigh more than female. I (5 ft. 8), weigh (just now) 7 stone (or 98 lbs.). You (how tall) weigh only 115-120 lbs. Normally, I weigh nearer 8 stone (112). You should be heavier. Eat better and butter. (*No milk.*) Very much love for Monday—I *am* glad I know you.

Yours always,

R. M.

[1] In his book *The Mind of the Missal* (p.22) Fr. C. C. Martindale states that he is " not disinclined to think " that *Communio Sanctorum* [' the Communion of Saints '] may mean " participation in the Holy Things, that is, the Eucharist."

[2] " Let the partaking of thy body . . . turn not to my judgment) . . ."

[3] *The Letters of Elizabeth Myers; with a Biographical Introduction and Some Comments on Her Books by L. C. Powys* (1951).

[4] *Llewelyn Powys; a Selection From His Writings Made by K. Hopkins* (1952).

June

20, *Hinde House, Hinde St., W.*1
8*th June*, 1952 †

My dear Hamilton,

I was about to follow up my birthday a[ir] p[aper] with an a[ir] l[etter] when arrived your further a.l. posted 3rd June. So now I have two interesting letters before me to answer. First, to continue my observations on letter 1. I haven't read *The Edwardians*[1] for years, and your letter makes me decide to read it again. I will then tell you what I think about it. I remember it interested me v. much at the time. I wish you could meet the author; she is a most loveable being. . . . I wish we met oftener; but she seldom comes to London, and I seldom go to Sissinghurst Castle (a fascinating old castle, which they bought some years ago when it was a ruin, in which farm buildings and cattle had their home; the Nicolsons dug up the buried walls and repaired the standing ones and planted the garden, unearthing an ancient nuttery in the process, and made it a lovely place). . . .

By the way, the only thing I found rather amiss in your very good and moving words on K. Adam's book was that you seemed rather to be content to accept a place of inferiority for the Ang[lican] Ch[urch], whereas you might have indicated that it is the better church of the two, more truthful, nearer the Gospels, more Christian, more reasonable, more open to the progressive leading of the Holy Spirit which is, in the end, to guide us all into all truth. That is a point which R.C.s don't seem to grasp; that Christianity is being *now* guided, led into new aspects of the knowledge of God and his laws; they seem to consider that being static is a merit not a defect. I am just now getting letters from R.C.s disagreeing with me about Sir H.

[1] Novel by V. Sackville-West (1930).

Slesser, and they keep saying that their strength is being a rock that can't be moved, whereas it ought to be a rock that progressively *does* move, on and upwards towards God. I think they and I are too far apart on this matter ever to meet, so I don't argue. But I do feel that we have the best of it! Besides having less *nonsense* (rather puerile and silly miracles, and infallibility, etc.). Oh yes, I do much prefer the C. of E., with all its faults. . . . By the way, I was interested, after our discussions recently, to find Steele of the *Tatler* writing in 1713, " I have not been at confession for some months." He was, of course, an Anglican. I rather like, don't you, the P[rayer] B[ook] admonitions (in the 1549 and '52 books) to people not to be offended either at those who practise private confession, or at those who don't. I am much interested in " *communio sanctorum*." I shall ask the R.C.s I know how many of them interpret it that way. Of course you are right about " *res* " not being implied; I wrote in unthinking haste. Anyhow I like to have that possible meaning, and shall mean it on Corpus Christi at Mass. What a good festival! In Italy we had a lovely procession always, and people threw down roses from their windows as it passed. We regard it at Grosvenor Chapel as more important than the other saints' days this week, and it is distinguished by a 7.30 Mass as well as the 8.15. By the way, why *shouldn't* you ask if someone is at peace with the Holy See? I hope you bear in mind that your cousin Rose likes *all* your forms of expression, and wishes not one of them altered in any direction. *Letter* 2 (in reply to): I am sorry about my handwriting being so cryptic; I know it is, and particularly on the rather flimsy paper of those a[ir] p[aper]s. But you shouldn't give it too much attention; make a rough guess at it, and it will doubtless be as rewarding as my actual remarks. That dinner at Dilly's went much astray about " *difficile est*," etc.; especially Mr. Wilkes.[1] I am sure your meaning is the right one; " it is hard to treat what is common knowledge in a way of your own." I will look and see what the Loeb translation has for it,

[1] See Boswell's *Life of Johnson*. Johnson first met the politician John Wilkes at a dinner given by the brothers Dilly, the booksellers, on 15th May, 1776, when they discussed " the contested passage " in Horace's *Art of Poetry*, " *Difficile est proprie communia dicere.*"

when next I get to the L[ondon] L[ibrary]. But I have always supposed that to be the sense. A pity we weren't at Dilly's that evening. Still, dinners where they discuss that kind of thing are a good kind of dinner to be at, whatever conclusions are reached by the *sensus communis* of the diners. By the way, shouldn't you think that possibly *sensus communis* bore two meanings in Latin, as it has in English certainly from the 16th century at least? I see in the O[xford] D[ictionary] that the Latin *sensus communis* is given as equivalent in meaning to common sense. It gives for meaning 1 (of common sense in English) " ordinary normal understanding of common things," and for meaning 2 " a feeling common to a community of people, or to the human race." Quotes in this meaning are given from Spenser on. I must certainly pray for Mr. Wilkes, that he may, besides resting in peace (improbable for he was seldom given to rest or to peace in life) grow in understanding, so that when Dilly gives dinner parties in the Elysian fields, he may not be so far astray in his guesses at meanings. Perhaps Horace may be there too, to elucidate his own passages and confound the critics and commentators. Dear me, what dinner parties, what social joys! And perhaps (talking of the Grosvenor Chapel deceased) Lady Mary [Wortley] Montagu and Pope also meet at such parties, and will (or long since have) make up their quarrels.[1]

Yes, what intensity those infant joys in beautiful things had! A kind of rapture, never quite to be recaptured (as Wordsworth says). " The earth and every common sight, To me did seem, Apparelled in celestial light, The glory and the freshness of a dream."[2] What Traherne called " new-burnisht joys."[3] Do you know that delightful poet, by the way? Delightful prose meditations, too. The rapture of childhood is nowhere better expressed than in his poetry. Teas in the garden and new green wheel-

[1] The friendship between Lady Mary Wortley Montagu and Alexander Pope was broken off *c.* 1730.
[2] William Wordsworth, "Intimations of Immortality from Recollections of Early Childhood."
[3] See "The Salutation" by Thomas Traherne (*c.* 1636-74), author of *Centuries of Meditations*.

barrows are part of it, but by no means all. The birthday I shall never forget was a rapturous day in Italy, when we were first given a canoe, and navigated it in the calm summer sea from morning till evening; indescribable beauty and joy and romance, that returns to me still in dreams.

Can there ever have been any wild heretics who asserted that there were " three Holy Ghosts " causing Athanasius to insert a clause against them in his Creed? This reflection is induced by Trinity Sunday, one of those days on which this Creed should be said. What contentious beings our Christian forefathers were! My mother used to sit down during the more minatory verses of it, embarrassing her offspring rather. To me Trinity Sunday recalls buttercup fields and punting on quiet University rivers among may bushes, very lovely, and very unlike the somewhat forceful denunciations and definitions of the good Athanasius. Here is the end of my paper, it seems. I must stop and answer some less interesting epistles.

Later. I have lost the post, and this can't go till to-morrow morning.

Much love,
R. M.

20, *Hinde House, Hinde St., W.*1
14*th June,* [1952]†

My dear Hamilton,

This is a page torn from my note book while I wait in the B[ritish] M[useum] reading room for the books I have ordered to arrive. I have now to use such scraps of spare time as turn up among my labours. The worst of *this* scrap is that I have left behind me your two letters—a[ir] l[etter] of a few days ago, and a[ir] p[aper] that came yesterday, so can't answer what you said till I rejoin them. When I get home, I will have to catch a train to Romford, and shall take the a.l. with me in case I can write a little (however badly) on the short journey by electric train. I do remember that both letters were full of interesting things, largely liturgical; and that in the a.l. you told me that you were having me sent the Pittenger book, which excited and delighted me hugely. How very generous you are to me: for, tho' you say you haven't any more book-space, you could easily have got yourself some nice *thin*, *small* book. But how lovely for R.M. that you decided otherwise; it is a book I badly want to read, and it seems can't be got here. It sounds exactly what I want.

I had an interesting liturgical letter the other day from a nice R.C., who enclosed with it a bibliography (compiled by him) of liturgical books, which is useful to have. He seems an expert. I might send you his letter, if it won't make mine too heavy. The primitive Mass he describes (celebrant facing congregation, no candles, etc., on altar) is sometimes executed at S. Thomas's, Regent St. They call it " basilican " there. Other letters I have had complain that we " filched " their churches. I reply, with dignity, that we did not *filch* them, we just *kept* them, as they were already ours, and the fact that we made some changes in our Religion was no reason for renouncing our churches. But this is, naturally, a perennial quarrel between the Churches.

Romford. Now I have got to Romford, and have your 2 letters with me, and my sister has had to go out to a patient for ½ an hour or so, so I will continue my letter. I have been reading again (in the train) your letters, and enjoying them. I like what you say about being *in* the Church: yes, isn't it a wonderful corporate feeling of being carried along, being part of the body, not looking at it from outside, from beyond a fence. And, as you say, everything in it fits gradually in, forming the pattern of the whole; and the bits one doesn't yet grasp, or that don't mean anything much to one, may one day. Anyhow, that doesn't matter to the whole pattern and movement in which one is involved, as if it was a great sweeping symphony that one can hear a little of the meaning of now and then.

The American P[rayer] B[ook] did wonderfully get hold of some things our P.B. had omitted; especially that consecration prayer. But, that being so, isn't it rather odd that they left out references to private absolution? This is so, isn't it? (I haven't got it with me here, but seem to have looked for this in vain.) I suppose they took some things out of the Scotch Episcopalian book, didn't they? (Again, I should know about this if I was in Hinde [House], with my nice annotated U.S.P.B. at hand). That Consecration they have is beautiful.

I like to have that Latin prayer you say secretly and mutter half aloud. I go on learning more of these. I should do well to carry a Latin Missal or Breviary about with me on journeys, etc., and read them in trains and buses (*not* when driving my car) as priests do. (By the way, don't worry about the vehicular skill of my driving companions, as it is *I* who drive, when it's my car, and you know, of course, how great *my* skill and care are.)

As to that *Tom Jones*—Mr. Thwackum confession reference, what a very odd source Mr. T. is for it! I must look it up. My *Tom Jones* (a 1st edition, in the family for ages) was burnt up in '41, but I must get a cheap one sometime—or no, I don't actually like it enough to want to possess it; I will refer to it in a library. I have had lately two very nice ruin-seeking drives; the one in Herts, and last Thursday a lovely one to Hampshire, alone. I saw Silchester (the old Roman town now completely overgrown with crops of wheat and hay—100 acres girdled by the broken Roman wall, nothing inside the wall but a Tudor farm-house, a Norman and Perp[endicular] church, and the buried city, with a white horse cropping the grass above it. I wish some millionaire would employ architects and archaeolgists to build the Roman city again there; would it not look glorious? And import some Italians (or use those whom our miners so churlishly reject) to live in it, and chatter in the out-of-door market places, and argue loudly in the Forum, and hold basilican Masses in—the basilica. What well-spent money it would be, instead of piling up those costly armaments. But too beautiful a scheme ever to come off. From Silchester I went on to Basing House (nothing but steep walled foundations, with wild roses climbing about them) and to Basingstoke, to see the ruined Chapel of the Holy

Ghost, in a weed-grown old burial ground. Very neglected and lonely and forsaken, but once a centre of monastic training and devotion. Now roofless and shattered. There is a nice 18th c. poem about it that I was reading to-day in the B[ritish] M[useum]. Those 18th c. ruin-poems are very pleasing. When they are about the ruins of abbeys, they are full of owls and bats and ghosts of monks, and rather smug execrations on " fell Super-stition " who reigned there of old.

Here is one I like:

> ' *Gothick* in style, and tending to excite
> Free-thinkers to a sense of what is right . . .
> Not like St. Paul's, beneath whose spacious dome
> Thoughts of a future life too seldom come . . ."[1]

That seems to me very nice. Do *you* feel that way about Gothic? With your Latinism, you ought to prefer the classical style, so *in*conducive to thoughts of a future life.

Myself, I am all for the Byzantine (clustered domes and mosaics). I have just been to see the Ravenna mosaic copies now being shown in London. They are marvellously done. Yes, on the whole give me Byzantine. Or Romanesque, with baroque façades! As to Dostoyevsky and the Brothers K., I admire without much devoted love. I quite see that the Powyses —the Brothers P.—would adore before that shrine.

I suppose Fr. Morse[2] is all for Chinese temples, with curved eaves, and balls; and I must say I sympathise. I like him, with his large beard and " large Asiatic views," and his devotion to lamas (which I take to be the human not the goatish kind). Did he convert them, or only tend their bodies? I doubt if it would be easy to convert lamas; they already have their rather high priestly status, and would feel it lowering to lose it. I *must* get that Elizabeth Myers book from the Library. If Fr. Cow[3] liked it, I should too, though I feel just now something of an anti-cow resentment, after my 8 weeks attack from them. But it is a nice

[1] William Woty, *Church Langton* (1768).

[2] Rev. Walter P. Morse, S.S.J.E., an American Cowley Father, working at that time at Kalimpong, near Darjeeling.

[3] Probably a reviewer.

name. I used to hear of a Fr. Bull, but not before of a Cow, who should, surely, be a *female* Religious.

I'll tell you what I think about *The Edwardians*, and whether I think V.S.W. and R.M. write at all similarly, when I've got hold of it. (It's years and years since I read it.) And *The Venture of Prayer*,[1] too. But most I want Pittenger, and that is coming to me. What with that, and what with *Stones of Venice* (1st edition, with pictures) that Roger Senhouse (a friend of mine) is just presenting me with because he has another copy, my good fortune is great, and better than anything I could have hoped for; *funes ceciderunt mihi in praeclaris*.[2]

I wrote part of this letter in the train, returning from Romford: I hope it isn't too apparent *which* part. But none of it is good writing, I fear. I wish I wrote like you . . . or like any other reputable minister of God's word. Do you know that I have taken to saying clargy, and clargyman, as was customary till the 19th century. We stuck to *clark*, but minced down clargy to clergy, which I don't think sounds so good. I like Shakespeare's " Look where he comes, between two clargie-men " (*Richard III*). I am now gotten so old that I can talk old-fashioned with impunity.

Well, my love and gratitude, and not only for the coming Pittenger. I like your cousin Mary's " but she never liked such people very well ! " I wonder how many she knew of " such people." It is bed-time and bath-time. I am reading in bed a large book about the Carlyles—both funny and sad.

Your most affectionate

R. M.

---

[1] H. W. Northcott, *The Venture of Prayer* (1950).
[2] " The lot is fallen unto me in a fair ground." Ps. 16.7.

My dear Hamilton,

Two grand letters from you, of 11th and 17th, both stuffed
with interesting things. I forget, by the way, what I said about
your review of K. Adam; but I thought it admirable; the only
thing I a little regretted was that you seemed to accept the place
of the unwilling exile, which I feared might stick him up rather.
How interesting if he was to see the review and answer it. *I* get
letters from R.C.s who are already stuck-up, and silly too—
I meant to send you one, which mentioned Fr. Andrew's position
with scorn (you remember—about " do you ask me to believe
in a God who," etc.).[1] But I have retired to bed with a slight
temperature, so will only write this air paper, and leave enclosures for another time. I think I shall be all right to-morrow.
But I am working too hard; this can't be helped at present; but
I hate having so little time for letters, seeing people, reading,
etc. This stupid, stuck-up R.C. says " Either the Pope *is* the
one and only Vicar of Christ, *or* he is a damned liar and the father
of lies." So silly: all black and white. Why shouldn't the Popes
have been genuinely *mistaken* all the time, in their view of the
Christian Church? I think they *were*, and *are*; but that doesn't
make them liars. I hate these crude dilemmas which some people
create. " *Either* Christ did say precisely what the Gospel says
he said, *or* the evangelists were liars." Good heavens, do people
know *nothing* of how history is made and developed? And
" either Peter is the one rock, or Our Lord was a liar." (I note
that Fr. Palmer says it's " *a* rock "; and that Knox has *this* rock
(but surely the Rock was the *acknowledgment*, not the man).
I've not looked up the Greek. Oh yes; *how* I agree with you
about the diversities of the gifts to the church that can be provided by different cultures within it; and " every spirit that
confesseth . . ." etc. Just what these bigoted people won't or
can't believe. As to the Pope's supremacy, I say with Fr. Palmer

[1] See *The Life and Letters of Father Andrew, S.D.C.,* p. 133; a letter " to
one thinking of joining the Roman Communion."

nequaquam.[1] It is all so unnecessary. (... said to one of his own confession lately, about recent Papal pronouncements—assumption, midwifery, etc.—"they certainly don't help at all.") This, I think, is what many R.C.s feel. We are fortunate to have no Dictator in our Church, only the Spirit of God to guide it and check excesses and animate it. I am delighted to see that my friend ... has re-appeared in Grosvenor Chapel, after some months' absence during which she was, I believe, looking into the Roman claims. She even went to Rome (the city). She will perhaps tell me soon what she feels about it all. I am to dine with her, and she has also asked ... a great friend of hers (and mine), who is R.C. So he and I can fight for her soul across the dinner-table. Oh dear, ought one to try and influence people for their good? I *don't* mean ... who isn't at all my responsibility; but a much younger friend of mine, whom I have known since she was a child and [who] ... has long affairs with men; she is in one now; they are away for a week together. It's not a case of profound love, but just of wanting a companion of that sort and sex. He is married, and it all has to be very secret and furtive. I wish she would get married; ....
She is *really* nice: frank, honest, intelligent. What ought I to say to her when she tells me about it? I don't think anything I said could have any effect; but perhaps one should try....
She was once a churchgoer ... but that was long ago, and now she has no beliefs. But she's socially *good*; ... wants social justice; ... [and] wants better living conditions for the poor. She is not really "in love."

23rd June. I seem recovered now; temperature gone. I will write a bigger letter soon, with enclosures.

Meanwhile, I read, mark, learn and digest every word in yours, even when I have no time to comment on them. My love always,

R. M.

[1] "By no means."

My dear Hamilton,

What do you think? Coming in this afternoon from my labours in the London Library, I found, beautifully shop-done-up in Vandam St., N.Y., your noble gift *The Christian Sacrifice*. I have only had time to read a little in it so far, while I had my tea. It seems to have everything, all the meanings and aspects and their development, and I shall read it with great care and attention and interest. . . . Turning the pages, I note with approval "One of the unfortunate accompaniments of the Catholic revival in the Anglican Communion has been the way in which the degraded piety of much post-Tridentine Romanism has been taken over by some Anglican leaders . . ." (p. 177 and 8). I am glad to see that he adds that Romans themselves are now mending their ways. One beauty of Cowley and Grosvenor is that one meets nothing of that kind there. And possibly not in the American Episcopal church either? But many R.C. and some A.C. devotions are what one can only call sissy: " degraded piety " is possibly an apter expression. Oh it was nice of you to send me this good book.

Since I wrote you an a[ir] p[aper] on Sunday, I have an a.p. from you dated 20th. In it you say more of that horrifying decadence of the roof of S. John's church. It makes one cold with horror, to think what might have happened. It would have been more dreadful for you than for those killed, actually. Thank God indeed. These disasters take one back to 10 years and more ago, when everything was tumbling around us in that horrible and fantastic way, and one said to friends, " Meet me for lunch at such and such a restaurant—if it's still there to-morrow." And now you are in the peace of a Retreat. I'm glad Fr. P. is so good. I should have supposed he might be. Talking of 18th century confession, I see that all Fielding's novels, not only *Tom Jones*, refer to it; probably Fielding practised it. It does seem to have been widely recommended in the devotional books of the time. What *can* Sir Henry Slesser (A[nglo-] C[atholic] nearly all his life) mean by now saying that the C. of E. doesn't provide for it in its system? ... One likes to think of its having gone on all down the Church's history, however much abused by my Fludd uncles and others.

My enclosures are (a) a foolish R.C. correspondent, whom I have no intention of answering again, but I thought might edify you to see; (b) a rather anti-episcopal comment from the *Observer* on Canon Ramsey's appointment to Durham. I believe it was inspired by ... who obviously doesn't care for most bishops. I'm not sure how fair it is; they are surely rather less unscholarly than that? Not that at the moment I recall many weighty works by them. But after all their main business is to direct and administer, not to study. Oh yes, and what about Dr. Kirk? I think "Pendennis" of the *Observer* should have excepted him.

That running water of Horace's: yes, and he had it, in the stream Digentia (now the Licenza); and the *fons* he had too, in the spring he called Bandusia, not far from his farm. These things I had meant to see in May—but instead lay and undulated. However, I shall some day, and hope to bathe in the stream and drink of the *fons*.

Between the Armada and the Powder Action? I think my well would have been that of the Recusants and the destroyed abbeys; especially if one was too young to remember the Marian persecutions, but heard often of the Tyburn ones. But it is very hard to say how one's mind would have been conditioned, in such a different set of circumstances, such a different climate. My only Elizabethan ancestor we know much about —one John Conybeare, a rather learned schoolmaster—was a Protestant; and the Macaulays were certainly Presbyterian clansmen; what the Roses were I have no notion; the Herricks were, I am pretty sure, Protestant (i.e. the ancestors of my father's paternal grandmother); the Fergusons too. So, if we had no R.C. unreformed Elizabethan ancestors, how should I have been one? But I feel I should have joined that church, and perhaps given shelter to priests such as John Gerard. And, looking on the destroyed and abandoned abbeys (even though one[1] was already the fine mansion of my Babington relations. I forgot the B's—there was Anthony B[abington], of course, who was a Cath[olic] conspirator; perhaps I should have joined him)— well, looking on the abbeys, even at Rothley Temple, I couldn't but have sided against those who had thus destroyed them. Could you? And it would have been very inspiring, despite the " degraded piety " of many of the prayers and most of the relic-worship (such as curing your illnesses by keeping in touch with the skulls of executed martyrs). Yes, I feel I should have been well in. The judicious Hooker might have influenced me the other way, and (later) Lancelot Andrewes. But oh those repugnant Puritans! Nevertheless, I dare say Anglicanism and the P.B. and the pleasing dignity and moderation of it all would have claimed me, despite the abbeys.

No I scarcely knew Q (who only came to Cambridge to deliver his few official lectures; he never lived there).[2] But such a likeable person; a critic of no profundity, but one of the now old-fashioned school of humane, urbane, cultured, widely-read (tho' never quite widely enough—he had little acquaintance with foreign letters, unlike Desmond MacCarthy) literary writers at large, of whom there [are] now too few of any eminence. He made mistakes and could be diddled into putting into *The O[xford] B[ook of] E[nglish] V[erse]* poems by Quarles that had been appropriated by Rochester; and a great deal of that anthology is very poor stuff; but it is a great work; and how one loved it when young! I see it has only one Traherne—" News from a foreign country came." I must look up that Daniels[3] poem; I remember it only vaguely, but like what you quote, it is very impressive.

Apropos " wells," and early Anglicanism, I should like to read a book like Wickham Legg's *English Church Life from* 1660

[1] Rothley Temple in Leicestershire.
[2] Sir Arthur Quiller-Couch (1863-1944), appointed Edward VII Professor of English Literature in 1912, lived during term time at Jesus College, Cambridge.
[3] Samuel Daniel (1562-1619).

to the Tractarians[1] extended back to the 16th century and early 17th. Do you know this book? I am reading it from the L[ondon] L[ibrary] (pub. 1914) and it is full of extraordinarily interesting details from contemporary sources about the religious life of the times, under such headings as: The Eucharist. Early celebrations. Daily celebration. Reverence to altar. Reservation. Daily service. Church Furniture. Manners and Customs. Confession. Books of prayers (many adapted from the Roman), etc., etc. All very interesting to those studying the periods in question, or the continuity of church life. But I would like to read an earlier one, say 1562-1662. I have a notion one might find a lot of Elizabethan High Churchery (of course Queen E. herself)—as there certainly was Jacobean. I think the suppression of the Church and P.B. under the Commonwealth probably gave Anglicanism a kick and a secret underground stimulus. But we know a good deal about that; what I, anyhow, am ignorant about is the later 16th century Anglicanism. What learned ecclesiastical historian can we get to write it for us? I should suggest it as a theme, if it hasn't already been done.

Nice fine weather now, and I, being recovered, bathe again after Mass—so lovely!

Well, much love, and all my grateful thanks.

Your affectionate
R. M.

July

[*Postmark: London, W.*1]
5th July, 1952 †

My dear Hamilton,

Moved by your full and interesting letters posted 25th and 30th June, I had it in mind to write a full (if not interesting) a[ir] l[etter] in reply, and had jotted down things I wanted to say.

[1] J. Wickham Legg, *English Church Life from the Restoration to the Tractarian Movement, Considered in Some of its Neglected or Forgotten Features* (1914).

But (as you know) I am approaching D-day with that wretched book, and simply have *no* spare moment—indeed, I have no business even to be writing this paltry a[ir] p[aper]. But never think I don't absorb and prize and ponder over every word in your letters, even when I haven't time to write. The fact is, I am leaving *everything* undone just now. How happy I will be when I have finished that opus, already far too long!

I thought that half-baked R.C.'s references to Fr. Andrew (who had said a very logical and good thing) quite intolerably muddled, and even rather rude. Why drag in the Crucifixion? But then he *is* half educated (if as much) and they *can't* think clearly or straight, I find. I didn't answer his letter—one can't argue with people who can't see a point.

I think you must be right about "*felix culpa*."[1] I see, in *The Oxford Book of Familiar Quotes*, the reference to the *Exultet* is given, as if that was the 1st one they knew about (not that they are infallible).

And now here we are again at the collect for Trin. 4—things temporal and eternal. I certainly like the Latin version better than ours[2]—"*sic transeamus per bona temporalia, ut non amittamus aeterna.*" I like the *good* things, which our P.B. has cut out, and I prefer not to lose "*finally*," implying a looking to the end rather than the day-to-day struggle to keep the *bona aeterna* always with us. It's one of the best collects, I think, and *so* difficult an ideal.

That's what I am feeling about . . . , whom I mentioned to you as having affairs with men that don't go deep and that she would be better without. Very dubious *bona temporalia*, and must hide the *bona aeterna*. I will try, sometime, to tell her what I think about it, in general terms. . . . But I don't believe I should, at present, have any effect on . . . , who knows what she wants, and is very strong of purpose. Oh dear, I wish she would get married to someone.

[1] " O happy fault (which was counted worthy to have such and so great a redeemer!)," from the *Exultet*, or " Paschal Praise," which in the Western liturgy is sung at the blessing of the Paschal Candle on Holy Saturday.

[2] " We may so pass through things temporal, that we finally lose not the things eternal."

I have read most of Pittenger, with great interest, a little at a time. I find the last 3 chapters particularly good. I like his moderate, tolerant, civilised attitude; and what he says about modes of celebration is very instructive. I got a little bogged in the " modes of Presence," but then that is always beyond me. Do you know, I can't feel that it really *matters*, so long as the Presence is there. But that is, no doubt, my weak grasp of Metaphysics. Anyhow, what an excellent work!

Your suggestion for a work of *mine*, that should travel with its characters down history, making them react to the changing periods as they would, with their characters, have done—is a v.g. notion. I would take a group of people—clargy and laity, high and low, and try to imagine them confronted with the circumstances of each century in turn. What fascinating speculations it opens. Keeping all through the running thesis that individual character is the axis on which lives move. I doubt now if poor . . . will ever be anything religiously intelligent, either R.C. or C. of E. It seems that she does half mean *in the end* to join the R.C. church, but (like St. Augustine) not yet . . . so perhaps the poor old C. of E. will retain her to the end, who knows? She doesn't grasp a *thing* about it. . . .

I like that Faber hymn. By the way, did you ever consider Rome, in 1899? No more space, but much love.

R. M.

20, *Hinde House, Hinde St., W.*1
11*th July*, 1952 †

My dear Hamilton,

I am having a slight relapse into Undulant Fever (only slight, I'm sure) and am spending to-day in bed, which takes me from my work and my typewriter but gives me a chance to write a letter (*no* such chance in my normal days just now). So I will amplify my last a[ir] p[aper] by an a[ir] l[etter] and answer also your two last a.p.'s of 3rd and 7th July, which I was delighted to get. I had meant to send you one or two reviews of various Powys works that I had seen—but, being in bed haven't now the energy to look for them. I gather your Retreat is now over: I am glad Fr. P[edersen] was so good. I wonder exactly what particularly moved him, years ago, to forsake Baptism for the Episcopal Church, and how he came in contact with it, and what points of difference specially struck him. I expect you remember it happening. Of course I find it easy to believe that any contact with a branch of the Catholic Church should move a Baptist to join it: but then Baptism, or any kind of Protestant nonconformity, is antipathetic to me—too much so, for there is so much real Christianity there. I would except Quakerism from this distastefulness—I suppose because they say less, are not dogmatic (in these days) and do wait on the Spirit. I see that Pittenger is broad-minded about Dissent. I was interested in your young paragon's views on Pittenger. I do see what he perhaps means about the Holy Spirit: would he mean that there is too little about the H.S. leading the Church into further truth, into progressive illumination? That he is (perhaps) too much tied up with tradition and the past? For my part, I *never* find as much as I should like about the H.S., in any theological work—except perhaps Wm. Law and Jakob Boehme. And I do feel that the Church hasn't yet fully enough adopted or realised that amazing *progressive* illumination. The R.C. Church in effect denies it altogether (do they know that they do? Probably not). But how can they hope to be " led into all truth " when they believe that they *have* THE TRUTH, all discovered and crystallised and unalterable? (As one of my R.C. correspondents informed me.) That seems to me to be the major heresy, because it denies hope. Here we are, they say, and here we stay, in spite of all our horrible defects and sins (cruelty, intolerance, refusal to pray with fellow Christians, etc., etc.). They do deny the Spirit, utterly.[1] But not Pittenger—goodness no. But your young man may have thought he didn't *stress* it enough. Or did he mean something

[1] This passage appears to have been provoked by the rude and aggressive letter from a Roman Catholic (dated 10th June, 1952) which R. M. sent to Father Johnson on 25th June.

quite other? What does Fr. Williams[1] think about this? When he said (about the young man) " He thinks the Holy Ghost can't be shut up in any church." Well, no more do you—*Nequaquam*! Of course we all believe the H.S. is working everywhere. But I suppose it's a question of emphasis. It is possible that I am nearer the young man's standpoint than you are, with your life-long experience of Catholicism. You know, *I* didn't even feel that Pittenger goes far—not really *far*—with the Biblical Critics. But then, I read *The Modern Churchman*,[2] which really does! Anyhow, P[ittenger]'s book is of great interest to me, and value. One wants to get the right balance between Protestantism (the individual seeking after God) and Catholicism (the seeking through the Church), neglecting neither. This is what I keep trying to do, and P. helps me to it.

I am greatly interested in Wickham Legg's book about Church practices 1660-1830—fascinating side-lights on the past. So, indeed, is Mr. Thwackum—who'd have thought to find in him a sacramentalist and an advocate of Private Absolution? It shows the Church atmosphere which must have been Fielding's background, and obviously *was*. Do you know Wickham Legg's book? It is really most enlightening.

Do you ever come across or read any of those huge American novels—*The Sheltering Sky*[3] and others, which are full of horrors and obscenities and the nasty talk of the Common Man (usually a soldier). You wouldn't like them—but their popularity is a portent. Actually I don't read them myself, but I am told they are very " powerful " and impressive. So is G. Greene. I half forget *The Ministry of Fear*.[4] But how completely those war years were his milieu. He loved walking the bombed streets, wrapped in a shabby mackintosh, admiring the craters, the fires, and the tumbling buildings. It is his setting. But to him the world was always horrific, squalid, sordid. No, he would have no affection for the C. of E. of his childhood; it was much too temperate and

[1] Rev. G. Mercer Williams, S.S.J.E., Father Superior of the Cowley Fathers' American Congregation.
[2] The monthly organ of the Modern Churchmen's Union.
[3] P. F. Bowles, *The Sheltering Sky* (1949).
[4] Novel by Graham Greene (1943).

mild and benign for him. The R.C. church broke in his ears with a darker, more catastrophic thunder, and caught him up in it. Had he lived in *l'an mil*, he would have lived daily in expectation of the End of the World. . . .

My [holiday] plan is the Isle of Wight in early August. I hope to have done the book by then. Do *you* have a holiday or change? I hope so. I hope to be all right in a few days—the 2nd go is never *much*, I am told.

Forgive this ill-written screed, and my love always.

R. M.

20, *Hinde House, Hinde St., W.*1
19*th July,* 1952†

My dear Hamilton,

Since I wrote to you about a week ago, from my bed, I have recovered (the attack only lasted a week) and have had from you an a[ir] l[etter], an a[ir] p[aper], and a very nice packet of assorted journals, cuttings, etc.; I was particularly pleased with the article on Catholic novelists . . . [by] Martin Turnell . . . and the one from *Blackfriars* on the working of the Mind of the Church in arriving at its strange conclusions—Immaculate Conception, Assumption, etc., etc.—all to safeguard the Incarnation, it said, which seems to me nonsense. Surely the Incarnation doesn't need to be bolstered up by all that semi-magic— and how does the Perpetual Virginity help, which seems directly contradicted by the Gospels? That " Mind of the Church " of which the Romans are so fond, harnessing to it their interpretation of the Holy Ghost, always seems to me like the Wild Goose —" I don't know where the wild goose goes, but I must go where the wild goose goes "—quite unpredictable, and (worse) directed by the very fallible Vatican. I thought the article (obviously sub-sceptical, if not ironic) very good. In the end, they will ruin the Church—their branch, I mean—by going too far in affronting *every one's* intelligence. I am much interested in your account of your " Infatuation," which seems to me so very natural and almost inevitable. I don't know if you used to go ever to the R.C. churches in Malta, or what their effect would have been. I suppose I was inoculated early, and never became infatuated, though I was fond of our Varazze churches. But they weren't " religion "; that was what we were taught by my mother at home in her admirable " Prayer Book lessons " on Sundays; never have I been more inspired by a desire to be Good and to please God. I like what you quote from *The Venture of Prayer*; when I have a moment I shall get it to read. . . . Yes, you are right: personal influences are the predominating factor in starting one on roads; either in life or in books. But in the background there is perhaps always that inevitability created by natural character, or by a long chain of circumstances, hereditary and other. If you *had* 'verted, I wonder if you would have been happy in it, and if you would have been a priest, and a Religious. Interesting speculations. And would you now (no) have been writing me such interesting a.l.s and a.p.s about the Holy Ghost? Your a.p. on this subject is masterly in conciseness and packed meaning. Now, what about those bodies which, feeling themselves led by the Spirit, do start independent churches, but as Christian, Bible-led and dogmatic as the Church they left? They don't all lead towards relaxation of doctrine and loss of faith in the Incarnation and sacraments; many are very devoutly orthodox, and have an evangelical saving belief in Christ, though not in the Catholic Church. I couldn't myself ever have been a member of such bodies; but because I don't care for their *style*, not because I doubt their orthodox Christianity. And I do feel that we might be willing to unite with them, as so many people feel we shouldn't; we needn't *concede* anything by letting them communicate in our churches, no point of faith, I mean. Or is this quite wrong? The matter seems to have rather come up lately. I value the contact with God through the Sacrament more than anything in the world; but I don't believe that I think the Sacrament is confined by God to those who receive it from apostolically ordained priests. You will perhaps be sorry I feel like this; I hope not! Perhaps I am too " protestant," am I? But I don't want to be intolerant like the Papists, with all their defences and walls to shut other Christians out, and their refusal even to pray with them—that *can't* be Christian; what would Christ have thought of it? When we were little girls going to the daily convent school at Varazze for a time, the nuns wouldn't even let us join in prayers with the other children; we had to sit down, lest the awful sin should be committed of praying with little heretics. My mother was much vexed by this. To my mind it is anti-Christ. Well, I am working at high pressure, having promised to let my publishers have a chunk of the Book by Monday (day after to-morrow). It isn't exactly healthy, but won't last long, I hope. . . . I shall go to the I. of Wight in the first week of August, for about a fortnight, which will be nice. I shall be with my sister. . . .

I want to read some Jakob Boehme, as well as the *Venture of Prayer*. It will be nice to read some books other than about ruins, and other than the going-to-sleep books I read in bed. I would like a long spacious time with no *duty* books to read; just books about places and history and ideas. And I would like to be in Italy, but that can't be, looking at beautiful things. . . . I am returning to my early swim now I feel better. . . . By the way, thank you for sending me that American Ordinary and Canon of the Mass; it is almost what we say in the Chapel, with a few differences, and of course not all the " propers " included. And it has the prayer for the dead in the prayer for the whole Church, that I so much [wish] we had. Why don't we? We don't only want to " bless thy name " for them, but to pray for them. Well, here is the end, and the end too of the afternoon, and I must go out a little for air before I work again. Your letters refresh me greatly. My love always. Please pray that I may get this book done.

Your affectionate
R. M.

My dear Hamilton,

Thank you so much for your splendid a[ir] l[etter] of 21st July *et seq.*, which came to-day, and which I took to Romford to answer in the train and (as now) waiting at the station. *And* for a[ir] p[aper] of 17th, telling of your perilous ascent to find Wickham Legg's book—I'm so glad you got safely to earth with it. Yes, isn't it a good and interesting work; I find a lot in it that I like to know, and wish it was mine, not the L[ondon] L[ibrary]'s! I find it useful in such discussions as I was having the other night with Harman Grisewood, the very nice, intelligent, cradle-Catholic talks Controller at the B.B.C. I and someone else were trying to convince him that the C. of E. and P.B. affirmed the Real Presence—I adduced the P.B. consecration prayer, and other communion prayers, and Article 28, and the Catechism. He thought we only believed in a memorial; how ignorant of us they are! But we had an interesting discussion—which started because I referred to " the Anglican Mass," and he said, very kindly and politely, that that was, surely, a contradiction in terms. I half promised to send him a P.B. A Canadian present said that the Canadian Episcopalians did only believe in a memorial (unlike the Americans). Can this be so? We had an affable theological evening and also discussed the growing illiterate speech among the young—e.g. " Let you and *I*——", " He told John and *I*," which is, it seems, becoming common even among young public school types. It seems very odd! They *wouldn't* say " Let I," " He told I "—it seems to need a second name. Our hostess said her son's friends did this. What *are* we coming to?

I am all right now; yesterday I got off a section of the Ruins; I am now working very hard on the next bit. I *had* to stop to go to Romford this afternoon and evening, for my sister's birthday; am now in the train back (forgive writing if you can). Yes, C. of E. clergy have a pretty rough time in G[raham]

G[reene]'s books—"false hasty intellectual force" indeed—what *does* he mean?

I *must* get hold of the *Raccolta*,[1] it sounds fascinating. I am ignorant about Our Lady of Pompeii; when was her shrine put up there, and is it a pilgrimage centre? Even that may, one supposes, be conducted by the Holy Ghost, who has led so many strange affairs. No: of course I mean *The Mind of the Church*, not the Holy Ghost. But even that may be led of the Spirit sometimes. Now which way is the Spirit leading the Church—towards exclusiveness or union? I do see your point about the dangers, and you know I don't want anything watered down. But all the time I remember those 3 little girls at the Italian convent school, who weren't allowed to join in the prayers because Catholics could not pray with Protestants, and somehow one *knows* that is wrong. But is it so different from the Church saying they can't admit dissenters to their worship? I don't feel the question of the church "becoming Presbyterian" is concerned. It is a question of admitting Presbyterians to our communion. (The 17th century C. of E. wouldn't have been *lastingly* Presbyterian, if the King had yielded to his enemies on that point, any more than it was *lastingly* so when it was forced to become Presb. during the Commonwealth.) But I don't (as you know) want any change in the Church in a nonconformist direction, only toleration and admission to its altars. But a schism would be dreadful. One would have no home—I couldn't join either section. I suppose that whatever Grosvenor Chapel did, I should feel impelled to do; but I should regret it. And we should be no nearer union with Rome, until we accepted the Pope as our infallible autocrat and head and I don't think we should ever do that, though Hugh Ross Williamson would (and no doubt soon *will*).[2] . . .

On Tuesday I am bidden to a party at Graham Greene's. Wouldn't it be interesting if at that party I was surrounded by G.G. characters—evil men, racing touts, false clergymen,

[1] (Ital. "collection"). An officially approved R.C. prayer book.
[2] Hugh Ross Williamson was received into the Roman Church in 1955.

drunken priests and with G.G. in the middle of them talking about Sin. . . .

Sunday. I meant to get this off before—but have been struggling with the Ephesus ruins, how they looked at different dates, before Wood began his 1869 excavations. I am still immersed in them (like S. Paul, I fight with beasts at Ephesus), but will go to post. So with love.

R. M.

August

20, Hinde House, Hinde St., W.1
2nd August, 1952†

My dear Hamilton,

(I am trying out a new pen, I hope its results will be legible and beautiful.) I sent you an a[ir] l[etter] last Sunday, and since then have had your a[ir] p[aper] posted 25th, for which so many thanks. I am off to Wight, that charming island, in a day or two, and shall be back somewhere round the 20th. (My letters will be forwarded from here—much better than giving addresses.) I shall like being there very much: it is so peaceable and pretty and 19th century (but a lot of C. 17 in the middle of the island). And the sea is lovely, though goes out miles and miles! But I do like to be beside the sea-side. I have been having rather a gruelling time, but have now told the publishers they can*not* have the book in time for Christmas publication; it will be hard work to give it them in time for the early spring, even. Don't *hunt* for old magazines—only if anything of interest *should* turn up, of course I would like to see it. I got a lot of interest out of your last package. I will find out if *Commonweal* is still extant; it is certainly v.g. Yes, their periodicals are certainly better than ours. I wonder why?

I am much interested in what you say about your " infatua-

tion " in Malta and elsewhere. I was thinking the other morning,
a morning I (a) hadn't my car, so couldn't get far so early, (b)
wasn't feeling very well, (c) wanted, all the same, to make my
communion—well, I thought, if I go to St. James's (R.C.
Church), Spanish Place, just round the corner, and not only
assisted at mass but *communicated*—would it be a terribly dishonest and ill-mannered thing to do? I think, on the whole, it
would, don't you? I hope *I* regard it as all the one Church, and
its differences man-made, [but] *they* don't; they don't think I
am " in a state of grace," or communion-worthy, and, tho' they
wouldn't know I wasn't, I suppose it would be mean to trick
them like that. So I struggled to the Annunciation, ½ mile away,
which I don't care for. Next time I shall get to St. Thomas's.

Sunday. I did so. After Mass there was a Hail Mary. Gerard
Irvine said they say it in Latin when only the celebrant and one
priest are there. I would rather like that. When I have the car,
I like to go to my Chapel, and just say my prayers there, before
the tabernacle. Then I say the prayers I like, and don't find myself
bothered by the ones I don't, as I do at these very Romanised
churches.

I went to drink with G. Greene last week; not a single priest
there! Can they have dropped him, or he them? . . .

Sunday. I think I shall soon send you a novel by someone I
know that might amuse you[1]; it is about her attempts to become
R.C. (to marry one) and her final decision not to. I believe her
conversations with the priests are very accurate; one of them
says so, I hear! It is otherwise a rather amusing book, and I like
its author, a very nice, cheerful young widow in her 30's. She
comes to the Chapel on Sundays often.

I shall send you word from the Island, sometime. Meanwhile,
thank you for your P.S. (" *pro te oro* . . .").[2] I do so value that.
And your " *prosperum iter.*"[3] I am sure it will be. Now I must
go and sort some clothes out for packing and taking. I have a
pair of lovely new rubber bathing shoes, striped blue and

[1] J. Hichens, *Noughts and Crosses* (1952).
[2] " I pray for thee."   [3] " Prosperous journey."

yellow, for camouflage in sea and sand (I don't wear them in the water, of course, but they are very useful on the shingly sands). I love the sea, I love swimming, I love it all. I expect you feel I should have outgrown it—but why outgrow anything one likes?

My love always,
R. M.

20 *Hinde House, Hinde Street, W.*1.
4th August, 1952†

My dear Hamilton,

This is only a P.S. to yesterday's letter, to say I had a letter from Mrs. Paine asking if we could meet in the middle of the month—11th, 12th, or 13th when she will be in London. I am very sorry I shall be away, I should have loved to see her. I have written to tell her so. It was nice of her to write. She says she is soon after that going back to America. It is bad luck.

Thank you for a[ir] p[aper] of 30th, that came this morning. *Anglican Orders:* yes . . . I will read Dix.[1] I liked his *Shape of the Liturgy.* I suppose opinions vary from those who think that any one who wants to follow Christ's teachings and [believes] that the communion will help them, can receive it, and those who feel it should be exclusively for valid members of the Church. There are all degrees, between those two views.

I shall be interested in *Our Language,*[2] and will try and get it. Does he think we shall end by saying " me " in the nominative? I rather like " he drive a car." I much prefer the Norfolk speech as you quote it to the horrible " for George and I." . . . Oddly, I'd rather have " for I," without the " George "—but that these semi-genteel people *don't* say, though probably Norfolk would. The question is, why do they feel it more of an accusative without the second name thrown in? I'm sure they wouldn't know. So it would be no use asking them.

---

[1] Dom Gregory Dix, *The Question of Anglican Orders* (1944); usually known by the sub-title *Letters to a Layman.*
[2] Simeon Potter, *Our Language* (1951).

Bank Holiday, and a rainy one. I hope it will be finer to-morrow and on the Island, for I and Jeanie.

I am reading *The Next Million Years*.[1] It seems we are to run out of food, coal, oil, everything and so will perish off the earth. Perhaps in the New Jerusalem, with its honey and milk(!) we shall revive our strength. Do you know that we get no more nourishment from eating a sheep than we should get from the grass that sheep had eaten, if we had the patience to eat it? But a mutton chop is more *concentrated*, as well as nicer, so I shall stick to it.

I shall be back by 21st. Much love.

R. M.

Yes, I like "a coat what's buttons" . . . [*sic*] or should it be, more logically, "*which's*"? . . . Canon Hood has now passed over Pusey [House] to Fr. Maycock (late vicar of Little St. Mary's [Cambridge], Crashaw's church.)

Westfield Park Hotel, Ryde, Isle of Wight
12th August, 1952†

My dear Hamilton,

(What a grandiose piece of paper this is! Scarcely suitable, really, for an air letter—but I have finished my note-block and must use this till I go to the shops and buy another.) Yours (posted 8th) came this morning—must have made Hinde House on 11th, which is quite good. It was nice to get it, on this island, where the tides are against early swimmers this week, being some miles out till late afternoon, so I bathe at odd places round the island whither we drive with our tea. To-day or to-morrow I may see J. B. Priestley, who lives the other side of the island. . . .

I got here after an enjoyable drive from London, via 3 abbeys—Romsey, Netley, Beaulieu. Netley looked very different from what it does (look up that use of "what" in your C[oncise] O[xford] D[ictionary]—I'm sure it is quite

[1] Sir Charles G. Darwin, *The Next Million Years* (1952).

illiterate) in the old pictures and the old descriptions (see Horace Walpole, and *all* the accounts of it till lately), when it was covered with ivy and sprouting with trees, and looked very "wild," "picturesque," etc. But the Ministry of Works took it over, and in 1922 stripped it of ivy and trees, and it now stands neat and stark and gaunt. I complained to the keeper at the gate. He said that "most people" prefer it like this, which I doubt. "Ivy is pernicious to ruins"; while as to trees—"well, you don't expect to see *trees* growing inside churches, do you." Actually, when it is a ruined abbey church, I do. But it is a grand ruin, and so is Beaulieu, lying like a foundered skeleton ship by its deserted past. I would like to see these abbeys—at least some of them—restored and rehabilitated. It wouldn't cost 1/100th part of what we now squander on weapons of war. And how nice to have Britain jewelled again with abbeys, bells pealing, vespers and Mass floating out, processions winding round them, wayfarers entertained! We could share them out with R.C.s, *we to get most*, which would infuriate them, as they hate us to have *any* pre-Reformation churches. I hate this smug, superior attitude. *Pax* is an exception, I always think; I'm glad they appreciate Dom Gregory Dix. And I'm glad he was a staunch C. of E. man. I shall certainly read the *Letters to a Layman* —I wonder if the layman did "go over" in the end. I suppose I am further from the Church than you, or than Dom Gregory. For I *don't* believe in what it has promulgated down the centuries because it has promulgated it: I think it wasn't necessarily guided into truth by the Holy Ghost, but often misunderstood, owing to its human, earth-bound limitations and prejudices (as when it thought it had to torture and burn unbelievers in the name of God—a practice *we* have repented of and disavowed as evil, but they *never have* in words). I think they derived the exaltation of Mary from very ancient sources—there has so often been a Virgin goddess and mother of heaven, in so many cults, it seems profoundly a human need. *To me* (is this arrogant?) it seems that this was the derivation of the whole cult. Now, in making her bodily assumption *de fide*, they have gone beyond all reason, and troubled even many of their faithful members. And *was* the apotheosis of Mary so very early? You will know better than I do about this; I suppose it developed gradually. But I see no *need* for it, and it seems inherently improbable, and surely irrelevant to the Incarnation. Don't think all this very arrogant and argumentative—what business have *I* to be arguing with *you* about it? But I have got into a habit of saying to you just what I think, and very likely I am quite wrong about most of it. Only that great Church does so often shock me. Look at the line it has taken about "miracles" that all its educated members *know* to be bogus—statues that move their eyes, the liquefaction of blood, etc., etc.—manipulated by priests, who pretend to the simple that it is genuine. Can they think the H[oly] G[host] wants them to lie like that? I am so thankful to belong to the C. of E., which has got so much nearer what seems like truth. Though 100 years ago, I should have liked it much less! And particularly its stupid intolerant abuse of Rome (in which I appear to be joining!). Forgive my intransigence. I think Rome is slowly moving towards more comprehension of truth, don't you? (Or not?)

Just after I last wrote to you, news came from India of the very sudden death of my sister[1] there. It was a bad shock to us. She was a splendid person; we have had the most wonderful letters about her and her work there. One from the Bishop of Chota Nagpur, her diocese, saying "My heart is heavy with grief at the thought that one of my best friends and most devoted fellow workers has gone from us." He is in England now; he came to Mass one morning, and when . . . [he heard] afterwards who I was, he said he wished he had known, as he would have waited and spoken to me about my sister; this was a month or two ago—we haven't yet had letters from Ranchi, giving details; but we assume it was her heart, which was poor. Anyhow she would have wished to go suddenly, while at the job, and among the people she loved and worked for. She was a v.g. linguist, and knew Hindi well, and did excellent translations into it of hymns, etc. She really had literary gifts, as her friends all say. It makes one heavy-hearted; she was to have come on leave

[1] Eleanor Macaulay.

349

next year. She wasn't a close companion and friend, like my other sisters and brothers—she had lived so much away—but I feel now that I should have put more into our relationship, written more often. She wrote more than I did; and I wish I had thanked her for a Kashmir dressing gown she sent me, in time for her to get the letter. Alas for chances missed, that can't return; they are bitter in retrospect.

I *am* sorry to miss Mrs. Paine. She says she will try again when next she comes over. She seems such a real person to me, after all you have told me of her.

I won't write on this side of this thin paper; it isn't good enough. Thank you for " *Per signum Crucis* . . ."[1] which is very good to use. Much love. I shall be home in 10 days.

Your loving
R. M.

I am telling Bumpus to post you *Noughts and Crosses*, that novel I spoke of. . . .

20, Hinde House, Hinde St., W.1
22nd August, 1952†

My dear Hamilton,

I have got home, and got your a[ir] p[aper] of 15th; thank you so much for it. It relieved my mind, because I felt I had been a little less than courteous about the B.V.M. (on whose assumption day you wrote). And you say you don't mind. You know I don't mean any discourtesy (and you should see me when, as last night, I am talking with convert cousins and have to watch my step). But I say to you what is in my mind, that ill-informed religious mind which is all I have in such matters. I expect, if you ever feared I might move Romeward, you have long ceased to do so! I have never been in danger of that. By no means only, or mainly, because of their (what seems to me) mistaken view of the B.V.M., but because of so much that

---

[1] " By the sign of the Cross."

they accept in the way of beliefs, and their intransigent attitude. Yet there is a small section of them that I am in great sympathy with; and, of course, much of their worship and ceremonial. I was wishing the other day that the Welsh had stuck, as their fellow-Britons in Ireland did, to that Church, instead of going over to Methodism, which I don't think suits them (? does it suit any one? One respects so much in it; but it is unlovely). The C. of E. could never have won the Welsh; they connected that (and still do) with the disliked Ascendancy (as the Irish do); but R.C.s they could well be. I haven't yet got hold of *Letters to a Layman*; the L[ondon] L[ibrary] copy is missing (but unentered, so must be stolen, I fear). It is out of print, but may turn up when advertised for, say Mowbray. . . .

The Monastic Orders, by David Knowles [is] a very interesting 2 vols. of historical research.[1] And another book by Knowles is just out—*Abbeys from the Air*, also a large book, illustrated with excellent photographs;[2] I must get hold of this at once, as it bears on my ruin book—what my sister calls " the valley of the shadow of ruins," in which she feels I have walked far too long. I would like to review this, and so acquire it, but haven't any time for this at present. But no doubt I shall get hold eventually of the Dix book, in which there is obviously a lot I should like to read, and prayers to transcribe too. Have you seen the *Church Times* letters from his brother and the Abbot of Downside, about the rumours in the R.C. press that he had been converted on his death-bed? Simply because the Abbot, an old friend, went to see him just before he died. The Abbot, as well as the brother, write denying it; indeed it would seem most improbable. I suppose " *sacramentum* " in the prayer you quote would be used in the sense of " pledge," wouldn't it? I like it; it calms fretting and striving too much, and tells us it's all there for us to appropriate if we will. I ordered you to be sent *Noughts and Crosses*; when you've read it (in bed after the bath)

[1] R. M. was referring to two separate works by David Knowles: *The Monastic Order in England; a History of its Development from the Times of St. Dunstan to the Fourth Lateran Council, 943-1216* (1940), and Vol. I of *The Religious Orders in England* (1948).

[2] D. Knowles and J. K. S. St. Joseph, *Monastic Sites from the Air* (1952).

tell me what you think of it. It's not a profound novel, of course; but it amused and interested me, especially the heroine's interviews with the priests. . . .

Well, here I am back from Wight; I enjoyed my drive back seeing en route several abbeys—Beaulieu, Romsey, Malmesbury, Lacock, Abingdon, Dorchester (Netley I visited on my way to the island). On the island I saw again the ruins of Quarr—very touching and wild and neglected in their fields above the sea, a little way from the brand-new pink abbey full of monks and seminarists (I think). Abingdon is enchanting, of course; I expect you know it well, and Dorchester. I passed a night at Dorchester, and went to Mass in the Abbey at 7.30; a grand place. It wasn't v.g. bathing weather on the island, on the whole; still, I bathed each day, being something, as you know, of a Hemerobaptist,[1] and holding with them that " *homo non posse* [sic] *vivere, nisi singulis diebus in aqua mergeretur, ac ita ablueretur et sanctificaretur ab omni culpa.*"[2] Cornelius à Lapide[3] comments on this view, with something of a shudder, " *Verum haec est anatum potius et piscium vita, quam hominum.*"[4] However, with the fishes I immersed myself, and shall soon be doing so with the ducks in the Serpentine, as it seems to be getting warmer again. Oh thank you for those papers; I have only had time to glance, so far, but shall look through them later. Now I am back at work, I must set to and finish this book if I can, trying *tranquillius operare*, but I don't find this easy. Since I began this letter I heard from the L[ondon] L[ibrary] that they have discovered who has Dix, and as it only went out yesterday, just before I asked for it, it can't be sent back for a month; but I shall have it then. Oh what happens to the dead? *Lux perpetua*, we pray; but in what mode, and what individual consciousness do they have of us? We can't know. I'd like my sister to know I

[1] One of a Jewish sect for which daily ablution was an essential part of religion.

[2] " Man cannot live unless on every day he plunge into the water and be washed clean and be sanctified from every sin."

[3] Cornelis Cornelissen van den Steen (1567-1637), Flemish writer on Biblical subjects.

[4] " Nay, but this is rather the life of ducks and fishes than of human beings."

was just going to write and thank her for the present she sent me, and that I value it. But apparently we aren't meant to know about them, or about what chances we shall ourselves have in that veiled future. One can only hope. Death is in one's mind, after that disaster at Lynmouth, which swept families apart so suddenly and terribly. Not as bad as the bombing, of course, but so unexpectedly. Though we should by now be used all the time to nature rounding on us in some horrible savage way, the old tiger. We walk precariously upon an earth that may open and swallow us, among waters that may rise and drown us, with the chance of lightning that may strike us dead. As good ways of dying, I dare say, as any others; but shocking to those left behind, who like warning and preparation. Now I must stop and work. Much love always from your coz.

R. M.

20, *Hinde House, Hinde St.,* W.1
29th August, 1952†

My dear Hamilton,

Your letter of St. Bartholomew's Day came yesterday; thank you so much for it. I'm glad you like *The Sea around us,*[1] for it has been giving me a lot of joy since I was sent it from America early this year. You are quite right in thinking it is my kind of book. Ellen Green's too;[2] only all the learned, informative part would be far above her head; she would just know what was in the sea, but not why, or when the different things arrived, or anything of that kind. I don't suppose she would get through it, as she was no reader. I, on the other hand, peruse every word with interest and pleasure, and I am glad it has come your way, even though you have so far only heard isolated sentences read too faintly by your inaudible brethren. For my part I am reading a book by R. A. Cram[3] (1906) called *The*

[1] Rachel L. Carson, *The Sea Around Us* (1950).
[2] See R. M.'s *And No Man's Wit.*
[3] Ralph Adams Cram (1863-1942), American architect.

Ruined Abbeys of Britain, which is good and vivid and informing; but his reading of history is rather odd and piecemeal, and he seems to consider life in the Middle Ages a very perfect business, when every one was good and learned and civilized, and life after the Renaissance and the Reformation (which seem equally anathema to him) one of rapacity, villainy, ignorance, barbarism, cruelty and irreligion. It would be good for him, and enlarge his point of view, to read some well documented and detailed and unbiassed history of the centuries between the 9th and the 15th. One could hardly find later more anarchy, barbarism, intolerant cruelty, ignorance, murder, serfdom, or greed. He should see (as I did yesterday) *Ivanhoe* in technicolour, and consider the goings on of Norman barons in England, Templars, crusaders, kings, even monks. He should read a detailed story of some of the crusades and the cruelties practised on them—while as for ignorance and vandalism, look at the way they sacked Constantinople in 1215 (was it?). You might guess Mr. Cram R.C., but he says he is Anglican, and indeed he went to Mass at Dorchester Abbey, with delight, after leaving the restored and rather Protestant Malmesbury Abbey in rage and disgust. What makes him angriest is the treatment of the Scottish abbeys by the reformers, and indeed it was detestable, the way they mutilated them and put up their hideous kirks in them. Henry can be understood, as he wanted money, and the abbeys had it; but the Scotch reformers were merely full of *odium theologicum*. I think Cram is American (or was). I am also reading Dom David Knowles's *The Monastic Order in England*—very interesting; this was lent me . . . I think I shall get it in the end, either from advertisement or the L[ondon] L[ibrary] copy when returned.

I do agree with you about the uninspired English of most translated Missal (and Breviary) prayers. The translators should take hints from Cranmer; but they write in a different and less beautiful linguistic age, and I suppose don't want to be archaic and affected. All the same, they could, while remaining modern, be clear and harmonious. Cranmer often deviates from the exact meaning, either from reasons of sound or of sense, but he is always good. By the way, where does that " *Respice* " prayer you quoted in an earlier letter come from? I wasn't clear if you copied it from Dix's collection of prayers, or from the Missal—the one with " *sacramentum* " in it, which I suppose means " holy mystery," as applied to the Church. I have no time just now to dig for it in the Missal, being busier than ever.

There is such a nice notice of my sister Eleanor in *Overseas News* written by one of her colleagues in the Ranchi mission. I think I would like you to see it, to show you a little of what she was; so, when I get hold of more copies of the O[verseas] N[ews] I will send you one. It makes me cry a little; but I like to see it. The S.P.G. are having a Requiem Mass for her in their chapel in Tufton St. on 18th Sept., to which I shall of course go. The Bishop of Chota Nagpur, a splendid person, is still in Sweden conferring on Faith and Order, I believe; but I shall see him later. A letter I had the other day from Ranchi repeats what a great affection and friendship he had for her, and how much he valued her work and her advice. It is all good hearing. It makes one feel very small and trivial by comparison, and selfish. . . .

Cram ends his book with an interesting suggestion for putting some of the abbeys in commission again to harbour a supply of mission priests for the under-priested parishes; to work not permanently in one place, but in turns. He is right that there aren't enough would-be monks and nuns to fill them, even if workers could be spared from the national life. But how carefully the buildings would have to be restored! They might be modernised in an ugly way, or in bogus Gothic. There are many pitfalls; and some must be kept as ruins. Are there any American ruined abbeys? Plenty of ruined Spanish mission churches, of course; but abbeys probably not. I do wonder if we shall ever have a real revival of Anglican monastic life, beyond what we have already had. Dear me, this seems the end!

Much love,
R. M.

September

20, *Hinde House, Hinde St., W.*1
7th September, 1952†

My dear Hamilton,

I am spending this Sunday morning in bed, with a slight temperature (I get these little undulant come-backs, but they're not prostrating me; I will be up this afternoon) so am writing to you in my beautiful hand instead of typing; forgive it.

Thank you so much for a[ir] p[aper]s of 29th Aug. and 3rd Sept., I gather you must now be in the turmoil of putting up the visitors to the American Church Convention—I shan't expect to hear until the Bishops and the priests depart, the tumult and the shouting dies.

I am *much* interested in what you say of R. A. Cram.[1] It confirms what one gathers from his book; that unbalanced and child-like enthusiasm—even fanaticism—and idealism, combined with such good architectural knowledge. He published it in 1906, and prints as a foreword a quotation from Dugdale's preface to his *Monasticon*[2]—" I humbly crave leave, before I advance any further, publicly to profess myself to be a sincere, tho' very unworthy, member of the Church of England, and that I have as true and hearty affection for her interest as perhaps any other person whatsoever. And yet I cannot but here publicly declare that I think it would have been more happy for her, as well as for the nation in general, had K. Henry VIII only reformed and not destroyed the Abbeys and other Religious Houses: Monastic Institution is very ancient, and it had been very laudable had he reduced the manner and worship to the primitive form." So at that date Mr. Cram was a loyal Anglican,

[1] He had been a personal friend of Father Johnson.

[2] *Monasticon Anglicanum,* a collection of monastic charters, etc., published by Sir William Dugdale in 1655, 1661 and 1673.

though may have had yearnings. Anyhow, it is a good and vivid book.

I heard this morning a reading from *John Inglesant*,[1] announced by the BBC announcer; who said that J.I. belonged to " an old Roman Catholic family." This struck me as very odd. I've not read the book for years; but surely John, a firm Anglican, was not a member of an R.C. family? Or was he a convert from that faith? I expect the announcer was just ignorant; I must look it up. People to-day are so ignorant!

I am going to send you *Overseas News*, with the reference to my sister—or else cut it out and put it in an envelope. Her Requiem Mass is on the 18th.

My sister Jean, alas, can't come up for it; she says the mornings are stiff with work, which she mustn't leave. She is just back from a Retreat (the last few days of her holiday) taken by Canon Browne-Wilkinson, who she says was v.g. She *says* he gave her absolution without his stole—can this be? I told her that, in that case, her sins were yet upon her, and she had better get done again at once. I believe he's not an extreme A[nglo-] C[atholic]; *he* told them a story of how he had gone to see a parish priest, who had greeted him with " Alas, we haven't got our Lord here," to which the Canon exclaimed, "My dear fellow, what *can* you mean? " What he meant, of course, was no R[eserved] S[acrament] in the church—I think the story was told to the retreatants (at Clewer) to warn them against taking a materialistic, R.C. view of the R.S. — God localized and enclosed. My sister isn't tempted to this, and nor am I, but I daresay some Clewer retreatants might be. . . . Did I tell you I got *Letters to a Layman* at last from the L[ondon] L[ibrary] and read it. I thought it quite interesting; though *for me* aimed at something irrelevant, as the question of " validity " never bothers me at all. Indeed, what mainly interested me was the insight it gave into the minds of the two correspondents—the very able and fine one of Dom G[regory] D[ix] and that of his friend, of whom nothing much is revealed but that such questions did bother him, and nearly (if not quite)

[1] Novel by J. H. Shorthouse (1881).

drove him to Rome. All that could drive *me* there would be a belief that it is the most Christian of the churches (incredible to me at present) or that God *meant* us all to join it (still more incredible), or a feeling for its traditions and liturgy, which I *have*. But " validity " no, the word has no meaning to me.

I'm *glad* you like to have my letters. Really 100? I think you'd better get rid of them, of any you have kept, in that incinerator! I own I have kept yours—but that is another matter. They are full of such good stuff—how good you have been to me these 2 years! But I will burn them before I die; they're not for other people to see. How I value all that liturgical world you have opened to me.

My love always,
R. M.

Genealogies

Bibliography

Index

GENEALOGY OF ROSE MACAULAY

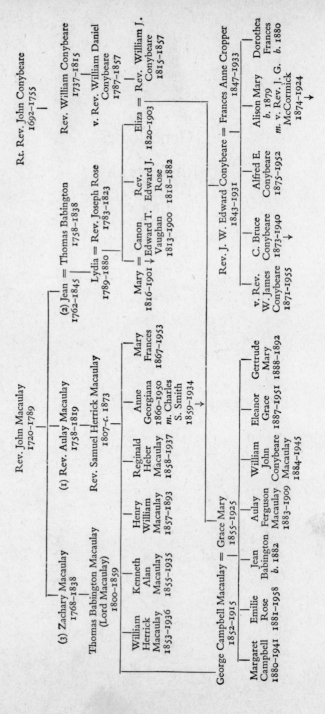

RELATIONSHIP BETWEEN ROSE MACAULAY AND FATHER JOHNSON

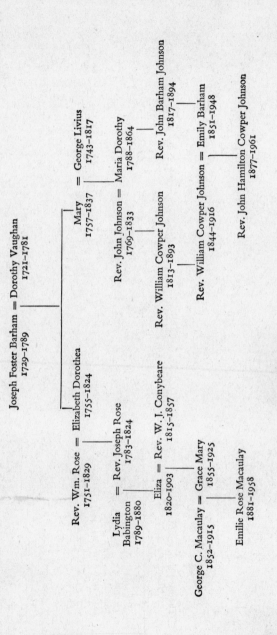

Joseph Foster Barham = Dorothy Vaughan
1729–1789   1721–1781

Mary = George Livius
1757–1837   1743–1817

Elizabeth Dorothea
1755–1824

Rev. John Johnson = Maria Dorothy
1769–1833   1788–1864

Rev. John Barham Johnson
1817–1894

Rev. William Cowper Johnson
1813–1893

Rev. William Cowper Johnson = Emily Barham
1844–1916   1851–1948

Rev. John Hamilton Cowper Johnson
1877–1961

Rev. Wm. Rose = Elizabeth Dorothea
1751–1829   1755–1824

Lydia   = Rev. Joseph Rose
Babington   1783–1824
1789–1880

Eliza = Rev. W. I. Conybeare
1820–1903   1815–1857

George C. Macaulay = Grace Mary
1852–1915   1855–1925

Emilie Rose Macaulay
1881–1958

Select Bibliography

NOVELS

Abbots Verney	*John Murray*	1906
The Furnace	*John Murray*	1907
The Secret River	*John Murray*	1909
The Valley Captives	*John Murray*	1911
Views and Vagabonds	*John Murray*	1912
The Lee Shore	*Hodder & Stoughton*	1912
The Making of a Bigot	*Hodder & Stoughton*	1914
Non-Combatants and Others	*Hodder & Stoughton*	1916
What Not: A Prophetic Comedy	*Constable*	1918
Potterism: a Tragi-farcical Tract	*Collins*	1920
Dangerous Ages	*Collins*	1921
Mystery at Geneva	*Collins*	1922
Told by an Idiot	*Collins*	1923
Orphan Island	*Collins*	1924
Crewe Train	*Collins*	1926
Keeping up Appearances	*Collins*	1928
Staying with Relations	*Collins*	1930
They Were Defeated	*Collins*	1932
Going Abroad	*Collins*	1934
I Would Be Private	*Collins*	1937
And No Man's Wit	*Collins*	1940
The World my Wilderness	*Collins*	1950
The Towers of Trebizond	*Collins*	1956

POETRY

The Two Blind Countries	*Sidgwick & Jackson*	1914
Three Days	*Constable*	1919

ESSAYS, CRITICISM, ETC.

ANTHOLOGY

HISTORY AND TRAVEL

Abbeys: Quarr, 176-7; Prinknash, 247; St. Michael's, Farnborough, 247; destroyed, 332, 333; Beaulieu, 347, 348, 352; Netley, 347-8, 352; Romsey, 347, 352; and Roman Catholics, 348; Abingdon, 352; Dorchester, 352, 354; Lacock, 352; Malmesbury, 352, 354; Scottish, 354; American, 355. See also *Ruined Abbeys of Britain, The*

"Abbot Daniel" stories, 84-5, 87, 89, 96, 100, 109, 118, 119, 316

Abinger, 255, 261

Acton, Lord, 91, 250

Adam, Dr. Karl, 139, 147, 163, 319, 321, 329

Addison, Daniel D., 147

Addison, W., 63n

Agnostics, 28, 101, 152, 190

Albert, Prince Consort, 287

Alfred, King, 281, 287, 289

Amalfi, 81n, 85

Ambrose, St., 254n, 263, 317

American Church Union, 211

American Prayer Book Commentary, see *Oxford American Prayer Book Commentary*

Americans: 139; publishers, 27, 212, 215-6; and English books, 67; and R.M.'s novels, 67; speech of, 119; schoolgirls, 149; soldiers, 209

Ananias (and Sapphira), 118

Andrew, Father: 97, 174, 180, 184, 191, 194, 329, 335; *Life and Letters of,* 97, 112, 174, 180, 184, 194, 200, 329

Andrewes, Bp. Lancelot, 159, 162, 333

Anglican Church, the: early development, 40, 170; "Romanism" in, 205, 331; L. Duchesne on, 205; mission to the world, 205; Prof. M. Simon on, 205; and Roman Catholic Church, 250, 319, 321-2, 349; Sir H. Slesser on, 312-13; and confession, 320, 322, 331-2; and "progressive illumination", 337; and the Real Presence, 312-73, 342; and Dissenters, 343; in 17th c., 343; monastic life in, 355, 356. *See also* Macaulay, Rose, return to Church

Anglican Dilemma, The (Sir H. Slesser), 312-13, 316

Anglican Society, The, 182

Anglicanism: in 17th c., 27, 36-7, 63, 154, 162, 225, 245, 333-4; in America, 28, 132, 154; ritual, 36-7, 84, 125, 126; R.M. and, 69, 99, 110, 138, 145, 148, 150, 182-3, 190, 271, 292, 322; in 18th c., 79-80, 154, 225; in 19th c., 79, 110, 186-7; "High, Low, and Broad", 79, 186-7, 202; compared with Roman Catholicism, 110, 131, 189, 257, 321-2; converts to, 124; variety of worship, 160-1, 168; and the Eucharist, 162, 225; different views within, 187; in 16th c., 225, 245, 334; "drift towards", 297; Anglican Catholicism, 320; "validity" of, 357

Anglicans: and Roman Catholic shrines, 87; and confession, 157; and Roman Catholics, 248, 301; "increasing confidence" among, 248; and Transubstantiation, 299; Canadian Episcopalians, 342; Protestant Episcopalians, 342; and communicating in Roman Catholic churches, 345; and persecution of heretics, 348

"Anglo-Agnosticism", 69, 138

Anglo-Catholicism: beginning of, 36-7; term "Anglo-Catholic", 79, 213, 225; "smarter than Roman Catholicism", 144, 148; Anglo-Catholic Ordinations Fund, 189, 202; Anglo-Catholic Progress Campaign, 189, 197, 202; W. N. Pittenger on, 331

Anglo-Catholics: 132, 312; and Roman Catholic usage, 173-4, 243, 357

Annan, Noel, 199, 214

Annunzio, Gabriele d', 175

Antipater of Sidon, 181

Apocrypha, The, 136

Apocryphal writings (New Testament), 163

Architecture: Indian, 309; Byzantine, 327; Chinese, 327; Gothic, 327; Romanesque, 327

Armstrong, Rev. B. J., 73n, 79, 80

Armstrong, H. B. J., 73n, 79, 102

Arnold, Matthew, 80

Arnold, Thomas, 80, 111

367

Mary-the-Less, Cambridge, 347
Protestant Episcopal: Church of S. John the Evangelist, Boston, Mass., 167, 219, 301n, 331
Roman Catholic: Our Lady & the English Martyrs, Cambridge, 40; St. James's, Spanish Place, 81, 83, 270, 345; St. Patrick's, Soho, 161
Church Times, 132, 187, 235, 239, 243, 248, 283, 351
Church Unity Week: opening meeting, 253; R.M.'s views on, 253
Cicero, 34, 56, 126, 142, 156, 181, 246, 273
Clapham Sect, the, 11
Class: and clergy, 105; in Middle Ages, 105; in 16th and 17th c., 106; in 18th c., 106; in 19th c., 106, 107; in Ancient Rome, 107; in New Testament, 107; in Norman Britain, 107; "class war", 195, 274
Claudel, Paul, 267
Clergy, English: R.M.'s acquaintance among, 19, 190, 248; younger generation of, 28, 246, 254; Anglican, 19th c., 79, 105, 107; in 17th c., 105, 247; in 18th c., 105, 106, 118; marriage of, 105; social status of, 105; in 16th c., 108, 245; pre-Tractarian, 118; celibate, 249; "gentility of", 249-50; and Class, 250; "new-style Anglican", 160, 161, 173-4; intelligent, 179, 189, 190; chaplains, 180, 245; "High, Low, and Broad", 79, 186-7, 202; "earthen vessels", 292
Cleveland, John, 298
Clifford, Lady (Mrs. Henry De La Pasture), 303
Cockin, Frederic, Bp. of Bristol, 267
Cod-liver oil, 96
Cole, Rev. William, 37, 118
Coleridge, Samuel, 53
Colet, John, 40, 169, 171, 260
Collects, *see* Prayers, collects
Common Prayer, The Book of: 40, 205, 302, 313, 315, 325, 333; revision of 1928, 32, 80, 81, 93, 133, 146, 316, 317; Baptism service, 32, 293; Psalms in, 43; American Prayer Book, 64, 70, 78, 80, 89, 108, 132, 147, 170, 302, 307, 316, 325-6; of 1662, 81, 113, 133, 173, 177, 250; of 1549, 113, 173, 217, 250, 322; Prefaces in, 113; language in, 130; Scottish Prayer Book, 140, 326; of 1552, 217, 250, 322; *Liber Precum Publi-*

carum (Bright & Medd), 142, 163, 246; commentaries, 170; commemoration of All Souls' omitted from, 216; "Cranmer's little work", 223, 225, 245; Catechism in, 248, 315, 342; Sir L. Jenkins on, 249; and Real Presence, 342. *See also* Prayers, collects
Commonweal, 344
Communism, 150
Community of the Resurrection, priests of, 253
Confession: R.M. and, 17, 39, 42-3, 47, 48, 49, 50-51, 52, 55, 57-8, 61, 62, 67, 69, 73-4, 88, 94, 101, 103-4, 109, 129, 140; in 18th c., 320, 322, 331; in *Tom Jones,* 326, 331; Henry Fielding and, 331
Conscience, awakening of: in Man, 284, 291, 294; in animals, 291
Conybeare, family of: 11-12, 13, 35, 68, 89, 124, 204, 218, 257, 289, 306; derivation of name, 299; pronunciation of name, 299, 303; and portrait of Lydia Babington, 308; family likenesses, 314
Conybeare, Alfred E., 305-6
Conybeare, Bruce, 32n
"Conybeare, Dr." (*They Were Defeated*), 35, 300
Conybeare, Dorothea, 265, 268, 272, 275-6, 286
Conybeare, Eliza (*née* Rose), 111, 204, 265, 268, 272n, 276, 279, 286-7, 288, 314
Conybeare, F. C., 35, 300
"Conybeare, Francis" (*They Were Defeated*), 298
Conybeare, John: 35, 332; *Letters and Exercises of,* 35n
Conybeare, John, Bp. of Bristol, 12
Conybeare, John Bruce, 31, 32n
Conybeare, Rev. J. W. Edward, 12, 56, 163, 239
"Conybeare, Julian" (*They Were Defeated*), 27, 35, 298, 300
Conybeare, W. D., Dean of Llandaff, 11, 35n
Conybeare, Rev. W. J.: 11, 79, 80, 135, 143; *Edinburgh Review* article on Church Parties, 79, 186-7, 204
Conybeare, W. James, Provost of Southwell, 12, 35, 56, 286
Cooking, 92, 138, 300
Cornelius à Lapide, 352
Coronation Stone, theft of, 48, 51

Genealogies, 272, 281, 282
George VI, King, 265-6, 270, 277, 287
Gibbs, Rev. G. C., 301, 303
Gide, André, 267, 277
Glass of Vision, The (A. Farrer), 112, 138-9
Glossography (Blount's), 273
God: the need for, 30; separation from, 39; pursuing purposes of, 71, 115, 175; and science, 90; communion with, 95, 289-90; and the Church, 219; "love for", 283; gifts of, 291, 292, 294; in men's souls, 311; balance in seeking after, 338; "through the Sacrament", 340
Godchildren, R.M.'s, 143, 149, 297
God so Loved the World (E. Goudge), 120
Gollancz, Victor, 42, 65, 96
Gondoliers, The, 165
Goudge, Elizabeth, 120
Great O's, the, *see* Liturgies: the greater Antiphons
Greek language, 65, 163
Greek Poetry for Everyman (F. L. Lucas), 181n
Greeks, the: 91; and the Mysteries, 37; and faculty for religion, 65-6
"Green, Ellen" (*And No Man's Wit*), 63, 69, 208, 353
Greene, Graham: 34, 98, 124, 135n, 179, 180, 196, 232, 297, 343-4, 345; and evil, 140; and sin, 124, 140, 344; and religion, 196; and sex, 196; and the Roman Catholic Church, 218-19, 339; and religious drama, 219; and the Church of England, 338-9, 342-3; and the war years, 338
Grisewood, Harman, 342
Groser, Rev. St. J. B., 161
Grosvenor Chapel, *see* Churches, Anglican
Guardian, The, 239
Gurney, Samuel, 214
"Guy" (*And No Man's Wit*), 209

Haley, Sir William, 144
Hall, George, Bp. of Chota Nagpur, 349, 355
Handwriting: R.M.'s, 27, 31, 37-8, 50, 59, 61, 65, 74, 75, 77, 81, 96, 129, 131, 134, 178, 190, 304, 310, 316, 317, 322, 328, 342, 344, 356; Fr. Johnson's 31, 38, 74
Harris, Wilson, 120
Hart-Davis, Rupert, 284n

Hartley, L. P., 255
Harvard College, 111
Harvard Co-operative Society, booksellers, 295
Heart of Jesus, The (P. N. Waggett), 40, 75
Heart of the Matter, The (G. Greene) 98-9, 196
Heber, Reginald, Bp. of Calcutta, 143
Hebrew language, 65, 158
Hemerobaptists, 352
Henry VIII, King, 354, 356
Herbert, George, 225
Heredity, 289
Here's a Church—Let's Go In (W. J. Conybeare), 35, 56, 73
Hermits, 85, 86, 92, 100
Herrick, family of, 124, 332
Herrick, Robert, 27, 143, 300
Hesketh, Lady: 78n, 82; *Letters of*, 78, 80
Hichens, J., 345
"Hilary, Mrs." (*Dangerous Ages*), 167
Hobhouse, Stephen, 248n
Holidays: Fr. Johnson's, ("day out") 115, 160; *R.M.'s:* 159, 160, 171, 175; plans for Italy, 285-6, 288-9, 294-5, 300, 306, 318, 332, 341; Isle of Wight (1952), 339, 341, 344, 345, 347, 352
Holmes, Oliver Wendell, 238-9
Holy Communion: R.M. and, 39, 61, 62, 74, 101, 108, 130, 134, 158, 340, 345; refusal of, 54-5, 283; midday, 81, 88, 91, 94, 214, 318; fasting, 95; infrequent, 101, non-fasting, 191; for the sick, 279, 285, 299, 305. For the Anglican rite *see* Eucharist
Holy Spirit, The: 182, 221, 292, 337, 340, 343, 349; invocation of (in the Eucharist), 317; and the Churches, 321, 330, 337-8, 339, 343, 348
Holy Wisdom (A. Baker), 221, 222, 236
Homosexuals, 267, 298-9
Hood, Canon Frederic, 155, 161, 179, 185-6, 188, 189, 197, 202, 211, 253, 347
Hooker, Richard, 225, 235, 333
Hopkins, K., 320n
Horace: 33, 68, 90, 100, 119n, 122, 231, 323; Milman's edition, 228; his farm, 231, 295, 332; and the Digentia, 239, 332; passage from *Art of Poetry*, 322n
Hound of Heaven, The (F. Thompson), 71

Roman Catholicism, 248, 255; ignorant, 248

228, 230-1, 234, 238, 315; character, 212-13, 230-1, 238, 257

Powys, Littleton C., 311, 315, 320n

Powys, Llewelyn: 231; *A Selection from his Writings*, 320

Prayer: 78, 95, 107, 110-11; after the Eucharist, 134, 139, 191; silent, 168; 'solitary', 174; during the day, 191, 222; mental, 191; natural gift for, 202; meditation, 202; as thanksgiving, 222; centred in one word, 222; personally congenial, 223; for the sick, 244-5; when ill, 280

Prayer Book, The, see *Common Prayer, The Book of*

Prayers: family, 13, 269; on celluloid, 30, 53; collects, 30, 32, 35, 38, 113, 139, 142, 147, 162-3, 172-3, 177, 189, 205-6, 222-3, 246, 302, 317, 335; Latin, 30, 32, 35, 38, 42, 53, 64, 81, 130, 134, 139, 142, 147, 158, 162-3, 173, 177, 206-7, 233, 246, 255, 256, 267, 271, 277, 280, 304, 308, 310-12, 326, 335, 350, 355; Eucharistic, 80-1, 93, 279, 309, 320, 343; R.M.'s collection of private devotions, 92, 117, 127, 162, 191, 214, 233, 236, 244, 280, 285, 302; R.M.'s daily, 100, 107, 111, 113, 197; memorizing of, 121, 127, 139; extempore, 223; Roman Catholic devotions, 223, 257, 331; collections of "brief prayers", 236, 244, 246, 251, 306; for emergencies, 244-5; "sissy" devotions, 249, 302, 331; memorized, 280; for the Queen, 307; the Epiclesis, 317; St. Ambrose's, 317; uninspired translations of, 354. *See also* Dead, prayers for the

Preces Privatae (Bp. L. Andrewes), 159, 162

Prelude to Adventure, The (H. Walpole), 124

Presbyterians: 11, 124, 343; and Church Unity, 253

Presence, the Real, 313, 315, 342; 'modes of', 336

Price, Bonamy, 286

Price, Lydia (*née* Rose), 286

Priest in the Family, A, 217

Priestley, J. B., 347

Primer of Medieval Latin (C. H. Beeson), 264, 266, 287, 294-6, 307, 314

Problem of Pain, The (C. S. Lewis), 233, 239

Procopius, 81

Pronunciation: of Latin, 143, 261, 270, 271; of English, changes in, 149, 153, 178; dictionaries of, 153; Shakespearian, 153, 260; and English dialects, 164, 274; of Aramaic, 164; St. Peter's, 164; of Cowper, 164, 303, 308; among the clergy, 164, 250; 17th c., 178; of Church Latin, 245, 258-261, (Italianate) 270, of *caeli*, 261; of tomato, 269-70; class feeling and, 274; of Conybeare, 299; of Donne, Romford, O'Donovan, Trevelyan, Cecil, Cowley, 303; of "clergy", 328

Propertius, 99, 229n, 230

Protestant Episcopal Church, 28, 132

Prudentius, 254n

Pryce-Jones, Alan, 167

Psalms, The: 58, 60, 100, 168; Coverdale's translation (P.B.), 43, 54, 179; Tyndale's translation (A.V.), 43; *Ps. 119*, 43, 51, 60, 100, 244, 290; *Ps. 73*, 43, 49-50; need for new edition of, 49; *Ps. 24*, 50; *Ps. 8*, 50; in Latin and English, 85, 100, 113, 244; in *Broadcast Psalter*, 179; as prayers, 222, 244; *Ps. 68*, 244; in the offices, 255; sung, 262, 290; and the 'way to God', 289-90; *Ps. 84*, 290; *Ps. 40*, 290; *Ps. 42*, 290; *Ps. 43*, 290; quotations from, 297, 328

Pseudodoxia Epidemica (Sir T. Browne), 273

Public Record Office, the, 123, 232

Publishers: 298; R.M.'s, 285, 341, 344; American, 27, 212, 215-16

Punctuation, R.M.'s, 201

Puritanism: 27, 154, 170; in America, 28, 81, 216

Puritans, 49, 91, 132, 162, 333

Pusey, E. B., 79, 99, 186

Pusey House, 186, 347

Quakers, 29, 63, 101, 188, 218, 337

Question of Anglican Orders, The (Dom G. Dix), 346, 348, 351-2, 357

Quiller-Couch, Sir Arthur, 123, 333

Raccolta, the, 343

Raine, Kathleen, 208

Rallies: United Church's (Hyde Park), 132; Church Union Prayer Week (Albert Hall), 211, 213

Ramsey, Canon A. M., 332

Raven, Canon C. E., 72, 90

Ruined Abbeys of Britain, The, (R. A. Cram), 353-4, 355
Ruins: artificial, 31, 254; quotations on, 31-4, 181, 327; R.M. and, 56, 60, 108, 118, 165, 175, 181-2, 183, 219, 224, 251, 290, 318, 341, 344; R.M.'s visits to, 176, 254, 326-7; Basing House, 326; Chapel of the Holy Ghost, Basingstoke, 327; 18th c. poems on, 327; in U.S.A., 355; restoration of, 355. *See also* Abbeys
Rutilius Namatianus, 177-8

Sackville-West, V., 19, 229, 315, 321, 328
Saints, the: 209-10, 302; minor, 169. *Individual saints are indexed alphabetically*
St. Anne's House, Soho, 161
St. Joseph, J. K. S., 351n
Salmon, Rev. George, 319
Salvation Army services, 164, 179
Samson Agonistes, performance of, 126
Savonarola, 9
Saye and Sele, Lord, 162
Sayers, Dorothy, 161
Scientific Temper in Religion, The (P. N. Waggett), 75n
Scotland under Charles I (D. Mathew), 234
Sea Around Us, The (R. L. Carson), 353
Self-analysis, 212-13, 238
Sellon, Priscilla Lydia, 179
Selwyn, E. G., Dean of Winchester 133, 146
Senhouse, Roger, 328
Sermones feriales et communes (James of Vitry), 266
Serpentine, the, 134-5, 141-2, 151, 158, 188, 191, 197, 206-7, 318, 352
Sex: and family relationships, 192; and friendships, 192; in literature, 156-7, 294; and half-literate readers, 294, 295
Shakespeare, William, 210
Shape of the Liturgy, The (Dom G. Dix), 346
Sheed and Ward, publishers, 108
Sheed, Maisie, 200
Sheltering Sky, The (P. F. Bowles), 338
Shorthouse, J. H., 357
Silchester, 326
Simon, Prof. Marcel, 205, 208, 225
Sissinghurst Castle, 321
Sitwell, Edith, 114, 148

Sitwell, Osbert, 114, 148
Sleep of Prisoners, A (C. Fry), 166-7, 170, 219
Slesser, Sir Henry, 312-13, 315-16, 317-18, 319, 321-2, 331-2
Smith, Mrs. C. S. (*née* Anne Macaulay), 28, 149n
Smith, Emily, 149n
Smith, Jean, 149n
"Social Joys", 263-4, 268, 277, 323
Society for the Propagation of the Gospel, 72, 355
Society of St. John the Evangelist: St. Edward's House, Westminster, 17, 21, 30n, 48, 87, 104, 227; in the U.S., 18, 21, 43, 87; Mission House, Boston, Mass., 21; The Monastery, Cambridge, Mass., 21, 55; *Cowley* (journal), 38, 80, 316, 319n; cemetery at Foxborough, Mass., 43, 247; R.M.'s attachment to, 109, 114-15, 126, 148, 331; *The Trumpet Shall Sound* (B. D. Wilkins), 64, 140; Rule, 183-4, 220-1; mission priests of (unnamed), 198, 248, 253; development of, 221. See also *Hours of Prayer*
Socrates, 65
Son of God (by Karl Adam), 147
Spectator, The, 63, 69, 120, 135-6, 148, 196, 293
Speech: English 17th c., 41, 261; English 16th c., 41; illiterate, 342, 347; Norfolk dialect, 346
Spelling: women's, 136-7, 261; Kitty Witham's, 115, 123, 128; of Macaulay, 318
Spenser, Edmund, 323
Spender, Stephen, 257, 276, 283
Sports and Games: hockey, 14, 40, 95; bicycling, 84, 141, 206, 267-8; tobogganing, 42; cricket, 90; croquet, 131; rowing, 141; tree-climbing, 141; walking, 141, 190; Boat Race, the (1952), 296; canoeing, 324. *See also* Swimming
Squire, J. C., 16
Stanton, Rev. A. H., 37, 79
Statius, 177, 178
Steele, Richard, 322
Stephen, family of, 204
Stephen, Sir Leslie, 199-200
Still the Joy of It (L. C. Powys), 315
Stockwood, Rev. Mervyn, 293
Stone, Rev. Darwell, 96-7, 99, 139, 146, 191

3g, Tyrrell, 152
        200
49
134
170

Tyrrell, 152